The
COOK'S
GARDEN

SHERIDAN ROGERS

Illustrations by Skye Rogers

VIKING

VIKING
Published by the Penguin Group
Viking Penguin, a division of Penguin Books USA Inc.,
375 Hudson Street, New York, New York 10014, U.S.A.
Penguin Books Ltd, 27 Wrights Lane,
London W8 5TZ, England
Penguin Books Australia Ltd, Ringwood,
Victoria, Australia
Penguin Books Canada Ltd, 10 Alcorn Avenue, Suite 300,
Toronto, Ontario, Canada M4V 3B2
Penguin Books (N.Z.) Ltd, 182–190 Wairau Road,
Auckland 10, New Zealand

Penguin Books Ltd, Registered Offices:
Harmondsworth, Middlesex, England

First American Edition
Published in 1992 by Viking Penguin,
a division of Penguin Books USA Inc.
by arrangement with CollinsAngus&Robertson Publishers
Pty Limited (ACN 009 913 517)
A division of HarperCollinsPublishers (Australia) Pty Limited

1 3 5 7 9 10 8 6 4 2

Text copyright © Sheridan Rogers, 1992
Illustrations copyright © Skye Rogers, 1992
All rights reserved

Poetry, prose and recipes reprinted by arrangement with the
copyright holders.

ISBN 0-670-84637-6
(CIP data available)
Printed in Hong Kong

SHERIDAN
To my mother and her mother before her
and all those who have been my mothers

SKYE
To my mother for being such an aesthete
and surrounding me with beautiful things to draw

CONTENTS

CONTENTS

THE GOOD HOST

You were sweeping the flagstones
When we came to lunch.
You offered us wine

Sunlight, paintings,
And a view of three cypresses
Up from the river;

Swimming, and talk,
More wine, melon,
Orange-trees, birds,

Long-necked bottles
And — still at lunch —
The mists of evening.

Rereading the poems
We are all late-stayers;
Guests in your country.

ROSEMARY DOBSON

Introduction

As a young child, it was in the garden that I found solace and peace. It was also the place that I often found my mother, a passionate gardener. The garden was her domain, her retreat from the world, the place she turned to for renewal. Like her mother, and her mother before her, she has always needed to be surrounded by gardens. Daily contact with the earth helped her to keep her balance, especially during the years when my father, a well-known media personality, was so busy and involved in his work. 'I get well when I can be alone in a garden,' was my mother's constant refrain.

My mother's enthusiasm for gardening and cooking was infectious and it is from her that I inherited those two passions. As a teenager struggling to make sense of the world around me I learned a lot from the vegetables in my vegetable patch about patience, endurance, joy, nurturing and struggle. Each plant had its own personality — frail baby lettuces were vulnerable and needed protection; sorrel on the other hand was much more independent and required hardly any pampering at all; bold, thrusting Swiss chard was assertive; and the lemon tree was joyfully abundant.

There was also knowledge to be gained from writings about the garden. As a child I had been enchanted by Frances Hodgson Burnett's novel, The Secret Garden. The idea of a secret, inner garden, hidden away behind walls appealed strongly to my imagination. Then as a teenager I read Voltaire's Candide in which he hinted at the importance of caring for one's own garden, both inner and outer. Today, as I watch my children grow, I realize more and more the importance of nurturing this inner garden, both in myself and in them.

As a teenager I set my vegetables out in neat rows. These days, my garden is rather rambling and informal as I have not adhered to a rigid separation between flower bed, vegetable bed, herb garden and fruit tree. My garden now has an element of surprise and unpredictability about it which I like.

It is important to create the sort of garden you are happy in and not to feel bound to set it out according to designs in books or to the latest fashion. It's also important to use available space — when it comes to a kitchen garden not everyone has a patch of earth just outside the kitchen door in which to grow vegetables or train fruit trees. Given a little sunshine, even the smallest garden, courtyard or patio should be able to produce a few herbs and vegetables or a fruit tree. The knowledge that what you grow is fresh as well as free from chemical sprays and pesticides, and the satisfaction derived from working the soil and eating the results, are just some of the more tangible rewards.

Ever since the first seed was planted, people have derived great satisfaction from cultivation, albeit at times from sheer necessity. In fact it took us a long time to light on the idea of growing food instead of just foraging for it. The first gardens arrived late in the world's history — not much more than ten thousand years ago in fact. Once hit upon it seems there was a spontaneous genesis of vegetable cultivation in different parts of the world (Central America, China, Southeast Asia and the Near East) over several thousand years.

Evidence exists that peas were grown in Turkey from the wild pea (Pisum elatus) by 6500 BC. In Central America, gourds, lima beans and maize are thought to have been growing by 5000 BC. Potatoes and possibly tomatoes were also probably being grown by then. By 3500 BC the cultivation of vegetables was firmly established among the Sumerians in the Valley of the Euphrates. They were largely vegetarians and their staple foods were barley, onions and beans. At the same time the Chinese were growing cucumbers, turnips and radishes. By 2000 BC the Egyptians were cultivating onions, garlic, peas, cabbages, celery, asparagus, radishes and exotic fruits, like dates, figs, pomegranates and melons. By the beginning of the first century BC, wealthy Greeks had elaborate gardens to supply their tables. Homer described a large walled garden in the town of Scheria which included a range of vegetables set out in beds, an orchard with apples, figs and pears, olive trees and a vineyard.

The Romans were great gardeners and, unlike the Greeks whose soil was becoming increasingly barren, were blessed with fertile soil and a good climate. Rich Romans cultivated vegetables in the gardens of their villas, although the poor also grew a wide variety of vegetables. As the Roman armies conquered new lands, local farmers began growing the vegetables the soldiers returned with — lettuces, onions, carrots, leeks, artichokes, garlic and cauliflower. Later, the Islamic invaders of northern Africa and Spain introduced citrus fruits, eggplants (aubergines) and spinach.

The contribution of monasteries to the increasing European knowledge about horticulture should not be underestimated. In the sixth century, St Benedict decreed that Benedictine monasteries should be self-supporting. As a result vegetable and herb gardens were established inside the monastery walls thereby helping to keep alive the growing of vegetables and herbs throughout the Dark Ages. By the Middle Ages vegetable farming was carried on extensively in Europe, especially in the Low Countries. New varieties of fruits, vegetables and grains, such as potatoes, tomatoes, corn, French beans, kidney beans, capsicums (sweet and chilli peppers) and Jerusalem artichokes, were introduced to Europe after the Spanish conquest of South America in the late fifteenth century.

The sixteenth and seventeenth centuries were a great time for gardening throughout Europe — and also for writing about it. This was the period of the 'herbals', scientific and pseudo-scientific treatises on the properties of different herbs and vegetables. Today, there are probably no new *species left to discover. The task now is to preserve the existing varieties. Industrialized agriculture (through large chemical trans-national companies) is promoting increased uniformity in all our food crops. Of the more than 7000 apple varieties that once grew in American orchards, 6000 are now extinct, while every broccoli variety offered through American seed catalogs in 1909 has now disappeared. The genetic diversity of many of our most basic food crops is being threatened. One way to help offset this insidious trend is to grow our own fruits and vegetables and join a local seed-saving network. It can be fun to grow unusual non-hybrid varieties and hence contribute to the preservation of the world's plant heritage.*

The joy of watching new shoots and buds appear is incalculable; the joy of transforming the food we have grown ourselves immeasurable. Where would the cook be without a garden?

PLANTING

Digging is so sensual —
worms squirm down
as if light were salt on a wound —
even the sound of the earth
and the spade is a pleasure

birds call yes they're thrilled
the plants are waiting quietly
as if they are pregnant
their time is coming
one by one they find their home
I press the earth down
with my yellow boots
it sinks like soft sin

my back aches
how do people plant rice all day —
the plants sit in their beds
like good children in hospital
all lined up
just how matron likes

and now to dig a big hole
for the Japanese maple
a tall red stick
waiting like dynamite

KATE LLEWELLYN

Vegetables

Leaf Vegetables

Through the open window he could see a flock of ducks
with their young. Waddling and stumbling, they were hurrying
down the road, apparently on their way to the pond. One
duckling picked up a piece of gut that was lying on
the ground, tried to swallow it, choked
on it and raised an alarmed squeaking. Another
duckling ran up, pulled the gut out of its beak and choked on
the thing too . . . At some distance from the fence,
in the lacy shadow cast on the grass by the young lindens,
the cook Darya was wandering about, picking sorrel
for a vegetable soup.

RAYMOND CARVER, 'SORREL' BASED ON ANTON CHEKHOV, 'AN UNPLEASANTNESS'

My father was delighted — for the first time ever, his lettuces had hearts! The cabbages that year also had hearts. In fact the whole garden was a joy to behold: there was spinach, parsley, broccoli and carrots. Living by the sea in a temperate climate, he is blessed with being able to grow a wide variety of vegetables all year round. We took our baskets and filled them with the fresh bounty, giving away the surplus to friends and neighbors.

That's one of the problems with a successful vegetable patch: over-abundance. The garden he'd been tending was based on the no-dig method and received plenty of morning and early afternoon sun all year round. When I asked him why the lettuces and cabbages had been so successful this time, he said it was the liquid fertilizer — 'they love it.' He seemed to enjoy the garden more that year, not finding it so much of a chore. Perhaps the vegetables were responding to his extra care and attention.

I've never had much luck with hearts either (I mean the vegetable kind). I'm in good company though. Heading lettuces (or those with hearts) are a relatively modern development although some claim the Romans taught lettuces to form heads! Emperor Diocletian was apparently very fond of lettuce, both to eat and to grow, and the heading variety seems to have been developed by his time (fourth century AD).

Earlier types, mostly of the romaine (Cos) variety, are very ancient, dating back to at least 800 BC when they are reported to have been grown in the gardens of King Merodach-Baladan in Babylon. Those lettuces put out leaves from a central stalk, in the same way our cultivated varieties do when they go to seed and send up seed stalks (or bolt). It was for this reason that the ancient Greeks called lettuce 'asparagus'. Some are depicted on the walls of Egyptian tombs and there are many references to them in Greek and Roman literature. During the early part of the Roman Empire, lettuces were eaten at the end of a meal, possibly because of their sleep-inducing properties. In contrast, towards the end of the empire, they were eaten as an hors d'oeuvre, in the belief that they aroused the appetite.

Today, garden lettuces are grown by the millions all over the world, and they come in all shapes, sizes and colors. In the West, they are fundamental to all manner of salads. In China, where they have also been grown for centuries, they are used more for cooking or for pickling.

There are many other varieties of leaf vegetable, like spinach, sorrel, sow thistle, watercress, land cress, arugula, raddichio, endive, Swiss chard (silverbeet), vine leaf, dandelion, celtuce, nettle, warrigal greens, and mustard and cress. Most are ideal for the home gardener and don't require a large patch of ground for growing, doing well in pots and boxes. Sensitive plants such as lettuce can be planted in the shade of other vegetables when it is hot and lattice can be used judiciously to screen out too much sun.

Lettuces are undoubtedly the most popular of the leaf vegetables. Yet many of the others, when picked young, can add zest and variety to a tossed salad. I particularly like baby spinach and sorrel, mizuna (a small cut-leaf mustard green, very popular in Japan), arugula and raddichio in a mixed salad. In France, mesclun (mixed wild leaves and grasses picked while very tiny) is sold in the markets. Mesclun need not only consist of wild plants; sometimes it is a mixed collection of greens picked at seedling stage, such as corn salad (mâche), arugula, different varieties of cress, mustard leaves and so on. Some of the seed companies now sell packets of mesclun. They are fun to plant because you can't be too sure just what will come up.

When talking about leaf vegetables, we mustn't forget the weeds. In her marvellous book, Honey from a Weed, *Patience Gray devotes a chapter to the many different weeds picked by the women and children on the island of Naxos and in Tuscany. These include dandelions, wild chicory, wild endive, milk thistle, several kinds of sorrel, and white and yellow arugula. Many are chosen for their medicinal properties which is why they are picked with a stub of root. Gray points out that Mediterranean people value bitterness in weeds, as once did all European peoples. Knowledge of which weeds to pick and their beneficial effects, especially as a balm for the liver, was once part of a common European heritage, handed down orally from mother to child. Admittedly the subject of wild greens amounts to a book in itself, though it is a shame more of us are not aware of these weeds and their properties.*

I find the growing of leaf vegetables one of the most rewarding and satisfying pastimes and would encourage everyone to try growing a few. It is possible to grow a wide selection and, because they attract few pests or diseases, they are good plants for beginners. You can grow them anywhere — in amongst the roses, or as a border along the flower bed. My mother grows various types of lettuces in polystyrene boxes and gives them away as gifts at Christmas time, wrapped in clear cellophane and tied with a bow.

Growing vegetables in containers also allows you the option of moving the plants around if the sun is too hot. Once you've had a little success, it is easy to become addicted.

Mostly leaf vegetables prefer cooler weather, thriving in spring, fall and even through winter in temperate climates. They need rich, moist, well-drained soil and most of them benefit from regular watering, applications of compost, and plenty of nitrogen and phosphorus. As with cabbages and broccoli, the secret is to grow them quickly (hence the liquid fertilizer) so that they don't become bitter or go to seed.

Lettuce
Lactuca *species*

The many different types of lettuce fall into four main categories, though there is some overlap: loose-leaf, butterhead (cabbage), crisphead and romaine (Cos). Loose-leaf don't have hearts and are the easiest to grow. They're ideal for the home gardener because you can snip off a few leaves at a time while the plant keeps growing, rather than harvesting the whole plant at once as with heading lettuce. The crisphead (or heading) variety is the one most of us buy at the greengrocer. They're crunchy and useful, without much flavor.

It's worth consulting different seed catalogues to explore the many different types now available. Some of my favorites include red and green oakleaf, lollo rosso (coral lettuce), red romaine, romaine verdi and mignonette.

With careful selection of varieties and successive sowings you can have lettuce every month of the year. Because they are shallow-rooted, however, they need frequent watering. Sugar content is 50 percent higher in the morning, so pick them early. Leaves should be washed carefully and dried thoroughly in a salad spinner or on tea-towels, then stored in the fridge. It's important to dry the leaves thoroughly so that they don't collapse, and also so that the dressing you use coats them. Baby lettuces are very fragile, so handle gently.

It wasn't until I started reading further about lettuces that I discovered, much to my surprise, that laudanum is an extract from lettuce stems, something known to the Romans. The content is highest in bolted lettuces (those which have gone to seed), so beware. They also had a reputation for cooling ardor and during the sixteenth century, Googe (author of a book on husbandry) suggested that they reduced lechery.

CYNTHIA ADEY'S SALAD

Restaurateur Cynthia Adey serves fresh greens picked daily from her garden, and tosses them together with various edible flowers. You can do the same with what you grow in your garden. One day when I visited her, she had prepared a salad made from the following: six types of baby lettuces including romaine (Cos), red and green oakleaf, lollo rosso (coral lettuce), buttercrunch and rabbit's ear; arugula (rocket), Lebanese cress, land cress, snow peas (mangetout), chervil and mizuna (a pot-herbed mustard green, popular in Japan). Tossed through these were edible flower petals — nasturtiums, borage, Johnny jump-ups, violets, pansies, geraniums, garland chrysanthemums and herb blossom.

A dressing made from three parts virgin olive oil and one part balsamic vinegar with some finely chopped garlic was tossed through this glorious salad.

Note: Mizuna is grown in the same way as lettuce, though it is more heat tolerant.

GOAT CHEESE AND WALNUT SALAD

Serve slices of good-quality fresh goat cheese (allow 2 slices per person) on a bed of tiny salad greens (corn salad, butter lettuce, mizuna). Toss the greens in a walnut oil vinaigrette and scatter with walnut halves.

In cooler weather, broil the goat cheese and if you wish, slightly warm the vinaigrette.

LETTUCE FRITTATA

This delicious Italian omelet is ideal for picnics or for lunch, served warm with a tomato and basil salad. Use a heading or romaine lettuce. Spinach or Swiss chard (silverbeet) are also good. In addition you can add cooked fresh peas, baby beans and asparagus. Grated zucchini (courgette) and zucchini flowers can also be used.

SERVES 6–8

2 ⅔ tblspns (1 ⅓ fl oz) olive oil
2 tblspns (1 oz) butter (optional)
1 onion, finely chopped
1 large crisphead lettuce
salt and pepper
6 eggs
1 ⅓ tblspns (⅔ fl oz) water
2 tblspns (½ oz) grated Parmesan cheese
handful each finely chopped basil and parsley

Preheat oven to 350°F (180°C/Gas 4). Grease a 10 in (25 cm) dish.

Heat the oil and butter in a frying pan and sauté the onion until soft. Wash and shred the lettuce and add to the pan. Cover and cook over low heat 10–15 minutes. Remove pan from heat. Drain the lettuce in a sieve, chop it, then drain again. Season well. In a large bowl, beat the eggs with the water, add the cheese, stir in the lettuce and then the basil and parsley. Pour into a greased earthenware dish or oven-proof frying pan and bake 20–25 minutes or until puffed and golden.

Note: If using the frying pan slide it from the pan onto a large plate when cooked.

SALAD SOUP

In Venice this soup is made from lettuce, spinach, celery or potatoes. Try it with the outer dark green leaves of romaine (Cos) and save the inner leaves for a salad.

SERVES 4

2 tblspns (1 oz) butter
1 small onion, finely chopped
½ head (10 oz) lettuce (any type), washed, drained and shredded
4 cups (1 qt) chicken stock (broth)
salt and pepper
3 tblspns (1 ½ oz) uncooked short-grain rice
1 tblspn (½ oz) grated fresh Parmesan

Melt the butter and sauté onion until soft. Add the lettuce and cook, covered, for about 10 minutes. Add stock and season to taste. Bring to a boil, add rice and cook, covered, for 10–15 minutes or until rice is cooked but not mushy. Remove from heat, stir in cheese until it melts, and serve.

SALAD GREENS WITH ORANGE POPPY SEED DRESSING

Choose greens with a firm leaf for this. They need to be sturdy to hold the dressing.

SERVES 6–8

1 lb mixed green leaves (romaine (Cos), iceberg, Swiss chard (silverbeet))
1 red (or Spanish) onion, peeled and finely sliced
2 oranges, sliced into segments (all pith removed)
DRESSING
1 cup (8 fl oz) plain yogurt
2 ½ tblspns (1 ⅓ fl oz) orange juice
1 ½ tblspns (⅔ fl oz) lemon or lime juice
2 ½ tblspns (1 ⅓ fl oz) vegetable oil
1 tblspn poppy seeds
zest (rind) of 1 orange, finely grated

Wash and dry the leaves. Put into a salad bowl with the onion rings and orange segments. Mix together the dressing ingredients and toss through the salad.
Variations: Grapefruit segments can be substituted for the orange for a tangy change. Some Belgian endive (witloof) is a nice addition as are a few borage flowers scattered over the top.

Swiss Chard (Silverbeet or Seakale)
Beta vulgaris

I love the bold assertiveness of Swiss chard (silverbeet), the way it thrusts up out of the ground and gleams in the sun. Once I lived in a unit on the third floor of a block of red-brick apartments. It was suitable only for one person and I felt very confined in it because I had no access to a garden, not even a balcony. Sometimes, as I was washing up, I would gaze out through the kitchen window onto the garden of the house opposite, yearning for a garden of my own.

Out the front, in amongst the flower patches, the owner kept a bed of bold, green clumps of Swiss chard. They stood there, the white and green against the brown of the earth (there was never a weed in this man's garden, so proud was he) and just looking at them would reinvigorate me. They were an assertion of life itself. I could then go back to the washing-up (and all the other chores).

Often mistakenly called spinach, Swiss chard differs from spinach by having a broad, white leaf-stalk, whereas spinach beet has a long, green stalk. Like beet, it is two vegetables in one: the green leaves can be cooked like spinach and the white stems like celery. Most people, though, tend to use both together. Swiss chard has a stronger flavor than spinach and is remarkably easy to grow, doesn't need much room, and yields well. It likes full sun and thrives on liquid manure. Mulch around the plants. It keeps the soil moist and enhances leaf growth. Outer leaves can be picked as required.

The most popular variety for the home gardener is the Fordhook Giant which has dark green leaves and creamy-white stalks; the beautiful Rainbow Chard (with its purple, red, pink and yellow leaves) and Ruby Chard (with its crimson stalks and bright green leaves) are splendid alternatives.

BROWN RICE AND SWISS CHARD

Quite often I find I get into a rut with my cooking. I keep doing the same dishes over and over. I have lots of cookbooks and am always thinking about food and yet I get stuck in these habitual patterns which can be quite deadly.

One night I looked in the refrigerator and found some leftover cooked brown rice and some Swiss chard. What could I do that would be delicious and a bit different? Here's what I came up with. It was very good.

I took a handful, 2–3 tblspns (1–1 ⅓ oz), of pinenuts (pignolias), tossed them until golden in a pan with some oil, threw in the rice, ⅔–¾ cup (4–5 oz), stirred it around, then added about 8 leaves of washed, shredded Swiss chard. I tossed that around for a bit, then sprinkled it all with a light soy sauce. Just before serving I scattered through 4–6 scallions (shallots, spring onions), cut on the diagonal. It's important these remain crisp, so take the pan off the heat immediately they are added.

This really could be a meal in itself and you can use English spinach or Swiss chard, brown or white rice.

SESAME SWISS CHARD SALAD

SERVES 4–6

1 small bunch Swiss chard (silverbeet), preferably the smaller leaves
1 tspn roasted sesame oil
4 tblspns sesame seeds
1 ⅓ tblspns (⅔ fl oz) lemon juice
salt to taste

Wash Swiss chard well; remove white stalks and dry leaves thoroughly. Tear up leaves and place in a large bowl, add oil and mix well — use your hands to do this.

Toast the sesame seeds in a heavy frying pan over medium heat, cool, then add to Swiss chard along with the lemon juice and salt. Toss together with your hands and serve. Even though there is so little oil, its flavor will go right through the salad.

SWISS CHARD AND CHICKEN TERRINE

I saw this being presented one night at a fashionable bistro. The chef had garnished it with snow pea (mangetout) sprouts and diced tomatoes. The sprouts were laid out around the slices of terrine in a hexagonal pattern, and the tomato placed in small mounds at the meeting of each corner of the hexagon.

You might be thinking, 'Oh no, nouvelle cuisine.' It wasn't. There was an abandon to the way the sprouts had been placed. It didn't have the stiff formality of nouvelle cuisine, though that was probably the original inspiration for this presentation. And the servings were generous.

This would make a lovely lunchtime or picnic dish, served with a tossed green salad to which you can add lots of avocado. It's also a good entrée or appetizer.

SERVES 10–12

8 thick slices of prosciutto
1 bunch Swiss chard (silverbeet) or spinach (12–16 leaves)
1 ½ lb chicken breasts
3 eggs
1 ¼ cups (10 fl oz) thickened cream
salt and pepper
freshly grated Parmesan cheese

Preheat oven to 400°F (200°C/Gas 6).

Brush an 8 cup (2 qt) terrine dish with oil. Line with slices of overlapping prosciutto. Wash the Swiss chard, cut off the stalks. Remove excess fat and membrane from chicken breasts. Pound lightly between two sheets of plastic wrap until flattened out a little.

Sprinkle the bottom of the dish with Parmesan, then make the layers: put some Swiss chard leaves along the bottom, then some of the chicken. Sprinkle with Parmesan. Keep doing this until you have 3–4 layers, finishing off with the chicken.

Beat together the eggs, cream, salt and pepper and pour over the top. Cover with aluminum foil and cook in oven in a *bain-marie* for 1 ¼ hours.

When you have removed it from the oven (and from the *bain-marie*), let it cool with a weight on top, then refrigerate overnight. Cut into slices and serve with a spicy fruit chutney like Spicy Peach Chutney (page 150).

Spinach
Spinacia oleracea

Like Swiss chard (silverbeet), spinach is easy to grow and attracts few pests and diseases. Its origins are obscure, though many say it comes from south-western Asia (Persia). The ancient Greeks and Romans did not know it. The earliest record comes from China, where the King of Nepal sent some ('a vinegar leaf vegetable') as a present to the Chinese in the seventh century AD. By the eleventh century, it had become popular in Spain and by the fourteenth century, prickly seed spinach was growing in monastery gardens throughout Europe. Smooth seed spinach was first documented in England in 1551.

Spinach likes a sunny position and does best in cooler weather, tending to bolt at temperatures above 75°F (24°C). It thrives in containers and also makes an attractive border for a flower garden if space is limited. It likes plenty of moisture, but is sensitive to fertilizer burn. An application of dolomite to the soil before planting will be necessary.

SPINACH AND PEAR PURÉE

One of the inventive (and good) combinations from 'nouvelle cuisine' days. Moist, smooth but grainy, and slightly sweet, it goes well with game and poultry. Best made just before it is needed when its colour is a delicate green.

Wash and destalk 13 oz fresh spinach. Cook 3 minutes in boiling salted water. Refresh in cold water and drain well. Peel, quarter and core 3 oz pears and poach for 15 minutes in boiling water. Purée spinach and pears in a food processor or blender and check the seasoning.

SPINACH SALAD WITH BACON, PINENUTS AND HARD-BOILED EGGS

The Bayswater Brasserie is one of Sydney's oldest and most popular brasseries. It is very alive and always busy, which is part of its attraction. The food is fresh and modern. This salad is a must for me whenever I visit and is really a meal in itself.

SERVES 6

4 bunches spinach
6 eggs, hard-boiled
10 oz bacon rashers
¾ cup (3 oz) pinenuts (pignolias), toasted
vinaigrette dressing
sea salt and freshly ground black pepper

Wash the spinach well and pat dry with paper towels. Chop off the stalks and tear leaves into thirds. Sieve hard-boiled egg yolks and chop egg whites. Remove the rind from the bacon and cut into julienne strips. Dry-fry until crisp, remove and drain on a paper towel.

Dress the leaves with a vinaigrette made with olive oil, white wine vinegar (3 parts oil:1 part vinegar) and Dijon mustard. Arrange them in a bowl, sprinkle with the egg whites then the yolks of eggs, the bacon and the nuts. Season with sea salt and pepper. Drizzle over a little more vinaigrette.

SPINACH WITH PANIR

Panir, or fresh cheese, is a staple in India where protein is often in short supply. It is also a way of stretching the life of milk. You can substitute Swiss chard (silverbeet) for the spinach.

SERVES 4

PANIR

8 cups (2 qt) milk
1 cup (7 oz) plain yogurt
2 ⅔ tblspns (1 ⅓ fl oz) lemon juice
salt

SPINACH MIXTURE

2 ⅔ tblspns (1 ⅓ fl oz) oil
1 green chilli, finely chopped
2 cloves garlic, finely chopped
1 knob ginger (1 in), peeled and finely chopped
¼ tspn cumin seeds
2 ripe tomatoes, chopped
2 bunches spinach, washed and chopped
salt
1 tspn each ground cumin, coriander (cilantro) and aamchur (dried mango powder)
¼ tspn ground turmeric

Bring milk to a boil on a low heat. Add yogurt, lemon juice and salt to taste, stir well. Allow to curdle and remove from heat. Let stand 2 minutes then pour though muslin or cheese cloth. Drain and place the panir (or curds) on a flat dish.

For the spinach mixture, heat oil in a medium saucepan. Add the chilli, garlic, ginger and cumin seeds. Let sizzle for 1 minute, then add the tomatoes. Cover and let cook 4–6 minutes or until tomatoes are soft. Add the chopped spinach and a little water and season with salt. Put lid back on and cook 10 minutes. Stir in the remaining spices and mix well, cook another 5 minutes.

Pour the spinach mixture over the panir and serve immediately.

Sorrel
Rumex acetosa

*Widely used in Europe until the seventeenth century, sorrel fell
from favor over the following centuries. It is almost unavailable these days,
except in France where it is much liked.*

*A pity, because it is very easy to grow. Once planted, this strong-rooted
perennial never gives any trouble, dying back in winter and bursting forth with new vigor each spring. The first
crop each year is the best of all. Picked small, it makes a good, astringent addition to a salad; picked large, the
leaves make excellent soup and sauces.*

*Because it wilts so quickly once picked, it is a good plant for the home gardener. If you've ever bought sorrel
from the greengrocer, you'll know how quickly it loses its freshness.*

*Most of the sorrels (of which there are about 100 species) grow wild in just about every part of the globe.
Some varieties have been cultivated. Sorrel is free from most pests, likes full or half sunlight and mulching when
the plants are small.*

SORREL AND POTATO SALAD

SERVES 4

Peel 3–4 potatoes — cook, cool and chop into cubes.
Wash a couple of good handfuls of young sorrel and
shred. Slice 2–3 scallions (shallots, spring onions).
Combine these in a salad bowl and dress. For the
dressing, mix together ½ cup (4 fl oz) sour cream, 1 ⅓
tblspns (⅔ fl oz) white wine vinegar, 1 tspn Dijon
mustard. Season to taste
with salt and pepper.

SORREL SAUCE

Sorrel goes well with fish and eggs. I like to shred it and
add it to an omelet filling. This sauce is good with
poached fish, though it's a pity it turns such an ugly
khaki color when it hits the heat.

Wash and dry two bunches (approx 4 oz) sorrel
leaves, remove the stalks and chop roughly. Melt some
butter in a pan, add the sorrel and some freshly ground
black pepper. Cook until soft then put into a blender
with ⅞ cup (7 fl oz) cream and blend until smooth.
Return to heat, thin out with more cream if too thick.

Endive
Cichorium endivia

There is much confusion over the naming of this vegetable, some claiming that endive is chicory, others that it is the straggly leafed green salad vegetable. For our purposes, I have chosen to call the latter 'endive'.

There are two main varieties of this leaf: the curly endive made up of a rosette of green curly leaves, darker at the tips, lighter in the middle; and the broadleaf Batavian, similar to the former, but with leaves that are toothed and wavy rather than curly (frisées).

Even more confusion reigns over its origin, some claiming its source as Egypt (or native to the Mediterranean region); others say it came from China or the Far East.

Whatever, its leaves add a slightly bitter taste to salad. The ancients appreciated it for its beneficial effect on the liver.

Like lettuce, it is best when grown quickly to avoid too much bitterness and pungency — in fact, it grows well in the same spot after a crop of lettuce. Endive likes full sun, but needs dappled shade in the heat of the summer. When the plant is half-grown and the head fairly well established, draw up the outer leaves and tie together with soft string to keep the heart out of the sun.

WARM SALAD OF ENDIVE AND QUAIL

Prepare the quail the day beforehand. Allow one quail per person. Split the quail down the back so that they lie flat. Marinate the quail in the Apricot Marinade (page 152) overnight. Remove from marinade and let drain. Char-grill the quail in a lightly oiled, ridged cast-iron pan. Or you can barbecue them, or cook them under a hot broiler. Cook 3–4 minutes on each side, keeping them pinkish.

Prepare a salad using curly endive. Wash and dry well, choosing the best tips. Put them in a bowl. A few leaves of butter lettuce, romana, baby sorrel or watercress can be mixed through.

Add 1 tspn roasted sesame oil and mix well — use your hands to do this.

Toast ¼ cup sesame seeds in a heavy frying pan over medium heat, cool, then add to leaves along with 1 ⅓ tblspns (⅔ fl oz) lemon juice and salt to taste. Toss together with your hands.

Warm Salad of Smoked Chicken (or Pheasant)

Smoked chicken is easier to find than pheasant and is a nice substitute.

SERVES 4–6

4 oz of a variety of lettuces (endive, mignonette, romaine (Cos), arugula, Belgian endive (witloof))

1 smoked chicken or *smoked pheasant, approx 2 lb*

8 oz large dark mushrooms, sliced

18 pieces mustard fruits (recipe below)

½ cup (4 fl oz) olive oil

2 tblspns (1 fl oz) balsamic vinegar

sea salt

pepper

Wash and dry lettuces. Make a vinaigrette to taste, about 4 parts olive oil to 1 part balsamic vinegar. Season to taste with sea salt and freshly ground pepper. Carve smoked chicken or pheasant off the bone and slice thinly.

In a frying pan, sauté mushrooms in 4 tblspns of oil until cooked and add sliced chicken or pheasant together with mustard fruits. Toss to warm only, then toss in a little vinaigrette to coat.

Compose the mixed lettuce leaves on serving plates, dress with vinaigrette. Divide chicken, mushroom and apricot mixture equally and spoon over top of lettuce leaves. Serve immediately while still warm.

Mustard Fruits

10–12 fresh apricots, washed, halved and pitted

2 ⅔ tblspns (1 ⅓ fl oz) water

1 tblspn (½ oz) sugar

2 tblspns (1 fl oz) white wine vinegar

1 ½ tblspns mustard powder

Put the apricots, water and sugar into a small saucepan, covered. Cook over medium heat 3–5 minutes, shaking the pan to dissolve sugar. Don't let apricots become mushy. Remove from heat. Mix vinegar and mustard powder together to form a paste and stir into apricots. *Note: Dried apricots can be used. Poach in a syrup made with equal quantities of water and sugar before using.*

Vine Leaves
Vitis vinifera

Vines grow well in most climates, depending on the variety. However, they do not like humidity. When grown in the backyard, make sure they are in an airy position with good drainage. Even if you don't have luck with the grapes, the leaves can be used in various dishes as enclosures (or envelopes).

VINE-WRAPPED QUAIL

Chef Phillip Searle once served a version of these at a Gastronomic Symposium held in Sydney. They were boned out, wrapped in lotus leaves and baked in the oven in a clay enclosure. Guests were each given a tiny hammer to crack them open. You can imagine the noise as 60 or so people cracked away! The quail can also be cooked in hot ashes in the barbecue for 25–30 minutes. Start preparation one day ahead.

SERVES 8

8 quail
½ cup (4 oz) butter, at room temperature
8 fresh large vine leaves (or 16 small), washed and dried
16 thin strips of pork back fat

MARINADE
½ cup (4 fl oz) soy sauce
1 tblspn fresh ginger, finely grated
2 cloves garlic, chopped
juice and zest (rind) of ½ orange
1 tspn roasted sesame oil

FILLING
¼ cup (2 oz) wild rice
¾ cup (6 fl oz) chicken stock (broth)
¼ cup (2 fl oz) water
1 ⅓ tblspns (⅔ fl oz) soy sauce
2 ⅔ tblspns (1 ⅓ fl oz) orange juice
½ cup (3 oz) golden raisins (sultanas)
2 cloves garlic, finely chopped
¼ cup (1 ⅓ oz) pinenuts (pignolias)

Combine marinade ingredients. Pour over quail and refrigerate, covered, for 24 hours.

Combine rice with the stock and water in a saucepan; bring to a boil, cover tightly, reduce heat to low and cook for 30 minutes without lifting the lid. Turn off heat and let stand 25–35 minutes or until rice reaches desired texture. Drain and combine with remaining filling ingredients.

Preheat oven to 400°F (200°C/Gas 6).

Drain quail and stuff body cavities with the filling, reshaping birds neatly. Lightly oil the vine leaves and wrap around quail. Place a piece of pork fat on each side of parcel and tie up with string. Wrap in foil and cook in oven for 25–30 minutes. To serve, remove foil, string and fat, and present quail still wrapped in the leaves.

VINE LEAF ROLLS

These are lovely and lemony. You can also use Swiss chard (silverbeet): plunge the leaves into hot water to make them limp, then roll up as for vine leaves. You will need to halve or quarter them, depending on their size. Place in a saucepan with the tomato slices on the bottom and the leftover Swiss chard stalks.

MAKES APPROX 40

1 bunch flat-leaf (Italian) parsley
1 tomato, finely chopped
1 medium onion, finely chopped
salt to taste
¼ cup chopped mint
1 cup (5 oz) uncooked long grain rice
½ cup (4 fl oz) lemon juice
½ cup (4 fl oz) oil
pinch allspice
40 fresh vine leaves, blanched
4 ripe tomatoes

Wash the parsley, trim stalks and chop coarsely. Combine in a bowl with all the ingredients except for the vine leaves and 4 tomatoes. Mix together well — make it a little salty to taste as the salt is absorbed during the cooking. Allow to soak for an hour then drain, reserving excess liquid.

Unroll the vine leaves, wash them under running water, then place a small amount of rice mixture in each leaf, fold in the corners carefully and roll up. Don't make them too big — about finger width is wide enough.

Slice the 4 tomatoes into ¼ in rounds and place in medium-sized saucepan with a few extra vine leaves. Place the rolls on top of the tomato slices. Pack the rolls close together so that there is no movement during cooking. Pour the reserved liquid over the packed rolls, then place a plate over them to hold them down, otherwise they will unroll as the mixture starts simmering.

Cook over a very low heat, for 30 minutes. Turn the heat off and allow the rolls to finish cooking in their own heat. When cool, cover with plastic wrap and store in the refrigerator.

Arugula
Eruca vesicaria (*or* sativa)

Variously known as 'ruccola', 'rocket', 'rughetta', 'roquette' and just plain arugula, this peppery, nutty green is a favorite of mine. In the Salentine peninsula in Italy, wild arugula (Eruca sativa) *is used for cooking. It has spiky leaves and a strong flavor. The cultivated version has larger leaves with a milder taste. Arugula is short-lived and best grown in early spring and autumn because it bolts in hot weather. Seed can be broadcast in the garden or sown first in seed trays and transplanted. Keep well watered and fertilize lightly for succulent growth.*

SALSA DI RUCCOLA

Use over freshly cooked pasta, gnocchi, jacket baked potatoes or with cooked white beans (borlotti, lima, cannellini), combined with tomatoes and shavings of Parmesan cheese.

SERVES 4–6

8 oz fresh arugula (ruccola), approx 2 bunches
⅓ cup (1 ⅔ oz) pinenuts (pignolias)
1 cup (4 oz) freshly grated Parmesan cheese
½ cup (4 fl oz) olive oil

Wash the arugula, dry well and put the torn leaves into the food processor. Add the pinenuts and process until mixture forms a paste. Add the Parmesan cheese and drizzle in the oil.

SPAGHETTI WITH ARUGULA

I love the flavor of arugula and like to eat it dressed with olive oil and a few shavings of Parmesan cheese on the top. It is also very good cooked, as in this simple, light dish. In southern Italy, a pasta known as orecchiette or 'little ears' is used and the dish is served very hot with a piquant grated cheese. They blanch the arugula in the pasta water first, but I prefer it this way.

SERVES 4

13 oz spaghetti
¼ cup (2 fl oz) olive oil
4 cloves garlic, finely chopped
1 small chilli, finely chopped
2 ½ oz arugula, washed and torn into pieces
salt and freshly ground black pepper

Cook the spaghetti until it is *al dente*. Meanwhile, heat the oil in a frying pan, add the garlic and chilli and cook until garlic is translucent, being careful not to let it burn.

Drain the pasta and put into a serving bowl. Toss the rocket leaves quickly in the pan, just to coat the leaves in the oil. Stir into the spaghetti in the bowl and mix. Add salt and pepper to taste. Serve immediately.

Variation: A little finely grated lemon zest (rind) is an interesting addition.

Watercress and other Cresses
Nasturtium officinale

Like the other leaves, watercress is easily grown and is especially suitable for gardens where space is at a premium. The ancient Greeks, Romans and Persians knew about watercress (they ate it for its health properties) but they gathered it wild, a practice which has continued ever since. Cultivated watercress is fairly recent, though during the mid-nineteenth century street vendors sold it in London and Sydney from baskets on the top of their heads.

Watercress is a close relative of the nasturtium, with dark green leaves and a pungent flavor. It is an aquatic plant which thrives in the wild in running streams, but is easily propagated from cuttings or divisions. Grow in the shade in pots or in a wet part of the garden. There are dry land cresses as well (those which grow on dry soils). These include Barbarea praecox *and* B. verna, *both of which are becoming increasingly popular. They are similar to watercress and sometimes confused with it. Their flavor is slightly more pungent. Mustard and cress is also popular, used as a pretty garnish or thrown into salads. Cress* (Lepidium sativum) *and mustard seeds (either the white,* Sinapis alba, *or the black,* Brassica nigra) *are grown together in small pots or punnets in well-drained, friable soil. They can be sown all year round and are ready for cutting with scissors in about three weeks. Because mustard germinates faster than cress, sow it a few days earlier. These seeds can also be grown on wet blotting paper, a fun thing for the children to do. Keep the seeds in a dark place until they germinate.*

BOILED TONGUE WITH SALSA VERDE (GREEN SAUCE)

It's a good idea to soak the tongue overnight in cold water, though not essential.

SERVES 4

1 tongue, approx 2–3 lb
2 ⅔ tblspns (1 ⅓ fl oz) vinegar
1 carrot, peeled
1 onion, peeled
1 stalk celery
bunch parsley
sprig thyme
1 bay leaf
few black peppercorns

SALSA VERDE
1 large bunch watercress, approx 1 lb
4 tblspns chopped parsley
1 small onion, chopped
1 clove garlic, crushed
1 ⅓ tblspns (⅔ fl oz) lemon juice
⅔ cup (5 fl oz) olive oil
4 anchovy fillets
2 (sweet) gherkins, chopped
salt and freshly ground pepper

Place tongue in a large pot and cover with fresh water. Add remaining ingredients, bring to boiling point, skim, cover and simmer for 2 hours or until tongue is very tender. Allow to cool in liquid, but while still warm, remove skin.

Slice the tongue thinly and arrange on a plate. Spoon over a little of the sauce and serve remainder separately.

SALSA VERDE
Wash the watercress and remove stalks. Blanch for 1 minute in rapidly boiling salted water. Drain and refresh immediately under cold running water. Process in a blender or food processor along with the parsley, onion, garlic and lemon juice.

When smooth, add oil very slowly, blending continually so that sauce does not separate. Add anchovies and blend a further minute or so until smooth. Place in a bowl and fold through the chopped gherkins. Season to taste.

POTAGE CREME DE CRESSON

Easy to prepare and cook, this is a beautiful, rich but delicate soup. It is versatile, too, as you can substitute sorrel or spinach for the watercress according to the season.

SERVES 4–6

1 onion, finely chopped
¼ cup (2 oz) butter
1 lb fresh watercress leaves
½ tspn salt
¼ cup (1 oz) all-purpose flour
6 cups (1 ½ qt) boiling chicken stock (broth)
2 egg yolks
⅔ cup (5 fl oz) cream
2 tblspns (1 oz) softened butter

Sauté the onion in the butter in a large saucepan until translucent. Wash and dry the watercress, add to onions along with salt and cook slowly for 5 minutes, covered, until leaves have wilted. Sprinkle over the flour and stir for 3–5 minutes. Remove from heat and stir in boiling stock. Bring back to a boil and cook for further 5 minutes, then place in blender or food processor and purée. You can prepare the soup a day ahead up to this stage. Cover and refrigerate.

Just before serving, reheat the soup. In a bowl, mix together the yolks and cream and gradually beat in 1 cup of the hot soup. Return to saucepan and stir over medium heat for 2 minutes to gently cook the yolks. Remove from heat, stir in softened butter. Serve decorated with watercress leaves.

Brassicas
Brassicaceae family

There was little of design in the garden originally, though one had formed out of the wilderness. It was perfectly obvious that the man was seated at the heart of it, and from this heart the trees radiated, with grave movements of life, and beyond them the sweep of a vegetable garden, which had gone to weed during the months of the man's illness, presented the austere skeletons of cabbages and the wands of onion seed.

PATRICK WHITE, FROM THE TREE OF MAN

Early morning in the Kangaroo Valley, on the south-east coast of Australia, the fog still lingering in nooks and crannies. Greg Thompson, in black Wellington boots, was out the back stooped over his cabbages, his young son alongside. Row upon row of silver-blue cabbages, the dew still on their leaves, greeted them. There was broccoli too, the heads not yet formed, rather like the stalwart young ones in my winter garden. The cabbage, chief of the brassica tribe and one of our oldest foods, has had a bad press for a long time, associated with evil smells and boarding school dinners. But who could ignore the beauty before us?

I recalled a table setting I once did for a Sunday lunch in which a mixture of the brassicas was laid out down the center of an old wooden table: a rainbow of purple sprouting broccoli, green broccoli, red cabbage, savoy cabbage, Chinese (Peking) cabbage, Roman broccoli (or cauli-broc), cauliflowers, kohlrabi, Brussels sprouts, and different varieties of curly kale. Their presence lent a majestic feeling to the occasion.

Greek myth acknowledges their majesty, claiming that the first cabbage sprang from the tears of King Lycurgus whom the wine god Dionysus (known as the 'raging god') punished for trampling his grapes. Not surprisingly, botanists have sought clues elsewhere. Many believe cabbage grew wild along the coasts of England and northern Europe (it still grows wild in some parts of England). Some claim that its ancestor is the sea kale (Crambe maritima) which is a native to those coastal areas.

There are many types of cabbage, now vanished, which were once considered very special. One of these is the musk cabbage, another the Dorsetshire kale.

Brassicas are members of the Brassicaceae (mustard) family, the flowers of which are four-petalled and cross-shaped. There are more than 40 species of the genus Brassica, *yet only one, B. oleracea, has found favor in Western kitchens. The variety of subspecies descended from it are one of the Old World's most valuable contributions to the kitchen garden.*

Broccoli, Brussels sprouts, cauliflower, collards, kale and kohlrabi are all cabbages which evolved not through mutation or hybridization but through the encouragement of one element or another already present in the original plant. Concentration on the flower resulted in both cauliflower and broccoli; swelling pith gave rise to kohlrabi.

Broccoli and cauliflower flourished in the early days of settlement in Australia, attaining 'a much superior degree of perfection' than those grown in England, according to leading statesman W.C. Wentworth. Cabbages also did well, and in a description of the colony published in London in 1820, Wentworth gives detailed advice on how to cultivate cabbages and other vegetables and fruits.

In China, the brassicas dominate the vegetable scene. The species in question are not those known to the rest of the world, and even botanists disagree as to their classification. They are all native Chinese cultigens, the dominant ones being B. pekinensis *(pai ts'ai): the long cylindrical-headed forms;* B. chinensis *(pak choi): the non-headed, white-petioled forms and* B. juncea *(kaai choi).*

The European cabbage (B. oleracea) *has only recently been introduced from the West. The Cantonese choi sum ('vegetable heart'), so essential to southern Chinese cooking, is a form of* B. chinensis. *Some consider this the best of the Chinese cabbages.*

These cabbages, along with mustards and radishes, are the most important minor crops of China. A bowl of rice, some beancurd and a dish of fresh or pickled cabbage is the staple meal of most southern Chinese. During the building of the Great Wall of China in the third century BC, *the men were fed on fermented vegetables, including cabbage (our version of sauerkraut), beets, turnips and radishes. If you prefer a more subtle-tasting cabbage, these are the ones to try.*

Chinese cabbage, broccoli, cabbage and cauliflower can all be grown from seed or seedlings. However, Chinese cabbage is less adaptable, tending to bolt if disturbed and seeds are best planted directly in the garden. Brassicas must be fed well — cauliflowers are particularly greedy. A highly fertile soil is necessary to give them a good start and they must be planted in firmly. If you are using the normal three-year rotation of crops, plant brassicas where peas and beans grew the previous year. If you are following the no-dig method, Esther Deans, author of Growing Without Digging, *suggests alternating leafy crops, like the brassicas, with tubers and root vegetables.*

Of the brassicas, the cabbages with solid heads are the most difficult to grow. This is because slugs and bugs can get up under the leaves and nestle inside. Once in, they're impossible to move, so they need careful watching. Dipel (Bacillus thuringensis) is one remedy, especially for the white butterfly and the cabbage moth larvae. Cabbages also need boosting with a liquid nitrogen fertilizer and to have the weeds removed from around them constantly (these attract the slugs and snails). They like good drainage and a high pH level in the soil. Broccoli and cauliflower aren't so susceptible to insects.

The mini varieties of cabbages and cauliflowers are good for balcony and rooftop growers, and have the widest planting period of any in the family.

Cabbages
Brassica oleracea *var.* capitata

If you've ever grown cabbages, you'll know how they grow out from their centers, just getting on with the job. Unlike the rose, which in some ways they resemble (their petals are rose-like, though their nature is not so vain), they are watery creatures, content to grow close to the earth.

The great novelist Patrick White captures their essence in The Tree of Man *when he speaks of how*

their blue and purple flesh ran together with the silver of water, the jewels of light, in the smell of warming earth. But always tensing. Already in the hard, later light the young cabbages were resistant balls of muscle, until in time they were the big, placid cabbages, all heart and limp panniers, and in the middle of the day there was the glandular stench of cabbages.

Home-grown ones have a much better flavor than those bought in a shop and are delicious shredded fresh through salads or added to soups. The tastes of all types are closely related, with a mustard-like flavor, though some can have a sweeter or musky taste, whilst others are more pungent with overtones of sulphur.

Snails and slugs love cabbages. So do caterpillars. In The Whole Art of Husbandry, *published in 1707, John Mortimer wrote 'If your Cabbages and Colliflowers are troubled with Caterpillars, mix Salt and Water, and water them therewith and it will kill them.' Picking the eggs off the undersides of the leaves is effective (the eggs are cream-coloured and about the size of a large pinhead).*

There are many varieties available, and juggling varieties and harvest times based on climate can be tricky. Consult local seed catalogs and nurserymen for specific advice. Having originated as loose-leafed wild plants, hard-headed cabbages were developed during the sixteenth century, after which horticulturalists developed types with different shaped heads: round, pointed (conical) and drumhead (solid, almost flat). Heads are usually 6–12 in in diameter.

Of all the cabbages, the reds are the most difficult to grow. Cabbages like well-drained soil and a sunny position, and will cross-pollinate with other brassicas. Seeds can be sown direct in clumps and each clump thinned to one seedling. Check local seed catalogs for best times to sow. Spacing depends on the variety: the smaller varieties need 16–20 in spacing, while the larger varieties need 23–30 in. You can make successive sowings over a long period and for the average family, nine to twelve plants are sufficient at each sowing.

All cabbages, especially the smaller hybrids like Superette, are ideal for growing in containers. The secret of success is to grow them quickly, otherwise they can run to seed (bolt). This can be achieved with good rich soil and regular applications of plant food.

CABBAGE AND LEEK STRUDEL

This is surprisingly easy and good.

MAKES 2 STRUDELS — SERVES 10

10 sheets phyllo pastry
1 large cabbage, approx 3 lb
1 leek, washed and sliced thinly
1 ½ cups (12 fl oz) sour cream
1 tspn caraway seeds
4 hard-boiled eggs, chopped
salt and freshly ground black pepper
melted butter

Allow 5 sheets of filo pastry per strudel. Stack them on top of each other, brushing melted butter between the layers. Keep covered with a damp tea-towel to avoid drying out.

Preheat the oven to 400°F (200°C/Gas 6).

Wash, shred and dry the cabbage, squeezing out any excess moisture. Mound half of it in the center of 5 prepared filo pastry sheets. Divide the other ingredients in half and arrange them along the top of the cabbage. Season to taste. Fold in the sides of one-half of the pastry and fold over the other flap. Brush with melted butter, sprinkle with water and bake for 20 minutes. Reduce heat to 350°F (180°C/Gas 4) and bake for another 10 minutes or until crisp and golden. Repeat for second strudel.

GADO GADO

I came across this delicious mixed vegetable dish with peanut sauce out on the Kedewatan Road, about three kilometers from Ubud in central Bali. We had bumped into some fellow Australians at Sanur, down on the coast, and they had told us about their fledgling new restaurant — the Kupu Kupu Barong, overlooking the Ayung River.

I was pleased we made the effort to go there. Not only was I shown how to make a number of dishes by Darta, the cook, but the restaurant was one of the most breathtaking I'd ever been to.

In typical Balinese style, it was open to the outside with a tiled floor and high, pointed roof. It sat on the side of a steep cliff, the river sparkling along below, and was surrounded by row upon row of terraced rice paddies. The thick heat, the vivid colors of the vegetation, and the gentleness of the people who looked after us will always remain with me. I had an intimation that day that I was close to heaven.

This cold mixed vegetable salad is an ideal meal for a Sunday lunch or you can use it to accompany a full meal of meat and rice.

Firmer vegetables need blanching first. Or you can steam them, if you prefer. The following is a selection which can be varied:

SERVES 6–8

¼ small cabbage, shredded

8 oz green beans

2 carrots, sliced diagonally

4 oz beansprouts

small bunch watercress or Swiss chard (silverbeet), shredded

1–2 medium potatoes, cooked until soft and sliced

2–3 hard-boiled eggs, sliced

1–2 tomatoes, sliced

6 pieces tofu (beancurd), fried and sliced

fried onion flakes for garnish

PEANUT (GROUNDNUT) SAUCE

4 cloves garlic, peeled

4 small knobs (½ in) ginger, peeled

1 in piece large red chilli, seeds removed

1 small hot red chilli

1 small knob (½ in) terasi (shrimp paste)

½ cup (2 ½ oz) toasted peanuts (groundnuts)

¼ small coconut, brown skin on (shell removed)

½ cup (4 fl oz) water

salt and pepper

⅓ cup (3 fl oz) hot water

fresh lime juice

Blanch cabbage, beans and carrots separately in rapidly boiling salted water. Refresh under cold water. Drain well, then arrange the vegetables on a round (or oval) platter. Put all the cabbage in one section, then place the beans beside it and work around the plate. Top with potato and tomato, then the egg. Arrange the tofu around the outside and serve with Peanut Sauce. You can either spoon the sauce over the vegetables and garnish with fried onion flakes or serve it in a separate bowl which can be placed in the center of the vegetables.

PEANUT SAUCE

Put the garlic, ginger, chillies and terasi into a dry, hot wok or frying pan. Cook until blackened. Alternatively, the ingredients can be broiled (grilled) until they begin to 'char'. (You can also secure each to a toothpick, or skewer, and heat it over a gas flame, as Darta did, until it begins to blacken, though this is time consuming.) Doing this helps to release the pungent flavors.

Remove from the heat, and add peanuts. Grate the coconut coarsely and process together with the wok ingredients in a food processor with ½ cup (4 fl oz) water.

Season to taste. Return to wok, add ⅓ cup (3 fl oz) water, bring to a boil, cook 5 minutes. Add more water if you like a runnier sauce.

If serving separately, put the sauce into a bowl, add a squeeze of lime juice and stir well. Garnish with a few fried onion flakes.

CABBAGE AND BACON

SERVES 6, AS AN ACCOMPANIMENT TO A MAIN MEAL

4 rashers bacon, rind removed and chopped
1 ⅓ tblspns (⅔ fl oz) vegetable oil
½ savoy or heading cabbage, approx 2 ½ lb,
shredded
3 tblspns (1 ½ oz) butter
2 tspns caraway seeds
black pepper and salt

In a large saucepan, cook bacon in oil until crispy. Add cabbage, butter and caraway seeds. Cover and cook over medium heat 10–12 minutes, stirring occasionally. Check for seasoning. Serve hot.

SAVOY CABBAGE AND BEAN SOUP

SERVES 6

1 onion
1 carrot
1 stalk celery
1 leek
2–3 ripe tomatoes
¼ cup (2 fl oz) olive oil
4–6 cloves garlic, crushed
1 ¼ cups (8 oz) haricot or cannellini beans, soaked overnight
8 cups (2 qt) chicken stock (broth)
¼ savoy cabbage, shredded (approx 8 oz)
3 zucchini (courgettes), sliced
salt
freshly ground black pepper

Peel the onion and carrot and slice. Chop the celery. Wash the leek well, slice. Peel tomatoes by plunging into boiling water for 1 minute and removing skins, chop coarsely. Heat the oil in a medium-sized saucepan, add the onion, carrot, celery and leek and cook until soft, then add the crushed garlic and cook for a couple of minutes longer. Add tomatoes and drained beans, combine well. Pour in the stock. Bring to a boil, lower heat and simmer gently for 1 ½–2 hours or until beans are cooked. Twenty minutes before the end, add the cabbage and zucchini and season to taste. Cook until they are *al dente*.

Pour into serving bowls and serve with a little pesto or olive oil. For a real peasant-style soup, put a slice of whole-wheat (wholemeal) bread in the bottom of each bowl, and pour the soup over this.

Chinese Cabbages
Brassica rapa pekinensis

In China, the word for 'cabbage' is the same as for 'vegetable' — 'choi'.

In autumn, all over China, you'll find cabbages piled up for pickling or drying in the sun in preparation for winter. They are everywhere, the streets filled with them, some people even storing them under beds.

There are many varieties available, though all are more tender and succulent than their European counterparts. They also develop more quickly. Some are heading cabbages and others, like 'pak choi', are loose-leaf. Many are mild in flavor, others more peppery or strongly cabbage-like. In China, individual villages and communes often have their own varieties, and if you've ever asked a Chinese market-gardener what the name is for a green he has grown and how you should use it, he'll usually grin at you and say 'Soup, soup.'

My favorite is 'pak choi' (Chinese white cabbage) with its succulent white leaf-stalks and tender leaves, though some consider choi sum (Chinese flowering cabbage) to be the best. Certainly in Hong Kong today, it is one of the most common and popular of the leafy vegetables. Peking cabbage, sometimes called pe-tsai, wong bok, Napa, Shantung or Tientsin is also a lovely cabbage with a sweetness that I like.

Pak choi is available as a non-hybrid and is a hardy, fast growing variety; kwan hoo choi and Santo are also available in the non-heading varieties and can be sown spring, summer and autumn; Nozaki, South China Earliest and wong bok are available in the heading varieties.

Chinese cabbages are grown in much the same way as ordinary cabbage but are not quite as adaptable. Seeds are best sown late summer and fall because seeds sown in spring and early summer tend to run to seed prematurely.

They are usually ready to harvest in 8–10 weeks from sowing. In the heading varieties, heads should be well formed but still give slightly if pressed with a thumb. Because of its finer leaf structure, Chinese cabbage won't freeze as well as European cabbage. It also won't smell like cabbage whilst cooking!

NORTHERN THAI GRILLED BEEF SALAD

SERVES 4–6

10 oz sirloin steak, with fat
3 ⅓ oz Peking (napa) cabbage, finely shredded
1 tblspn roasted, ground small dried chillies
2 tblspns roasted ground rice
2 tomatoes, quartered
4 scallions (shallots, spring onions), sliced on the bias
12 shallots (brown onions), finely sliced
fresh mint and coriander sprigs

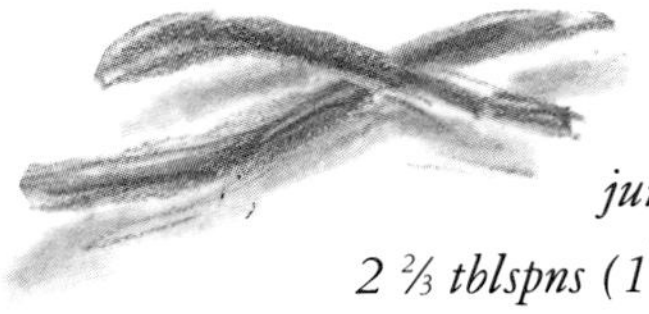

DRESSING
juice of 4 limes
2 ⅔ tblspns (1 ⅓ fl oz) Thai fish sauce
2 tspns jaggery (or use brown sugar)

Heat the grill to very hot and grill the beef on both sides until medium rare. Remove and rest until lukewarm. Cut into ⅛ in slices. Put into a dish with remaining salad ingredients and combine lightly with the salad dressing.

To make the dressing, put the ingredients into a screwtop jar and shake well.

STIR-FRY CABBAGE WITH PEANUTS

Have all the ingredients ready before you start cooking. Use a Peking (napa) cabbage.

SERVES 4

2 ⅔ tblspns (1 ⅓ fl oz) peanut (groundnut) oil
¾ cup (4 oz) fresh shelled unsalted peanuts (groundnuts)
2 cloves garlic, finely chopped
2 carrots, peeled and sliced on the diagonal
1 lb Peking (napa) cabbage, chopped in 2 in pieces

1 ⅓ tblspns (⅔ fl oz) light soy sauce
1 ⅓ tblspns (⅔ fl oz) dry sherry
½ tspn salt

Heat the oil in a wok. When hot, throw in the peanuts and stir until golden. Add the garlic and the carrots, stir-fry 30 seconds, then throw in the cabbage.

Stir-fry 1–2 minutes over high heat to coat cabbage in oil. Add the soy sauce, sherry and salt, stir well to combine. Put on the lid, turn off the heat and let sit 3–4 minutes before serving. The cabbage should be cooked but still crunchy.

SESAME CHINESE CABBAGE

Use a Peking (napa) cabbage for this dish. Its sponge-like texture absorbs flavors beautifully. Stir-frying is a good method of cooking cabbage because it brings out its sweetness. This one is quick, easy and nutritious. Have everything ready before you start cooking. Add water only if the cabbage needs moistening.

SERVES 6

2 ⅔ tblspns (1 ⅓ fl oz) vegetable oil
1 clove garlic, peeled and finely chopped
1 in knob ginger, peeled and grated
½ cup (2 ½ oz) sesame seeds
½ Chinese cabbage, approx 1 ½ lbs finely shredded
½ tspn salt
1 ⅓ tblspns (⅔ fl oz) water (optional)
1 ⅓ tblspns (⅔ fl oz) roasted sesame oil

Heat the oil in a wok. Add the garlic and ginger and stir-fry 30 seconds. Throw in the sesame seeds and stir until golden, being careful not to let them burn.

Add cabbage and toss over high heat, coating the cabbage with the oil. Add salt and water (if needed). Put on the lid and steam for 5 minutes with heat turned to low. Remove lid, turn up heat, add sesame oil, stir well. Serve immediately.

Broccoli
Brassica oleracea *var.* botrytis

Some call it the 'endless food', which refers both to its vigorous, year round growth (though it doesn't like hot weather), and to the fact that it is packed with nutrients and vitamins.

The Romans were keen on broccoli and it was probably they who developed it from its ancestor, the cabbage. Apicius, the ancient Roman food writer, was known for his skill in cooking it. The name 'broccoli' is derived from the Italian brocco, *meaning shoot or arm, and was introduced into France by Catherine de Medici. The French, however, understand the word to mean the flower stalk which pushes upward from the center of the ordinary cabbage at the end of its life.*

Broccoli is probably an intermediate development on the way to the cauliflower, different broccolis showing different stages in that evolution. I know a man who once grew some white broccoli, a rarity in Australia. The bees had cross-pollinated the seeds of his cauliflower and broccoli. Both are grown for their immature flower heads.

In the nineteenth century there were many varieties of broccoli grown in the kitchen garden — brown, red and cream heading types; green, purple and white sprouting ones. The green sprouting Calabrese is the best known today. It can be sown at any time, and likes plenty of water. Di Cicco and Green Goliath are available as non-hybrids; a Chinese variety (Fat Shan) is also available. It is the Chinese who have in fact mastered the art of cooking broccoli so that it comes out crisp, green and delicious. In the West only the Italians can rival them.

Broccoli does best in areas with a cool winter, but is adaptable and grows in most climate zones. Like its relative the cauliflower, it is a heavy feeder, requiring plenty of water and nitrogen. Nine to twelve plants at each sowing is sufficient for the average family, with sowings at four to six week intervals. It likes a sunny spot.

SPAGHETTI PRIMAVERA

In keeping with its name, this crisp, colorful pasta dish should include the young sweet vegetables of spring. However, it is still delicious using whatever vegetables are in season.

There are a number of steps in its preparation: the cooking of the spaghetti, the preparation and blanching of the vegetables, making of the tomato sauce and the final assembly. It's a good idea to toast the pinenuts ahead: you will need a couple of handfuls. Put them into a hot frying pan and toss well over medium heat until golden. The vegetables listed can be varied.

SERVES 6–8

6 ½ oz broccoli, cut into florets
3 ½ oz stringless beans, sliced into thirds
2 small green zucchini (courgettes), sliced on the diagonal
2 small yellow zucchini (courgettes), sliced on the diagonal
3 ½ oz fresh baby peas, petits pois (approx 10 oz unshelled)
8 stalks young asparagus, sliced into thirds
3 cloves garlic, crushed
¼ cup (2 fl oz) olive oil
1 tin tomatoes (14 oz), drained
6 ½ oz mushrooms, sliced
sea salt
freshly ground black pepper
⅔ cup (5 fl oz) cream
1 ½ lb spaghetti

GARNISH
fresh basil, fresh Parmesan cheese and toasted pinenuts (pignolias)

Blanch the broccoli, beans, zucchini, peas and asparagus in boiling salted water for 1 minute, refresh immediately under cold water. Alternatively, steam the vegetables, making sure they remain very crisp.

Sauté the garlic in the oil in a frying pan for 1 minute, add tomatoes, stir well. Add the mushrooms, season to taste, cook 3–4 minutes, then throw in all the blanched vegetables. Pour in the cream and heat gently on top of stove. Keep warm.

Cook spaghetti in plenty of rapidly boiling salted water until *al dente*, about 10 minutes. Drain, keep hot in a large warm bowl.

Pour the vegetables over the spaghetti and toss together well. Scatter with freshly chopped basil, grated or shaved Parmesan cheese and a handful or two of toasted pinenuts.

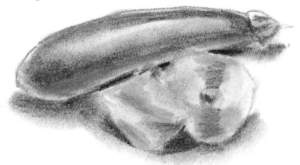

BROCCOLI WITH WALNUT SAUCE

SERVES 6–8

1 ½ lb broccoli
WALNUT SAUCE
1 cup (3 ½ oz) fresh walnuts
2 slices whole-wheat (wholemeal) bread, crusts removed
½ cup (4 fl oz) olive oil
2 ⅔ tblspns (1 ⅓ fl oz) vinegar
1–2 cloves garlic, crushed
paprika and cayenne to taste

Cut the broccoli into florets. Peel the stalks and slice thinly on the diagonal. Blanch in rapidly boiling salted water and refresh under cold water.

Put the walnuts into the food processor and process until fairly fine. Soak the bread in water, squeeze dry and crumble it. Add to the ground walnuts along with remaining ingredients. Process until smooth and creamy. Serve in a bowl with the blanched broccoli florets and stems on a platter around the bowl.

Note: This sauce is also delicious with other steamed or blanched vegetables like cauliflower, green beans, zucchini (courgettes) and squash.

VEGETABLE CURRY

This curry comes from Calcutta and the food from that area is not as rich or creamy as that from other parts of India. This is a mild curry — you can add more freshly chopped hot chilli if you like. Good with dhal (lentil purée) spooned over the top.

SERVES 6–8

¾ cup (6 ½ fl oz) vegetable oil
4 large onions, peeled and sliced
1 in knob fresh ginger, grated
2 cloves garlic
1 tblspn each turmeric and coriander (cilantro) powder
2 tspns garam masala
2 large hot green chillies, chopped
3 ripe tomatoes, peeled and chopped
3 medium potatoes, peeled and diced
1 lb carrots, scraped and diced
½ small cauliflower, broken into florets
1 small head broccoli, broken into florets

6 ½ oz green stringless beans, halved
2 tspns tomato paste
salt
13 oz sliced zucchini (courgettes), approx 6 untrimmed
2 oz snow peas (mangetout)
toasted slivered almonds
freshly chopped coriander (cilantro)

Heat the oil in a large pot and brown the onions over high heat, stirring often, for about 15 minutes. Make a paste of the ginger and garlic — do this in a blender with a little water. Add to onions. Cook 5 minutes on medium heat. Add the spices and chillies. Stir-fry 3 minutes on low heat. Stir in the tomatoes.

Throw in the potatoes and add water to cover. Cook on medium heat until potatoes are half-cooked, then add carrots, cauliflower, broccoli, beans and tomato paste. Add salt to taste and simmer until almost cooked. Throw in the zucchini and snow peas and simmer a further 5 minutes.

Remove from heat and garnish with the almonds and coriander. Serve with steamed basmati rice and dhal.

Cauliflower
Brassica oleracea *var.* botrytis

Dr Johnson is said to have remarked 'Of all the flowers in the garden, I like the cauliflower.' Elizabeth David, however, had an entirely different view, damning it for its 'normal coarse flavor and soggy texture' and consigning it to soup. Properly cooked, the cauliflower has many virtues, not least of which is its beautiful appearance.

The word comes from two Latin terms and means cabbage flower or stalk flower. It is a cultivated descendant of the noble cabbage family. Although some claim the cauliflower originated in Cyprus, most seem to think it was developed in Asia Minor. The Romans grew it but it was forgotten until the Arabs re-invented or re-imported it during the Middle Ages. By the eighteenth century, it was highly regarded, trouble being taken to produce it both early and late in the growing season.

Most people eat only the creamy white flower buds, known as the 'curd', which nestle in around a bed of leaves that can also be eaten, being, after all, cabbage. The leaves can be blanched, steamed or added to soup.

In India, where they curry the cauliflower, it is not uncommon for a single head to be 28 in across and to weigh up to 20 lb. You needn't be so ambitious for your kitchen garden, however!

Cauliflower likes a sunny spot and is best sown in late summer and autumn. They are liberal feeders and need to be kept well-watered. They mustn't be allowed to suffer a setback through lack of moisture. Paleface can be planted in most places throughout the year; Phenomenal Early is suitable for warmer climates; Deepheart is the old standard variety, taking five months to mature; Purple Head has deep purple heads when growing and turns green when cooked; Snowball Elite is a select strain, with pure white heads.

Cauliflowers require more care and are slower growing than broccoli. Sow three varieties that mature consecutively, so that curds can be harvested over a period of 12 weeks. Depending on the variety, they will take 12–26 weeks to mature. Allow 20–30 in for growth in each direction between the plants.

CAULIFLOWER IDEAS

I once read a story by French chef Louis Diat, in which he stressed the importance of carefully cleaning vegetables like cauliflower, cabbage and broccoli. He told of an embarrassing experience on his first job at the Hotel Bristol in Paris. Queen Amelia of Portugal had ordered cauliflower with a mousseline sauce for dinner.

A beautiful, firm white head was cooked and arranged on a napkin with the sauce in a sauceboat. When the maître d' cut through it with a serving spoon, he uncovered a big, ugly-looking worm. Fortunately, he was quick enough to hide it by covering it with a corner of the napkin and by serving a piece from the other side, but as you can imagine, everyone got the rounds of the kitchen later.

A whole head of cooked cauliflower is a majestic thing. Traditionally, the French have served it with either a cream or mousseline sauce or a polonaise butter.

I like the idea of cooking it whole and pouring a bolognaise (Italian) style sauce over the top and around it. You need to put the parboiled cauli head into a greased casserole dish — it needs to be deep and round so that the cauliflower fits snugly. Pour over the sauce and then sprinkle thickly with grated cheese, ground pepper and dot with butter. Cook it in a fairly hot (400°F/200°C/Gas 6) oven on one of the lower racks (this is so it will fit into the oven) until the cheese turns golden. Serve with a green salad and crusty French bread.

The Lebanese are keen on cauliflower and use it in a variety of ways. One that is particularly delicious is to steam the cauliflower, break it into florets and deep-fry it. The cauliflower is then scattered with freshly chopped coriander (cilantro) and smothered with tahini. This is fiddly but worth it.

Vegetable Pie

This sounds very basic (which it is) but is also creamy and luscious. It makes a good Sunday lunch with lots of homemade whole-wheat (wholemeal) bread. The vegetables listed are suggestions only. Use fresh vegetables in season.

Serves 6–8

1 ½–2 lb mixed vegetables
(cauliflower, cut in florets; broccoli, cut in florets; zucchini (courgettes), cut diagonally; carrots, cut diagonally; good handful beans, cut in 1 in pieces)
4 eggs
1 ¼ cups (10 fl oz) cream
⅔ cup (5 fl oz) plain yogurt
3–4 tblspns chopped fresh green herbs — chives, basil, parsley, coriander (cilantro)
pinch freshly grated nutmeg
salt and freshly grated black pepper
1 cup (4 oz) grated Cheddar (tasty) cheese

Preheat oven to 300°F (150° C/Gas 2).

Prepare the vegetables by chopping into bite-sized pieces, then blanch 2–3 minutes in boiling salted water, refresh under cold water. Drain on paper towels.

Lightly grease a baking dish and put in the vegetables. Beat together the eggs, cream, yogurt, herbs and nutmeg, season to taste and pour mixture over vegetables.

Bake for 45 minutes or until custard is set. Check occasionally to make sure it doesn't brown too quickly. Sprinkle with grated cheese 10 minutes before removing from oven. Serve hot.

Variation: In winter, substitute 2–3 tblspns pesto for the fresh herbs.

Jardinier

This is another lovely way of preserving home-grown vegetables. They look beautiful too, swimming in the golden oil. You can use any vegetables — those listed are just given as a guideline. Pick them when young and sweet. The given quantity of vegetables will fill a 12 cup (3 qt) container.

There are two main steps involved: the pickling of the vegetables in a vinegar infusion which allows them time to mellow; then the preservation with herbs and spices under oil.

These are so good, they are hard to keep in the store cupboard.

Pickling Solution
8 cups (2 qt) white wine vinegar
½ cup (4 oz) sugar
1 stick cinnamon
5 crushed juniper berries
5 whole black peppercorns
3 whole cloves
2 cloves garlic, peeled and bruised
1 bay leaf

1 tspn coriander (cilantro) seeds
½ tspn fennel seeds

VEGETABLES
¼ cauliflower, cut into florets
3 onions, peeled and cut in wedges
6 oz green beans, topped and tailed
4 oz baby okra
1 red sweet pepper (capsicum), seeded and cut into finger lengths
1 yellow sweet pepper (capsicum), seeded and cut into finger lengths
2 cucumbers, cut into finger lengths, seeds removed
3 green squash, quartered
3 yellow squash, quartered

THE OIL
good-quality olive oil
fresh herbs of choice (basil leaves are good)
3 whole red chillies
3 whole cloves garlic, peeled

PICKLING SOLUTION
Put all the ingredients together in an enamel saucepan. Bring to a boil and simmer 5 minutes. Leave to infuse for a day or two, then use for pickling the vegetables.

VEGETABLES
Wash all the vegetables and dry thoroughly first. Pack the prepared vegetables into sterile glass jars or a sterile bucket with a tight-fitting lid.

Strain the pickling liquid and pour over the vegetables. Seal and leave for 10–14 days. Taste the vegetables after 10 days. If they have mellowed, but are still crunchy, they are ready for putting under oil. If you like them more mellow, leave them to stand, tightly covered, for another few days.

OIL
When vegetables are ready, remove from pickling liquid, pat dry with paper towels and re-pack in clean sterile jars. Insert leaves or sprigs of herbs, chillies and garlic between the layers. Cover with oil. Seal and store for a week before eating.

NIÇOISE VEGETABLES

This salad can be served as an entrée and is a good lunch dish.

SERVES 8

1 small or ½ large cauliflower
8 oz French beans
2 medium tomatoes
4 oz button mushrooms
handful black olives, pitted
a few capers
3 anchovy fillets, drained
¾ cup (6 ½ oz) vinaigrette dressing
lettuce leaves for garnish
2–3 tblspns fresh chopped green herbs (parsley, oregano, marjoram, chives)

Break the cauliflower into florets. Top and tail the beans and cut in half. Blanch separately in boiling salted water (or steam), and refresh under running cold water.

Peel and seed tomatoes, cut into eighths. Wipe the mushrooms. Put cauliflower, tomatoes, mushrooms and olives into a salad bowl, add capers and drained anchovy fillets. Toss together with vinaigrette, allow to stand 2–3 hours in refrigerator to marinate. Add beans just before serving, otherwise they will discolor. Toss well.

Serve on lettuce leaves and garnish with fresh chopped herbs.

Shoot and Stalk Vegetables

I notice that it is only when my mother is working in her flowers that she is radiant, almost to the point of being invisible — except as Creator: hand and eye. She is involved in work her soul must have. Ordering the universe in the image of her personal conception of Beauty.

ALICE WALKER, FROM *IN SEARCH OF OUR MOTHERS' GARDENS*

Here we have a mixed bouquet from the garden — asparagus, celery, fennel, globe artichokes, cardoons, and sea kale. Wrapped in a crisp white linen cloth, each makes a beautiful offering when freshly picked.

At first sight, they have little in common, except perhaps that most of them have enjoyed, at one stage in their history, a reputation as aphrodisiacs.

Some call them the undisputed aristocrats of the kitchen garden, the asparagus being the noblest of all. Some, indeed, are a luxury in the garden, taking up a lot of time and space. Growing asparagus, for example, requires initial patience: to ensure the plants become well established you mustn't cut them during the first three years of growth. Once in the kitchen, though, such efforts are well rewarded. The taste and aroma of freshly steamed asparagus in spring is not easily forgotten.

Asparagus is often called 'the king' of the vegetables and has inevitably been treated as an aphrodisiac throughout much of its history. Known to the ancients, it is believed to have originated in the eastern Mediterranean and Asia Minor, though some say it developed from Asparagus prostratus, *a rare sub-species which grows on grassy sea cliffs in the British Isles. The Romans were the first to cultivate it from the wild, growing it in trenches to blanch the young stems. Pliny recorded that three of these fat spears weighed a pound. The main centre of cultivation was at Ravenna, where some stalks weighed in at 10 oz each. Even today, the best asparagus in Italy is still produced at Ravenna.*

The Greeks also cultivated asparagus and invented a myth about it — that it grew from a ram's horn stuck in the ground, the starting point perhaps of later ribaldry which associated asparagus with cuckoldry. The myth lingered: in the seventeenth century, John Worlidge wrote in Systema Horticulturae *that 'some curious persons put Rams-horns at the bottom of the Trench, and hold for certain, that they have a kind of Sympathy with Asparagus which makes them prosper the better'. There may be some truth in it. Horns do have plenty of nitrogen.*

There are about 20 varieties of asparagus, the most common being the green, followed by the fat white.

Like the asparagus, the artichoke has long been a contender in the aphrodisiac stakes, which may explain Catherine de Medici's passion for it. Artichokes are the plant's unopened flower buds. Legend has it that a jealous god converted a beautiful woman into a thistle and hence the artichoke was born. The ancient Romans certainly loved artichokes and they were also admired by the Greeks. Many varieties exist, the Green Globe and Purple Globe being the most common. Italy has a wealth of varieties including extremely small ones and medium-sized ones with purplish leaves. The small purple ones are served raw, sliced thinly, with olive oil and lemon juice.

Closely related to the artichokes are cardoons, the stalks of which are similar to celery and can be eaten raw or braised as a vegetable. In Turkey, where they grow wild, children eat the stalks raw; in Italy, they are often deep-fried. In Australia, however, they are something of a curiosity.

Unlike cardoons, asparagus and artichokes, celery is an everyday vegetable and would certainly be missed in the kitchen by most cooks, be it in the form of stalks, seeds or salt. Being so popular, it can do without testimonials from the ancients, all of whom held it in high regard as a food, flavoring and medicine. The Romans even believed that a celery wreath worn around the head would help a hangover and I particularly like the story about the medieval magicians who put celery seeds in their shoes — they apparently believed this could help them to fly!

Wild celery is a native of Britain and other temperate Eurasian countries, thriving in seaside soils impregnated with brackish water. The cultivated version is distinguished as Apium graveolens *var.* dulce *and has come a long way from its wild state to the succulent stringless varieties we have today.*

Similar in texture to celery, though very different in taste, is another shoot vegetable, Florence fennel, the most versatile variety being Foeniculum vulgare *var.* azoricum *commonly known as Florence fennel. The stem, base, foliage and seeds of Florence fennel are all usable, though the feathery leaves are sometimes mistaken for dill. Fennel's origins are clouded by mystical legends. The Greek for fennel was 'marathon', the place where the famous battle was fought. It was so called because the battle ground was overgrown with fennel. It was regarded as one of the good magical herbs and is one of the ingredients (along with cardamom, star anise, cloves and Szechuan pepper) in Chinese five-spice powder. It is a native of the Mediterranean region as well as other parts of Europe, including sea cliffs in Ireland, Wales and England.*

*Also native to those parts is sea kale (*Crambe maritima*), almost completely unknown in the*

United States and Australia. It is a relative of the cabbage and belongs to the Brassicaceae family. Its yellowy-white shoots are easy to grow and to force. It has a delicate, nutty flavor with a succulent texture and is eaten like asparagus.

Rhubarb is a member of the Polygonaceae family and is closely related to wild dock and sorrel. Commonly thought of as a fruit, it is in fact a stalk or stem vegetable. The long tender tangy stalks (the edible part) can be either red or green and are usually served cooked in well sugared pies (a common name for rhubarb is the 'pie plant'). Eskimos and Afghanistanis are known to eat the stalks raw — but then, they don't have the Western 'need' for sugar.

Celery
Apium graveolens *var.* dulce

The celery (or 'sellery' from the Latin name) we know today with its succulent leaf stem was developed by sixteenth century Italian gardeners. Previously it had been a rather bitter and foul-tasting weed, used by the ancient Greeks for medicinal purposes. Chinese celery, although belonging to the same species, is stronger and tougher, the product of 1500 years of Oriental cultivation. In Europe, celery was only widely grown towards the end of the eighteenth century. By the middle of the nineteenth century, there were green, white and reddish sorts available, as well as varieties with heavily frilled leaves.

Celery is a cold season vegetable which can be difficult to grow. If it is not constantly fed, watered and mulched, the stalks can become tough, stringy and bitter, losing the lovely succulence of prize specimens. It prefers a temperate or cool climate and requires a heavy, loamy soil, plenty of water and a lot of space. Some people prefer the self-blanching types which don't require trenches to be dug or earthing the vegetable up. However, the self-blanching varieties are less hardy and have a milder flavor than ordinary celery, though they are ready earlier and have a shorter season than the white, pink and red varieties. You can blanch celery by wrapping newspaper around the stalks when near full size. Do this three weeks before harvesting. This will modify the taste and color of the stalks.

Celery grows best in temperate areas. Seeds can take three weeks to germinate and are best started off in punnets, as slugs and snails love this vegetable. Sixteen to

20 plants at each sowing are ample for a family. Grow it quickly, otherwise the stems will be of poor quality. Water each day in hot weather and keep well mulched, letting one lot go to seed while the next lot is growing. Even when seeding, parts of the stalk are good for soups, stews and in salads.

Celeriac (Apium graveolens var. rapaceum), though often mistaken as the root of celery, is a separate vegetable, which grows under the same conditions as celery. Its globular root, which can grow up to 6 in across, has white flesh with the flavor of celery. It takes longer to mature (up to five months), but is less demanding than celery.

LENTIL SOUP

This is a delicious and wholesome soup and is very easy to make.

SERVES 4–6

1 cup (6 oz) brown lentils

4 cups (1 qt) stock (chicken broth)

2 stalks celery (leaves on), chopped

1 onion, peeled and chopped

1 carrot, peeled and sliced

2–3 cloves garlic, crushed

1 tin tomatoes (14 oz), chopped or 6–8 fresh ripe tomatoes, peeled and chopped

⅓ cup (3 fl oz) olive oil

¼ cup (2 fl oz) tomato paste

1 tblspn freshly chopped oregano

salt and freshly ground pepper to taste

Put the lentils into a large saucepan and cover with water. Bring to a boil, drain and return lentils to pan. Add all the remaining ingredients. Bring to a boil and simmer until lentils are soft, 25–30 minutes.

Remove from heat. Purée in the food processor or blender, but don't make it too smooth. Check the seasoning, reheat and serve hot. Garnish with oregano leaves.

STIR-FRIED CELERY WITH OYSTER SAUCE

Celery is often overlooked as a vegetable. Here is a simple, quick dish and one that goes well with meat, poultry and seafood. Have all the ingredients prepared before you start as the cooking is very rapid.

SERVES 4

1 ½ lb celery

2 tblspns vegetable oil

2 cloves garlic, finely chopped

2 tblspns (1 fl oz) oyster sauce

1 tspn roasted sesame oil

Wash the celery, remove string on the tougher stalks, and slice on the diagonal. Make the slices about ¼ in thick.

Heat the oil until very hot in a wok. Add the garlic, stir well for 15–30 seconds, then throw in the prepared celery. Stir well to cover with oil and cook, stirring all the time, for 2–3 minutes. Add the oyster sauce, stir well, then stir in the sesame oil. Put a lid on the wok, turn off the heat and let stand 3–4 minutes. Serve immediately.

RICE VERMICELLI WITH PORK FILLETS AND VEGETABLES

Pork fillets prepared in this way can be used in many dishes: in soups with pak choi, in fried rice, or added to rice vermicelli and vegetables. The celery lends a nice crunch. This dish is what my mother's friend poet Kate Llewellyn would describe as 'wet food'. She relishes such dishes for breakfast.

SERVES 4

1 ⅓ tblspns (⅔ fl oz) mirin or dry sherry
1 ⅓ tblspns (⅔ fl oz) hoisin sauce
1 ⅓ tblspns (⅔ fl oz) light soy sauce
2 tblspns (1 fl oz) honey
1 clove garlic, crushed
½ tspn salt
sprinkling of Chinese five-spice powder
1 pork fillet
4 oz rice vermicelli
2 ⅔ tblspns (1 ⅔ fl oz) oil
1 in piece ginger, grated
1 red chilli, chopped (optional)
3–4 stalks celery, cut on the diagonal
1 green sweet pepper (capsicum), slivered
small bunch scallions (shallots, spring onions), cut
on the diagonal

Start marinating the fillet the day before. Combine the mirin (or dry sherry), hoisin sauce, soy sauce, honey, garlic, salt and five-spice powder. Place fillet in mixture and marinate overnight, turning occasionally.

Preheat oven to 400°F (200°C/Gas 6).

Remove the pork fillet from the marinade, reserving marinade. Roast the fillet for 15 minutes, remove and let stand 10 minutes, then slice thinly on the diagonal.

Soak the vermicelli in hot water for 5–10 minutes, or until soft. Drain well. Heat the oil in a wok, throw in the ginger and chilli and toss well. Add the celery and sweet pepper and toss for 1–2 minutes or until the vegetables are coated in oil; add the scallions. Add the vermicelli and mix in well. Pour in the marinade from the pork fillet and toss. Put on the lid, turn off the heat and let stand for a couple of minutes.

Serve garnished with the sliced pork.

CRUNCHY SALAD OF CELERY, ORANGE AND APPLE

A very pretty and delicious salad, easy to make. Cut all the fruits into crescent shapes.

SERVES 4–6

½ bunch celery, approx 1 ¼ lb
1 red apple, quartered
2 oranges, peeled
Orange Poppy Seed Dressing (page 6)

Trim the celery and wash well. You should have about 12 oz. Slice the stalks on the diagonal, about ¼ in in thickness. Put them into a salad bowl.

Remove pips from the apple and slice thinly into crescent shapes (the salad looks prettier if you leave the skin on). Make sure all the white pith is removed from the oranges, then cut into the orange with a small sharp knife to remove the segments. Add cut apple and oranges to celery and toss with the Orange Poppy Seed Dressing — you will need about two-thirds of the recipe quantity. Serve immediately.

Asparagus
Asparagus officinalis

Considering how easy it is to grow once established, it is surprising how rarely asparagus is seen in the kitchen garden. It sounds fiddly, but really all that's required is constant mulching. Even a row or two (or about 20–25 plants) will give the average family bonne bouche *(a good feed). It does best in mild–cool climates, likes sandy soils and plenty of mulching. The plants die off each fall and remain dormant through winter. In warm areas, help keep the soil cool for spring cropping by applying a heavy layer of mulch in late winter before the soil has started to warm up.*

Establishing the plants is the hardest part, but once done, they are perennial and will keep on producing for 20 years or more. Asparagus can be grown from seed, but it is quicker to buy seedlings or 'crowns' which will give a limited picking in about a year. Sow the crowns in a sunny spot in a separate bed during spring. The bed should be well prepared beforehand with plenty of compost or animal manure plus a complete fertilizer. Dig a trench about 12 in wide and 8 in deep, and set the crowns 12–20 in apart at the bottom. Rows should be about 4 ft apart. Cover the crowns with 2 in soil. Keep well watered, well mulched and fertilized. Asparagus will also thrive in a 'no-dig' style garden.

You won't be able to pick the plants until they're three years old, by which time the spears should be thick and plentiful. Don't cut them the first spring after planting and cut sparingly during the second.

Green asparagus is cut when spears are 4–6 in long. For white asparagus, heap the soil over the row of growing asparagus to a depth of 12 in. When the tips appear, cut the spears with a sharp knife, about 6 in below the surface.

During winter, when the plants are dormant, grow a crop of lettuce in some compost on top of the asparagus, or plant a winter crop of peas between the rows.

Ken Hom's Vegetable Pasta

The Canadian–Chinese chef Ken Hom has a marvellous way of simplifying complex techniques. Here is one example. All the vegetables here are cut into long thin, spaghetti-like strips and then stir-fried. Olive oil has a lower burning temperature than most other cooking oils, so is combined with peanut oil here.
The dish can be made ahead of time and served at room temperature with a splash of lemon juice or mild vinegar. For a nuttier flavour, add 2 tspns of sesame oil and increase the peanut oil.

SERVES 6–8

2 lb baby zucchini (courgettes), cut into long
julienne strips
1 tblspn coarse salt
2 ⅔ tblspns (1 ⅓ fl oz) olive oil
1 ⅓ tblspns (⅔ fl oz) peanut oil
⅔ tblspn (⅓ fl oz) ordinary sesame oil
4 garlic cloves, peeled and sliced thinly
8 oz thin asparagus, cut into 2.5 in lengths
3 red or yellow sweet peppers (capsicum), or a combination of
the two, seeded, de-ribbed and shredded lengthwise
1 lb peas, shelled and blanched
2 large handfuls basil leaves
salt and freshly ground black pepper

Put the zucchini into a colander and sprinkle with salt. Let sweat 30 minutes. Wrap in a tea towel and squeeze out the moisture. Set aside. In a wok or large frying pan, heat the oils, add garlic and stir-fry for 15 seconds. Add the asparagus, peppers and peas. Stir-fry for 1 minute. Add zucchini and stir-fry for 2 more minutes. Toss in the basil leaves and, when they wilt, add salt and pepper to taste, and serve. Freshly grated Parmesan cheese is nice to serve with this mock pasta.

Asparagus with Parmesan Cheese and Olive Oil

A simple, delicious way of cooking and eating fresh asparagus.

SERVES 4

1 lb asparagus
extra virgin olive oil
shavings of fresh Parmesan cheese
freshly ground black pepper

Trim any woody ends from the asparagus and wash well. Steam or cook in boiling salted water until just cooked. Refresh under cold water.

Divide asparagus between four plates, drizzle over the oil, sprinkle with shavings of Parmesan cheese and freshly ground black pepper. Serve immediately.

Asparagus Stir-fry

This is the best way I know to cook asparagus.

SERVES 4

1 lb asparagus
2 ⅔ tblspns (1 ⅓ fl oz) vegetable oil
2 ⅔ tblspns (1 ⅓ fl oz) water
2 tspns roasted sesame oil

Trim off the tough woody ends of the asparagus. Wash and dry well, then cut into 3 in lengths.

Heat the vegetable oil in a wok and when hot, throw in the prepared asparagus and stir-fry for 30 seconds or until all the spears are covered in the oil. Add the water, bring to a boil, turn down heat and put on the lid and cook 2–3 minutes or until asparagus is cooked but still crisp. Remove lid, turn up heat and boil away any remaining water. Add the sesame oil and stir well to coat. Serve immediately.

ASPARAGUS RISOTTO

I am a fan of risotto, its creamy texture is so satisfying, especially on a cold winter's day. Once you understand the basic principle behind preparing it, you can add any type of vegetable. Mushrooms are good, especially if combined with sweet, young peas. Freshly chopped herbs are a good addition. For classic Risotto alla Milanese, a few strands of saffron are added to perfume and color the rice. The rice should always be creamy when cooked but still slightly chewy (*al dente*).

SERVES 6

3 bunches asparagus, approx 1 lb
2 ⅔ tblspns (1 ⅓ fl oz) vegetable oil
3 tblspns (1 ½ oz) unsalted butter
1 onion, finely chopped
2 cloves garlic, crushed
1 ½ cups (11 oz) arborio (short grain) rice
½ cup (4 fl oz) dry white wine
6 cups (1 ½ qt) boiling chicken stock (broth)
salt and freshly ground pepper
extra butter (optional)
½ cup (2 oz) finely grated Parmesan cheese
freshly ground pepper, extra
Parmesan cheese, extra

Steam the asparagus spears until just cooked, and cut into 1 ¼ in lengths. Reserve some of the tips for garnishing.

Heat the oil and butter in a large heavy frying pan and sauté the onion and garlic until translucent. Tip in the rice and stir until all the grains are coated with the butter and onion mixture. Pour in the wine and stir with a wooden spoon until the wine has almost disappeared.

Add a ladleful of the boiling stock and stir into the rice. Once the liquid has disappeared, add another ladleful. Continue like this, stirring frequently with a wooden spoon, until the rice is creamy but still *al dente* and all the liquid has been absorbed (it may take the smaller quantity of stock). This will take about 30 minutes. Season to taste.

Add the asparagus and extra butter (if using) and combine well, being careful not to damage the tips. Stir in the grated cheese.

Serve immediately. Garnish with freshly ground black pepper, reserved asparagus tips and shaved Parmesan cheese.

Note: It's the starch content in Arborio rice which makes a risotto so creamy. Make sure the stock is simmering in a separate pan alongside the risotto.

Fennel

Foeniculum vulgare *var.* azoricum

Florence fennel (or finocchio) is easy to grow. Its delicious sweet aniseed flavor is a great boon in salads. Grown as an annual for its swollen stem bases, it prefers cool weather though it can also be grown through summer. Pull out the swollen bulbs as you need them when they are about the size of tennis balls. Don't leave them in the ground too long or they will become stringy and taste very aniseedy. Fennel can become a pest in many areas, so you may need to concentrate more on controlling rather than growing it. The lovely feathery leaves make splendid decorations on platters and as garnishes. With a sunny position and a soil rich in humus and decayed manure, it will grow from 3–16 ft high. Seeds can be sown directly into the soil from midsummer to early fall. Fennel is usually free from most pests and diseases, the most likely pest being aphids.

KOFTA WITH RAITA

These meatballs are good served hot with drinks before dinner. Provide toothpicks to pick up the meatballs and put the Raita in the center of the dish.

MAKES 30

½ medium onion, chopped
1 ½ in knob ginger, peeled and roughly chopped
2 cloves garlic, peeled
1 small green chilli
1 lb very lean ground (minced) lamb
2 tblspns fresh coriander (cilantro), finely chopped
2 tblspns scallions (shallots, spring onions), finely chopped
1 tblspn dried ground fennel
salt
flour (for rolling)
oil (for frying)

RAITA

1 cup (6 ½ oz) plain yogurt
1 small cucumber, chopped and seeded
½ bunch mint, chopped
½ onion, finely diced
lemon or lime juice

Put the onion, ginger, garlic and chilli into the blender and blend until almost liquefied. Mix together with the remaining ingredients and season to taste. Shape into walnut-sized balls, roll in flour and fry in hot oil. When cooked, remove and drain on paper towels.

For the Raita put the yogurt into a bowl. Mix through the cucumber, mint and onion. Add a squeeze of lemon or lime juice and combine well.

TUSCAN FENNEL

SERVES 6–8

1 onion, finely sliced
2–3 cloves garlic, finely chopped
olive oil
4 fennel bulbs, washed and finely sliced
6 ripe tomatoes, peeled and chopped
salt and pepper
1 cup (2 oz) fresh breadcrumbs
½ cup (2 oz) freshly grated Parmesan cheese
1 tspn lemon zest (rind), finely grated
2 tblspns (1 oz) butter, melted

Preheat oven to 400°F (200°C/Gas 6).

Sauté the onion and garlic in oil until soft, add fennel and cook until the fennel begins to brown and is almost cooked. Add the tomatoes, season well and simmer gently for 5 minutes. Put fennel mixture into a greased earthenware dish. Mix together remaining ingredients and scatter over the top of the vegetables. Bake for 15–20 minutes or until golden on top.

FENNEL, RED ONION AND SWEET PEPPER SALAD

Fennel is always a good crunchy and refreshing addition
to a salad. It is also delicious on its own, sliced, dressed
with vinaigrette and strewn with shavings of fresh
Parmesan cheese.

SERVES 4–6

2 fennel bulbs, washed and finely sliced
1 medium red onion, finely diced
1 green sweet pepper (capsicum), cut into rings
vinaigrette

Put the fennel, onion and sweet pepper into a salad
bowl. Mix together your favorite vinaigrette and pour
over the top. Toss together well.

Artichokes
Cynara scolymus

*If you think of the globe artichoke as a thistle, rather than as some exotic epicurean vegetable, it won't seem quite
so daunting. It is also quite simple to grow and, because it is so decorative, looks pretty in the flower garden.
Artichokes may grow up to 5 ft, so put them at the back of a flower bed. Flower heads not harvested bloom as
large purple heads which can be dried and used as indoor decorations. The parts that are eaten are in the
immature flower head: the delicate heart and inner petals. The hairy center, or choke, is not eaten.*

*For the average family, four to six plants are ample (providing the children like them, often a moot point).
Globe artichokes like a well-drained, rich soil and sunny position. They prefer cool, moist summers and mild
winters. The plants last for three years so prepare the soil well by mulching first and fertilizing. Suckers can be
sown from autumn through early spring (the plants don't grow true from seed). Plant firmly at least 3 ft apart
and water well. For tender heads, keep the roots moist and mulch well each summer.*

*Heads can be harvested in spring and summer — the younger the bud, the more tender it is to eat. Cut out the
center head first. If you want larger center heads, prune out some of the lateral heads when they are about the*

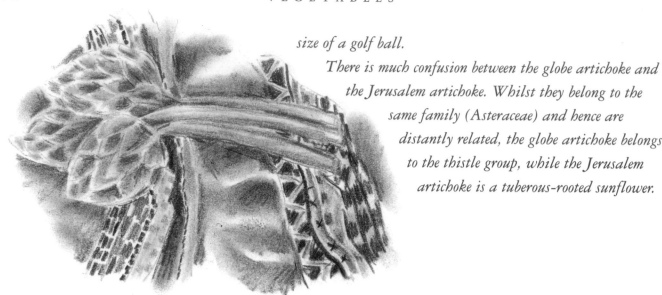

There is much confusion between the globe artichoke and the Jerusalem artichoke. Whilst they belong to the same family (Asteraceae) and hence are distantly related, the globe artichoke belongs to the thistle group, while the Jerusalem artichoke is a tuberous-rooted sunflower.

ARTICHOKES À LA GRECQUE

Perfect for tiny artichokes, picked before the chokes have formed and cooked whole. Serve as part of an antipasto or through a mixed salad.

SERVES 4

20 baby artichokes
juice of 3 lemons
½ cup (4 fl oz) olive oil
1 tblspn freshly chopped dill
1 tspn fennel seeds
8 peppercorns
bouquet garni (bay leaf, sprig thyme, celery stalk)
1 tspn salt
2 ½ cups (22 fl oz) water

Drop the artichokes into a pan of rapidly boiling water to which you have added the juice of 1 lemon. Simmer 5 minutes. Drain in a colander and rinse under cold water. Drain well, heads down, and set aside.

Put remaining ingredients into a saucepan and bring to a boil. Add the artichokes and when liquid returns to a boil, reduce heat, cover and simmer 7–8 minutes or until artichokes are tender.

Remove from pan with a slotted spoon and put into a bowl. Increase heat to high and boil until liquid is reduced by half. Strain the liquid through a sieve over the artichokes. When cold, cover the bowl and chill in the refrigerator until needed.

PRESERVED VEGETABLES

A superb way of preserving vegetables is *sott' olio* (or 'under oil') — olive oil, that is. The better the quality of the oil, the better the preserve. The liquid seals the food off from the air and if you add spices and herbs, they also flavor the oil.

Home-grown vegetables can be kept for months this way in lovely jars full of golden oil. Blanch them first in a mixture of good-quality vinegar, water, sugar and salt mixed to suit your taste. Bring to a boil then blanch the vegetables briefly. Drain and dry well, add spices and herbs of your choice, pack into jars and cover with olive oil.

All sorts of spices and condiments can be added — a twist of lemon or orange zest (rind), chilli peppers, Szechuan peppers, coriander (cilantro) seeds and juniper berries, bay leaves and cloves of garlic. They make wonderful gifts.

Herbs can also be preserved this way — basil is especially good. Put a layer of washed, dried leaves into a sterile screw-top jar, pour in some oil and repeat the layers until the jar is full. Make sure the oil covers the leaves at the top. The leaves will blacken, but the flavor is stunning.

Baby artichokes are lovely packed in jars. Trim the stems, remove any old leaves and snip off the tip of each leaf with scissors. Cut in half vertically and place in a bowl of acidulated water (water to which you've added freshly squeezed lemon juice) so they don't discolor. Cook them covered with water, a little vinegar, salt and a bay leaf until tender. Drain well and dry on paper towels. Pack into sterile jars and cover with oil. Coriander seeds and sprigs of rosemary are a nice addition. Open after four weeks and serve as part of an antipasto.

Artichoke hearts can also be preserved in oil. Remove the outside leaves of medium-sized artichokes and with a sharp knife, cut off the top two-thirds of the artichokes. Take out the choke and trim around the outside so that only the heart is left. Proceed as for baby artichokes in oil (above).

STUFFED ARTICHOKES

Start the preparation for these the day before.

SERVES 6

6 medium artichokes
4 cups (1 qt) water
juice of 1 lemon

STUFFING

1 ¼ cups (5 oz) dry breadcrumbs
½ cup (2 oz) freshly grated Parmesan cheese
3 cloves garlic, finely chopped
freshly ground pepper
4 stalks mint, leaves removed and chopped
handful of freshly chopped parsley
3 anchovy fillets, chopped
2 oz prosciutto, chopped
1 small chilli, finely chopped (optional)

TO COOK

½ cup (4 fl oz) olive oil
butter
water

Prepare the artichokes: remove the tough outer leaves and snip off the tips with a pair of scissors. Put tips and leaves into a saucepan and cover with the water. Bring to a boil and simmer 25–30 minutes. Remove from heat and strain.

Peel about 5 in of each artichoke stalk with a vegetable peeler, discarding peelings. Put the artichokes and their stalks into a large bowl of water and add the lemon juice. Leave to soak overnight.

Next day, make the stuffing by mixing all the ingredients together in a bowl. Season to taste, but don't add any salt (because of the cheese, anchovies and prosciutto). Stir well to combine. Remove the artichokes from the water. Turn them upside down and, holding the stalk firmly, beat the heads to soften the petals. Do this over the sink.

Cut off the stalks (reserving them) and use your thumbs to open the petals out. Fill each artichoke with the stuffing.

Choose a saucepan into which the artichokes will fit snugly. Sit them inside with the stalks between. Drizzle with the oil and top each with a knob of butter. Turn on the heat, cover and cook over low heat for 10 minutes. When warm, add water to come to at least 1 in from the top of the artichokes. Bring to a boil and simmer, half covered, until water is reduced and a leaf from near the base can be easily pulled out, about 30–45 minutes. There should be about 1 ¼ in water left in the bottom of the pan. Remove from pan and allow to cool. Dress with slices of prosciutto, shavings of Parmesan cheese and some freshly chopped parsley.

STEAMED GLOBE ARTICHOKES

SERVES 6

A tender globe artichoke makes a good, simple first course served hot with melted butter or hollandaise sauce, or cold with a vinaigrette or herbed mayonnaise.

For six people, you'll need 6 large or 12 small artichokes. Soak them in a large bowl of acidulated water (for every 2 cups (½ qt) water, add 1 ⅓ tblspns (⅔ fl oz) lemon juice) for 1–2 hours before trimming and put them back into the water each time they are cut (the cut surfaces turn brown if not treated in this way).

Cut off the stems, pull off any of the hard outer leaves and snip the tips with a pair of scissors. Cut across the top and scoop out the hairy choke. Put into a steamer and cook until the artichokes are just tender, about 35–40 minutes.

Alternatively, drop the artichokes into a large pan of rapidly boiling salted water and simmer gently, uncovered, for 35–40 minutes. Drain thoroughly, heads down, in a colander.

Rhubarb
Rheum rhaponticum

The most beautiful rhubarb I have seen is grown in Australia on Tambourine Mountain in the hinterland of Queensland's Gold Coast. Whenever we go to my mother's farm in Queensland, we try to make one trip to this magnificent part of the world.

I was surprised to find such succulent rhubarb growing so well there, because this is a subtropical area where the days can get very hot. Originally from Siberia, northern China and Tibet, rhubarb was brought to Europe on the caravans through Baghdad. It reached the West about the beginning of the Christian era, but unfortunately the wrong parts were eaten. The roots were used for medicinal purposes well into the eighteenth century, and then the leaves were eaten. Both these parts contain oxalic acid and should never be eaten.

Rhubarb is popular in America, Australia and Britain, but is not eaten much in France. Unlike other ancient vegetables, it hasn't gathered a literature around it, though Kingsley Amis's Lucky Jim *had a love–hate relationship with it. For most people, it is either love or hate, but in its favor it is easy to grow and very productive.*

Rhubarb loves organic matter and plenty of mulch. It's a good idea to grow rhubarb in a separate bed. These days, with winter-cropping varieties that crop year round, you can harvest indefinitely. It likes full sun, but will tolerate a shady position — though not full shade. Plant crowns in winter in soil just deep enough to cover. Leave about 2 ft between each crown. As soon as leaves appear, mulch the plants well and pinch out any seeds. Pick stalks from the outside inwards.

RHUBARB MARMALADE

A marvellous way of using rhubarb. Good on toasted cornbread.

MAKES ABOUT 16 CUPS (4 QT)

2 lb rhubarb, trimmed, chopped, approx 3 lb,
untrimmed
⅓ cup (3 fl oz) fresh orange juice
⅓ cup (3 fl oz) fresh lemon juice
2 in knob fresh ginger, bruised
grated zest (rind) of 1 lemon and 1 orange
3 cups (1 ½ lb) warmed sugar
2 oranges, peeled and cut into segments
1 lemon, peeled and cut into segments

Make sure the rhubarb is well washed. Put into a big pan with the orange and lemon juice, the bruised ginger and the grated orange and lemon zest. Bring to a boil, cover and reduce heat to low. Cook until rhubarb is tender, about 15 minutes, stirring from time to time.

Meanwhile, warm the sugar in a baking dish in a moderate oven. Add to the pan when rhubarb is cooked, stirring until all the sugar is dissolved.

Bring to a boil and boil rapidly for 10 minutes, being careful it doesn't catch. Stir in the orange and lemon segments. Turn off heat and let cool, stirring occasionally. Remove knob of ginger.

Pour into sterile jars and seal.

RHUBARB CRUMBLE

3 bunches rhubarb, approx 2 ½ lb
zest (rind) and juice of 1 orange
⅓–½ cup (3–4 oz) sugar, depending on sourness of the fruit
1 knob fresh ginger, peeled and grated (optional)
½ cup (2 oz) all-purpose (plain) whole-wheat
(wholemeal) flour
½ cup (3 oz) brown sugar
½ cup (1 ½ oz) shredded coconut
½ cup (2 oz) rolled oats
½ cup (1 oz) wheatgerm
½ cup (4 oz) butter, softened
1 tspn cassia cinnamon

Preheat oven to 350°F (180°C/Gas 4).

Remove tops, wash the rhubarb and chop it into 2 in lengths. Put it into a saucepan with the zest, juice, sugar and ginger. Cover and let simmer gently until just cooked. Pour into an ovenproof dish.

Work the remaining ingredients together with your fingertips. Don't overwork or they will become oily. Cover the rhubarb with the topping and bake in the oven for 20–30 minutes or until golden.

Pods and Seeds

Now it was plain that this must be a real Princess, since she had been able to feel the three little peas through the twenty mattresses and twenty feather-beds. None but a real Princess could have had such a delicate sense of feeling.

So the Prince made her his wife, being now convinced that he had found a real Princess. The three peas were, however, put into the royal museum, where they are still to be seen, if they have not been stolen.

Notice that this is a true story.

HANS CHRISTIAN ANDERSEN, FROM *THE PRINCESS AND THE PEA*

I had a passion for growing beans as a teenager. There's a photo of me, head peeping out from amongst the vines and bare-footed, proudly showing off my new crop of stringless green beans. I'd built my vegetable patch on difficult terrain — a rocky slope, to be exact — and after much hoeing, tilling and mulching was justifiably pleased with the results of my endeavors. I also grew corn there. When pulled back, the green, silken husks revealed the pale buttery yellow cobs, so sweet we ate them raw. The beans, too, were so fresh and sweet they'd be eaten en route to the kitchen.

I never lost that early love for growing vegetables. It wasn't something I was directly encouraged to do, but rather something handed on to me by mother and grandmother. They have always been great gardeners. My grandmother had tins full of cuttings she'd struck from other people's plants all around her house. As children, whenever we didn't know where our mother was, we'd look for her first in the garden. And that's where she'd be, whether it was early morning or evening. I am convinced that's why, to this day, I love to feel the garden creeping into my house, almost spilling over onto the table.

Beans, of course, come in so many shapes and sizes that a book could be devoted to them alone. There are the soy beans (Glycine max) of Asia, the American haricot (Phaseolus vulgaris) and the

European broad bean (Vicia faba). *The haricot, native to Central America and cultivated since at least 5000 BC, reached Europe in the sixteenth century and was widely grown there soon after. It is the most versatile of the beans, comprising tall climbing plants (in the style of Jack and the Beanstalk) and low bush types. Some beans are round, others flat, some fat, others long, kidney-shaped or oval. They come in all sorts of colors too — green, yellow, white, red, pink, purple, black, mottled or multicolored. There are beans meant to be eaten young, pods and all (like my green stringless ones), and others which are meant to be picked when mature and only their pods consumed.*

The European broad bean is the one variety unknown to the Americas. Grown throughout Europe and the Middle East since prehistoric times it has, being such an ancient crop, acquired much religious and magical significance. These beans were used as dedications to Apollo and to honor the wife of Janus. Overindulgence was, however, thought to dull the senses and cause bad dreams. Upper-class Greeks and Romans regarded them as harmful to their vision.

Another pod, the pea, is so ancient that its place of origin is unknown. Recently, an archeological expedition reported finding peas (Pisum sativum *var.* hortense) *near the Burma–Thailand border in what archeologists call the 'Spirit Cave'. They were carbon dated at approximately 9750 BC. Indeed, peas were probably the earliest cultivars: evidence also exists that they were grown in Turkey by 6500 BC, from the wild pea* (Pisum elatius).

It was not, however, until the Norman Conquest of England that 'green peas' are mentioned. Before that, the 'pease' eaten were mainly dried and were popular in both France and England as Lenten dishes. Pease porridge, a purée or soup made from dried peas, was a standard ration for the poor. (The word 'pea' comes via Sanskrit to the Greek pison. *Until the sixteenth century, peas were known as 'peason' in England, which was shortened to 'pease' during the reign of Charles I, becoming 'pea' in the seventeenth century.) The English developed many fine varieties, including the Hotspur, Hastings, rose, rouncival, sickle and tufted, many of which were no longer available by the nineteenth century. The delicious sugar pea, once again popular, was known in the sixteenth century, and the* petits pois *was developed in Italy during the Renaissance. All derive from* Pisum sativum, *of which there are now hundreds of varieties.*

Corn (or maize), along with another of the pods, the haricot bean, was indigenous to America and, like the haricot bean, it is a plant of great versatility. After the tomato, corn remains the most popular vegetable in the United States where the different varieties are made into all manner of products — corn syrups, tortillas, succotash, cornbread, hominy and popcorn to name just a few. Some ears of corn hold as few as 16 kernels and are tiny, while others can hold up to 500.

Native Americans often called corn 'sacred mother' and considered it a gift from the gods. Temples were dedicated to corn deities. For them, it has always represented much more than food — for some tribes it symbolized fertility, for others renewal. Sometimes kernels of different colors (be they white, yellow, blue, red, purple, brown, near-black or rose) represented different families or tribes. Generally, corn is yellow or white, but sometimes different colored kernels grow on the same cob. One thing is for certain — without corn, the Mayan, Aztec and Inca cultures as we know them would have had a difficult time surviving.

Within 50 years of Columbus taking corn to Italy, it was growing across Europe, in Africa, India and even China. The first English settlers to North America were shown by the American Indians how to use and prepare it, thereby saving many of them from starvation.

Peas, beans and corn are well worth growing in the kitchen garden. Their sweetness and succulence when picked young and fresh is a revelation.

Peas
Pisum sativum

I eat my peas with honey,
I've done it all my life.
It makes the peas taste funny
But it keeps 'em on the knife!

Food lovers must cringe! Picked fresh when young and sweet, peas shouldn't need honey to make them palatable. Many people, in fact, wax lyrical over the pea, one writer (James de Coquet, gastronomic writer for the Parisienne Figaro*) calling a dish of peas 'an allegro', another claiming they possess 'freshness of soul'. They are referring to the* petits pois *(or* piselli novelli*), the sweet, small succulent peas taken to France by Catherine de Medici in 1533 when she married Henry II. At that time they were referred to as a 'royal dish' and are not to be confused with the 'pease' eaten by peasants. Peas, however, also have the dubious honor of being the first vegetable to be canned and, later, deep-frozen.*

*If you grow your own peas, you'll understand why the French love the small, young, sweet ones. These are the shelling peas which include both round-seeded and wrinkled. The latter, though less attractive, are much more flavorsome than the round. Then there are the edible-podded peas (*P. sativum var. macrocarpon*) which include the snow pea (mangetout) and the sugar snaps. They are all delicious. Look around for different varieties, but don't plant them close to each other as they tend to cross-pollinate. (If you studied botany at school, you might remember that Mendel cross-pollinated dwarf peas with tall peas in 1866, proving that the distinct characteristics of each type were inherited in precise and predictable ways.)*

The versatility of the pea has been rather underestimated — the blossoms themselves are edible and look very elegant as garnishes. The shoots, too, are stunning. Crisp, green and tasting very much like the peas themselves, they are much prized in Asian countries.

Pea plants are either long climbing vines or short bushes — both benefit from support. Even the dwarf varieties produce better if they have something to lean on. Try planting them next to maturing corn. Peas like cool weather and do best if sown to mature in spring. In cool areas, they can be grown at other times too. They like a well-limed soil, good drainage and are adaptable to both heavy and light soils, but will not thrive in cold, wet soil. Plant them about 2–2 ½ in apart with about 16 in between the rows.

Birds can be a problem (knowing a good thing, they are attracted by the pea's sweetness). Colorful lengths of material woven between the supports act as a deterrent, perhaps because they remind the birds of snakes.

ANITRA DI CAMPAGNA

SERVES 8–10

An Italian picnic dish, delicious served cold. Ask the butcher to bone out the duck for you.

STUFFING

1 onion, chopped

1 clove garlic, chopped

2 ⅔ tblspns (1 ⅓ fl oz) vegetable oil

liver and heart from the duck, chopped (optional)

3 ½ oz veal, chopped

1 oz ham, chopped

10 leaves fresh sage, chopped

small sprig fresh rosemary, chopped

2 ⅔ tblspns (1 ⅓ fl oz) white wine

1 small zucchini (courgette)

3 leaves spinach, chopped

2 ⅔ oz peas, shelled, approx 8 oz in pods

2 tblspns (1 oz) rice

2–3 eggs, well-beaten

salt and pepper to taste

THE DUCK

1 medium duck, approx 3 lb

2–4 tblspns (1 ⅓–2 fl oz) oil

2–3 stalks celery, chopped

1–2 carrots, chopped

2 onions, chopped

½ cup (4 fl oz) white wine

1 tspn honey

1 cup (8 fl oz) orange juice

Prepare the stuffing: sauté the onion and garlic in the oil. Add the chopped liver, heart, veal, ham, sage and rosemary. Cook until offal and meat are browned, stirring constantly, then pour in the wine. Bring to boiling point, add vegetables and cook for 8–10 minutes. Remove from heat and cool. Process in the food processor but don't let it become mushy. Boil the rice and stir into the meat/vegetable mixture along with the beaten eggs. Season to taste.

Fill the duck carcass with this mixture and stitch together firmly or tie with string.

Heat the oil in a frying pan, add the duck and brown it all over, sealing in the stuffing.

In a large pot, add the duck and the vegetables. Put on the lid, cook for 30–35 minutes on top of the stove over medium–low heat. Add wine, honey and orange juice, cook for 5 minutes, remove lid and baste with the liquid. Cook another 20 minutes half-covered, basting frequently. Lift out, cool and refrigerate. Serve cold, cut in slices.

GREEN PEA AND APPLE SOUP

SERVES 6

2 lb green peas, in pods
6 cups (1 ½ qt) chicken stock (broth)
2 Granny Smith apples (or *greening apples*)
butter
1 tspn ground cumin
1 ¼ cups (10 fl oz) fresh cream
green or *white peppercorns*
salt
fresh mint
croutons

Wash the peas well, shell them and place the pods in a large saucepan. Add the chicken stock and simmer until the pods are soft. Drain stock from the pods, pressing on the pods to extract their flavor.

Simmer the shelled peas in the stock from the pods until soft. Meanwhile, peel, core and slice the apples and sauté the slices in a little butter until they turn golden.

Add the apples to the stock and purée in the blender or food processor until smooth. Add cumin, cream, ground peppercorns and salt to taste. Bring to simmering point, but don't let boil. Serve piping hot, in bowls, garnished with mint leaves, croutons and a little extra ground cumin.

MEERA'S SPICY PEAS AND POTATOES IN YOGURT

SERVES 4 AS AN ACCOMPANIMENT

8 oz fresh shelled peas, approx 1 ½ lb in pods
1 ⅓ tblspns (⅔ fl oz) vegetable oil
1 tspn fenugreek seeds
1 tspn black mustard seeds
1 tspn cumin seeds
1 in knob fresh ginger, peeled and finely chopped
1–2 chillies, finely chopped
8 oz potatoes, peeled and cut into small cubes
½ cup (4 fl oz) water
1 tspn ground cumin
1 tspn ground coriander (cilantro)
1 tspn aamchur
½ tspn turmeric
salt
1 cup (7 oz) plain yogurt, whipped with a little water
½ bunch fresh coriander (cilantro), chopped

Cook the peas in boiling water until they are *al dente*.

Heat the oil in a wok. When hot, add the fenugreek, black mustard seeds, cumin seeds, ginger and chilli. Let sizzle for a few minutes, add peas and potatoes and stir well. Add ½ cup water to cover and cook on low heat for 15–20 minutes or until potato is nearly cooked.

Stir in the spices and salt and cook another 10 minutes. Remove from heat and stir in the whipped yogurt. Garnish with the coriander.

GREEN PEA AND WALNUT SALAD

SERVES 8

7 oz sugar peas, snow peas (mangetout) and shelled young peas
5 oz snow pea (mangetout) sprouts
1 small bunch white radish sprouts (optional)
1 ¼ cups (4 oz) walnut halves

1 ⅓ tblspns (⅔ fl oz) vegetable oil
2 tspns finely chopped rosemary
pinch cayenne

DRESSING
⅓ cup (3 fl oz) walnut oil
3 tblspns (1 ½ fl oz) safflower oil
3 tblspns (1 ½ fl oz) wine vinegar
1 tspn Dijon mustard

Blanch sugar peas and snow peas for 30 seconds, and green peas for 2 minutes, refresh under cold water, drain. Fry walnuts in oil in a frying pan with fresh rosemary and cayenne. Toss well to coat. Drain on paper towels. Cool. Toss salad vegetables and walnuts together. Just before serving, heat dressing ingredients together in a small saucepan, season to taste and pour over salad.

STIR-FRY BEEF AND SNOW PEAS

It is easier to cut the meat if it is partially frozen beforehand.

SERVES 4

1 lb sirloin, chuck or round
⅓ cup (2 ⅔ fl oz) oil
½ cup (3 oz) blanched almonds
1 medium onion, cut in eighths
2 cloves garlic, finely chopped
1 small chilli, finely chopped (optional)
1 large carrot, sliced on the diagonal
6 ½ oz snow peas (mangetout) or sugar snaps,
topped and tailed
2 ⅔ tblspns (1 ⅓ fl oz) oyster sauce

Slice the meat across the grain into thin strips. Put aside. Prepare all the vegetables and have them ready alongside the wok. Heat half the oil in the wok, throw in the almonds, and toss around until just golden. Add the onion, garlic and chilli and cook over high heat, stirring constantly, for 1–2 minutes. Add carrot and

cook another 1–2 minutes. Keep tossing so that nothing burns. With a slotted spoon, remove the vegetables from the wok and set aside.

Heat remaining oil in the wok, throw in the meat and stir-fry over high heat until brown all over. Return vegetables to the wok, throw in the snow peas, toss well, add the oyster sauce. Put the lid on the wok, turn off the heat and let stand for a couple of minutes. Serve immediately with brown rice.

RISI E BISI

This delightful combination of rice and peas comes from Venice, Italy.

SERVES 4 AS AN ENTRÉE (OR APPETIZER)

¼ cup (2 oz) butter
1 small onion, finely chopped
1 stalk celery, finely sliced
2 rashers bacon, approx 3 ½ oz, rind removed
1 clove garlic, finely chopped
10 oz shelled peas (2 lb in pods)
2 cups (6 oz) arborio or short-grain rice
2 cups (½ qt) boiling chicken stock (broth)
½ tspn salt
pepper
1 tblspn freshly grated Parmesan cheese

In a large heavy frying pan, melt the butter. Add onion, celery, bacon and garlic and sauté until vegetables are soft and bacon is cooked.

Add the peas. Cover and braise for about 5 minutes, stirring occasionally.

Remove lid, add the rice and cook for 2–3 minutes, stirring to coat all the grains with butter. Add the boiling chicken stock, salt and pepper (to taste). Bring to a boil, cover and turn down the heat. Cook very slowly (a simmer pad is helpful) for 25–30 minutes or until liquid is absorbed and the rice and peas are moist. Stir in the Parmesan cheese. Serve at once, offering additional grated Parmesan cheese.

Beans
Fabaceae family
Faboideae sub-family

My early successes in the garden were with green stringless beans (Phaseolus vulgaris). *They have a confusing number of names, being known as French in Australia and snap, string and green in North America. They are the ancient bean of the New World, made popular by the French, who called the dried seeds of the beans haricots, because they put them in 'ragouts' or 'haricots' of mutton. The young pods, eaten whole, were called* haricots verts *and the shelled beans, eaten young, became known as flageolet beans (this name being a corruption of the Latin* phaseolus).

To add further to the confusion, not all green beans are green. Some are purple, changing to green when cooked; others are purplish-green and waxy yellow (wax or yellow beans, miscalled butter beans); others are flat and some are round. Butter beans are in fact lima beans (Phaseolus lunatus), *which are flat and kidney-shaped. They are named after Lima, in Peru, from where they originated. The green or French bean we eat is the immature pod of the navy and kidney beans, picked while the seeds are tiny.*

Like peas, beans are nitrogen-fixers — they manufacture nitrogen in their roots thus enriching the soil. However, the better the soil initially, the better the crop. A handful or two of lime or dolomite sprinkled over the soil before planting will help as they don't like an acid soil.

Although they can be grown on the same spot year after year, they are usually grown as annuals. Seed should be sown in spring 1 in deep and 4 in apart. Rows for climbing types should be 5 ft apart, 2 ft for bush types. The latter can also be grown in containers. They like a sunny position and must be kept well watered when flowering.

Then there are the broad beans, Vicia faba, *as old and venerable as the pea. They grow in large thick pods with soft, furry linings. Only the beans are cooked, unless you pick the pods when very young. They are cool-season crops, for eating in spring when other vegetables are either too old or too young. Broad beans can be either dwarf or regular, and both types require support in the form of a fence or trellis. They are a valuable stand-by. If you want dried beans, leave the pods on the plants until they are dry, then pick, shell and store in a dry place.*

MINESTRONE

The best of all vegetable soups and great for warming you up on a cold winter's night. There are many versions, those including beans, bacon or ham and basil being the most flavorsome. The Genoese claim to have invented minestrone, and when served in Liguria it contains more vegetables than elsewhere. They serve it with pesto, which is a last-minute addition. A really good minestrone is a meal in itself.

SERVES 6–8

⅔ cup (4 oz) dried haricot beans
2 onions, finely chopped
¼–⅓ cup (2–2 ⅔ fl oz) olive oil
4 cloves garlic, crushed
2 oz bacon or well smoked ham, chopped
2 stalks celery, chopped
2 carrots, chopped
2 potatoes, peeled and chopped
2 zucchini (courgettes), sliced
2 ⅔ oz shelled peas, approx 5 oz in pods
4 large ripe tomatoes, peeled and seeded
8 cups (2 qt) chicken stock (broth)
bay leaf
parsley sprig
salt and freshly ground black pepper
⅓ cup (2 ½ oz) plain white uncooked rice
2–3 tblspns pesto (see page 129)
½ cup (3 oz) Parmesan cheese, grated

Bring 4 cups of water to boiling point, add beans and boil for 2 minutes, remove from heat and allow to soak for 1 hour. Return to heat and cook over low heat, uncovered, for 1–1 ½ hours or until just tender. Drain and set aside.

Sauté the onions in the oil and when translucent, add the garlic, bacon, celery, carrots, potatoes and zucchini. Cook until soft over medium heat. Add the peas, coarsely chopped tomatoes, chicken stock, bay leaf and parsley sprig, salt and pepper. Throw in the rice, bring

to a boil, reduce heat and simmer gently for 30 minutes. Check seasoning and stir in pesto. Pass the cheese separately.

STIR-FRIED GREEN BEANS WITH SUNFLOWER SEEDS

Simple, crunchy and delicious. Have all the ingredients ready before cooking. Also good cold.

SERVES 4

1 lb green stringless beans, topped and tailed
2 ⅔ tblspns (1 ⅓ fl oz) vegetable oil
½ cup (2 oz) sunflower seeds
2 ⅔ tblspns (1 ⅓ fl oz) water
1 tspn roasted sesame oil

Wash and dry the beans well. Heat the oil in a wok until hot, throw in the sunflower seeds and stir-fry for about 1 minute until golden. Throw in the beans and stir well until coated in oil, about 1 minute.

Pour in the water. Cover the wok with a lid, turn heat to low and cook for 3–4 minutes or until beans are cooked but still crunchy.

Turn up heat and boil away any remaining water. Stir through the sesame oil and serve immediately.

BEANS AND TOMATOES

A simple Italian family dish. When fresh ripe tomatoes
are in season, it's good to use them. You'll need 4
medium–large ones, plus ¼ cup (2 fl oz) water.

SERVES 6

¾ lb stringless green beans, topped and tailed
2 medium potatoes, thinly sliced
½ cup (4 fl oz) olive oil
1 medium onion, sliced
2 cloves garlic, finely chopped
2 medium zucchini (courgettes), cut in ½ in pieces
1 tin tomatoes (14 oz)
2 tblspns freshly chopped basil
2 tblspns freshly chopped flat-leaf (Continental) parsley
salt and pepper

Cut the beans into 2 in lengths. Bring a pan of water to
a boil and throw in the beans and potatoes. As soon as
the water returns to boiling point, remove vegetables
and drain.

In a large heavy frying pan, heat the oil and sauté the
onion and garlic until soft. Put in all the remaining
ingredients and season to taste. Cover and cook for
15–20 minutes or until vegetables are tender.

Corn (Maize)
Zea mays *var.* saccharata

Sweet corn is easy to grow and, although a warm season plant, it grows in all climate zones. It likes an open site
with the greatest possible amount of sun. Time of planting is governed by local climatic conditions, but in both
temperate and cold climates it is best to delay sowings until the soil is warm enough (70°F/20°C) to germinate
the seeds quickly.

Corn is usually planted from seeds directly into the soil — the seed is easy to handle and germinates quickly,
though birds can be a problem in some areas. Sometimes the seeds are treated with a fungicide, however most
gardeners do well with untreated seeds. It's a good idea to grow the corn in a block of short rows about 2 ft
apart, rather than in one long row. This increases the chances
of pollination from male tassels
falling on the female silks
below.

If you stagger the crop by
sowing a few weeks apart,
you can have a continuous
harvest throughout the
growing season. Corn needs a good soaking

in hot weather and mulching helps keep the soil moist. It is a heavy feeder and requires high levels of nutrients, especially nitrogen.

Sweet corn begins to lose its sweetness as soon as it is picked, so don't pick it until you are just about to cook it. If this is impossible, put the corn into the refrigerator with its husks still on. Most corn can be harvested when immature and used as baby corn, but there are varieties available bred specially for use as tiny ears.

A number of varieties of corn are available, including the popcorn which is fun to grow and eat. Some hybrids have been specially developed to retain their sweetness long after harvest.

Meal ground from whole, dried corn kernels comes from corn which has a high content of soft starch. This makes it easy to grind and it can then be cooked or baked, as in cornbread, to make a digestible and delicious food.

In America, it is possible to find yellow, red, white and blue cornmeal, ground from different colored kernels. Native Americans treated corn in an amazing variety of ways, parching it, drying it, popping it (not all corns will pop) or eating it as we know best — on the cob. I remember it wasn't until I saw the film Pollyanna *that I tried it like that, and to this day, I still love hot buttered corn on the cob.*

VEGETABLE KEBABS

Marinated vegetables, cooked on the barbecue are delicious.

Soak bamboo skewers in water for 30 minutes before using to prevent burning.

Cut fresh corn into 1 in slices using a large heavy knife and parboil in rapidly boiling water. Other vegetables might include chunks of eggplant (aubergine), salted for 1 hour beforehand with the salt washed off, then added to the marinade, and onions cut into quarters, chunks of zucchini (courgettes), squash or parboiled pumpkin and potatoes. Red and green sweet peppers (capsicums) cut into squares and fresh mushrooms are also good.

MARINADE

This quantity is sufficient for about 1 ½ lb prepared vegetables and makes 6–8 skewers. Double ingredients for a larger quantity.

½ cup (4 fl oz) olive oil
2 tblspns (1 fl oz) light soy sauce
2 cloves garlic, crushed

1 tblspn freshly grated ginger
3 tblspns freshly chopped coriander (cilantro) or *parsley*
3 tblspns freshly chopped basil, oregano or *marjoram*

Mix the marinade ingredients together in a bowl, stirring well to combine. Add the vegetables and marinate for 6–8 hours or overnight to allow marinade to permeate.

Thread the vegetable pieces onto the skewers, alternating the color and type. Brush with the marinade and cook on barbecue until vegetables are *al dente*, turning and basting frequently.

BARBECUED CORN

Corn is good cooked on the barbecue. Cook it un-shucked (that is, with the husks still on). Soak the corn cobs in cold water for 1 hour, peel back the husks and brush the kernels with a herbed oil. Put the cobs directly onto the charcoal at the edge of the barbecue and cook for 30–40 minutes, sprinkling with water and turning frequently.

MIXED VEGETABLES IN COCONUT MILK

A colorful, interesting, one-dish vegetarian meal of Indian origin. I remember Margaret Fulton being very excited by it when she returned from a trip to India. This is my version of her recipe. You don't have to stick with the vegetables listed (pumpkin, zucchini (courgettes) and squash are good substitutes), but do get out a large pot to cook it in.
Serve the vegetables heaped up in a pyramid shape on a big platter. Spoon the coconut gravy over the vegetables, then scatter some freshly chopped coriander (cilantro) and a handful or two of toasted cashew nuts on top. Good with chapatis.

SERVES 8

8 oz stringless green beans, topped and tailed
8–10 corn cobs
3 medium potatoes, peeled
3 medium pink sweet potatoes (kumara), peeled
½ small cauliflower
1 cucumber, washed
1 small bunch spinach, washed
1 bunch fresh coriander (cilantro)
10 oz baby carrots, peeled
5 tblspns (2 ½ oz) ghee or butter
4–6 small hot chillies
2 ½ in piece fresh ginger, grated
approx 4 cups (1 qt) coconut milk
salt
unsalted cashew nuts
fresh coriander (cilantro), extra

Cut beans into halves. Using a large, sharp knife, cut each corn cob into rounds about 1 ½ in in length. Cut potatoes and sweet potatoes into cubes; break cauliflower into florets. Cut cucumber in half lengthwise, remove seeds and chop into lengths the same size as the beans. Remove spinach leaves from stalks, then chop leaves and coriander leaves. Leave baby carrots whole.

Melt the ghee or butter in a large, heavy pot, add the chillies and grated ginger and cook for 3–4 minutes. Add the pieces of corn, scatter over half the greens, add cubed vegetables and carrots, and scatter with remaining greens. Add coconut milk to reach a quarter of the way up the pot, season with salt and cover. Simmer very slowly for 50–60 minutes or until vegetables are tender. Serve as described.

SWEET CORNBREAD

This is good toasted, drizzled with honey and eaten with fresh figs.

MAKES 1 LOAF OR 12 MUFFINS

1 ½ cups (6 oz) self-raising flour
1 tspn each baking powder and salt
1 cup (5 ⅓ oz) fine yellow cornmeal
¼ cup (2 oz) sugar
2 eggs, beaten
1 cup (8 fl oz) milk
¼ cup (2 oz) butter, melted

Preheat oven to 400°F (200°C/Gas 6).
Sift together the flour, baking powder and salt. Add the cornmeal and sugar and make a well in the center. Pour in the eggs, milk and butter and stir until the ingredients are well combined and form a smooth thick batter. Spoon into a greased standard loaf tin or muffin tins, place on a tray and bake for 25–30 minutes for the loaf or 15–20 minutes for the muffins. Remove and cool.

Fruit Vegetables

. . . What takes flight
into fruits? Gives us, in the circling intake
of tasting, its worth? What to us communicates
aroma?

RAINER MARIA RILKE, FROM 'DECEMBER 1925'

No matter where I turn in my garden during summer, I find a tomato plant. They're in amongst the roses, pushing up through the violas, and asserting themselves with the daisies. In fact, they become just another weed. Don't get me wrong, I love tomatoes. Especially home-grown ones. It's just that I can't get rid of them. I use a lot of compost in the garden and it's this that gives rise to the tomatoes.

The ones I like best are the self-sown cherry tomatoes. These, unlike other tomato varieties, never seem to attract pests and will grow to a deep red color, when left on the vine. Their flavor is exquisite: sweet, and tasting of the sun. They are superb dried and preserved under oil.

Where would the modern cook be without the tomato? Yet when first introduced to Europe from South America in the sixteenth century, the tomato was treated with much disdain. The English cultivated them for two centuries as garden ornaments and decorative plants.

Early botanists classed it as poisonous, recognising it as a member of the Solanaceae (or deadly nightshade) family. Perhaps someone had eaten the leaves instead of the fruit, which would explain its wicked reputation, for its leaves and stems are toxic. It was in Italy that the culinary barrier was first broken and the habit of eating tomatoes spread around the Mediterranean and gradually northwards. It was called mala aurea *or* poma amoris *(Latin for golden apple or love apple). Red, yellow and white tomatoes were all known, the red in two varieties: small and round, and large, flat and lobed (part of the Marmande group).*

Here I must say that most tomatoes available in shops today are a sorry apology for the real thing: tasteless, lifeless and dull. Which is why, if you're serious about your food, you'll plant a few today. Poor tomatoes, I feel really sorry about what's happened to them commercially.

Tomatoes are botanically classed as fruits, as are avocados, eggplants (aubergines), sweet peppers (capsicums) and chilli peppers. Breadfruit, akee and plantains also fall into the same category. Tomatoes and eggplants are, in fact, berries; avocados are drupes, but both are commonly used as vegetables because they are not sweet. Mind you, some of the home-grown tomatoes I've eaten have been quite sweet.

Like the tomato, eggplants also got off to a difficult start. They, too, are members of the Solanaceae family and were treated with much suspicion when introduced to Europe in the sixteenth century. Early names included 'mala insana' or mad apple. Elizabeth David once wrote an article about eggplants entitled 'Mad, Bad, Despised and Dangerous', which gives you an idea of the way in which they were regarded. And yet a thirteenth century Chinese dramatist, Kuan Han-chi'ing, could write, 'The fall harvest is gathered in. Let's set a feast out under the gourd trellis, drink wine from earthen bowls and porcelain pots, swallow the tender eggplants with their skins, gulp down the little melons, seeds and all. The turnips are sliced in a salty sauce; the country wine goes down by the bowlful . . . '

Clearly they weren't despised in China. In fact some writers claim the eggplant was first domesticated in either China or India, the earliest Chinese records dating from the fifth century BC. It seems they were introduced to Europe courtesy of the Arabs, reaching there via North Africa and Spain.

The Chinese were slow, though, to accept the tomato and the pepper. It's only been during the past 100 years that these two have been used in Chinese cooking. Their adoption has actually transformed the taste of southern Chinese cooking.

Historically, fruit vegetables seem to have caused a number of headaches for cooks: are they fruits? are they vegetables? Do we add sugar to them? or salt? Take the avocado, for instance. Some writers class it as a fruit, others as a vegetable. Imagine if you were being introduced to it for the very first time, what would you do? Would you peel it like an apple? Turn it into an ice-cream? Cut it in half and dress it with a vinaigrette? Spread it on a sandwich (my favorite)? Or perhaps you might try it with a dob of redcurrant jelly, or even use it as a facial? All these are possibilities.

And peppers. Imagine if you bit into one of the small, very hot chillies. You'd probably never want to use it in your cooking, let alone handle one again. When my son was three, he picked up a cut red chilli from the kitchen bench and accidentally rubbed it near his eye. It created great anguish for hours afterwards. He had been tempted by the glossy red color, but what a nasty awakening. Yet it is these very peppers that give the added fire to the spicy dishes of many Latin American and Asian cuisines (Indian, Thai and Singaporean to name a few).

Peppers, of course, are found in considerable varieties. The most familiar are the sweet ones (capsicums) which come in a glorious array of colors: red, green, yellow, orange, black, white. What a beautiful display they make in the garden.

None of these fruit vegetables are difficult to grow, though tomatoes can attract a number of pests and diseases. All need warm to hot weather to thrive. In fact, tomatoes, eggplants and capsicums need similar conditions and are best planted when all danger of frost has passed. The ideal soil temperature for germination is 65–75°F (18–23°C).

Avocados, being native to Central America, also need a warm climate. They have become very popular over the past 10 to 20 years, so that there is now often a glut of them in Australian markets. I remember as a child that they were considered very exotic. Now I see both the trees and the fruit all over the place. Avocados don't like salt-laden winds, so are best planted away from seaside areas.

Tomatoes
Lycopersicon esculentum

Did you know that there are hundreds of varieties of tomatoes to choose from? It was only a decade ago that I really became aware of this. Until then, a tomato was a tomato for me and not a vegetable I gave much thought to.

Like most of us, I hadn't had much exposure to a real tomatoey tomato. But as more and more people have begun demanding tomatoes they remembered from their childhoods, growers are responding by growing better and different varieties. You see them around the place now — the tiny yellow teardrops, the vine-ripened, juicy red ones.

The best place to start experimenting is at home. They are probably one of the most popular of all home garden crops. If you don't have a lot of space, they grow well in pots, especially the small varieties like Tiny Tim, Small Fry Hybrid and Patio Hybrid.

I suggest you start experimenting with the different varieties now available. Many home gardeners grow Grosse Lisse, but have you tried the San Marzano's and Rouge de Marmande? By selecting the correct varieties you can grow tomatoes all year round.

You may find, though, that a specific variety differs from region to region, season to season or garden to garden. They can even vary from plant to plant within the same garden

which does make choosing a variety a process of trial and error.

Tomatoes prefer open, sunny positions and dislike wind. They germinate poorly in cold soil and are best started indoors and transplanted when soil temperature is 70°F (20°C). For full flavor, don't water them too much as they begin to ripen, otherwise they tend to turn into bags of water. Mulching is good to retain moisture: less water means intensified flavor.

PASTA WITH PROSCIUTTO AND DRIED TOMATOES

For a delicious and simple lunch (or supper) for four, try the following: toss 7 oz of dried, halved cherry tomatoes in a little warmed olive oil. Add 1 ¾ cups (7 oz) toasted pinenuts (pignolias) and about 7 oz of prosciutto, cut into thin strips. Combine with 13 oz of cooked fettuccine and toss well.

Note: If using fresh pasta, you will need 1 ⅓ lb, about 5 ½ oz per person

DRIED CHERRY TOMATOES

I have a friend who lives on a farm in Tuscany. She is a wonderful cook, one of those gifted creatures who instinctively knows what to put with what. Once, when visiting her, she told me how, during summer, she picks the surplus cherry tomatoes from her garden, strings them up in bunches and hangs them against the walls of her stone house.

This surprised me because I had never thought of drying cherry tomatoes, even though they sprout so abundantly from my compost. I'd only ever associated egg tomatoes with being dried and had often wondered what all the fuss was about, as I'd found the imported variety tough and leathery.

Then, a couple of years ago I was given a pot of dried cherry tomatoes. They looked wonderful, red and bright amidst the golden olive oil and they tasted even better — like potted summer sunshine. Interestingly, they weren't sun-dried, but oven-dried. In a humid climate,

it is difficult relying on the sun to do the drying as too often the mold gets to the fruit or vegetables first. These make splendid gifts.

vine-ripened cherry tomatoes
flaky sea salt
white sugar
chopped fresh thyme or oregano
garlic cloves
olive oil
sterilized jar

It is best to use a convection (fan-forced) oven, either gas or electric, set at the lowest possible temperature. It needs to be low enough to enable you to put your hand in without burning. Some people have had success with clothes' drying closets, again set at the lowest temperature.

Wash the tomatoes and dry them, remove the calyx. Cut into halves. Place them cut-side up on cake racks and sprinkle with equal quantities of sea salt (ordinary salt is too harsh) and white sugar. Add a little finely chopped thyme or oregano. For every 9 oz tomatoes, also allow two peeled, whole garlic cloves.

Put the tomatoes and garlic on the racks into the oven, with a tray underneath to catch the water, and leave them to dry up to 24 hours. The time will vary; sometimes they may need only 8–10 hours, depending on your oven. The first batch will require experimentation for you to get the heat and timing right. The tomatoes should be dry and fleshy, but not withered. Remove and allow to cool, then place in jars with branches of thyme or oregano (which have been washed and dried); cover with olive oil and seal. You can also dry egg tomatoes like this.

SPAGHETTI AL SALSA DI POMODORO CRUDO

The success of this lovely, simple dish depends on the freshness and quality of the raw ingredients. Prepare the sauce a few hours ahead to develop the flavors. Rich red egg or plum tomatoes are best.

SERVES 4

10–12 medium very ripe tomatoes, approx 1 lb
2 cloves garlic
small bunch fresh basil
⅓ cup (3 fl oz) best quality virgin olive oil
13 oz spaghetti
salt
freshly ground black pepper

Peel the tomatoes with a sharp knife. Don't plunge them into boiling water. If you have trouble, it's better to leave the skin on. Chop roughly and put the pieces into a bowl. Add the bruised garlic cloves and torn basil leaves. Pour on the olive oil, mix well and leave to marinate for 3–4 hours, covered.

Cook spaghetti in plenty of rapidly boiling salted water until cooked. Drain and tip into a serving bowl.

Season the sauce with salt and pepper to taste and remove the garlic cloves. Tip sauce over hot spaghetti, combine well and serve immediately.

Variation: A nice substitute for the basil is torn, fresh arugula leaves.

TOMATOES STUFFED WITH TUNA

I very much like the Italian combination of tomatoes with a tuna mayonnaise. You can either cut raw fresh tomatoes into halves, or cut a lid off their tops. Scoop out their insides and stuff with a tuna mayonnaise. Make the tuna mayonnaise by pounding 4 oz tuna fish in oil and gradually adding this mixture to 1 cup (8 fl oz) homemade mayonnaise. Scatter with freshly chopped parsley.

PASTA AL PESTO DI OLIVA

This is a wonderful way to use your dried cherry tomatoes. I decided to try the idea with pasta and it, too, is delicious.

SERVES 2–4

13 oz fresh spaghetti
2 ⅔ tblspns (1 ⅓ fl oz) olive oil
2 cloves garlic, crushed
2–3 tblspns olive paste
dried tomatoes
fresh goat cheese

Cook the spaghetti in rapidly boiling, salted water until *al dente*. Drain and reserve, keeping hot.

In a frying pan, heat oil and sauté garlic 1–2 minutes, just so that it sizzles. Don't let it burn. Remove immediately from heat, stir in the olive paste and toss this mixture through the spaghetti. Some olive pastes are oilier than others, so use your judgment when mixing this through the spaghetti.

Toss the halved, dried cherry tomatoes through the spaghetti with some roughly broken pieces of fresh goat cheese. Serve with green salad.

Eggplants (Aubergines)
Solanum melongena

I love the glossy sensuous beauty of eggplants (aubergines). I recall once seeing a mound of them piled on an old wooden platter at a very stylish beachside restaurant. They glowed, and I could not resist stroking them.

I'm referring to the purple-black, oval-shaped fruits, yet the name 'eggplant' derives from the smaller, white-fruited varieties. The French name 'aubergine' derives from the Catalan 'alberginies'.

Eggplants are popular nowadays, yet they've had a checkered history. In sixteenth century England, John Gerard was telling readers of his Herball *'. . . to content themselves with the meate and sauce of our owne country than with fruit and sauce eaten with such perill; for doubtless these apples have a mischievous quality; the use thereof is utterly forsaken.'*

Its greatest devotees are the southern Italians and the Arabs of the Middle East, where it is referred to as 'poor man's caviar' or 'poor man's meat'. In Turkey, it has been customary for a young bride to know how to prepare eggplant at least twenty-seven different ways if she is to be considered worthwhile by her husband-to-be. In American jazz singer Michael Franks's quirky song about his girlfriend, she cooks it nineteen different ways. He has it raw with mayonnaise.

A member of the potato family, eggplants do well in the vegetable patch. They like full sun and a rich soil. Because they look so beautiful, you can plant them as a border or in a handsome container. The climate requirements are similar to those for tomatoes and they are very susceptible to frost, especially when germinating.

The very tiny pea-sized eggplants used in Thai cooking have become more widely available recently.

Soupe à la Victorine

A good, hearty peasant soup from France, one which is a meal in itself. The eggplant–tomato garnish adds an interesting touch.

SERVES 6–8

4 cups (1 qt) water
3 oz white beans
1 lb leeks or *onions*
¼ cup (2 fl oz) olive oil
1 bay leaf
sprig each fresh thyme and sage
½ lb green bacon in one piece or *unsmoked pork shoulder* or
Italian sausage (optional)
salt and freshly ground black pepper
2½ cups (20 fl oz) chicken stock (broth)
handful fresh basil, chives and parsley, chopped

EGGPLANT AND TOMATO GARNISH
1 lb eggplants (aubergines)
salt
1 lb firm ripe tomatoes
¼ cup (2 fl oz) olive oil
4 cloves garlic

Bring water to a boil, add beans and boil for 2 minutes. Remove from heat, cover pan and let soak for 1 hour.

Slice leeks or onions and cook gently in oil until translucent. Raise heat and brown lightly. Add to beans with the herbs, bacon or sausage, salt and pepper. Bring to simmer and cook slowly for 1 ½ hours or until beans are cooked, keeping the pan partially covered. Remove bacon or sausage and set aside. Remove herbs.

Just before serving, bring soup to simmering point and thin out with the chicken stock. Slice bacon or sausage and add to soup along with Eggplant and Tomato Garnish. Simmer 3–4 minutes to incorporate all flavors, check seasoning and finally add the fresh green herbs. Serve immediately.

EGGPLANT AND TOMATO GARNISH
Peel eggplant, cut into small cubes. Sprinkle with salt and let stand 15–20 minutes. Wash off salt, drain and dry on paper towels. Meanwhile, peel and seed the tomatoes and cut pulp into small cubes. Heat the oil in a heavy frying pan and add eggplant. Cook until lightly browned, stirring occasionally. Add tomato pulp and crushed garlic. Cover pan, simmer 10–15 minutes until eggplant is tender but still holding its shape.

Baked Eggplant with Pesto

This is a simple, lovely dish.
SERVES 4–6

*3 medium eggplants (aubergines), approx 1 lb each, washed
and trimmed of stalks*
salt
homemade pesto (see page 129)

Cut the eggplants in thick slices (about 2 ½ in). There'll be 2–3 thick slices per eggplant. Cut a cross into the flesh at each end and salt well. Put into a colander to drain for 1 hour.

Preheat the oven to 400°F (200°C/Gas 6).

Wash off the salt and dry. Lightly oil a baking dish and place the eggplant slices on the tray. Cover each one with foil, folding down around the sides. Cook 25–30 minutes or until the flesh feels soft.

Remove from the oven, take off foil and top each slice with a generous tblspn of pesto. Turn down oven to 350°F (180°C/Gas 4) and return the eggplant slices, uncovered. Cook another 10–15 minutes. Pierce eggplant with a sharp knife or skewer to ensure it is cooked through to the middle. Serve hot.

EGGPLANT PRESERVED IN OLIVE OIL

This takes a bit of preparation but the effort is worth it. You can eat it immediately but it's best left to mellow for a week. It will keep for 2–3 months in the refrigerator. You can use large eggplant too, cut into finger lengths.

Preserved like this, eggplant is excellent sandwiched between bread with sliced tomatoes and fresh basil leaves. Slices of salami or mortadella are also very good. It's also good on crostini, which can be made by slicing a French loaf diagonally into ½ in slices. Brush on one side with olive oil and bake in a moderate oven until golden brown.

MAKES APPROX 4 CUPS (1 QT)

4 lb baby eggplants (aubergines), peeled
salt
4–6 cloves garlic, peeled and halved
3–4 red chillies, halved
sprigs of oregano
¼ cup (2 fl oz) white wine vinegar
virgin olive oil

Slice the eggplants into half lengthwise. Put them into a glass or stainless steel bowl and sprinkle liberally with salt. Toss well, cover and refrigerate overnight.

Drain and rinse well. Squeeze well, using a tea-towel if necessary. Be careful not to damage the eggplant.

Put eggplant halves into sterile glass jars, inserting the garlic, chillies and oregano sprigs as you go, making a pretty pattern. Press down, pour over the vinegar and oil and seal. Refrigerate. Check occasionally to see if it needs topping with more olive oil.

GREEN CURRY OF CHICKEN

SERVES 4–6

2 x 14 fl oz tins coconut cream
4–6 tspns Thai green curry paste
6 chicken fillets, sliced into strips
6 fresh kaffir or lime leaves
1 stalk lemongrass, cut into 2 ½ in lengths and bruised
2 oz Thai pea eggplants (aubergines)
1 cup (8 fl oz) water, if needed
1 ⅓ tblspns (⅔ fl oz) fish sauce
1 ⅓ tblspns (⅔ fl oz) lemon juice
¼ cup chopped fresh coriander (cilantro)
2 fresh red chillies, bruised, for garnish

Put 2 tblspns coconut cream into a pan, and reduce until oily, then add the curry paste and fry for 1–2 minutes. Stir in the chicken and add the remaining coconut cream, together with the citrus leaves, lemongrass and pea eggplants. Simmer very gently until the chicken is cooked, about 10–15 minutes adding the water if the curry reduces too much. Just before serving, stir in the fish sauce, lemon juice and coriander leaves and garnish with the red chillies. Serve with boiled or steamed jasmine rice.

Note: If the pea eggplants are unobtainable, use large peas or 1–2 small green eggplants, quartered. Thai green curry paste is available in tins from Asian food stores.

RATATOUILLE

Poet Kate Llewellyn gave me this recipe for a
different version of this lovely traditional dish. She in
turn had been given it by gourmet Geoff Parsons, who
says it improves with standing overnight in the
refrigerator, and will feed an army.

SERVES 10–12

⅔ cup (5 fl oz) olive oil
4 onions, coarsely chopped
10 cloves garlic, peeled and bruised
1 green sweet pepper (capsicum), seeded and sliced
2 red sweet peppers (capsicums), seeded and sliced
5 zucchinis (courgettes), sliced
2 large eggplants (aubergines), cut into chunks, skin on
2 bulbs fennel, sliced
few whole black peppercorns
1 tblspn coriander (cilantro) seeds
2 tspns fennel seeds
6 ripe tomatoes, peeled and chopped
1 bunch freshly chopped basil
1–2 chillies, chopped (optional)
bay leaf
1 tblspn freshly chopped ginger

Heat the oil in a large pan. Add onions and cook gently
until they soften. Don't allow them to brown. Add
garlic and sweet peppers and let soften. Add zucchini,
eggplant and fennel and simmer 10–15 minutes,
stirring occasionally. Add the tomatoes, spices and
herbs. Continue cooking very slowly for a couple of
hours. Let the vegetables meld together slowly, without
losing their shape — vegetables should not be served
mushy.

BABA GHANOUGE

A delicious dip, or good spread on flat, freshly baked
bread and topped with sliced tomatoes and chopped
basil.

SERVES 6–8

2 large or 3 medium eggplants (aubergines)
2 cloves garlic, crushed
¾ cup (6 fl oz) tahini
½ cup (4 fl oz) lemon juice
½ cup (4 fl oz) oil
sea salt

You can either bake or broil (grill) the eggplants. If you
broil them, they will have a lovely smoky flavor which
won't be so pronounced if baked. Prick them over with
a fork and place under the preheated broiler or in a hot
oven. If broiling, turn frequently. You can also cook
them over a gas flame, using a long fork, and turning
frequently. They will cook in their own juices.

When soft — and cool enough to handle — scoop
out the pulp and mash to a coarse consistency. Add the
garlic and tahini, then the lemon juice and continue
stirring until the mixture turns a grayish-white color.
Stir in the oil and salt to taste.

Peppers
Capsicum *species*

Like eggplants, peppers in all their myriad shapes and sizes are a glorious addition to the garden. Their glossy red, green and yellow colors will brighten any patch, be it the vegetable or flower garden.

Native to South America, they were discovered by Christopher Columbus who was on his way to Asia, the land of pepper. When the Indians gave him a hot spice on his food, he called it pepper and the name has stuck. What he was given was powdered chilli of the genus Capsicum.

There are hundreds of varieties of capsicum peppers, ranging from sweet to mild to hot in flavor. To simplify things, we can divide them into major categories: the sweet (capsicum) pepper (Capsicum annuum) *and the* chilli pepper (C. frutescens).

Of the sweet peppers, the bell is the most popular because of its shape, size and sweetness. They can develop through a wide range of colors, from green to purple to red; green to yellow to red; or green to black to red. In Hungary, the red ones are used to make paprika and in Spain to make pimento.

Chilli peppers are much smaller and also come in a huge variety of shapes, colors and sizes. In Italy, you often see them tied in bunches, hanging from eaves. As they dry, they wrinkle and look most attractive. Cayenne pepper, Tabasco sauce and chilli powder are by-products.

Like tomatoes and eggplants, peppers are a warm to hot weather fruit vegetable. Like them, they look good in containers. They won't tolerate frost and need a long growing season. They require deep rich soil and regular watering and fertilizing, though it is best to avoid fertilizers that are rich in nitrogen. Nitrogen tends to encourage leaf development at the expense of fruit development.

RED SWEET PEPPER SOUP

This is surprisingly good.

SERVES 6–8

3 large red sweet peppers (capsicums), approx 1 ½ lb,
washed, seeds removed
1 medium onion
2 tblspns (1 oz) butter
8 cups (2 qt) chicken stock (broth)
¼ cup (2 oz) butter, extra
½ cup (2 oz) all-purpose (plain) flour
½ cup (4 fl oz) cream
extra blanched red sweet pepper (capsicum) for garnish

Chop the sweet peppers and onions and sauté in butter in a medium saucepan until soft but not colored. Add the stock, bring to a boil, then simmer for 30 minutes or until the sweet pepper flavor is prominent through the stock. Strain the stock, reserving the vegetables.

In a separate saucepan, make the roux: melt the extra butter, remove from heat and add flour. Stir together well, return to heat and cook until it is an even, sandy color, 1–2 minutes.

Add about a quarter of the stock a little at a time to the roux, mixing continuously with a wooden spoon to avoid lumps. Return to remaining stock, bring to a boil and simmer for 30 minutes, stirring occasionally.

Put vegetables into the blender and process until smooth, then add to the thickened stock. Bring back to a boil, add the cream, season to taste and serve hot with a swirl of cream and some shaped red sweet pepper pieces.

CHICKEN SALAD WITH OLIVES, TOMATOES, SWEET PEPPERS AND BASIL

I like to use the whole of the chicken in this salad, though you could just use 2–3 chicken breasts poached for 8–10 minutes. It is a good one for taking on a picnic. It can be prepared the day before and stored in a plastic container, with a tight-fitting lid, in the refrigerator.

SERVES 4–6

1 medium chicken (size 12)
1 onion
1 carrot
1 bay leaf
6 peppercorns
3 parsley stalks
2 slices lemon
2 tomatoes, cut into wedges or 6 ½ oz halved cherry tomatoes
½ green sweet pepper (capsicum), cut into squares
handful black olives
1 garlic clove, crushed
lots of freshly chopped basil
salt and pepper to taste
2 ⅔ tblspns (1 ⅓ fl oz) good olive oil

Remove any fat from the chicken and put it in a pot. Cover with the water and add onion, carrot, bay leaf, peppercorns, parsley and lemon.

Bring to boiling point, skim off any froth, turn down to gentle simmer and cook for approximately 1 ¼ hours or until tender. Remove immediately and set aside to cool. For quicker cooking, you can joint the chicken and then cook it.

When chicken is cold, remove flesh from bones, discarding skin. Cut into nicely shaped pieces. Put into a bowl or plastic container along with remaining ingredients, toss together and store in the refrigerator. The flavor will improve overnight. Freshly chopped parsley can be added.

Variations: Substitute coriander (cilantro) for the basil, omit the olives and add some freshly chopped chilli; substitute the green sweet pepper with roasted red, yellow or green sweet peppers; substitute the olive oil with ½ cup (4 fl oz) of a good, homemade mayonnaise. When young asparagus or beans are in season, quickly blanch, cut into 1 ½ in lengths and toss them through the salad as well.

PRESERVED SWEET PEPPERS IN OIL

Pickling is a common method of preservation in the Middle East, especially in hot, isolated areas. There, grocers prepare their own and offer a taste of the newly mellowed pickles to their customers. Different people use different proportions of salted water to vinegar, depending on their taste. The sight of large glass jars shimmering with a myriad of differently colored vegetables is wondrous.

You don't need a precise recipe, just some guidelines. For every 2 parts white wine vinegar (choose a good-quality one — some vinegars are very acidic), allow 1 part water, ⅓ cup (3 oz) rock salt per 4 cups, some peeled cloves of garlic and a chopped stalk of celery.

Wash and dry fresh whole sweet peppers (capsicums) and put a split in them to help them drain. Use a sharp knife and run the split from the bottom of the sweet pepper to about half way up. Put them into sterile glass containers or into a large sterile bucket and cover with the solution. Put a plate or saucer on top to hold them down (otherwise they float to the top) and cover tightly. After 7–10 days, taste to see if they are crunchy and mellowing — if left too long, they start to become soft and vinegary.

Drain off the solution and re-pack in glass jars, interspersing with slivers of garlic, bay leaves and dried oregano or basil sprigs. Cover with olive oil and seal tightly. They'll be ready for eating after 2–3 days.

CHILLIES IN OLIVE OIL

Chillies can be dried by threading them onto string and hanging in the sun to dry. There is an amusing scene in Federico Fellini's film *Juliet of the Spirits* where the women sit around a table threading peppers onto string and chatting away madly.

They are also good preserved in olive oil. You can do this with either the pre-dried or fresh chillies, washed and dried thoroughly. You need a sterile glass jar with a screw-top lid. Fill half of it with dried or fresh chillies and pour in sufficient olive oil to fill the jar. Seal and leave for a few weeks.

The resultant oil is wonderful used in cooking. Try it brushed over a chicken before roasting. Or brush over meats on the barbecue.

Chillies can also be preserved under vinegar. Use a white wine vinegar. Pack washed and dried chillies into sterile jars. Insert a few sprigs of parsley (or herb of choice), a few peppercorns and pour over the vinegar. Seal well. Recently I've come across chillies in the shape of baby squashes. They look particularly decorative preserved in this way.

OCTOPUS SALAD

Octopus used to bother me — the cooking of them, I mean (the look of them has always terrified my children who run screaming from the kitchen when they're around). Cooking them like this is very good. Char-grilling is also a delicious way to cook them, but you must use the baby ones. Check with your fishmonger that they've been pre-tenderized. Quite often this is done in a cement mixer. Around the Mediterranean, they do it by bashing them on the rocks, which I guess would tenderize anything.

I like the addition of a couple of chopped fresh chillies to this cold seafood salad. It gives a bit of a kick and makes it more interesting. This is a nice one for summer picnics, lunches and boat parties, but make sure you pack it into a cooler (or icebox) to keep it chilled. These proportions are a guideline and you can also mix and match your seafood. Freshwater crayfish and squid would make nice additions or alternatives.

SERVES 6

2 lb baby octopus
1 carrot
1 onion
1 bay leaf
2 ⅔ tblspns (1 ⅓ fl oz) white vinegar
2 lb fresh mussels
1 lb medium-sized jumbo shrimps (prawns), cooked
½ cup (4 fl oz) olive oil
¼ cup (2 fl oz) lemon juice
1 clove garlic, crushed
salt and pepper
1 red chilli, chopped (optional)
1 green chilli, chopped (optional)

Put octopus into a medium–large saucepan, cover with water, add carrot, onion, bay leaf and vinegar. Bring to a boil, skimming off any scum, turn off immediately. Let sit in the water until cool. Drain well, wash the octopus, discard the vegetables.

Scrub and clean mussels then steam open in a covered frying pan, shaking the pan as you do so.

Discard any unopened ones. Shell and de-vein shrimps.

Combine the seafood in a bowl. Combine olive oil, lemon juice and garlic, and season with salt and pepper. Pour dressing and chillies over seafood and toss. Allow to stand for 2 hours in the refrigerator.

CHICKPEA SALAD WITH RED SWEET PEPPER

Try this combination: cooked chickpeas (garbanzo beans) tossed together in a vinaigrette with chopped red sweet pepper, scallions and diced or finely sliced hot salami. Mix together well. Sprinkle with chopped parsley. A little powdered cumin added to the salad dressing is a nice addition.

ROASTED SWEET PEPPERS

Red sweet peppers (capsicums) are especially good done like this, their sweetness and flavor being drawn out by the heat.

Wash medium red sweet peppers, cut them in half and remove the seeds. Heat the broiler (griller) to high and cook them, skin side up, until the skin is blackened and blistered. Move around with tongs to distribute the heat. Remove from broiler and put them in a plastic bag. Seal the bag. After 10 minutes or so, remove from the bag, scrape off the skins and cut the sweet peppers into strips.

Put into a bowl and dress with vinegar and olive oil to taste. Crushed garlic is a good addition. Season with salt and pepper. Serve as an accompaniment or use through pasta dishes and in salads.

PANTHAY KAUKSWE

An unusual meal-in-one dish inspired by Doris Ady, a Burmese-born cookery expert. It is very delicious (egg noodles in a creamy coconut and chicken soup) and a great success at dinner parties.

SERVES 8–10

1 medium chicken (size 12)

5 cups (1 ¼ qt) water

¼ cup (2 oz) ghee or butter

4–5 large onions

4 cloves garlic, chopped

1 piece ginger, approx 2 in, chopped

2 tspns turmeric powder

¼ tspn chilli powder

4–6 chicken stock (bouillon) cubes

¼ cup (1 ¼ oz) lentil flour

cold milk

3 oz frozen coconut cream

salt

fresh coriander (cilantro) or parsley

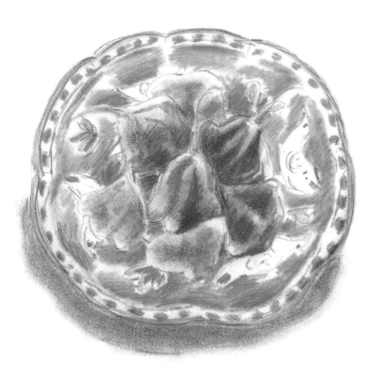

ACCOMPANIMENTS

1 lb fine egg noodles

4 hard-boiled eggs, chopped

large bunch scallions (shallots, spring onions), sliced (include green parts)

12 red dried or fresh chillies, seeded and chopped

4 oz extra fine egg noodles

oil for deep frying

lemon wedges

Joint the chicken and place the pieces in a large pot along with the water. Bring to a boil, turn down and simmer until chicken is tender. When cooked, remove from stock and cut the meat from the bones. Put stock aside.

Heat the ghee or butter in a large frying pan and add onions, garlic and ginger. When they begin to brown, add turmeric and chilli powder. Put this into the chicken stock and add stock cubes for extra flavor. Cover and simmer 30 minutes.

Meanwhile, put the lentil flour into a bowl, add a little cold milk and mix until it forms a smooth paste. Add a small cupful of the stock from the pan and when the paste is liquefied, add it to the stock. Bring to boiling point, then turn down to simmer. Put the chicken meat into the soup, add the coconut cream and allow to dissolve slowly. Add salt to taste and a good handful of chopped, fresh coriander.

Cook the egg noodles in boiling salted water until tender. For the accompaniments, fry chillies in a little hot oil, adding a little vinegar towards the end (½ tspn per person is sufficient of these). Break the extra fine egg noodles into 1 in lengths and deep-fry in hot oil until crisp, drain on paper towels. Place hard-boiled eggs, scallions, chillies, fried noodles and lemon wedges in separate small bowls.

To serve, put a spoonful of the egg noodles into a large soup bowl and ladle the hot soup over. Each guest then helps themselves to each of the accompaniments, sprinkling these over the soup.

Note: Extra-fine egg noodles are also available pre-fried.

PHILADELPHIA HOTPOT

If you like tripe, you're sure to love this soup. If, however, the very thought of it makes you feel squeamish, do try this recipe. The betting is you won't even notice the tripe as the flavor is so good. This is a traditional soup in the United States, apparently created by the head cook of George Washington's army during the winter of the Valley Forge campaign in 1777. Washington is believed to have named the soup 'Pepper Pot' because of its ingredients, and Philadelphia after the cook's home town. In Bermuda and the West Indies, they make a soup similar to this one, but it is more highly spiced. A gay, colorful dish indeed.

SERVES 8

1 lb honeycomb tripe
1 veal knuckle
freshly chopped parsley
1 sprig each fresh thyme, marjoram, basil and chervil
1 bay leaf
1 clove
10 peppercorns
1 medium onion
1 stalk celery

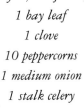

1 carrot
1 green sweet pepper (capsicum)
1 medium potato
2 ⅔ tblspns (1 ⅓ fl oz) oil
salt and freshly ground black pepper
handful or two of uncooked short-grain rice
4–6 ripe tomatoes, peeled and chopped
1 ½ red sweet peppers (capsicums), diced
2–3 small red chillies, finely chopped
freshly chopped parsley, extra

Blanch the tripe and veal knuckle: put into a large pot, cover with cold water, bring to a boil, and drain. Dice tripe and put back into the pot along with the veal knuckle. Add water to cover and parsley. Tie the herbs, clove and peppercorns in a muslin bag and add to the pot. Simmer very gently for about 2 hours or until tripe is tender, being sure to skim the soup of any scum after it has reached a boil.

Chop the onion, celery, carrot, green sweet pepper and potato, and cook gently in the oil in a heavy frying pan until soft. Add to the soup and cook very gently for 30 minutes. Add rice, tomatoes, red sweet pepper and chillies.

Season the soup well and cook for further 15–20 minutes. Remove the veal knuckle before serving, and sprinkle with chopped parsley.

Avocados
Persea americana

Do you remember when avocados were considered a luxury and their soft buttery flesh was much sought after? Over the past couple of decades, however, we have witnessed so much planting by commercial growers that we often have a glut. As a result, we tend to take these lovely fruit vegetables for granted.

According to English food writer Tom Stobart, the avocado has only come into its own rather recently, due to the work of American breeders, and is now grown in most tropical and subtropical countries. Avocados are native to Mexico, Guatemala and perhaps Nicaragua. They may be round or pear-shaped, black–purple or green, smooth-skinned or rough. In Mexico they sometimes weigh in at 2–4 lb, which has no doubt led to the nickname 'poor man's breakfast'.

There are many varieties: the Fuerte (the Spanish name for hardiness and strength), which is pear-shaped with a thin green skin; the Rincon, which is pear-shaped with a smooth, shiny thin skin and large seed; the Hass, which may be either ovoid or pear-shaped with a purple to black skin and a pebbly texture; and others like the Hazzard, Wurtz and Sharwil.

These are all suitable for the home garden and can be planted at any time of the year. They like a sheltered position and should be planted in holes just big enough to take the root system. A nitrogen-rich artificial fertilizer is necessary to encourage growth, the Hass variety needing almost twice as much as other varieties.

AVOCADO SALAD

This unusual combination comes from the Middle East, the oiliness of the avocados contrasting with the acidity of the grapefruit. For a more substantial dish add some flaked crab flesh.

⅓ cup (2 ⅔ fl oz) olive oil
juice of 1 lime or lemon
1 tblspn honey
salt and pepper
2–3 ripe avocados
2–3 small grapefruit
1 small pomegranate or fresh coriander (cilantro)

Combine oil, lemon juice, honey, salt and pepper in a salad bowl, stirring well to combine. Cut the avocados in half, remove the stones and peel. Slice them and drop into the dressing. Peel the grapefruit, removing all the pith. With a small sharp knife, cut out the segments and add to the avocado. Toss well to combine and chill before serving. Strew the top with the seeds from the pomegranate. Alternatively, scatter freshly chopped coriander over the salad.

AVOCADO SALSA

This colorful, delicious dish goes well with barbecued or char-grilled (broiled) meats, poultry and sausages. It's also nice on its own with some crusty bread.

2 medium, ripe avocados
juice of 1 lime or lemon
2 medium, ripe tomatoes
1 Lebanese cucumber or ½ telegraph cucumber
1 green sweet pepper (capsicum)
½ red (Spanish) onion
olive oil
flaky salt and freshly ground pepper

Halve, peel and seed the avocados. Dice into large pieces and put into a salad bowl. Squeeze over the lime or lemon juice, tossing to coat well.

Chop the tomatoes and cucumber into large dice and add to the avocado. Halve and seed the sweet pepper and dice. Dice the onion. Add sweet pepper and onion to the other ingredients. Sprinkle the salsa with olive oil and season to taste with salt and pepper. Toss gently.

AVOCADO DIP

This is lovely with crudités. Put the dip into a bowl or hollowed out shell of a golden nugget pumpkin and place the raw vegetables around it.
It is also delicious with shrimps, either hot or cold.

2 firm ripe avocados, halved, seeded and peeled
1–2 chopped green chillies
juice of 1 lime or lemon
1 tomato, peeled and diced
1 scallion (shallot, spring onion), finely chopped
2 cloves garlic, crushed
salt and pepper to taste
freshly chopped coriander (cilantro), for garnishing

Mash all the ingredients together roughly but keep some texture in it. Garnish with the coriander. Spoon into serving bowl or cavity of golden nugget pumpkin.

JANICE'S NACHOS

Good with drinks. Choose a good quality corn chip, preferably low-salt and organically grown, available from health food stores.

2 large avocados
2 cloves garlic, crushed with salt
squeeze lemon juice
dash Tabasco or chilli sauce
6 scallions (shallots, spring onions), finely chopped
salt and freshly ground pepper
1 small tomato, seeded and diced
7 oz packet plain corn chips
¾ cup (3 oz) Cheddar cheese, grated

Peel avocados, cut in half and remove stones. Purée or mash the flesh, add garlic, lemon juice, Tabasco or chilli sauce, scallions and season to taste. Fold through the tomato.

Put the corn chips in an ovenproof serving dish, sprinkle with cheese, place in a moderately hot oven (375°F/190°C/Gas 5) for 5–7 minutes or until cheese has melted. Spoon the avocado mixture over the warm corn chips and serve immediately.

Variation: 1–2 tblspns freshly chopped coriander (cilantro) is a nice addition folded through the avocado.

Squashes
Cucurbita *species (or Cucurbitaceae family)*

. . . I'm holding one foot up, looking
for somewhere
amongst this vine. And find
the pumpkin —
segmented like a peeled mandarin
or leather
on the back seat of a thirties tourer.
I break the stem
and lift the heavy, warped pumpkin,
just when the vine's become

too dark.
In between pink and yellow,
its orange tone
can be added easily to the sunset
that's been going on.
I put the pumpkin beneath my arm.
Like a bad painting, this magnificent
sunset.

ROBERT GRAY, FROM 'PUMPKINS'

It would be hard to beat the pumpkin for cheekiness, though admittedly the chayote (choko) is a close rival. Even in the most barren of back lanes, I have espied a pumpkin tentatively putting out its tendrils through the grey slats of a wooden fence. Its very presence dispelled the surrounding gloom. My mother tells me a quaint story of a pumpkin vine growing on a tall fence — the grower of the vine had built steps alongside the fence to stand or rest the pumpkins on as they became swollen and enlarged.

In nineteenth century Australia, pumpkin was the chief vegetable, growing at times to the size of a large bucket. To this day, it is still highly regarded and used in all sorts of imaginative ways. The English mostly continue to scorn it whilst the French still don't understand it, though I recently came across some exciting recipes in a French women's magazine. Chef Alain Passard of Arpege in Paris proclaimed he loved pumpkin for the very reason many French people don't — its subtle taste and mild manner in the kitchen. 'Because pumpkin doesn't have a very powerful taste, you have to find ways to push it,' he said. In one recipe in the magazine, pumpkin was steeped in syrup flavored with vanilla, lemon and orange, then drizzled with balsamic vinegar. I also found a recipe for pumpkin cheese (similar to guava and quince cheeses), which was photographed in a slab, sprinkled with sugar.

Pumpkin has come a long way from the days when it was fed to pigs. In France, the best pumpkin is from Brittany where, it is said, the winds 'oxygenate' it, bringing it to a perfect state of ripeness. According to

Passard, what gives pumpkin its unique taste is a barely discernible petit point *of acidity — without this, it is bland and characterless. Whatever, pumpkins remain disliked in France, except in the south. There, as food writer Waverley Root points out, they are more receptive to rustic foods, a category into which pumpkins, and the squashes in general, are placed.*

In America, pumpkins and Halloween go hand in hand and pumpkin pie was first cooked there, subsequently becoming a Thanksgiving tradition.

In Australia, Queensland Blue variety is popular, prized for its flavor and color. Senator Flo Bjelke-Petersen, wife of former controversial Queensland premier, Joh Bjelke-Petersen, is well known throughout Australia for her use of this vegetable in scones. Pumpkin scones are a lovely golden color and very delicious served hot with thick cream and homemade jam. The color alone will entice you.

Pumpkins are members of the squash family, which consist of three major groups: marrows, gourds and squashes. They are all varieties of a single species which in general favor warm climates, dislike frost and whose fruits are watery and mild. The terms 'winter' and 'summer' squash can be confusing, but it is helpful to remember that summer squash refers to those that are picked when immature and usually don't need peeling, like zucchini (courgettes), baby squash (with scalloped edges), straight and crooked neck yellow squash, and pineapple or pattypan squash. Winter squash generally need to be peeled as the skin is thicker and the squash longer and more mature. These include the butternut, Hubbard, acorn, Turk's cap, Queensland Blue, banana and the sugar pumpkin, which is the one used to carve jack-o'-lanterns at Halloween. Winter squash grow slowly and are harvested late. Their tough skins protect the pulp inside which means they can be stored for three to four months before eating. They are also sweeter and tastier than summer squashes.

Sorting out the members of the squash family is, however, a mighty task and best left to the taxonomists. It is not so difficult tracing their origins. Fossilized squash seeds and rinds have been found in Andean sites dating back several millennia. Archeological finds in Mexican caves dated between 9000 BC and 4000 BC reveal squash seeds of cultivated varieties whilst the beans found with them were still from wild plants. Pre-Incan pottery vessels in the shapes of pumpkins and gourds show the many varieties known to the Indians.

As the Indians migrated north, they took squash seeds with them, planting them as they went. The Pueblo Indians of the south-western United States were cultivating squashes at least 2000 years ago and, along with the pumpkins, they became a staple in the diet of Indian tribes throughout the Americas. They were baked,

boiled, fried, made into cakes, soups, dried and ground into meal and even the seeds were eaten. These squash were originally thought to be melons by the Europeans. Friar Bernardino de Sahagún reported squash seeds and squash flowers on the table of Montezuma. Both are still eaten, indeed relished, today. The Spanish Conquistadores quickly spread pumpkins and squashes worldwide, causing some to think that they had in fact originated elsewhere.

Winter squash is used to some extent in Chinese cooking. They are only fairly recent arrivals in Asia and will probably never usurp the 'most-favored' status of the white-fleshed summer melons there.

You'll need plenty of space in your garden if you want to grow pumpkins and squashes. Their creeping vines spread rapidly, taking over anything in sight. Those not for eating purposes, like the gourds, look splendid in a wooden bowl or as ornaments for decoration. In American Indian ceremonies, different dried varieties are used as rattles.

Pumpkins and Winter Squash
Cucurbita species

'I regard pumpkins as the most domestic of vegetables, the classic sprawlers over the back fence, the traditional autumn harvest', writes organic gardener Jackie French. They are easy to grow, often germinating from seeds in the compost heap. 'A gardener has something to show very early with a pumpkin,' Jackie declares. Even children will find much delight and satisfaction from growing these vegetables.

Pumpkins and winter squash need to be sown in warm soil. If sown in cold soil, they'll rot. Feed heavily with animal manure, keeping well watered until the fruit is developed. As pumpkins and winter squash are very similar differences aren't important when it comes to growing. There are many varieties available, most taking up a lot of room. Several bush varieties are available like the Golden Nugget, which grows to the size of a grapefruit on a non-running bush, Butterbush and

Bush Table Queen. Miniature pumpkins like Jack Be Littles are also available. They are about the size of an apple and make very appealing decorations, keeping up to eight months.

Others, like the Jumbo Banana Pink, can grow up to 3 ft in length and weigh 40 lb. Its skin is pink and its flesh dry and sweet.

Mildew may be a problem and can be prevented by limited overhead watering. It's also a good idea to stake the fruits and provide supports for them as they are less likely to pick up moisture from the ground that way.

VEGETABLE COUSCOUS

A spectacular, delicious Moroccan dish, great for entertaining. Use the pre-cooked couscous which is available from health food stores and delicatessens. It only needs soaking in hot water for a few minutes.

SERVES 8

4 oz chickpeas (garbanzo beans), soaked overnight
1 cup (8 fl oz) chicken stock (broth)
2 onions, quartered
2 carrots, peeled and cut in halves lengthwise
salt and freshly ground pepper
½ lb pumpkin, peeled and cut in
1 ¼ in chunks
3 baby yellow squash, quartered
2 zucchini (courgettes), cut in halves lengthwise
4 baby eggplants (aubergines), cut in halves lengthwise
4 tomatoes, peeled and quartered
pinch saffron (optional)
2 ¼ cups (13 ⅓ oz) medium couscous
½ cup (3 oz) seedless or golden raisins (raisins or sultanas)
1 cup (8 fl oz) boiling water
6 tblspns freshly chopped parsley
2 tblspns each freshly chopped coriander (cilantro) and mint

HARISSA SAUCE

1 tspn each ground cumin and ground coriander (cilantro)
½ tspn chilli powder
2 ⅔ tblspns (1 ⅓ fl oz) tomato paste
2 ⅔ tblspns (1 ⅓ fl oz) hot chicken stock (broth)

Drain the chickpeas and cook in fresh, salted water until tender, about 1 hour. Drain well.

Put chicken stock in a medium–large pot and bring to a boil. Add onions and carrots, salt and pepper, cover with a lid and cook for 10 minutes. Add pumpkin, cover, cook 10 minutes, then add the squash, eggplants and zucchini. Don't worry if stock doesn't cover all the vegetables — they will be steamed if you keep on the lid. Cook for another 15–20 minutes or until all the vegetables are tender but not mushy. Add tomatoes and stir through to become warm. Stir chickpeas and saffron through the vegetables.

Meanwhile, prepare the couscous: put couscous and seedless or golden raisins in a bowl, pour over the boiling water. Leave to soak for 3–5 minutes. Keep warm, covered with foil in the oven. Fork through the couscous just before serving to ensure the grains are all separated, then shape into a mound with a well in the center. Ladle over a little of the broth, keep warm. Alternatively, pile the couscous into a pyramid shape and proceed as before.

Place cooked vegetables around couscous in a pretty pattern and scatter with the freshly chopped herbs.

For the sauce, mix all the ingredients together, stirring well. Put into a small bowl and pass around at the table.

CARBONADA CRIOLLA

A colorful, unusual dish from Argentina which is served in a pre-cooked pumpkin shell. It is really a casserole, made with either beef or veal. The recipe belongs to the cuisine of the Latin American Creoles, and it is interesting to note that the word 'creole' is derived from the Latin *creare* which means 'to create'. Some versions include zucchini (courgettes) and sweet potatoes, apples and grapes which are optional. The corn, potatoes and peaches are a must, though. Use what is in your garden at the time. Serve with hot fluffy rice.

SERVES 8

1 pumpkin, weighing about 10 lb, washed and scrubbed or 8
baby Golden Nuggets
olive oil
2 lb beef or veal, trimmed and cut into
rectangular pieces
3 cloves garlic, crushed
2 onions, chopped
2 small green sweet peppers (capsicums), sliced
1 large stalk celery, chopped
1 fresh medium chilli, chopped finely
3 ½ cups (1 ¾ pints) beef or veal stock (broth)
bouquet garni (parsley stalk, oregano branch and bay leaf)
3 tomatoes, peeled, seeded and chopped
salt and ground pepper
3 potatoes, peeled and cut in chunks
2 small sweet potatoes, peeled and cubed
2 corn cobs, husks removed and cut in 1 in rounds
3 small zucchini (courgettes), washed and sliced
2 apples, peeled and cut into wedges
4 peaches, peeled and halved
8 oz black grapes

Preheat oven to 350°F (180°C/Gas 4).

Choose a pumpkin with a stem on it. This will serve as a handle. Cut into the top of the pumpkin to make a lid about 6 in in diameter, lift out and, using a spoon, scrape out the seeds and stringy inner parts from the pumpkin. Put the lid (or lids if using the Golden Nuggets) back. Place pumpkin in a roasting dish and bake in oven for 1–1 ½ hours or until the pumpkin is tender but still firm. Remember that the shell has to hold the filling so don't let it get too soft. If using Golden Nuggets, cook for about 50 minutes. When done, scoop out some of the cooked flesh to allow more room inside, being careful not to damage the skins.

Meanwhile, heat a few tablespoons of oil in a large heavy frying pan. Add the meat and brown on all sides, turning frequently. Remove meat from pan. Add more oil to pan if necessary and then throw in the garlic, onions, sweet peppers, celery and chilli and cook until soft. Pour in stock and bring to a boil. Return meat to pan, add the bouquet garni, tomatoes, salt and pepper and cook gently for 45 minutes. If sauce seems too thin, thicken with a little cornstarch (cornflour).

Add potatoes, sweet potatoes and corn to the meat, cover and cook for 15–20 minutes. Add zucchini and apples, cook a further 10 minutes. Finally, add the peach halves and grapes and cook a further 5 minutes, still covered.

Spoon the meat, vegetables and fruit into the pumpkin shell, place pumpkin in baking dish and bake another 15–20 minutes in oven. Remove pumpkin from roasting dish and transfer to a large serving dish. Remove bouquet garni before serving.

GOLDEN NUGGET SOUP

Pumpkins make marvellous containers for all kinds of foods, including all sorts of vegetable mixtures. You can stir-fry the vegetables or curry them and pile them into pre-baked Golden Nugget shells. They add color and interest to any meal. This is a rich soup.

SERVES 4

4 Golden Nugget pumpkins
1 onion, finely chopped
¼ cup (2 oz) butter
⅔ cup (3 ½ oz) Swiss cheese, finely diced
pinch nutmeg
pinch cayenne pepper
12 leaves fresh sage
approx 2 cups (½ qt) cream

Preheat oven to 400°F (200°C/Gas 6).

Wash the outer skins of pumpkins and with a large sharp knife, cut off a lid. The bottoms may also need leveling if they don't sit straight. Scoop out all the seeds and stringy inner parts.

Cook the onion in the butter in a frying pan until soft and translucent. Put an equal amount of the onion mixture into the cavity of each pumpkin. Do the same with the cheese and sprinkle with the spices and sage. Fill cavities almost to the top with the cream. If you pour in too much cream, it will overflow when cooking.

Put on the lids.

Place on a baking dish and cook for approximately 1–1 ¼ hours. Test if the pumpkins are cooked by lifting off lids and inserting a sharp knife into the flesh. If soft, then your soup is ready.

WHISKEY SQUASH

Small butternut squash baked with a little whiskey are a nice addition to a winter meal. Cut the pumpkins in half lengthwise, scoop out their seeds, cover with foil and place on a tray. Bake in a moderate oven until soft and pour some whiskey into the cavities before serving.

PUMPKIN AND ORANGE SOUP

The flavor of this soup is enhanced if you use a sweet-fleshed pumpkin. Don't discard the seeds — toast them and use them to garnish the soup.

SERVES 6

2 tblspns (1 oz) butter
1 medium onion, chopped
1–2 tblspns freshly grated ginger
3 lb pumpkin, unpeeled
grated zest (rind) and juice of 1 large orange
6 cups (1 ½ qt) chicken stock (broth)
salt and pepper to taste

GARNISH
cream (optional)
nutmeg
toasted pumpkin seeds

Melt the butter in a large pan and sauté the onion and ginger until soft. Peel the pumpkin and cut into chunks, reserving the seeds. Put pumpkin into the pan along with the orange zest, juice and chicken stock.

Bring to a boil, cover and simmer gently until pumpkin is cooked, about 20 minutes. Purée in batches in a blender or food processor and return to pan. Season to taste. Bring back to boiling point. Ladle into bowls and serve immediately, garnished with a swirl of cream. Sprinkle over some fresh nutmeg and the toasted pumpkin seeds.

Note: To toast the seeds, rinse them well, removing excess pulp. Place on a baking sheet and toast in moderate oven (350°F/180°C/Gas 4), for 20 minutes. These are also good on their own with a little salt. The soup improves in flavor overnight.

AUSTRALIAN PUMPKIN FRUIT CAKE

Steam the pumpkin rather than boil it — this means less moisture when it is mashed. You'll need about 10 oz unpeeled pumpkin.

1 cup (8 fl oz) strong hot tea
½ cup (4 oz) butter
1 cup (8 oz) raw (demerara) sugar
1 tblspn golden syrup
2 cups (1 lb) mixed dried fruit
grated zest (rind) of 1 orange
6 ½ oz cold, mashed pumpkin
2 eggs, beaten
1 cup (4 oz) self-raising flour
1 cup (4 oz) all-purpose (plain) whole-wheat
(wholemeal) flour
1 tspn baking soda (bicarbonate of soda)
1 tspn cinnamon

Preheat oven to 350°F (180°C/Gas 4).

Put the tea, butter, sugar, golden syrup, dried fruit and zest into a medium saucepan. Stir together well with a wooden spoon and bring to a boil over medium heat, stirring. Simmer for 10 minutes, remove from heat and cool.

Stir in pumpkin and eggs, then gently stir in the sifted flours, soda and cinnamon.

Spoon mixture into a lined and greased 8 in or 9 in cake tin (either round or square) and bake in oven for 30 minutes, then reduce temperature to 250°F (120°C/Gas ½) for a further 1–1 ¼ hours. Test with a skewer to see if it is cooked. It may need the longer time if you have used the smaller tin.

PUMPKIN SCONES

If your family like scones, they will love these, so you might want to double the mixture. I like my scones to stand high (somehow it feels more generous), and always bake them close together, packed side by side, so that they rise well.

MAKES 12

1 tblspn (½ oz) butter, softened
½ cup (4 oz) sugar
grated zest (rind) of ½ orange
6 ½ oz steamed mashed pumpkin
1 egg, well beaten
3 cups (12 oz) self-raising flour
½ tspn nutmeg (optional)
½ tspn mixed spice (optional)
milk, if necessary

Preheat oven to 425°F (220°C/Gas 7).

Cream together the butter, sugar and zest. Stir in the pumpkin and egg. Sift together the dry ingredients and stir into the pumpkin mixture. Add a little milk if mixture is too dry.

Turn out onto a lightly floured bench or board and pat mixture out to 1–1 ½ in thickness. Cut them out with a glass or round cutter dipped in flour and place close together on a greased tray. Cook for about 20 minutes or until golden.

Try them with homemade Raspberry Jam (page 166) and thick cream. Heaven!

Marrows and Zucchini
Cucurbita pepo

These belong in the category of summer squash and come in a variety of shapes and sizes. Zucchini (courgettes) are marrows picked when very young and have become increasingly popular over the past decade or so. In France and Britain they are known as courgettes. Dark zucchini like the Blackjack and the Fordhook are most common, but Lebanese zucchini, with their pale green skins and sweeter flesh, are becoming increasingly popular. Zucchini need to be grown quickly and picked as young as possible. The flowers can also be eaten, either fried in batter or used in salads and frittatas. Left too long, zucchini will grow into marrows. They like a rich soil, and regular but not overhead watering, because they are prone to mildew. Zucchini are frost sensitive.

Other summer squashes can be harvested when large enough and the skin is hard. Large marrows are tasteless and need to be stuffed with a spicy filling to enhance their palatability. One recipe by the Roman author Apicius contains 13 ingredients for stuffed marrow, including pepper, cumin, coriander (cilantro), mint, honey, vinegar and oil, and the marrow was sprinkled with pepper again before being served.

Spaghetti squash is an amusing marrow for the home gardener, many claiming it as an excellent low kilojoule substitute for pasta. The vegetable is cooked whole for 30 minutes and the flesh scooped out in long strands and served with a spaghetti sauce. It can also be used chilled through salads. It's fun to explore the many varieties available. Ask at your local nursery or find out through local seed catalogues.

Every fourth Saturday in August, an International Zucchini Festival is held in New Hampshire in the United States. The idea behind the fair is to salute the prolific summer squash and so end the ennui that its plenitude sometimes causes. Ribbons are given to the longest and heaviest, and there is a zucchini peel-off, where adults race to scrape the skins off their squash. I like the sound of it. A good communal get-together, a lot of fun, and a way of celebrating nature's bounty.

ZUCCHINI AND TUNA PATTIES

Nice for lunch with wedges of lemon and a green salad.

MAKES 10 PATTIES

3 medium zucchini (courgettes), approx 10 oz, grated
1 cup (8 oz) cottage cheese
1 x 6 oz tin tuna, bones removed and broken
into pieces
¾ cup (4 oz) fine semolina
1–2 tblspns freshly chopped mint, parsley or basil
1 large onion, finely chopped
vegetable oil
salt and pepper
whole-wheat (wholemeal) flour

Put the grated zucchini, cottage cheese and tuna into a sieve over a bowl to drain. Let drain 15–20 minutes. Mix together in a bowl with the semolina and herbs. Sauté the onion in a little oil until soft, then add to the mixture. Combine well and season to taste. Form into patties and roll in whole-wheat flour.

Heat 2 tblspns oil in a frying pan and cook the patties on both sides until golden.

MEDLEY OF FRESH VEGETABLE RIBBONS

Choose fresh vegetables from the garden: zucchini (courgettes), asparagus, carrots, and baby turnips.

Using a vegetable peeler, scrape the carrots and turnips, then go deeper into the vegetables, peeling off long, thicker strips. Do this with the zucchini, but leave its skin on. Cut the asparagus into lengths to match the lengths of the other vegetables.

Set a pot of water on the stove, bring to a boil and add salt. Blanch each vegetable for 30 seconds, remove with a slotted spoon or tongs and refresh under cold water.

Mix all the vegetables together, toss with a vinaigrette and marinate in the refrigerator for a few hours. Before serving, make some squiggles of radish skin and lemon peel to add color on the top.

CONNIE'S ZUCCHINI SNACK

Unlike the Lebanese, the Italians prefer the dark green zucchini (courgette). These are more bitter than the white or pale green variety. This is a simple but delicious way of cooking zucchini. It is nutritious and infinitely variable.

Put 1–2 tblspns of olive oil in a frying pan (enough to cover the bottom), add a large diced white onion and sauté until clear. Then add 3–4 medium diced zucchini, some salt and cracked pepper and a tspn of sugar.

When the zucchini are cooked, beat 2–3 eggs with some salt and pepper and pour them into the pan, stirring all the time. The eggs are meant to be scrambled, not to lie flat as in a frittata. Remove from the pan and serve garnished with chopped parsley. This is good hot or cold or for dinner with crumbed chicken breast and an arugula salad. It is also very good as a snack on toast which has been spread with butter and soft avocado.

ZUCCHINI PASTA WITH PESTO

If you cut zucchini (courgettes) into long thin julienne strips, it's a wonderful substitute for pasta as in this dish.

SERVES 2–4

4 medium green, yellow or white zucchini (courgettes),
approx 11 oz
2 ⅔ tblspns (1 ⅓ fl oz) olive oil
2 tblspns (1 fl oz) pesto (see page 129)
1 tblspn (½ oz) pinenuts (pignolias)

Wash the zucchini, trim off the ends and cut into long fine strips. Put them into a colander, sprinkle with salt and let sweat for half an hour. Rinse off the salt and dry well.

In a large heavy frying pan, heat the oil, throw in the zucchini and toss for 2–3 minutes, coating well with oil. Don't let the zucchini brown. The idea is that they 'wilt'.

Add the pesto and toss well to combine. Remove from pan onto a warm dish. Brown the pinenuts quickly in the pan and strew over the top.

FRITTATA PRIMAVERA

Beppi's is one of Sydney's most successful Italian restaurants. Originally a cheap Italian eatery, Beppi's is now a sophisticated, friendly restaurant in the true Italian style. It was to Beppi's that my father took my sister Brett and me on the night our sister Skye was born. So thrilled was everyone by the news of her safe delivery that Beppi ordered a zabaglione to be whipped up and taken posthaste to my mother over at the hospital (it was her favorite dessert).

As well as the restaurant, Beppi now owns a farm at Orchard Hill in the foothills of the Blue Mountains. One midsummer's day, when the peaches were in full glorious bloom, I went with my other sister, Justin, for a picnic to the farm. Beppi had prepared this delicious frittata which we ate with rosette, the Italian bread rolls. He used duck eggs, which made it very rich, but you can use large hen eggs.

SERVES 6–8

¼ cup (2 fl oz) olive oil

2 tblspns (1 oz) butter

4 medium onions, chopped

1 large zucchini (courgette) or 2 small, approx
3 ½ oz, sliced

5–6 leaves spinach, washed and chopped

2 oz fresh shelled peas, cooked
(approx 4 oz unshelled)

6 eggs

2 tblspns (½ oz) Parmesan cheese, freshly grated

salt and pepper to taste

Sauté the onions in the oil and butter in a large heavy frying pan until transparent. Add remaining vegetables, cook for 5 minutes, stirring frequently.

Break the eggs into a bowl and whisk them together with the cheese, salt and pepper. Be careful with the salt as the cheese is already salty.

Turn the heat to medium–high, tip in the eggs and mix them together with the vegetables until well amalgamated. Turn the heat to medium–low and cook for 5–10 minutes. Put the pan under the broiler (grill) to finish the cooking. Remove when golden.

Transfer to a plate, let cool, then cut into wedges.

IJJEH

The Lebanese use every part of the zucchini — white zucchini, that is. Even the seeds. They stuff the zucchini to make Koussa, and with the seeds they make a sort of small egg omelet or crispy pancake. What they do is mix the chopped seeds (which have been removed with an apple corer) with a beaten egg and some freshly chopped mint, parsley and scallions (shallots, spring onions), salt and pepper. Then they fold in enough flour to make it hold together and drop it by the spoonful into hot oil in a frying pan. Drained on paper towels, it's good hot or cold and is nice with a homemade fresh tomato sauce as an entrée.

To make about 20 small ijjeh you'll need the seeds of 5 zucchini, 1 egg, 2 scallions (shallots, spring onions), 2 tblspns each of parsley and mint and ¼ cup (1 oz) flour.

SWEET ZUCCHINI BREAD

Nice spread with butter.

½ cup (4 oz) butter
½ cup (3 oz) brown sugar
2 eggs, beaten
5 oz zucchini (courgettes), approx 2 medium
zucchini, grated
¾ cup (4 oz) plain whole-wheat (wholemeal) flour

1 cup (4 oz) all-purpose (plain) white flour
1 tspn baking soda (bicarbonate of soda)
½ tspn baking powder
2 tspns cinnamon
pinch salt
¾ cup (6 fl oz) buttermilk
1 tspn vanilla extract (essence)

Preheat oven to 350°F (180°C/Gas 4). Grease a standard loaf tin — or line with non-stick baking paper.

In a mixing bowl, cream together the butter and sugar. Add eggs one at a time, then stir in the grated zucchini. Combine well.

Sift together the dry ingredients and fold into the zucchini mixture alternately with the buttermilk and vanilla. Pour into prepared pan and cook for 50 minutes or until a skewer inserted in the middle comes out clean. Turn out onto a rack and cool. Cut into slices and spread with butter.

Cucumbers
Cucumis sativus

Cucumbers grow in gardens when the moon is full, and their growth is as visible as that of sea-urchins.

ATHENAEUS, FROM *THE SOPHISTS AT DINNER*

Cucumbers belong to the Cucurbitaceae family to which the squashes, gourds and melons also belong. They are an ancient cultivated fruit thought to originate in central Asia. In 1970 the seeds of peas, beans, water chestnuts and cucumbers were found during an expedition at Spirit Cave near the Burmese border of Thailand, suggesting they were cultivated as long ago as 9750 BC. The Ancient Romans were fond of cucumbers. Pliny records they were 'a wonderful favorite' with the Emperor Tiberius who ate them every day. Apicius provided a number of recipes for them, one of which was to boil them with brains, honey, cumin, celery seed, oil and eggs.

The many varieties can be divided horticulturally into five types: green slicing (ordinary), Lebanese, pickling,

Italian and apple. Like their cousins, they are warm-seasoned plants which like a lot of mulching and water, are prone to mildew and dislike frost. Without ample water during the growing season, they tend to become bitter. If you stake them, they will mature more quickly and will be less likely to get mildew.

Pinching out the growing tips once they are established will produce more cucumbers. Bush varieties are ideal for home gardens. Trailing varieties do well on a trellis.

CUCUMBER FINGERS

SERVES 6

India is synonymous with heat and dust. It was in India one hot summer that my mother came across this way of serving cucumbers. They became a big hit in our household.

Choose 3 small–medium cucumbers. Wash them well. Halve and quarter them lengthwise so that they resemble fingers. You might need to slice some into eighths.

Sprinkle the cucumbers with paprika and serve on a platter garnished with coriander.

CUCUMBER GRAVLAX

Cucumber, cut into julienne strips or sliced thinly lengthways, is delicious mixed through strips or pieces of gravlax salmon or ocean trout. Wash well and leave the skin on — it adds to the color and texture. You'll need to salt the cucumber after slicing to rid it of excess water. Put into a colander and let drain for 1 hour or so, then wash off the salt. Put onto a white platter with the gravlax and toss together with freshly chopped dill and a light dressing.

CUCUMBER AND TOMATO SALAD

As a delicious side salad for four to six people, peel, seed and dice 4 Lebanese cucumbers. Chop 4 ripe tomatoes and combine in a salad bowl with the cucumbers. Chop up some Italian (flat leaf) parsley, basil and scallions (shallots, spring onions) and scatter over the top. Make a dressing with olive oil and lemon juice and toss together well. You could add some chilli powder or paprika if liked.

CUTTLEFISH AND CUCUMBER SALAD

SERVES 4 (WITH OTHER DISHES)

One day when I went to the markets to buy calamari it was far more expensive than the cuttlefish on sale alongside. A number of Chinese women were hovering around, so I knew it must be fresh and good. But little did I realise what was involved in cleaning them — it wasn't just the kitchen sink that was splattered with black ink! Once cleaned, the final quantity of flesh is about half of the purchased weight.

You can use calamari, if you don't want to go to so much trouble. Honeycomb it and cut into 1 in cubes. It is a refreshing and delicious dish for a summer's day.

2 lb cuttlefish, uncleaned
1 telegraph cucumber, peeled and cut in half lengthwise
handful of fresh coriander (cilantro) and mint
½ green sweet pepper (capsicum), cubed

VINAIGRETTE
olive oil
lemon juice
salt
cumin

Clean the cuttlefish, turn soft side up and, using a sharp knife, cut lengthwise through the body. Open the body, carefully pulling out the insides (watch that ink sac). Remove cuttlebone. Pull skin off firmly, and cut tentacles below eyes, removing the beak. Cut flaps into halves and honeycomb them.

Put flaps and tentacles into a saucepan with water to cover. Add a tblspn of white vinegar, some celery leaves, half a carrot and a bay leaf. Bring to a boil, remove scum and turn off heat immediately. Let the cuttlefish sit in the water until cool.

Strain when cool, and discard the vegetables. Put the cuttlefish into a salad bowl.

Remove the seeds from the cucumber and cut into half-moon slices about ⅛ in thick. Add them to the cuttlefish. Chop up the coriander and mint and add to the bowl along with the sweet pepper. Toss with the vinaigrette: make this to taste with olive oil and lemon juice, salt and about ¼ tspn cumin powder (or to taste). Chill for an hour before serving.

CUCUMBER AND DILL SALAD

Simple and refreshing.

SERVES 6

2 medium cucumbers
salt
juice of 1 lemon
½ cup (4 fl oz) olive oil
pepper
bunch of dill (or chives), finely chopped

Peel the cucumber and slice paper thin in the food processor. Sprinkle liberally with salt and leave to stand in a colander for an hour. Wash and drain well.

Beat together the remaining ingredients and toss together with the cucumber.

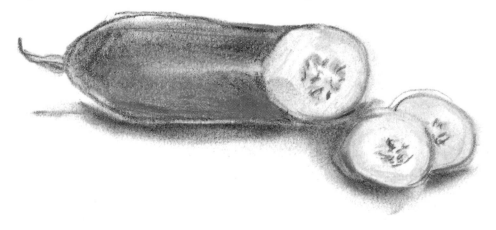

Bulbs

Allium *species*

Wel loved he garleek, oynons, and eek lekes,
And for to drinken strong wyn, reed as blood.

CHAUCER, *THE CANTERBURY TALES*

Where would the cook be without onions? Or without the other members of this old and noble family, which includes the rather grand leek, the scallions (shallots, spring onions), chives and garlic? Yet they rarely receive the attention they deserve. Perhaps their very versatility and widespread influence means we just take them for granted. Or perhaps it's their strong odor?

It seems to be for that reason they were deemed taboo by certain religious orders in China, India and Tibet. In China, these members of the genus Allium *were known as the 'five strong-odored foods' (wu hun), and included garlic, onion and scallions (shallots, spring onions). The avowed reason for such a taboo was the promotion of physiological harmony, though they were used in T'ang cookery (618–907 AD) and highly recommended for their warming, tonic properties.*

Dubbed 'the king of vegetables', onions have enjoyed a very long reign, having been regarded as a food and flavoring longer than almost any other vegetable. Along with roots like turnips and radishes, and members of the cabbage family, onions are amongst the oldest vegetables of the world. Their antecedents cannot be dated by historians, having been cultivated by prehistoric humans when they were still in the collecting stage — which preceded the pastoral and agricultural stages — when roots and bulbs were easy to gather.

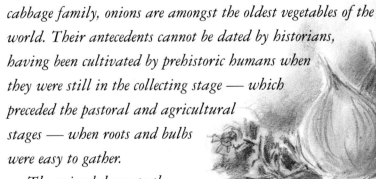

The onion belongs to the Alliaceae family and originated somewhere in central Asia, probably Afghanistan. A Turkish fable attributes its creation to the devil, dating it from the time he was thrown out of heaven and landed on earth. According to the

fable, garlic sprouted where he put his left foot, and onions where he placed the right. More reliable authorities have speculated it may have come from North America, because both the tree onion and the Welsh onion grow wild there.

Wherever it first grew, it was one of the best known vegetables in Mesopotamia, though eaten mainly by the poor who put it on bread. With its myriad layered skins, it was regarded by the ancients as a symbol of eternity, a sacred object to be invoked when swearing an oath. In the Old Testament, Israelites longed for onions while in the wilderness. The Egyptians were great onion and garlic eaters. Onions were a staple part of their diet and were depicted in much of their art and temple decorations, though it is unlikely that they were also onion worshippers. Folklore and medieval herbals prescribe it as a cure for many ills, including exorcising toothaches and even vampires.

Like onions, garlic also belongs to the Alliaceae family and probably originated in central Asia. It is also found wild in the Americas and was apparently eaten as a vegetable by pre-Columbian Indians. The seeds of the garlic plant are infertile and the different varieties are propagated by cloves. Recently, however, botanists in Soviet Central Asia have discovered garlic samples with fertile pollen. Ancient Egyptian records of garlic dated from 3200 BC exist as do ancient Chinese records. The ancient Greeks considered garlic one of their most important vegetables and by Roman times, many distinct cultivars existed as cited by Pliny the Elder.

Garlic has had its detractors, not the least of which were the British up until the middle of last century. There, it was thought of more as a medicine than a food. Medieval medicine thought it cured blood pressure, rheumatism, snakebite, freckles, lung problems, toothache and even baldness (by rubbing its juice on the bald spot). Tibetan Buddists say it blocks the channels of energy in the body. Some French chefs treat it with caution, those espousing 'haute cuisine' barely touching it. In that country, it is most important in the cooking south of the Loire. In Italy too, its use is confined mostly to the south.

Leeks, however, are popular in the British Isles. They are the national emblem of Wales and St Patrick is believed to have transformed reeds into leeks, thereby curing a sick woman. Wild leeks grow around these regions, especially on the islands off Wales. In the north-east of England, annual leek shows are held every September, a Freudian competition amongst local miners and shipbuilders to see who can grow the biggest ones. They also grow around the Mediterranean, and it is probably from the eastern Mediterranean that the cultivated types originate — they were being cultivated in Egypt when its history began, were admired by the Romans and were a favorite vegetable during the Middle Ages.

Despite its lowly associations as the 'poor man's asparagus' (because its flavor is less fine and more robust than that of asparagus), leeks fresh from the ground have a wonderful flavor. In China, the fragrant leek (Allium odorum) is eaten in many forms. No satisfactory English name for it exists, but they are highly esteemed both for eating and medicinal purposes. The Chinese are also fond of the common onion, garlic, the famous ts'ung or green onion (A. fistulosum) — which is the 'Welsh' or 'bunching' onion of the West — and A. tuberosum, Chinese or garlic chives. These are a very popular flavoring herb, one of the few commonly used.

The Chinese phrase 'chive-cutting mentality' derives from these chives: a reference to the state of mind of those who feared, during the early Communist days, that any wealth or property they accrued would be redistributed or taken away from them, just as any chive stalk that sticks up is picked for cutting.

Onions and Shallots
Allium cepa *and* A. ascalonicum

An onion under the pillow tonight —
will bring a vision of one's wife to be.

I came across this amusing yet thought-provoking observation by French writer Raymond Dumay: 'Garlic is peasant, rustic; the onion is urban. The onion brings to the kitchens of the cities a little of the countryside . . . the onion offers always, and especially in winter, a little of the springtime of the soil, preserved in its bulb.'

If you plant different varieties of this versatile bulb, you can have onions all year round. Few people grow enough. Cultivated onions are sensitive to day-length for the formation of flowers, so it is important to select varieties for specific regions, depending on the length of the day. Most development should be already made by the longest day of the year. Early varieties are short-day onions, mid-season varieties are medium-day onions and late varieties are long-day onions. If you plant them out of season or sequence, they may bolt or run to seed.

The phrase 'to know one's onions' indicates the huge variety of this species. Some are propagated by seed, others without seed. The latter produce clusters of side bulbs which grow beneath soil level. These include shallots or eschalots (Allium ascalonicum), recognizable by their small, brown-skinned bulbs and much favored by the French; the potato onion (A. cepa aggregatum), similar to shallots; and the tree or Egyptian onion (A. cepa proliferum).

Those propagated by seed include spring onions or scallions (A. cepa, incorrectly labeled 'shallots' in Australia); the delicious sweet red or Spanish onions, the light brown Creamgold or Pukekohe pickling onions, and many others. Make sure you check whether they are early, mid-season or late varieties. Keeping quality also depends on variety, later varieties keeping better than others.

Spring onions and bunching onions should be grown quickly — hill the soil around them to blanch the stems. The others take a long time to grow, usually from 24–34 weeks depending on the maturity of the varieties. Weeds can be a problem for this reason. A good way to eliminate these is to cover the ground with black plastic for a month before planting. The most important thing is to prepare the beds properly. With most other vegetables you can get away with minimal preparation but when it comes to onions, you can't. If you think you can catch up by feeding them as they grow, this will only encourage large tops and small bulbs. Too much nitrogen makes them susceptible to neck rot. This disease causes the greatest losses in onion crops and enters the onion through a wound, so never use forks or spades when digging around them, just mulch them and pull out the weeds.

Bulbs are ready when the tops start to die off and fall over. Let them dry on the ground, protected from sunburn, for a week or so before storing, then store in wire baskets or open mesh bags in a cool dark, ventilated spot. You can also plait the tops and hang them up to dry.

DEEP DISH ONION TART

Very good for lunch or Sunday supper, this goes well with a glass of red wine, a green salad and crusty French bread.

SERVES 6–8

2 cups (8 oz) all-purpose (plain) flour
pinch salt
½ cup (4 oz) butter, frozen and cut into pieces
2 eggs
1 ⅓ tblspns (⅔ fl oz) water, if necessary

FILLING
¼ cup (2 oz) butter
3 lb onions, peeled and finely sliced
3 eggs, beaten
¾ cup (3 oz) Gruyère cheese, grated
nutmeg
1 ⅓ tblspns (⅔ fl oz) dry sherry
freshly ground pepper
cream (optional)

Place flour, salt and butter in food processor and process until mixture resembles breadcrumbs. Add the eggs and continue to process until mixture forms a ball. Add a little water to bind, if needed. Wrap the dough in greaseproof paper and refrigerate for 1 hour. Roll out to line a spring-form cake tin or deep flan dish about 9–9 ½ in in diameter, reserving remainder for further use. Crimp edges and prick with a fork. Return to refrigerator to relax for a further 15–20 minutes. Heat oven to moderate (350°F/180°C/Gas 4). Line pie shell with aluminum foil and put in a layer of beans or rice. Cook for 10 minutes, remove foil and beans. Cook a further 5 minutes until golden. Remove and cool.

FILLING
Melt the butter in a deep pan and cook the onions gently, covered, until they are golden and transparent. This will take 30–45 minutes.

When the onions are cooked, let them cool a little and then stir in the eggs, cheese, nutmeg and dry sherry. Grind in some pepper and add a little cream if you like.

Fill the prepared pastry case with this mixture and bake on a rack in a moderate oven (350°F/180°C/Gas 4) for about 1 hour or until filling is set and browning on top.

Variation: This pie is good topped with strips of anchovies, stoned black olives and extra grated Gruyère cheese. Lay the anchovies and olives out in a decorative fashion.

GREEN COUSCOUS

SERVES 4–6

This is a stunning and simple dish. You can eat it hot,
at room temperature or cold. A good accompaniment to
the Marinated Melon Balls (page 211). Have all the
vegetables chopped and ready because you need to work
quickly once the oil is hot.

1 cup (6 ½ oz) pre-cooked couscous
2 tblspns (1 oz) seedless or golden raisins (raisins or sultanas)
1 cup (8 fl oz) boiling water
½ cup (4 fl oz) oil
⅔ cup (2 ½ oz) pinenuts (pignolias)
2 cloves garlic, crushed
1 tspn ground cumin
1 tspn ground coriander (cilantro)
1 bunch scallions (shallots, spring onions), sliced on the
diagonal
2 large zucchini (courgettes), sliced
1 green sweet pepper (capsicum), cut into 4 in cubes
1 red chilli, finely chopped
sea salt
freshly ground black pepper

Put the couscous and seedless raisins in a bowl and pour
over the boiling water. Leave to soak for a few minutes
until all the water is absorbed.

Heat the oil in a wok or large frying pan. When it is
hot, add the pinenuts. Stir constantly until golden, then
add the garlic and spices. Keep stirring for another 30
seconds (don't let them burn), then throw in the scallions.
Stir well, then add the zucchini, sweet pepper and chilli.
Cook, stirring constantly, for 1–2
minutes. Stir in the couscous
mixture, tossing to fluff up the
grains. Stir to combine for
another 2–3 minutes.
Season to taste.
Serve
immediately.

MEGADARRA

This makes a wonderful vegetarian meal. Food writer
Claudia Roden describes it as a modern version of a
medieval dish called 'mujadarra'. It is good served with
a finely sliced cabbage salad dressed with plain
yogurt, lemon juice and crushed garlic.
You can use long-grain rice, but a mixture of rices
makes for a more complex and interesting dish.

SERVES 8–10

1 cup (6 ½ oz) brown lentils, uncooked
1 cup (6 oz) basmati rice or Thai jasmine rice, uncooked
1 cup (6 oz) wild rice or Thai black rice, uncooked
4–5 large red (Spanish) or brown onions, finely sliced
6 cloves garlic, slivered
1 cup (8 fl oz) olive oil
6 tblspns (3 oz) butter
2 tspns each cinnamon, hot paprika, cumin powder and
ground coriander (cilantro)

Rinse lentils and cook in 3 cups (24 fl oz) water for
25–30 minutes, or until soft.

Rinse the basmati rice. Put it into a saucepan, add
1 ½ cups (12 fl oz) water and a pinch of salt. Bring to a
boil and cover. Turn down heat to very low (use a
simmer pad). Cook 10 minutes. Remove from heat, let
stand for 5 minutes, then remove lid. (The jasmine rice
can be cooked the same way, using 1 ¼ cups (10 fl oz)
water.)

Wash the wild rice. Cook according to directions on
packet.

In a large, heavy frying pan, cook the onions and
garlic in the oil, butter and spices for 1 hour or until the
onions have collapsed and caramelised. Toss through the
cooked grains and serve hot.

Note: If using black rice, you will need to first soak it a few
hours or overnight in water to cover. Next day, bring 5 cups
(1 ¼ qt) water to a boil, add the drained rice and cook,
uncooked, for 20–25 minutes. Drain well before adding to the
Megadarra.

WHOLE SNAPPER WITH ONION RINGS AND PINENUT SAUCE

Cooked in this classic manner, a baked fish is delicious served with just a tossed salad and some baby potatoes, scattered with chives.

For something different, try it with this delicious Lebanese-style sauce. The onions are placed over the top of the fish like a loosely crocheted brown wrap. You can use walnuts instead of pinenuts (pignolias), but make sure they are very fresh.

SERVES 6–8

1 large snapper, approx 6–8 lb, cleaned and scaled
1 clove garlic, crushed
1 ⅓ tblspns (⅔ fl oz) lemon juice
freshly ground pepper
3–4 fresh parsley and coriander (cilantro) stalks
1–2 scallions (shallots, spring onions), sliced
knob of butter
½ cup (4 fl oz) white wine or vermouth

THE TOPPING
4 lb brown onions, finely sliced
cooking oil
1 small breadstick
2 cups (8 oz) pinenuts (pignolias)
2 cloves garlic, crushed
juice of 1–2 lemons

Preheat the oven to 350°F (180°C/Gas 4).

Wash snapper and pat dry with paper towels. Make some diagonal slashes in the skin to allow it to cook more evenly. Rub the flesh with a mixture made from the garlic, lemon juice and pepper.

Place the herbs, scallions, butter and some more ground pepper into the cavity. Wrap in well-oiled or buttered foil, adding wine or vermouth before making final folds. Seal well to prevent juices leaking.

Put the fish on a baking tray in the oven and test for doneness after 20–30 minutes. Do this by putting a sharp knife into the thickest part of the shoulder and when done, you will see that the flesh has begun to flake. If it's a big fish, it may take 45–60 minutes.

While the fish is cooking, fry the onion rings in batches in a wide frying pan filled with about ¾ in heated cooking oil, until they brown. Lift out and drain on paper towels. Keep warm.

For the sauce, cut 3–4 thick slices off the breadstick, soak them in water and then squeeze dry. Grind the pinenuts finely in the food processor. Add bread and garlic. Add juice of 1 lemon, or more to taste. Continue processing, adding some of the liquid the fish was cooked in, until you have a smooth creamy paste. Taste for seasoning.

To serve, remove fish from its parcel and place on a large platter. Smother with pinenut sauce and arrange onion slices thickly all over the fish.

Garnish with finely chopped parsley or coriander (cilantro).

JENNY'S PUFF PASTRY PIZZAS WITH ONION AND PROSCIUTTO

leftover puff pastry scraps
2 medium onions
1 ½ tblspns (⅔ oz) butter
6 thin slices prosciutto
½ cup (2 oz) freshly grated Parmesan cheese
2 tblspns finely chopped (or snipped) chives
freshly ground black pepper

Preheat oven to 375°F (190°C/Gas 5).

Roll out the puff pastry thinly on a floured surface. Cut out the circles, whatever size you like (listed ingredients make one large pizza). Drape rolled pastry onto a baking tray and cut out the circle, using a saucer or dinner plate (depending on size) to trace around. Prick all over with a fork and chill for 20 minutes.

Slice the onions finely and fry in butter until soft and golden. Drain very well. Trim any fat from prosciutto and slice into strips.

Cover pastry circle/circles with the cooked onion. Sprinkle prosciutto all over, then the cheese, chives and a good grinding of pepper. Bake until crisp and golden, 15–20 minutes.

Leeks
Allium porrum

Because they're easy to grow, leeks are a good introduction to other members of the onion family. You're hardly ever likely to fail with them and for cooks who garden, leeks are a vegetable which deserves greater popularity. Disaster with main crop onions is far more likely and can put you off growing them for years.

Leeks are not as greedy as onions, though no harm is done by giving them the same treatment. Onions need to be harvested and stored; leeks can be left in the garden from one spring to the next. They are also more adaptable to climate variations than onions. In addition, they can be picked whenever you want them and are especially good when young and sweet. They do, however, require feeding, and the more feeding, the better the leek. They don't need to be put into prepared beds like onions and will grow anywhere. They do well in a compost trench (which needs to be kept filled as they grow, and to be kept moist) or well-manured ground. If you hill them up with compost, they will do very well. They can be dug up with a fork and are very hardy.

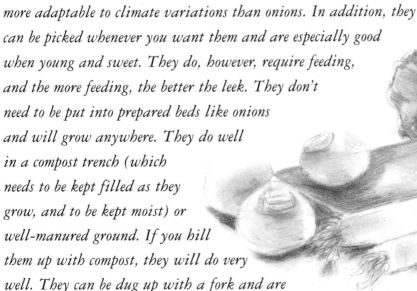

HERB POLENTA

Delicious served for lunch with a green salad.

SERVES 6

¾ cup (5 oz) cornmeal (polenta)

¼ cup (1 oz) all-purpose (plain) flour

1 tspn baking powder

½ tspn baking soda (bicarbonate of soda)

¾ cup (2 oz) grated sharp Cheddar cheese

¼ cup (1 oz) Parmesan cheese, grated

¾ cup (6 oz) butter

2 leeks or 1 large onion, chopped

2 cloves garlic, crushed

6 ½ oz button mushrooms, sliced

1 small bunch parsley, chopped

½ bunch basil, chopped

½ bunch chives, snipped

1 small red chilli, chopped

1 red sweet pepper (capsicum), chopped and seeded

1 egg, lightly beaten

1 cup (8 fl oz) buttermilk mixed with ½ cup (4 fl oz)
water

Preheat oven to 400°F (200°C/Gas 6).

Combine dry ingredients with cheese in a bowl. In a frying pan, melt half the butter and sauté leeks or onion until translucent. Add mushrooms and cook until softened. Add chopped herbs, cook 1 minute, set aside.

Process chilli, sweet pepper, egg and buttermilk in a blender until fairly smooth. Add to dry ingredients with vegetables.

Melt remaining butter in a heavy 9 in non-stick ovenproof frying pan or flameproof dish. Pour half into polenta mixture and mix well. Heat remaining butter until foaming, spoon polenta mixture into pan and cook over low heat until mixture bubbles. Place in oven and bake for 35–45 minutes or until a skewer inserted in the middle comes out clean. Rest in pan for 2 minutes, then turn out on a serving plate.

STEAMED LEEKS

Baby leeks are delicious steamed. I love to cook them with baby turnips, adding the turnip tops towards the end so that they don't overcook. I do mine in a bamboo steamer over a wok of gently simmering water. Make sure they are well washed and trim the green ends.

Serve hot with butter and sprinkled with parsley. Also nice dressed with a vinaigrette, crushed black pepper and shavings of Parmesan cheese.

SMOKED SALMON WITH LEEK VINAIGRETTE

Julienne the white part of leeks: blanch in rapidly boiling salted water for 1–2 seconds, drain well. Toss through a French dressing mixed with horseradish cream. Good served with smoked salmon, or any smoked fish.

JUMBO SHRIMP PARCELS

Leeks and jumbo shrimps team very well. A delicious way of serving them is to wrap the blanched white part of a halved leek around a raw, de-veined jumbo shrimp, and cook in sizzling butter, 1 minute on each side. Serve immediately, seasoned with freshly ground black pepper and some flaky sea salt.

Note: Slice the leeks in half lengthwise and separate out the white leaves, one from the other. Remove any tough leaves. Wrap around the jumbo shrimps as if putting on a bandage.

COCK-A-LEEKIE

A traditional Scottish soup which not only tastes good, but looks good too: creamy chicken flesh is offset by the deep black of the prunes, contrasting with the green and white of the leeks. Originally it was eaten only by servants and the lower class and was made with a capon.

SERVES 6–8

1 lb prunes
1 chicken, weighing approx 3 lb
1 bay leaf
1 stalk parsley
3 lb leeks
salt and pepper
freshly chopped parsley

Soak the prunes in water for 6 hours or overnight. Joint the chicken and place into a pot. Cover with water, add bay leaf and parsley stalk. Bring slowly to a boil, skimming off any scum that comes to the top.

Meanwhile, clean, and wash the leeks, being careful to wash out all of the grit. Slice half of the leeks and set aside. Leave the remaining half whole and tie into a bundle. Add bundle to the pot after skimming. Simmer until the chicken is almost cooked. Season to taste.

Add pitted prunes, and sliced leeks. Simmer another 15 minutes. Remove chicken and cut the flesh into small pieces, return to pot. Discard the whole leeks and serve soup hot with chopped parsley sprinkled over the top.

Note: You can add 2 lb shank of beef for more flavor if you like. Put it on to cook before the chicken as it will need more time.

BRAISED LEEKS

SERVES 6–8

24 baby (or 12 medium) leeks, cleaned and washed
2 x 14 oz tins peeled tomatoes, drained
1 cup (8 fl oz) red wine
1 cup (8 fl oz) olive oil
2–3 tblspns (½–1 oz) sugar (optional)
6–8 slices prosciutto
¾ cup (3 oz) Parmesan cheese

Preheat oven to 350°F (180°C/Gas 4).

Trim the green leaves of the leeks to about ¼ of their length. Slit the green part down the middle and soak in a tub of cold water — this should remove all of the dirt. Put the leeks into a large earthenware dish. Purée the tomatoes along with the wine, oil and sugar (add the sugar, to taste, if the leeks are bitter, using your judgment as to how much to add). Pour this mixture over the leeks and cover with foil. Bake in oven for 1 hour (or 1 ½ hours if using medium-sized leeks) until the leeks are really tender.

Meanwhile, prepare the garnish by laying the prosciutto on a foil-covered baking dish and crisping it under the broiler (grill). Remove and crumble into small pieces. With a sharp knife, shave the Parmesan cheese into longish, slender pieces. Scatter prosciutto and cheese over the leeks just before serving.

Garlic
Allium sativum

Most of us have never seen or tasted fresh garlic, and yet it can easily be grown from a clove. Divide heads into individual cloves, plant about 1 in deep and about 4 in apart. Once you've seen and tasted the succulent, fresh heads, you'll wonder why more people don't grow it.

Like all bulbs and root crops, garlic likes a rich soil, well drained, with all organic matter well-decomposed. It will grow in a poor soil, but the cloves will be smaller (though pungent); the better the soil, the larger and more succulent the bulbs. It prefers a cool, mild climate. Some claim that if you plant it on the shortest day of the year it will be ready for harvesting on the longest. Ample water is required for the first four to five months of development, as well as full sun. Dry and store as for onions.

The tops can be eaten too and are good in salads. It's a pity, in fact, to discard the tops of most vegetables (this is where the Chinese are wiser than we in the West). Other edible tops include beetroot, fennel and turnip. The latter is particularly good steamed. For the cook, garlic has a strange 'Jekyll and Hyde' character. If you crush one or two and add them to a salad, their pungency is unmistakable; but if you cook them slowly with a casseroled chicken or duckling (left whole, peeled but not pierced), their flavor will be transformed into a delicate sweetness. (A number of rustic French recipes are famous for including 30–40 cloves in the one dish.) They are also good cooked whole alongside a leg of lamb or piece of roast beef.

PARSI-STYLE DRUMSTICKS

These are marinated overnight in a mixture of yogurt and spices, baked in a moderate oven and served hot or cold.

SERVES 4–6

12 chicken drumsticks
1 in piece fresh ginger
4–6 cloves garlic
1 tspn cumin seeds
½ cup (3 ¼ oz) plain yogurt
1 onion, finely chopped
juice of 1 lemon
½ tspn each cinnamon, chilli powder, salt, ground pepper and ground cardamom
melted butter or ghee for basting

Slash the drumsticks with a sharp knife to allow the marinade mixture to penetrate. Peel the ginger and garlic and chop finely.

Put cumin seeds in a frying pan and dry-fry them until they smell fragrant. Combine with ginger and garlic and pound to a paste, or blend together in a blender with a little of the yogurt. Put into an earthenware dish along with the yogurt, onion, lemon juice and spices and mix together well. Rub this mixture over the drumsticks and allow to marinate a few hours or overnight.

Cook in a moderate oven (350°F/180°C/Gas 4) in a greased baking tray for 40–45 minutes or until cooked, basting occasionally with the melted butter.

TANDOORI CHICKEN

A tasty way of preparing chicken and a dish which works well either hot or cold.

SERVES 4–8

2 small chickens, approx 1 ½ lb
2 cups (13 oz) plain yogurt
6 cloves garlic, crushed
1 ½ tblspns fresh ginger, grated
¾ cup (6 fl oz) lemon juice
2 tblspns ground coriander (cilantro)
1 tblspn ground cumin
1 tspn paprika
1 tspn powdered garam masala
½ tspn chilli powder
salt

Mix all ingredients together, rub chickens inside and out with the mixture, scoring skin heavily to allow it to penetrate. Place chicken in a dish and pour over the remaining marinade. Put in refrigerator and marinate for 24 hours, turning the chickens occasionally. Cook on a rack in a hot oven (400°F/200°C/Gas 6) for 45–60 minutes, basting occasionally with marinade. Serve chicken cut into halves or quarters with wedges of lemon or lime.

Root Vegetables

... He said, All that's important
is the ordinary things.
Making the fire
to boil the bathwater, pounding rice, pulling weeds
and knocking dirt out of their roots,
or pouring tea — those blown scarves,
a moment, more beautiful than the drapery
in paintings by a master.

ROBERT GRAY FROM 'TO THE MASTER, DŌGEN ZENJI (1200–1253 AD)'

Many years ago, when I was a child, the very first vegetable I ever grew was a radish. Such a delight it was to see the leafy green tops and to pull the little red root out of the soil. It was my introduction to the pleasures of growing vegetables, and in retrospect, a wise choice: radishes are just about indestructible and can be grown anywhere in almost any type of soil and any type of climate. They are also one of the quickest growing vegetables.

The name 'radish' comes from the Latin radix, *meaning 'a root'. There are a number of members of this group, the most popular today being the carrot. Then there's the turnip, the beet, horseradish, celeriac, parsnip, swede, salsify, burdock, arrowhead and Chinese artichoke. Edible roots were one of the very first foods eaten by humans. Some object that they're too sweet, though the radish escapes being condemned for this due to its sharp, peppery flavor.*

In ancient Greece, certain roots were used as votive offerings to Apollo at Delphi — turnips were presented on lead dishes, beet on silver ones and radishes on gold. Perhaps this said something about the esteem in which each was held. No carrots, though. These originated in

Afghanistan and, though mentioned by Greek writers as early as 500 BC, were not highly thought of. The Romans preferred the turnip.

These days, the carrot, along with the onion, is a foundation vegetable in Western cooking. It is used as a base for stocks, soups, stews, and casseroles and is also popular in cakes and grated raw through salads. Its high sugar content was recognised early and, during the Victorian period in particular, many recipes were devised using carrots in puddings, pies, flans and charlottes. Carrot cake is one of the few survivors of this once extensive cuisine. The only vegetable with a higher sugar content is beet.

Interestingly, orange-colored carrots are an eighteenth century invention. Once the most popular types were purple or violet (these are still widely grown in Asia Minor, India and South-East Asia), and the red variety was the most preferred up until the mid-eighteenth century. White or yellow ones are still occasionally seen in Europe, though most are fed to animals. Carrots weren't always conically shaped either — in Roman and medieval times, they were probably as branched as the wild types. Present-day conical-shaped carrots most likely originated during the tenth or eleventh centuries in Asia Minor.

Of the other roots, my favorite is beet. As a child I loathed it because I'd only ever tasted the canned, sliced version. But both the root and the leaves seem to have regained popularity as fresh vegetables over the past few years. I love it grated and added to a salad sandwich; or cooked and chopped, then tossed with fresh mint or coriander (cilantro), a little olive oil and chopped orange. Along with its close relatives, the chards and spinach beets, beet developed from Beta maritima, *a European seashore plant. Early Romans ate only the leaves and the root wasn't developed for food until the early Christian era.*

Root crops thrive in soils rich in humus and plant food. Organic gardeners find they often enjoy some root crops which they formerly disliked because they have a better color, taste and are of a superior quality. They need to be well watered early in their growth and the watering needs to be a good, soaking one.

Radishes
Raphanus sativus

Historically, the radish was one of the first recorded cultivated vegetables. In fact it's so old that even its wild ancestor has disappeared. The small round types, so popular today, were probably developed in eighteenth century France. They come in shades of red, pink, rose and white. Black-skinned sorts are shown in Egyptian tomb paintings and are described by Herodotus who saw an inscription there honoring the radish, leek and onion as the foods which supplied strength to the workers building the pyramids. Black winter radishes are still available

today and grow to the size of a small turnip. They are used mostly as a winter salad vegetable.

Wild radishes grow as a weed around the Mediterranean, though most botanists think that the radish probably originated in China. Even today the enormous-rooted varieties (luo-po *or* lo pak) *are one of the most important minor crops of China.*

SLICED RADISH AND BLACK SESAME SEED SALAD

Easy and rather stunning. Goes well with the Fish in Lemon Leaves on page 184.

SERVES 4–6

12–18 radishes
1 tspn salt
1 tblspn black sesame seeds

Trim radishes and slice thinly. Sprinkle with salt and leave to drain and soften in a colander for 30 minutes. Rinse briefly and pat dry on paper towels. Dry-fry or toast the sesame seeds until they are fragrant and starting to pop, 2–3 minutes. Chop or crush roughly and stir through the radishes just before serving.

RADISH HORS D'OEUVRE

In France, a platter of washed young red radishes, their green stems and leaves still attached, is served with crusty bread, flaky sea salt and a pot of butter. You can dip the radish in salt and eat with buttered bread or spread butter on the radish, dip it in salt and eat with bread. The leaves and all are consumed.

RADISH, CUCUMBER AND NASTURTIUM SALAD

SERVES 4–6

nasturtium leaves and a few nasturtium flowers
2 cucumbers
bunch fresh radishes
vinaigrette dressing

Wash nasturtium leaves and flowers. Line a salad bowl or platter with the leaves. Peel cucumbers and slice finely. Wash radishes and slice finely. Toss together with the dressing and spoon into the nasturtium leaf-lined bowl or platter. Garnish with a few of the flowers. *Variation: Also nice with dressing made with yogurt, oil and lemon juice.*

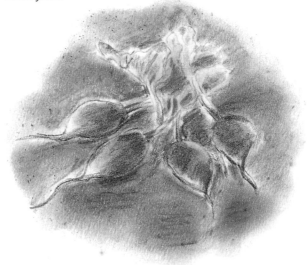

Carrots
Daucus carota

Carrots can be grown in the vegetable patch, along flower borders or in containers. Their lovely feathery tops make a pretty addition on platters and as garnishes. In Elizabethan and early Stuart times, there was an amusing fashion of substituting the tops for feathers in the hair!

Carrots belong to the Umbelliferae family, which explains the pretty tops. Chervil, parsley, fennel and anise are also members.

If you've never tasted a carrot fresh-picked (and unscraped) from the garden, you've missed a real delight as they are sweet and crunchy, very moreish (as is anything fresh-picked). They can be sown directly, ⅜ – ⅝ in deep with 8–12 in between rows, and thinned out to 2 in apart. Beds built up to give deeper soil help produce better roots.

There is a surprising number of carrot varieties available, and not all are of the tapering conical shape. There is a Mini Round carrot available for those who have trouble growing carrots. It is particularly good for pots and heavy soils, and saves space because it can be sown twice as thickly as other varieties. In the non-hybrids, Western Queen is popular with home gardeners. It has a full-bodied root with many red cores. Chantenay, Amsterdam Forcing, Nantes and Royal Star are others. Of the standard types, Western Red is the dominant carrot variety.

Some people worry about growing carrots in the no-dig garden, believing they will not grow a long tapering root. This can happen in very heavy soils (not a problem in the no-dig garden where there is plenty of straw and lucerne hay) or when fresh manure is applied, making the carrots fork and split. They like well-drained deep soils, and plenty of sun and moisture. In the no-dig garden, they can be ready for picking every two months if the seeds are planted regularly in small patches. In very hot weather, it's a good idea to assist germination by covering the seeds with newspaper, thereby keeping the earth moist underneath. Remove the paper at the first sign of germination.

CARROT PUDDING

You can make the pudding two or three days ahead.
Refrigerate it, then steam on the day needed.

SERVES 8–10

½ cup (4 oz) butter
1 cup (8 oz) sugar
finely grated zest (rind) of ½ lemon and ½ orange
1 egg, well-beaten
1 cup (3 ⅓ oz) grated raw carrots
1 cup (5 oz) grated potatoes
1 cup (4 oz) grated tart apple
1 cup (5 oz) seedless or golden raisins (sultanas)
1 cup (4 oz) chopped walnuts or pecans
1 cup (4 oz) all-purpose (plain) flour
1 tspn baking soda (bicarbonate of soda)
1 tspn cinnamon
½ tspn each allspice and nutmeg
pinch ground cloves

You will need an 8 cup (2 qt) pudding basin, well-
greased. In a bowl, beat together the butter, sugar and
citrus zest until creamy, then add the egg and beat until
light and fluffy. Stir in the carrots, potatoes, apple,
raisins and nuts. Sift together the dry ingredients and
fold them through the mixture until well combined.
Spoon into the pudding basin. Cover top with greased
brown paper or two thicknesses of waxed (greaseproof)
paper. Put a pleat into the paper to allow the pudding
to expand. Tie firmly with string. Set on a rack in a
large deep saucepan containing hot water. Bring to a
boil and steam, covered, for 2 hours and 45 minutes.
Check to see there is enough water from time to time
and add more boiling water if necessary.

Remove pudding, loosen sides and unmold onto a
platter. Serve with custard or cream.

CARROT MUFFINS

This recipe can be divided easily in half for a
smaller quantity.

MAKES 24

4 cups (13 ⅓ oz) grated carrot
2 Granny Smith apples (or greening apples), peeled,
cored and grated
4 cups (1 lb) all-purpose (plain) flour
4 tspns baking soda (bicarbonate of soda)
4 tspns cinnamon
1 tspn salt
1 ⅔ cups (13 ½ oz) sugar
1 cup (3 oz) shredded coconut
1 cup (6 oz) mixed peel
1 ½ cups (7 oz) pecans, chopped
6 large eggs
2 cups (16 fl oz) vegetable oil
2 tspns vanilla extract (essence)

Preheat oven to 350°F (180°C/Gas 4) and grease the
muffin tins.

Put the carrots, apples, sifted dry ingredients, sugar,
coconut, mixed peel and chopped nuts into a bowl. Stir
well to combine.

In another bowl, beat the eggs with the oil and
vanilla, then stir this into the flour mixture. Stir with a
wooden spoon until just combined.

Spoon batter into tins until ⅔ full and bake in the
oven for 35 minutes or until
springy to the touch.

HOT AND SPICY CARROT SALAD

A delicious Moroccan dish. Harissa is a hot Moroccan red pepper sauce, available from good food outlets. Or make your own — see page 77.

SERVES 6

2 lb whole medium carrots, scraped
1 clove garlic, peeled and halved
¼ cup (2 fl oz) lemon juice
½ tspn harissa, sambal oelek or cayenne
1 tspn each ground cumin and paprika
¼ tspn each cinnamon and sugar
salt to taste
olive oil
freshly chopped parsley or coriander (cilantro)

Cook the carrots with the garlic in a large pot of boiling water until carrots are just tender. Drain, cut into halves lengthwise. Mix together the lemon juice and spices, seasoning with the salt. Combine well and pour over the carrots, tossing until the carrots are well coated. Cool to room temperature, cover and place in refrigerator.

Just before serving, sprinkle the salad with olive oil and toss well. Strew with chopped parsley or coriander.

CARROT AND GINGER SALAD

A refreshing combination. The dressing for this can be made in advance and stored in a jar in the refrigerator.

SERVES 4

4 large carrots
½ cup (2 ½ oz) seedless raisins or golden raisins (sultanas)
½ cup (2 oz) slivered toasted almonds
⅓ cup (3 fl oz) vegetable oil
2 ⅔ tblspns (1 ⅓ fl oz) lemon juice
2 tspns finely grated fresh ginger
1 tspn finely grated lemon zest (rind)
1 tblspn honey

Peel the carrots and grate coarsely into a bowl. Add the raisins and almonds and mix together lightly. Combine remaining ingredients in a screw-top jar and shake well. Pour dressing over carrots just before serving.

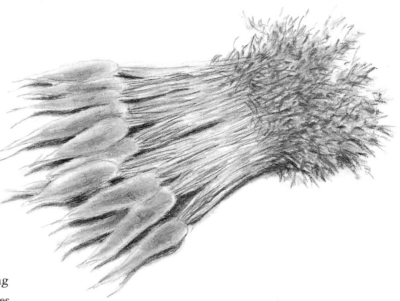

CARROT COOKIES

MAKES 20–25 COOKIES

1 large egg
⅓ cup (3 fl oz) vegetable oil
¼ cup (2 oz) sugar
finely grated zest (rind) of ½ an orange
1 medium-sized carrot, approx 3 ½ oz, peeled (scraped), boiled and mashed
¾ cup (3 ½ oz) all-purpose (plain) flour
⅔ tspn baking powder
generous pinch salt
½ tspn either ground ginger or cardamon
⅓ cup (2 oz) golden raisins (sultanas)

Preheat oven to 350°F (180°C/Gas 4). Put the egg, oil, sugar and orange zest into a mixing bowl and beat together well. Add the mashed carrot. Sift together the dry ingredients. Add to the egg/sugar mixture and mix well. Fold in the golden raisins. Drop by teaspoonfuls onto a greased baking tray, allowing room for spreading. Bake 10–12 minutes.

Beet (Beetroot)
Beta vulgaris

Beet is closely related to the sugar beets, mangolds, spinach beets and chards, which are believed to be derived from the wild subspecies, Beta maritima. *A native of the Mediterranean region,* B. maritima *was closer to chard than is today's table beet. The Greeks knew it, preferring the leaves, though the roots were eaten with lentils and beans (with mustard to give them flavor). The Romans ate only the leaves, not developing the root for food until around the beginning of the Christian era.*

The first modern record is from a German source of 1557 where beets are still referred to as Roman beets. Old beets came in a number of different colors (anything from orange to white) and tended to be tough, nasty, earthy and oversweet. Mostly they were roasted, though by the eighteenth century there were recipes which combined them with Seville oranges and parsley. However, it wasn't until the early nineteenth century that Vilmorin, the famous French plant breeder, put them on the gastronomic map.

Beet is one of the easiest vegetables to grow, and is particularly delicious when picked young. Both the leaves and the root make a lovely salad — remove baby ones when thinning out. It likes an open, sunny position and a well-limed soil (this should be done a few months before sowing). Sow seed 1 in deep in rows 12 in apart. Regular watering and thinning are important to prevent the development of thin straggly beets. They also like plenty of food when growing, particularly liquid seaweed and liquid poultry manure.

There are a number of varieties available to the home gardener. These include the Globe, which has deep red round roots; the Mini beets (good space-savers); Chioggio, which has pretty concentric circles of pink and white and holds well over a long period; and the Golden Beet, which has golden roots which don't bleed and leafy tops which are also delicious.

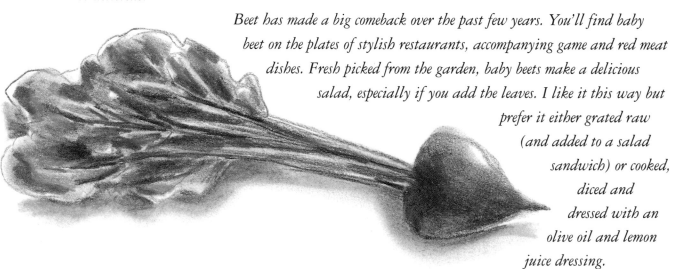

Beet has made a big comeback over the past few years. You'll find baby beet on the plates of stylish restaurants, accompanying game and red meat dishes. Fresh picked from the garden, baby beets make a delicious salad, especially if you add the leaves. I like it this way but prefer it either grated raw (and added to a salad sandwich) or cooked, diced and dressed with an olive oil and lemon juice dressing.

SHREDDED RAW BEET AND YOGURT SALAD

SERVES 6–8

6 large beet (beetroot)
1 small bunch coriander (cilantro)
½ bunch mint
½ bunch dill
juice of 1 ½ oranges or 2 lemons
flaky sea salt
freshly ground black pepper
2 cups (13 oz) plain yogurt

Peel, trim and grate the beet. Chop up the coriander, mint and dill and toss through the beet until well combined. Add the juice of the oranges or lemons and season to taste. Arrange on a salad platter leaving a hole in the middle and spoon the yogurt into the center.

CHLODNIK (BEET AND SOUR CREAM SOUP)

Pale pink, garnished with shrimp, cucumber and fresh herbs, this is one of the prettiest soups I know. The veal is optional.

SERVES 4–6

small bunch beet tops, approx 3 ½ oz, chopped
1 carrot, peeled and sliced
leafy tops of 2 celery stalks, chopped
1 small onion, chopped
3–4 sprigs parsley, chopped
6 cups (1 ½ qt) chicken stock (broth)
8 oz cooked, diced beets
6 ½ oz veal steak, pounded flat or leftover diced veal
roast (optional)
1 ½ cups (12 fl oz) sour cream
6 ½ oz cooked jumbo shrimp, peeled

salt and pepper
1 small cucumber, thinly sliced
freshly chopped chives and dill

Put the beet tops, carrot, celery tops, onion and parsley into a medium–large saucepan. Cover with the stock and bring to a boil, then simmer for 15–20 minutes or until vegetables are tender. Skim off any scum that may accumulate. Add beets. Cook a further 5 minutes.

Heat the broiler (grill) and cook the veal quickly, then cut into bite-sized pieces.

Strain the vegetables, reserving the stock. Purée vegetables in the blender until very smooth, then return to the stock, stirring well to combine.

Allow the soup to cool. Put into a blender or food processor and blend in the cream until the soup is smooth and a pale pink color. Add the veal pieces and the jumbo shrimp (reserve a few for garnishing) and season to taste. Chill in the refrigerator. When ready to serve, float the reserved jumbo shrimp and cucumber slices on top and sprinkle with the chives and dill.

BEET AND CITRUS SALAD

In the Middle East, beet is served like this with yogurt and freshly chopped parsley. Sometimes the lemon juice is omitted and a little orange blossom or rose water and some cinnamon are added instead.

All are delicious.

SERVES 4–6

2 lb beet (beetroot)
1 medium Spanish (purple) onion
vinaigrette made with olive oil, lemon juice and crushed garlic
zest (rind) of 1 large orange, finely grated or julienned
freshly chopped mint or coriander (cilantro)

Cut the tops off the beets, wash well and cook in boiling salted water until tender. The time needed will vary depending on their size. Drain and remove skins while still warm under cold running water. Cut into cubes and put into a salad bowl.

Dress the beet with the vinaigrette, add the orange zest and a couple of handfuls of freshly chopped mint or coriander (or to taste). Toss well, check for seasoning.

Parsnips
Pastinaca sativa

Parsnips are native to much of Europe, though in their wild state they are acrid and inedible. Quite a contrast to the cultivated ones which are sweet. In medieval cookery, they were an important ingredient, used as a sweetmeat (preserved in honey or made into fritters) and for medicinal purposes. It wasn't until the Middle Ages, in fact, that a really fleshy parsnip developed. These didn't have a woody core and formed a staple food during the Lent fast when served with salt-fish dishes.

Parsnips are not so popular today. Like a number of the root vegetables (the turnip, swede, salsify and celeriac), they are rather neglected. Perhaps this is due to the fact that it is difficult to find good ones, which is all the more reason to grow your own. Even if you're not particularly fond of them, it would be worth planting a row or two of freshly bought seed. Try them baked or made into a soup. Both are delicious.

Growing parsnips is similar to growing carrots. Like carrots, they can be ready for picking every two months if planted regularly and in small batches. They are one of the hardiest root vegetables. Frosts add sweetness to their flavor. It is advisable to keep the tops of roots covered to avoid canker.

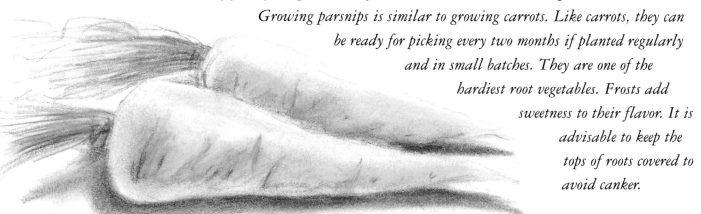

PARSNIP AND POTATO PANCAKES

Use your food processor to do the grating — it is
quicker and easier that way. Use any fresh herb you like.
You can add a beaten egg, whisked with 1 tblspn of
flour, to the mixture.

SERVES 6

1 brown onion, peeled
1 lb potatoes, peeled
2 medium parsnips, peeled
garlic, crushed
3 tblspns chopped fresh coriander (cilantro) or chives
1–2 small red chillies (optional), chopped and de-seeded
sea salt
freshly ground pepper
cooking oil and butter

Grate the onion, potatoes and parsnips. Squeeze out all
the moisture with your hands then put them into a tea-
towel. Squeeze out remaining moisture and put them
into a large mixing bowl. Combine with the garlic,
coriander or chives, and the chillies. Season to taste.

Heat the frying pan and add a few tablespoons of the
oil and an equal quantity of butter. When hot, add a
ball of the parsnip mixture, flattening it with an egg
slice. Let it cook until golden brown underneath, then
flip over and cook on other side. Make sure they are
cooked in the middle before turning out (approx 4–5
minutes each side). Keep warm in a hot oven until ready
to serve.

PARSNIP PUFF

Something nice to do with parsnips — the flavor is
delicate, not what you'd expect with parsnips.

SERVES 6–8

4 large parsnips, weighing approx 2 ½ lb
¼ cup (2 oz) butter
¼ cup (2 fl oz) milk
finely grated zest (rind) of one orange
2 eggs
salt and pepper
1 cup (2 oz) dried breadcrumbs
handful freshly chopped parsley
¼ cup (2 oz) melted butter

Preheat the oven to 350°F (180°C/Gas 4).

Peel the parsnips and cut them into chunks. Cook in
rapidly boiling salted water until tender. Drain well.
Process until smooth in the food processor with the
butter, milk, orange zest, and salt and pepper to taste.
Spoon into a greased ovenproof dish and sprinkle with
the combined breadcrumbs and parsley. Pour the melted
butter over the top. Cook for 30 minutes.

Turnips
Brassica rapa

Poor old turnips. So long held in contempt, so long associated with poverty (Roman armorials sometimes depicted turnips to denote a benefactor of the poor) and artistic flops (from the French navet, *meaning a dud). Such references must be to big old turnips, the type fed to cattle, especially in England during the eighteenth century. Yet there are many varieties of turnip, the best of all being the small sweet white ones, delicious both for their roots and tops. The tops are actually a real bonus and very good for digestion as they absorb fat in the stomach. There are, in fact, varieties of turnips which have been solely developed just for their tops, which are especially good steamed with baby leeks and need no peeling.*

Turnips come in many colors (scarlet, yellow, white, black) and shapes and sizes. Like beet, they probably originated from sea kale, which makes them a native of northern European coasts. Those grown for their leaves probably originated further east, in Afghanistan or Pakistan.

My preference is for the fast-growing baby white turnip, ideal for the home gardener and almost as easy to grow as radishes. They are best grown to reach maturity in cooler weather and should be grown quickly for tender roots. Sow ½ in deep in rows 12 in apart. The Tokyo Cross Hybrid is five weeks earlier than other common varieties and is an exceptionally fine variety.

PICKLED TURNIPS

I first came across these pretty pink pickles in a Lebanese restaurant. They were served before the meal, as part of mezes, the Middle Eastern version of hors d'oeuvre. Crunchy and moreish, easy to make.

MAKES ABOUT 8 CUPS (2 QT)

2 lb fresh small turnips, peeled
2 small beet (beetroot), peeled

4 cups (1 qt) boiling water
1 ½ cups (12 fl oz) white vinegar
⅓ cup (3 oz) cooking salt

Cut the turnips and beet into quarters. Place the vegetable pieces into a sterilized jar. Mix the water, vinegar and salt together in a jug, then pour over the vegetables. The liquid should cover them. Seal with a screw-top lid and allow to sit for 7–10 days before opening.

GLAZED TURNIPS

These are nice with roast duck or lamb. Top and tail small—medium turnips, wash well and dry. Glaze them in a frying pan in a mixture made from half butter/half vegetable oil. Cook very slowly, uncovered, tossing occasionally, until tender but firm.

Ginger
Zingiber officinale

This pungent-rooted plant is actually a rhizome (or an underground stem), and is an indispensable vegetable and spice in Chinese cooking. In Cantonese cooking, it is as ancient and traditional as the wok.

Ginger thrives in the heat and grows like bamboo to about 3 ft. It likes long hot summers and will not tolerate frost. Its exotic flowers, be they yellow or white, are exquisite and highly perfumed. The leaves, too, are very decorative. A large jar or vase of these beauties will fill your house with fragrance and joy.

Buy ginger roots from a Chinese grocer or your local greengrocer, plant in very rich soil in a fairly shady spot and keep well watered whilst growing. After five to eight months, the plant will produce tubers and you can dig these up. The young tender shoots are also good to use in cooking. To store, put the roots in damp sand in a cool dark place or peel and chop into pieces and preserve in a bottle covered with dry sherry. Grated ginger can also be frozen.

The Chinese make a distinction between ginger (geung) and stem ginger (tsee geung). The latter is the newest spring growth of the ginger rhizome and is moist and pinkish. The old, mellowed ginger with its dry, brown skin is used for seasoning; the young stems are eaten as vegetables in their own right or as pickles. They are tender yet crisp and have a fresh, fragrant flavor. The older ginger is used for its aromatic and chemical effects — it helps to mask unpleasant odors and flavors in fish, seafood or organ meats, and is often added to hot oil to sweeten it before cooking meat or vegetables.

Steamed whole fish, cooked with slivered pieces of fresh ginger, freshly chopped scallions and coriander (cilantro) is delicious.

GINGER WATER

Sometimes in winter when I am cold, I make a thermos flask full of hot ginger water. I find the aroma of the hot water hitting the ginger revivifying, and I am told that this drink is very good for frozen bones.

You will need to decide how much ginger you like to use. Start with a smallish knob, peel it and cut it into julienne strips. Put these into the bottom of a thermos. Pour over the boiling water, straight from the kettle (even better if it's purified water). Then toss in a handful of organically grown golden raisins (sultanas) to sweeten the water. As the day goes on, the ginger will become more pungent, and the water will begin to taste quite fiery and hot.

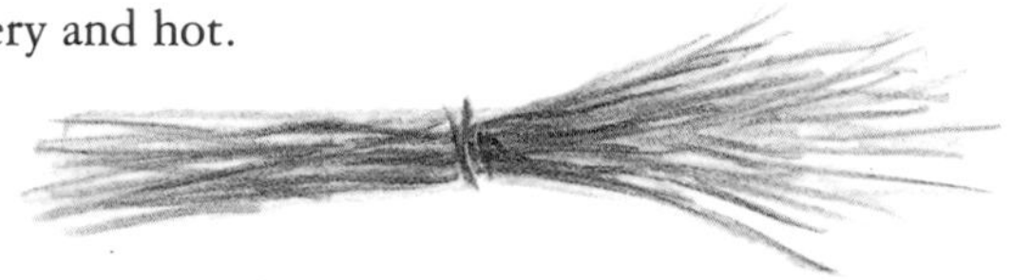

CRAB SOUP

This is an unusual mix due to the addition of the beaten eggs. It is a good lunch dish served with crunchy bread. The addition of coconut cream makes a rich soup.

SERVES 4

2 ⅔ tblspns (1 ⅓ fl oz) vegetable oil
8 oz fresh crab meat, chopped
2 ripe tomatoes, peeled and chopped
4 tblspns freshly grated ginger
4 cups (1 qt) chicken, lobster or crab stock (broth)
2 eggs
3–4 tblspns (1 ⅓–2 fl oz) dry sherry
⅓ cup (2 ⅔ fl oz) fresh lime juice
grated zest (rind) of 1–2 limes
chilli sauce to taste
3 scallions (shallots, spring onions), sliced diagonally
½ bunch fresh chives, snipped
salt and pepper to taste
⅓ cup (3 fl oz) coconut cream (optional)

Heat oil in a large pot and when hazy, stir in the crab meat. Sauté 2 minutes, add tomatoes and ginger, cook

for 1–2 minutes, then pour in the stock. Bring to a boil, stirring well, then reduce heat and simmer for 10 minutes.

Beat the eggs in a bowl, add the sherry and lime juice. Pour mixture into the soup in a slow steady stream over low heat, stirring all the time. Do not let the eggs curdle or overheat.

Add the remaining ingredients to the mixture, stir well, remove from heat and serve immediately.

WARWICK'S GINGER BREAD

A delicious bread for those who like ginger. Because the bread rises with the sun, you have to start your preparation the night before.

MAKES ONE SMALL LOAF

⅓ oz fresh compressed yeast
1 ⅓ tblspns (⅔ fl oz) dark honey
⅔–¾ cup (5–7 fl oz) warm water
1 ⅔ oz fresh ginger
1 ⅓ tblspns (⅔ fl oz) molasses
1 tspn sea salt
2 ⅔ cups (13 ⅓ oz) finely sifted organic whole-wheat (wholemeal) flour

Cream the yeast with one teaspoon of the honey and 2 tblspns of water. Set aside. Peel and grate the ginger, add remaining honey, molasses and salt. Rub this through the flour. Make a well in the center and pour in the yeast. Pour in the warm water, using only enough to bring the dough together. Knead to combine, about 5 minutes. Put dough into a bowl, cover with a cloth and leave overnight.

In the morning, punch the dough down. Knead for 5 minutes into a ball, roll in a small amount of flour and place in a lightly oiled ovenproof dish (a bowl makes a nice shape). Slash the top, let sit and rise another hour (or more, depending on warmth of the day). Put into a very hot preheated oven for 5 minutes, then turn down to 425°F (220°C/Gas 7) for a further 15 minutes.

Tubers

Oh the delight, ever new, out of loosened soil!

RAINER MARIA RILKE, FROM 'THE SONNETS TO ORPHEUS', II, 24

I'll never forget the sight of those aerial potatoes. Flying nuns, flying potatoes, now I'd seen everything. Brown, pendulous, and irregularly shaped, they were growing from the axils of the leaves of a twining green vine which had wound its way over a wire near the citrus trees.

Aerial potatoes? Another of my mother's quirky ideas, I thought. She'd put them in some time before and told me that on my arrival at her farm they would be waiting for me. They were. I steamed a few for dinner that night, brushed them with melted butter and browned them in a pan. They were very good. The texture was waxy and there were purplish patches inside. Not like the potato we are accustomed to, because in fact they belong to the yam family (genus Dioscorea*).*

The one in question is Dioscorea bulbifera *and seems to have originated in central Africa and been much cultivated in tropical Asia and the Caribbean, thriving in warm, temperate–tropical areas. I subsequently discovered that aerial potatoes also grow under the ground, though the best eating is provided by the aerial tubers (or bulbils). The* Dioscorea *family covers an almost unbelievable variety of plants, the number of which is usually underestimated. More recently I came across a Yacon, another interesting tuber, and one of the lost crops of the Incas. This was delicious peeled and eaten raw. It reminded me a little of the Nashi pear, succulent and crunchy, though not with the sweet pear flavor. In South America, the children eat it as a fruit.*

'Tuber' is really just a convenient, though not strictly accurate, category for a number of different vegetables which all belong to different families. Potatoes are members of the Solanaceae

family which also includes tomatoes, peppers, eggplants (aubergines) and the deadly nightshades. The sweet potato (Ipomoea batatas) *belongs to the Convolvulaceae family and is exceptional in being the only member of the family raised for human food (despite its name it is not related to the potato, though potatoes and* I. batatas *hail from the same area — Central America. Then there is the Jerusalem artichoke* (Helianthus tuberosus), *related to the sunflower; yams* (Dioscorea); *sweet cassava* (Manihot dulcis) *and taro* (Colocasia esculenta).

Of all the tubers, the potato is the best known and most widely used today, though when first introduced to Europe, it was regarded with much suspicion. In Italy potatoes were considered tasteless and only fit for the poor; in Germany and France, they were believed to be unhealthy, even poisonous. The Irish were the first Europeans to cultivate potatoes extensively and, by the eighteenth century, it had become their staple food. It was only due to the famine of 1770 and the persistence of Antoine Parmentier, a French military pharmacist, that the potato became more widely accepted. Today his name is still associated with a soup, a hash and an omelet, all containing potatoes.

Potatoes, Jerusalem artichokes and sweet potatoes are all easy to grow, though the sweet potato likes a good deal of heat (at least 140 days of hot weather is needed to produce a good crop). Potatoes don't grow well in extreme heat and are also very susceptible to frost damage. In the no-dig garden, you can grow them all year round and the yields are very rewarding. In her book on the no-dig garden, Growing Without Digging, *Esther Deans tells of how she grew 50 lb of potatoes in an area 4 x 6 ft. She put the potatoes in a little compost on hay, under straw. The green tops push up through the straw and you can lift this up from time to time to check on their progress.*

Potatoes take up a fair bit of room, so you might consider a separate patch for them. Good drainage is essential. Because they are susceptible to disease, it is important to buy government certified tubers, harvested from crops known to be free from virus and other diseases.

Sweet potatoes also need a lot of space in the garden as their vines spread a great deal. Like potatoes, they need plenty of water. As the vines grow, it's a good idea to lift them up occasionally to discourage rooting at the nodes along the stem —these tend to restrict the development of the main tubers on the parent plant. Sweet potatoes spoil more easily than ordinary potatoes.

Jerusalem artichokes also require a fair amount of space, as they can reach a height of 6 ½ ft or more. They need only the most rudimentary care during the growing season and, once planted, can be hard to get rid of. The tall stems have broad, heart-shaped leaves and bear large, yellow flowers in mid-summer, rather like sunflowers. The tubers grow up to 4 in long and are irregularly shaped. They can be dug up in fall, or heavily mulched and left in the ground to be dug up as required.

Don't wash tubers when storing — leave the dirt on as they will stay fresher and keep better.

Potatoes
Solanaceae family

I have a special fondness for potatoes, though I know there are some who find them cloddish (it is true that they're not among the great-lookers of the vegetable kingdom). The Tibetans say they are a 'cold' food and as such, are not good for the kidneys.

It's the transformation that takes place when you cook them that makes the difference. Something about their wholesomeness appeals — their starchy sustenance. I love them baked in their jackets, mashed or roasted. I particularly like them in salads: boiled (or steamed), then cut up whilst hot and tossed with some good-quality olive oil, and some flaky salt and pepper. Chopped scallions (shallots, spring onions) or chives are always a good addition.

Potatoes have certainly been around a long time: it is possible they were being harvested as far back as 5000 BC. Reay Tannahill, the author of Food in History, *says the potato had been domesticated in Peru by 3000 BC and it was there that Pizzaro's men first saw it around 1530. Pedro de Cieza wrote about it in his* Chronicle of Peru *and it was probably he who took the first potatoes to Europe.*

Apparently the early Peruvians slit and sun-dried their potatoes, which they called tunta. *By 1000 BC the Incas were using a more advanced technique whereby they first froze the potatoes in the snows of the Andes. They then allowed them to thaw and squeezed out the juice until they were dry. The resulting* chuno *was a staple when potatoes were out of season. It predated modern freeze-dry techniques by 3000 years.*

It is in Peru today that the full genetic diversity of the potato is being explored through the Centro Internacional de la Papa (CIP). Australia has a potato research station where new potato varieties are being developed. As in Peru, they are always looking for improved varieties for French fries.

New potato varieties developed by Australians include the Desiree (a Dutch variety, red-skinned with yellow flesh, good for baking, roasting and mashing); the Toolangi Delight (purple-skinned, white-fleshed variety suitable for home gardens, which cooks up dry and is therefore good for baking, boiling, chipping and mashing); the Patrone (another Dutch variety with a creamy skin and yellow flesh, good for salads and casseroles, but not good for mashing). Other varieties include the ubiquitous Sebago, the Pontiac, Russet Burbank (which is good for baking and French fries), the Kennebec, Kipfler, Coliban, Bison and Exton. It could be an interesting project to try and grow, then to cook and taste all the different types now available. After all, the varieties available in the shops are sometimes limited and have often been sitting around for weeks. Freshly cooked potatoes are a real treat.

Potatoes grow extremely well in the no-dig garden. Tubers for planting should be about 2 oz in weight and there should be at least one 'eye' or sprout on each. It's a good idea to let the sprouts harden before they are planted: before planting, spread the tubers (or cut pieces) out on the ground in a shady spot for a week or two, then discard any which have developed weak growths or rotten areas. A 14 lb bag of certified potatoes will provide 50–60 plants, which is plenty for the average family.

WARM POTATO SALAD WITH SESAME AND SUNFLOWER SEEDS

SERVES 6–8

This is a nice, simple thing to do with new potatoes.

For six to eight people, you will need 2–4 lb of medium size new potatoes. Wash them well, then steam or boil unpeeled until just cooked. Whilst still hot, cut them into quarters and put into a salad bowl. Sprinkle with a good-quality olive oil, flaky salt and ground pepper. Add vinegar and cayenne to taste (both optional).

Heat a frying pan. Throw in a handful or two of sesame and sunflower seeds and shake or stir with a wooden spoon until toasted. Add to the hot potatoes and combine.

Homemade mayonnaise is nice with this if you omit the oil and vinegar. Commercial mayonnaise — with its added sugar — is best avoided.

KAREN'S RÖESTI POTATOES

Chef Karen Kerby makes the best röesti I've tasted. This is how she does them. She uses best-quality Pontiacs which are parboiled (skins on) the night before. You need six to seven medium-size potatoes.

SERVES 6

1 ¼ lb grated Pontiac potatoes, parboiled
6 tblspns (3 ⅓ oz) butter
½ tspn salt
1 rasher bacon, finely chopped

After the potatoes have sat overnight, peel and grate them.

Melt half the butter in a large, heavy based frying pan until it starts to bubble. Don't let it burn. Sprinkle over the chopped bacon and swirl to spread evenly all over the base. Add all the grated potato and season to taste. Use an egg slide to shape the potato around the edge of the pan, but do not press the potato down. Shake pan to prevent potato from sticking.

Cook on the first side for 5 minutes over medium–high heat. Turn by placing a plate on top of the potato and tipping potato onto plate. Melt remaining butter in the pan and slide the röesti back into the pan.

Cook a further 5 minutes then slide out of the pan onto a plate.

Note: Karen tosses the röesti with the butter on top to turn, but this is quite an art and takes some practice!

POTATOES IN CREAM WITH BASIL

I don't normally associate potatoes with basil, but in this adaptation from a recipe of Julia Child's, you will find it a luscious combination.

SERVES 4–6

2 lb potatoes, peeled and cut into slices
⅓ in thick
3 tblspns (1 ½ oz) butter
1 ½ tblspns (⅔ oz) all-purpose (plain) flour
1 cup (8 fl oz) milk
½ cup (4 fl oz) cream
bunch fresh basil, chopped
2 cloves garlic, crushed
flaky salt and freshly ground black pepper
freshly chopped basil (extra)

Blanch the potatoes in rapidly boiling salted water for 3 minutes, drain (a non-stick or stainless steel saucepan is best for this).

Make a roux by melting the butter in a saucepan and working into it the flour, cook over low heat for 1 minute. Heat the milk and whisk it into the roux, off the heat.

Add the cream, basil, garlic and salt and pepper to taste. Return to the heat and keep whisking until it comes back to a boil. Simmer 2 minutes, then gently fold in the parboiled potato slices. The sauce should cover the slices. Add more milk or cream if it doesn't.

Place saucepan over low heat and simmer for 10–15 minutes or until potatoes are tender, stirring occasionally to prevent sticking. (A simmer pad comes in handy to prevent burning.)

Serve straightaway scattered with more freshly chopped basil. It can also be reheated.

Note: Put the potatoes into a greased, shallow serving dish, dot with butter and reheat in oven before serving. Fresh tarragon is a wonderful alternative when fresh basil is not in season.

BUBBLE AND SQUEAK

Good for Sunday brunch and a wonderful way of using up leftover vegetables. It's especially good with hot buttered toast and some chilli or tomato sauce.

You'll need a wide, heavy-bottomed frying pan so that the heat is evenly distributed. Melt a few tblspns of butter in the pan, then add 6 rashers of bacon, trimmed and cut into pieces about 1 ½ in long. Let cook slowly.

Now add any of the following: cooked potato, pumpkin, sweet potato, cabbage, broccoli, baby squash, Brussels sprouts, cauliflower, onions, parsnips, cooked peas. Tomatoes are too watery and mushrooms are not so good. Cut root vegetables into slices, divide cauliflower and broccoli into florets.

Add to the bacon in the pan, keep turning and squashing down with a spatula. Add freshly ground pepper to taste and more butter or bacon fat if needed. Keep on frying the vegetables until the starchy ones begin to get crispy.

Serve hot with all the crunchy bits from the bottom of the pan.

MADHUR JAFFREY'S POTATOES WITH WHOLE SPICES AND SESAME SEEDS

I love most potato dishes, but this is one of my very favorites. Use a wok and have all the ingredients ready before you start the cooking. A green vegetable, like pak choi or English spinach, stir-fried in a little hot oil and finished off with a little sesame oil, is a good accompaniment.

SERVES 4–6

10 medium-small potatoes
2 tspns whole cumin seeds
¼ tspn whole fenugreek seeds
2 tspns whole black mustard seeds
½ cup (4 fl oz) vegetable oil
⅛ tspn ground asafoetida (optional)
1–3 dried red chillies
2 tblspns sesame seeds
¼ tspn ground turmeric
2 tspns salt
freshly ground black pepper
2 tsps ground aamchur or lemon juice

Boil the potatoes in their jackets, drain and allow to cool thoroughly. Peel and then cut into ¾ in cubes.

Combine the cumin, fenugreek and mustard seeds in a small cup and arrange all the ingredients near the stove in the order in which they go into the wok.

Heat the oil in the wok and when very hot put in the ground asafoetida and let it sizzle for 3 seconds; then put in the combined cumin, fenugreek and mustard seeds and let sizzle for another 5 seconds; add the red chillies and stir the spices around for 3 seconds; put in the sesame seeds and stir spices for another 5 seconds; finally, add the turmeric, stir once and put in the potatoes. Turn heat up to medium–high, stir-fry the potatoes for another 5 minutes. Add salt and pepper to taste, then the aamchur or lemon juice. Stir-fry for another 3–5 minutes. Serve warm.

Sweet Potatoes
Ipomoea batatas

In China, the sweet potato has saved millions from starvation when wheat and rice crops have failed. It's not a vegetable I associate with that country (I usually think of the West Indies), yet in the streets and lanes of every Chinese city, street vendors sell freshly baked sweet potatoes, a favorite with children and adults.

Noodles made from sweet potato starch are popular and many Chinese eat sweet potato slices as they would fruit. The baked sweet potato (kaobaishu) of Beijing is well known and dried sweet potato slices are stored for year-round use.

The sweet potato found its way to China in the sixteenth century either through India or Burma or by way of the Philippines. It arrived from Central America before the common potato and was highly regarded.

Sweet potatoes are often incorrectly called yams, but yams belong to a different species and family. It seems *that the early explorers had trouble distinguishing the difference and this mistake is still frequently made. Vasco da Gama's 'cooked roots that had the flavor of chestnuts' were probably yams.*

There are two types of sweet potato: a moist-meated, red-colored one, and a dry-meated, pale fawn-colored one. My preference is for the moist, red one, which New Zealanders call 'kumara'.

Stem cuttings or shoots from the roots should be planted 12 ft apart. In tropical areas, two crops a year can be grown.

BAKED SWEET POTATOES

Sweet potatoes combine very well with oranges. Peel and slice 1 ½ lb of sweet potatoes thickly and steam until they are soft but still firm. Pour over the potatoes the juice of one orange and 2 tblspns (1 oz) melted butter. Sprinkle with nutmeg, ground ginger and a little brown sugar. Bake in a hot oven 30–40 minutes, basting occasionally.

SWEET POTATO PUDDING

If you use the orange kumara for this, you will have a beautiful golden pudding. You'll need about 1 lb unpeeled potatoes.

SERVES 6

13 ½ oz sweet potatoes, peeled, cooked and mashed
1 cup (8 fl oz) orange juice
¾ cup (6 oz) sugar
½ cup (4 oz) butter, melted
6 egg yolks, beaten
1–2 tspns preserved ginger in syrup, finely chopped (optional)

1–2 tspns lemon zest (rind), finely grated
¼ tspn cinnamon or nutmeg
2 egg whites, stiffly beaten

Preheat the oven to 350°F (180°C/Gas 4).

Combine all the ingredients except for the egg whites in a bowl and beat together well. Fold in the egg whites and bake in a greased pudding dish for about 1 hour.

Note: Preserved ginger in syrup is available in jars from delicatessens. In Australia, it is manufactured in Buderim, Queensland, where ginger is grown.

MASHED SWEET POTATOES

Steam or boil sweet potatoes in their skins. Peel and mash with a potato masher. Add some butter, salt, hot milk and whisk until very light.

If you fold through some chopped dates and walnuts or pecans, this dish is a good accompaniment to a baked ham.

SWEET POTATO SALAD

I came across this recipe in an informative article on potatoes by Raymond Sokolov in *Natural History* magazine. It is Eileen Yin-Fei Lo's variation on a traditional Chinese salad preparation. Turnips, young ginger and white radishes can also be prepared in this way and left to marinate overnight. Lovely with chicken or meat dishes or to accompany a barbecue.

SERVES 4–6

1 lb sweet potatoes
¼ cup (2 fl oz) white vinegar
1 ½ tblspns sugar
1 tspn roasted sesame oil
tspn salt
1 tspn freshly chopped coriander (cilantro)

Peel, wash and dry the potatoes and cut into juilienne strips about 2 in long.

Mix together the vinegar, sugar, sesame oil and salt. Toss in the potato strips and combine well. Cover and refrigerate overnight.

Before serving, add the coriander and toss well. Serve chilled.

Jerusalem Artichokes
Helianthus tuberosus

The first time I set eyes on these gnarled tubers I was amazed. They reminded me of knotted-up, arthritic old men. And when I first saw how they grew, I was amazed again, because they looked to me like lovely small sunflowers, bowing and moving in the wind. It is the whitish-yellow tubers underneath that are edible.

In fact, like the sunflower, the Jerusalem artichoke is native to North America and was introduced to Europe in the seventeenth century. Although from the same family as the globe artichoke, it is only distantly related. Nor does it have any connection with the city of Jerusalem. Perhaps the name came about through some confusion or mispronunciation, girasole *being the Italian word for sunflower.*

Native Americans ate Jerusalem artichokes (sometimes called 'sunchokes') for centuries. Their flavor is sweet and mildly herbal, and they have a lovely crunch. They are fabulous in soup and are also good when pickled or eaten raw, tossed through salads. They can also be fried, baked and roasted.

Like potatoes, Jerusalem artichokes take up a fair amount of room and, once planted, can be very hard to get rid of. They will do well in ordinary, well-drained garden soil with full sun or partial shade whilst the tubers (or pieces of tuber) can be planted in late winter or early spring. Choose good-quality tubers, about 1 ½ – 2 in in diameter and length. Each should have two eyes or buds. Ten to twelve plants will be ample for an average family.

JERUSALEM ARTICHOKE SOUP

The English themselves have been quite confused by this vegetable, which is why it has such an odd name. During the nineteenth century, they invariably called this soup 'Palestine Soup' under the mistaken assumption that the artichokes came from Jerusalem.

SERVES 4

1 ½ lb Jerusalem artichokes
1 large onion
¼ cup (2 oz) butter
2 ½ cups (20 fl oz) milk
2 ½ cups (20 fl oz) water or *chicken stock (broth)*
salt and freshly ground black pepper
1 egg
¼ cup (2 fl oz) cream

Scrub the artichokes, leaving on their skins (to add flavor and fiber). Slice the onion and cook until translucent in the butter in a medium–large pot. Slice the artichokes and add to the pan with the milk. Bring to a boil, cover and cook for about 10 minutes, stirring occasionally. Add the water or stock, season to taste and simmer for another 20 minutes. When the artichokes are cooked, put the mixture into the blender or food processor and blend until reasonably smooth — leaving some texture in it. Season to taste — this soup needs plenty of seasoning. Beat the egg in a small bowl, stir in the cream and add slowly to the soup. Serve hot.

PICKLED JERUSALEM ARTICHOKES

The lemon flavor of these pickles cuts through rich or oily meats and fish. The pickles are also good tossed through a salad of snow pea (mangetout) shoots and avocado, dressed with walnut oil and raspberry vinegar.

MAKES APPROX 6 CUPS (1 ½ QT)

2 lb Jerusalem artichokes
zest (rind) of 1 lemon, peeled
2 bay leaves
1 seeded chilli or *a few juniper berries*
4 cups (1 qt) white wine vinegar

Peel the artichokes and cut them into pieces of the same regular size. Drop them into acidulated water to prevent discoloring. Steam until just tender — don't overcook as they will become mushy.

In an enamel saucepan, put the zest, bay leaves, chilli or juniper berries and the vinegar. Bring to a boil and simmer gently for 10 minutes.

Arrange the artichokes in sterile jars with the zest, bay leaves and chilli or berries. When the vinegar is cold, pour over to cover. Store for 2 weeks before using. *Variations: Vary the spices: slices of fresh root ginger are an interesting addition, so too is mustard and celery seed. Omit the other spices if you use these, or make up a combination that suits your taste.*

Mushrooms
Agaricaceae family

Dōgen received, they say, his first insight
from the old cook of some monastery
in China,

who was on the jetty
where they docked, who had come down
to buy mushrooms

among the rolled-up
straw sails, the fish-nets, brocade litters,
and geese in baskets.

ROBERT GRAY FROM 'TO THE MASTER
DŌGEN ZENJI (1200–1253 AD)'

The most delicious mushrooms I have ever eaten were in the woods of Umbria one September. We gathered them from the wild during the morning, and ate them grilled (broiled) with olive oil over a wood fire for lunch. The flavor was stunning — intense and meaty. Served with a salad and some crusty bread, they were all that was needed for a satisfying and delicious lunch.

Such porcini are much prized in Italy, though of course you need to know (or be with people who know) which are edible and which are poisonous. Until that time, I'd only tasted cultivated mushrooms which hardly bear comparison. I'm inclined to agree with Colette when she wrote, 'I am in revolt against the mushroom of Paris, an insipid creature born in the dark and incubated by humidity. I have had enough of it, bathing chopped in all the sauces it thickens. I forbid it to usurp the place of the chanterelle or the truffle; and command it, together with its fitting companion, canned cocks' combs, never to cross the threshold of my kitchen.'

Since that time in Italy, I've been fortunate to try wild mushrooms closer to home in the Blue Mountains, west of Sydney. A number of varieties grow and thrive there and it is a wonderful fall day's outing to look for mushrooms under the trees.

Mushrooms have been eaten for thousands of years. Wild varieties were recognized by the Sumerians in 3500

BC *and the Greeks exported their edible varieties. The Egyptians allowed only the Pharaohs to eat them, since they were considered too good for ordinary people, and the Romans thought they were a food for the gods. The French knew the wild chanterelles, morels and cèpes of the forests and regarded them as a delicacy. The first to be cultivated was the shiitake mushroom by the Japanese at least 2000 years ago. They are called after the shii tree but also grow on oak and hornbeam trees. In the West, the French only began cultivation 300 years ago in the caves around Paris.*

Mushroom hunting is a favorite pastime in many countries, though the mushrooms vary greatly. In France, Finland, Russia and Germany, certain areas are kept wild so that the mushrooms may thrive. In America there are 50 edible wild species including the beefsteak mushroom (so-called because of its similarity to a steak in flavor), the oyster mushroom, the morel, the shaggy-mane, the milky-cup and the puffball (some of which grow to the size of a football). At the famous funghi markets of Trento in Italy, up to 230 varieties of funghi can be found. This market is not subject to the controls exerted by the local commune in other districts, where only 15 of the most widely recognized types are allowed to be sold.

The most widely eaten cultivated mushroom is the agaric (Agaricus bisporus). *It is usually harvested young either as a button mushroom (or champignon), a large button, a cap or cup (where the cap has partially opened), or an open flat mushroom. Other cultivated varieties include the shiitake, oyster, straw, the Japanese golden mushroom and the wood or cloud's ear mushrooms. The latter, also known as Chinese black fungus, is usually sold in dried form and is reconstituted in water. Soaked in hot water for 10 minutes, it swells to translucent blackish-brown shapes rather like prettily shaped ears. It is used more for texture than as a flavoring ingredient, though it does absorb subtle flavors from food with which it is combined.*

Some of these varieties — like the oyster and the golden mushroom — have only recently become cultivated. 'The domestication of mushrooms is always a challenge,' Dr Kai Yip Cho, a microbiologist at Sydney University, told me. 'This is because we don't yet know enough about their exact nutritional requirements.' He has been experimenting for a number of years with different oriental varieties and has had success with the oyster, straw and Japanese golden mushrooms.

Because mushrooms have no leaves and no chlorophyll, they cannot absorb and use carbon dioxide from the air. They live on dead matter and start life as spores from the parent mushroom. On germination the spore puts out minute threads called hyphae, which branch in all directions forming mycelium (the white fluff on moldy bread). The amateur gardener starts a cultivation by buying mycelium as spawn — either composted manure or grains inoculated with mycelium. Amateur mushroom growers can purchase pre-prepared boxes and full cultivation instructions are given with each box or bag of mushroom compost. Mushrooms will grow just about anywhere, even under the bed. I know people who have boxes tucked away in their laundries and garages.

Optimum temperatures for growth are between 60°F and 66°F (15°C and 18°C). Ventilation must be good but draughts and direct sunlight should be avoided. When successfully cultivated, mushrooms crop in flushes at intervals of 10 days or so and may continue for two months. Be careful not to pick the mushrooms too early — the open flat ones have more flavor than the buttons. Do not be surprised, however, if sometimes they do not come up because although exciting to grow, they can be unpredictable. The exhausted compost is very good for the garden.

Cultivated mushrooms do not require washing because they are grown in sterilized conditions. They only need wiping over with a cloth although extremely dirty ones can be peeled.

> Shyly the silver-hatted mushrooms make
>   Soft entrance through,
> And undelivered lovers, half awake,
>   Hear noises in the dew.
>
> JOHN SHAW NIELSON, FROM 'MAY'

BLACK AND WHITE FUNGUS SALAD

SERVES 4–6

9 ½ oz bean sprouts
2 whole silver fungus (or white fungus)
½ oz dried black fungus (or cloud ear fungus)
3 scallions (shallots, spring onions), thinly sliced, including some of the green tops
½ oz sliced water chestnuts
½ tspn chopped fresh ginger
¼ tspn finely chopped garlic
1 ⅓ tblspns (⅔ fl oz) light soy sauce
1 ⅓ tblspns (⅔ fl oz) rice vinegar
1 tspn roasted sesame oil
½ tspn sugar
⅓ cup (2 ⅔ fl oz) peanut (groundnut) oil

Trim bean sprouts, rinse, drain and pat dry. Cover silver fungus and black fungus with warm water and soak for 20–30 minutes. Drain the silver fungus, cut out and discard the hard core, slice into strips and pat dry. Drain the black fungus, trim off any hard portions and pat dry. Combine sprouts, fungus, scallions and water chestnuts in a bowl, cover and refrigerate. Combine remaining ingredients in a screw-top jar and shake thoroughly. Just before serving, pour dressing over and toss.

Note: Don't discard the soaking water for the dried mushrooms. It is useful for soups and stocks.

MARINATED MUSHROOMS

Good served as part of an antipasto or as an accompaniment to cold meats.

SERVES 4–6

½ cup (4 fl oz) olive oil
⅓ cup (3 fl oz) water
juice of 2 lemons
1 bay leaf
2 cloves garlic, crushed
1 tspn salt
a few whole peppercorns
1 lb baby mushrooms

Put all ingredients except mushrooms into a saucepan, bring to a boil and simmer for 10–15 minutes. Strain and return to saucepan, bring back to boil, drop in mushrooms and cook for 5–7 minutes. Allow the mushrooms to cool in the liquid and serve cold, drained of liquid. Scatter with freshly chopped parsley.

MUSHROOM STRUDELS

SERVES 8

8 oz streaky bacon
1 medium onion, finely chopped
1 clove garlic, crushed
16 oz button mushrooms, sliced
¼ cup (1 oz) all-purpose (plain) flour
1–1 ½ cups (8–12 fl oz) chicken stock (broth)
1 tspn dried tarragon
pinch cayenne or hot paprika
salt and freshly ground black pepper
16 sheets phyllo pastry, approx 8 oz
melted butter
1 egg, beaten with 1 tblspn water

Preheat oven to moderately hot (400°F/200°C/Gas 6).
Remove rind from bacon and dice. Sauté in a frying pan, reduce heat and add onion and garlic, cooking until soft but not colored. Add mushrooms and cook until soft, then add flour and cook a further minute, stirring constantly.

Remove from heat, add stock, stir well and return to heat. Bring slowly to boiling point, stirring all the time. Add herbs and seasonings to taste, being careful to taste for saltiness, remove from heat and allow to cool.

Take a sheet of phyllo pastry, brush with melted butter, place another sheet over the top and fold sheets in half to make a square. Brush well with melted butter, then place 2 tblspns of the mushroom mixture into the center of each square. Draw up the edges of the pastry so that it looks like a sack. Brush the pastry with beaten egg and bake in oven on greased baking trays for 10–15 minutes.

MUSHROOM SALAD

SERVES 4–6

1 lb mushrooms, wiped and sliced
1 red (or white) onion, finely sliced
½ each green and red sweet pepper (capsicum), sliced
½ cup (4 fl oz) olive oil
¼ cup (2 fl oz) lemon juice
1 clove garlic, crushed
flaky sea salt
freshly ground pepper
½ bunch freshly chopped parsley

Put the mushrooms, onion and sweet pepper into a salad bowl. Mix together the oil, lemon juice and garlic. Season to taste. Toss through salad ingredients. Strew with freshly chopped parsley.

Variation: Try a mushroom and shrimp salad. Combine equal amounts fresh, finely sliced baby mushrooms and small shrimp with the above vinaigrette. Substitute freshly chopped mint, basil or tarragon for the parsley.

COLD CHICKEN PIE

This delicious recipe from my friend Janice Baker is ideal for picnics. You will need to make it the day before and chill it overnight in the refrigerator. Its keeping qualities are good. I like to add a generous scattering of freshly chopped tarragon or sage to the onion–bacon mixture for extra flavoring.

I took it on a picnic to Mosman Bay on Sydney Harbour one day when working on a photographic shoot for a magazine. We had decided to base the idea for the food around one of Tom Roberts's most famous paintings, *Mosman's Bay* (1894), which is now part of the Howard Hinton collection. The painting is a joyous celebration of one of the many lovely bays in Sydney Harbour, full of light and color.

The pie was one of a number of dishes included in the picnic. There was a superb gravlax of ocean trout, a salad, a large Italian-style salami, olive pâté, dried tomatoes and a large loaf of crusty bread. We had trouble keeping the ducks away from the food. Every time the photographer was ready to press the button, these cheeky creatures would dart in and devour something. As well, the tide was creeping in and the waves kept lapping onto our beautiful Indian quilt.

SERVES 6–8

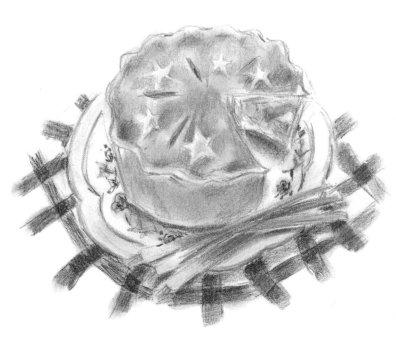

1 cup (4 oz) all-purpose (plain) flour
1 cup (4 oz) self-raising flour
pinch salt
¾ cup (6 oz) unsalted butter
1 egg, beaten with 1 egg yolk
1 ⅓–2 ⅔ tblspns (⅔ –1 ⅓ fl oz) iced water

FILLING
6 chicken fillets
3 large onions, thinly sliced
6 tblspns (3 oz) butter
6 rashers bacon, rind removed and diced
8 oz mushrooms, thinly sliced
2 tblspns freshly chopped tarragon or sage, or to taste
sea salt and freshly ground pepper
⅓ cup (3 fl oz) thickened cream
1 egg, beaten (for glaze)

Sift flours together with salt. Rub in butter until mixture resembles breadcrumbs. Add eggs and egg yolks and mix to a pliable dough, adding as much water as is necessary. Shape into a ball, wrap in greaseproof (waxed) paper and chill until needed.

Divide pastry, allowing a little more than half for bottom crust. Roll out on a lightly floured surface and line the base of a 9–10 in pie plate. Chill. Keep remaining pastry wrapped and chilled too.

Preheat oven to 425°F (220°C/Gas 7).

Remove skin and any fat from the chicken fillets, set aside.

In a large frying pan, sauté the onions in the butter until translucent; add the bacon and mushrooms and sauté for a further 5 minutes. If adding herbs, do so now. Stir in well, remove from heat and cool.

Spread onion mixture over base of pie shell, top with chicken fillets and season with salt and pepper to taste. Dribble over the cream.

Roll out remaining pastry and cover top of pie. Prick top with a fork. Trim edges, crimp and seal. Brush pie with beaten egg and bake in hot oven for 10 minutes. Reduce heat to moderate (350°F/180°C/Gas 4) and bake for a further 45–50 minutes. Remove and cool. Chill overnight.

Herbs

. . . Here's flow'rs for you:
Hot lavender, mints, savory, marjoram;
The marigold, that goes to bed wi' th' sun
And with him rises weeping; these are flow'rs
Of middle summer, and I think they are given
To men of middle age . . .

WILLIAM SHAKESPEARE, FROM *THE WINTER'S TALE*, PERDITA, ACT IV, SC 4

It wasn't until I lived in Italy that I realized the value of having my own pot of basil. I'd gone to Perugia to study at the university and was living with an Italian family. Lunch was the main meal of the day and a substantial, simple meal was always prepared. Often there was a pasta dish, and always a plate of tomatoes, dressed with olive oil and fresh sweet basil from the garden.

The flavor of that herb lived in me so strongly that to this day I can't go through a summer without at least two basil bushes somewhere in my garden. Fresh basil continues to evoke hot summer days, sweet ripe tomatoes, clear blue skies, terracotta pots and geraniums.

Despite my associations, the many different species of basil are native to India. This surprised me at first, because basil is not a herb used much in Indian cooking. Apparently it was sacred to Vishnu and Shiva and a pot grew in every courtyard. As it spread to the Mediterranean, the legends grew and changed. In Italy, it was customary for a pot of basil to be placed in the window by a lady as a signal to her lover that she was expecting him. In the famous poem 'Isabella', by Keats, Isabella kept the head of her lover in a pot of basil. In Greek, the world basileus *means 'king' and some call it the king of herbs, a claim I wouldn't dispute.*

These days, as I weed, water and cultivate the different herbs throughout my garden, brush against their leaves and inhale their fragrant scents, I wonder how anyone can live without fresh herbs. The pungency of a few crushed leaves in my hand fills my nostrils and helps to clear my head. Parsley, basil, lemongrass, marjoram, sage, rosemary and rose geranium are only some of the herbs I like to have around me.

Even before the written word, primitive people used herbs instinctively in cooking and for medicinal purposes. They were used in a variety of ways, as dyes for cloth and aids to crop-growing and farming; as antiseptics to help purify and sweeten the environment; to be imbibed, or used as salves, poultices, and simple remedies for illness.

A clay tablet from Sumeria dated around 3000 BC gives formulas for mixing different herbs with water, wine, mustard and milk to make poultices. The first Chinese herbal, the Pen ts'ao Kang-mu, said to date from the third millennium BC, gives an encyclopedic account of thousands of plants, including herbs, and the notes about each herb include a statement concerning their edibility and healing properties. China has fewer culinary herbs than southern Europe (the world center of herb use) though their use of herbal medicines and teas remains extensive.

The ancient Egyptians used anise and marjoram for embalming, and living herbs were entombed with the dead. The first European to write on plants, Theophratus, was born in 370 BC. He is called the father of botany and was a pupil of Plato and later of Aristotle. He describes how perfumes were made from mint, saffron, sweet marjoram, thyme, bergamot, lilies and iris. The ancient Greeks used herbs in other ways too — athletes celebrated their victories with crowns made of bay leaves and parsley; rosemary garlands were commonplace at festivals.

The ancient Romans also used herbs extensively — for culinary purposes, for scented herbal baths, for stuffing pillow cases, and to aid digestion. Wealthy citizens created elaborate courtyard gardens where they planted herbs and flowers such as roses and violets. Small gardens were made to seem bigger by the addition of murals depicting sweeping vistas filled with trees and flowers.

During the Middle Ages, walled gardens became popular. In the courtyards of castle strongholds sealed off by moats and walls, herbs and other plants were grown to feed the inhabitants. Monastic gardens also flourished. These were usually self-supporting and became important centers for the dissemination of knowledge about herbs. I remember coming across the recreation of the mood of a medieval courtyard garden at The Cloisters in Manhattan. There, plants cultivated by monks before 1520 are grown today. It was a grey, drizzly day and, after the speed of New York, the feeling of peace in this lovely courtyard was blissful.

The three most important writers about plants in classical times were Claudius Galen, Dioscorides (his De Materia Medica, *written in AD 77, records cures involving 600 plants) and Pliny, whose* Natural History *has delighted and amused scholars from his day to ours. Out of these classical writers about herbs grew the herbals, ponderous tomes which mixed medicinal remedies, botanical descriptions and recipes. Probably the best known of these is John Gerard's* The Herball *which appeared in 1597. Just how much Gerard wrote himself and how much he pinched from other sources is disputable. Perhaps the most notorious of all was Nicholas Culpeper, whose* Complete Herball *of 1651 was full of celestial ramblings.*

The popularity of herbs continued until the mid-nineteenth century. With the rise of the industrial revolution, the population's move to the cities and the growth of supermarket food, interest waned. During the 1950s, for example, only the most adventurous cook would have had more than fresh parsley or mint in the garden.

Today, the growing of herbs has become popular again and their natural qualities are once again prized. Most herbs are easy to grow, preferring lean soils and hardy conditions which help to produce their essential oils.

Potted Herbs and Containers

Here bloweth thyme and bergamot

WALTER DE LA MARE

Where you grow your herbs will depend on how much room you have. Even if it's only a tiny space, they'll do well — you can put them in pots and containers along windowsills and many will do well indoors if kept in a light, sunny spot.

Scented geraniums, for example, make excellent houseplants as do many others, such as thyme, rosemary, marjoram, parsley. Pots help to contain herbs with spreading roots like mint, and even those with long taproots like dill and borage will thrive if the container is deep enough. Bay trees can be shaped or trained as standards to decorate the terrace or garden. However, tall herbs like lovage and angelica are impractical in pots.

Use a good-quality, friable potting mix for the pots (which must have drainage holes at the bottom) and make sure there are some stones or pieces of crockery at the bottom to help with drainage. Remember that potted plants dry out faster than those in the garden and must be kept well watered. A diluted, liquid organic fertilizer applied once a month will help to provide necessary nutrients.

In the Garden

My own garden has herbs creeping up the driveway, a bay tree within the petunias, a bush basil with the alyssum. They're all over the place, and perhaps next time I'll plant them in a more orderly fashion.

Many people use wheel or ladder gardens for compact plantings. For a wheel or circle garden, lay an old cartwheel on prepared ground and plant the herbs of your choice between the spokes. The Tibetans (and in the West, Carl Jung) attribute a protective value to the perfect circle or mandala. Put the tallest herbs in the center (rosemary, French lavender, lemongrass), then plant another circle with medium-sized growers like lemon balm, Italian parsley and marjoram and, finally, plant the low border plants at the edge (parsley, pennyroyal and thyme). If the circle receives a lot of sun, put the shade-loving herbs like angelica, bergamot and chervil under a tree or in a shady corner.

For a ladder garden, lay a ladder along the ground and plant herbs between the rungs.

If you like more formal displays, you will need to establish crisp-edged beds and limit the herbs you grow to those with neat growing habits, keeping them well clipped. Such gardens can be simple or grand, large or small, limited to herbs alone or a combination of neat patterns of herbs, vegetables and flowers.

One of the most spectacular formal displays I've seen is the potager *(or kitchen garden) at the Chateau of Villandry in France. It covers two acres and is made up of nine squares, each planted in a different pattern. I like to admire gardens like these, but prefer a rambling garden for myself.*

Basil
Ocimum

Of the many varieties, the most commonly grown are the sweet and bush basil. The bush basil is only quite small, about 6 in high, whereas the sweet basil can grow up to 2 ft.

Basil likes a sunny spot and plenty of water on a hot day as the leaves wilt.

Try some of the other varieties as they are bound to delight you, especially the curly-leafed and purple types.

PESTO

Make lots of this summery paste when basil is in season and store in sterile, screw-top jars in the refrigerator. A film of olive oil on top will help seal it.

MAKES 1 ¼ CUPS (10 FL OZ)

2 bunches fresh basil, approx 7 ½ oz
2 cloves garlic, peeled and roughly chopped
⅔ cup (2 ½ oz) pinenuts (pignolias)
½ cup (2 oz) Parmesan cheese, freshly grated
½ cup (4 fl oz) olive oil

Remove basil leaves, wash and dry well. In summer, dry the leaves in the sun, spread out on clean tea towels. Put into the food processor with the garlic and pinenuts and process until mixture forms a paste. Add the cheese and drizzle in the oil.

RHONDA'S PASTA AND BASIL SALAD

Pasta salads have become very popular over the past decade or so, which is understandable because there are so many different types of pasta available and because it combines so well with many different types of food.

SERVES 6

6 oz corkscrew (spiral) pasta
¼ green cabbage, finely shredded

6 radishes, thinly sliced
1 small green sweet pepper (capsicum), seeded and thinly sliced
8 oz cherry tomatoes, halved if large
½ telegraph cucumber, thinly sliced
1 ripe avocado, peeled and sliced
½ bunch chives and extra basil leaves for garnish

DRESSING
2 bunches fresh basil
4 cloves garlic, peeled
2 tspns Dijon-style mustard
juice of ½ lemon
¾ cup (6 fl oz) olive oil
salt and freshly ground black pepper

Cook pasta in rapidly boiling salted water until *al dente*. Drain and cool. Prepare the vegetables.

To make dressing, wash basil and strip leaves from stalks, reserving a few for garnishing. Put leaves in container of food processor with garlic, mustard and half the lemon juice and blend until finely chopped. Slowly add oil through the opening of the container with motor still running and process until dressing thickens. Season and add remaining lemon juice to taste.

Toss all salad ingredients together in a bowl with the dressing. Snip over the chives and garnish with reserved basil leaves.

BELINDA'S SAVORY TART

This tart is excellent, perfect for lunch with a green salad. It is important to use the right-sized pastry shell, otherwise the filling won't set.

SERVES 6–8

1 lb mascarpone (Italian cream cheese)
1 ½ cups (¾ lb) ricotta
3 x 2 oz eggs
3 tblspns (1 ½ fl oz) cream
1 ½ tspns flaky sea salt
freshly ground black pepper
1 small bunch basil, freshly chopped, or
3-4 tblspns (1 ½ –2 fl oz) pesto (see page 129)

½ cup (2 oz) Parmesan cheese, freshly grated
pre-baked pastry shell (see glossary), either a deep, loose-based
9 in or shallow-based 11 in version
fresh tomato slices

Preheat oven to 350°F (180°C/Gas 4).

Put all the ingredients (except pastry and tomato slices) into the food processor and process until mixed together. Do not over-process. Pour into the pre-baked shell and cook in oven for 35–40 minutes, or until set and slightly puffed. Remove and let settle.

The tomato slices can be added for decorative effect, placed around the edges of the tart halfway through baking so that they don't drop to the bottom.

Bay Tree
Laurus nobilis

The bay is a perennial evergreen tree and is not, strictly speaking, a herb, although it is used extensively in bouquet garnis for flavoring. It grows up to 49 ft.

Bays like a sunny spot but will tolerate some shade. Though slow growing, they are not difficult to grow and like pots. They like to be fertilized occasionally and you mustn't let them dry out.

FRESH HERB WREATHS

I remember once in late spring coming across a flower stall at the markets in Salamanca Place, Hobart. The flowers were all freshly picked and some were arranged in posies, others tied together in big bunches. It was one of the most beautiful flower stalls I'd ever seen, not just because of the myriad colors and abundance of the display, but because the arrangements were so natural, spilling out hither and thither. It was clear that

someone really cared.

I asked the man who was serving where the flowers were grown. To my dismay, he was rather gruff and grumpy, but he did tell me they were grown on his herb and flower farm just outside Woodbridge, south of Hobart.

A few days later, en route to the salmon and ocean trout farms on Bruny Island, we made a slight detour to the Woodbridge flower farm. It was set high up on a hill looking out over the d'Entrecasteaux Channel to the island. The house was large and gabled and surrounded by the most magnificent garden in the rambling 'cottage garden' style; down one side ran a vegetable and herb patch.

As a memory of this beautiful place I bought a herb wreath from the small shop inside the house and it hangs in my kitchen to this day. It is made from both herbs and flowers. You can make yours with a mixture of both, or just with herbs, or perhaps with just one herb. A wreath made just from bay leaves is a lovely gift for a cook because the leaves can be snipped off and used in cooking.

1. Make or buy a base. Many small handcraft shops sell ready-made vine wreaths. If making one, use grape, lantana or wisteria vines and start making a circle (of whatever size you want), then another. Now twine the vines in and out, going around and around until you reach the desired thickness. The wreaths can be either thick or thin.

2. Pick herbs (and flowers, if you like) and attach in bunches to the wreath or work the stems in to follow each other in a circle. Alternatively, group the herbs or flowers at the bottom. Lavender, bay, rosemary, sage, flowering chives and thyme are all good.

3. When you have finished, add a large bow or attach a small wire loop to the back and hang up to dry.

CASSOULET

A rich French dish of baked beans. In typical French fashion, its composition is the source of endless dispute.

Originally from the south-west of the country, just about every town has its own version, the major variations being from Toulouse (where preserved goose is considered essential), Castelnaudary (beans, pork and sausages) and Carcassonne (where leg of mutton, preserved goose and partridge are a must). Here is a simple, but very delicious, version. Start the preparation the day before.

SERVES 8–10

1 ½ lb cannellini beans
1 ½ lb bacon pieces, cut in chunks
2 lb pork skin, diced
1 smoked neck of pork
14 good-quality pork sausages, approx 2 lb
1 pig's trotter
3 small onions, peeled
3 bay leaves
1 clove
4 black peppercorns
dried breadcrumbs

Soak the beans overnight in water to cover.

Next day, brown the bacon pieces in a large, ovenproof casserole dish. Add all the meats, onions, bay leaves, clove and peppercorns and cover with water. Bring to a boil, turn down the heat and cook gently for about 1 ½ hours.

Remove meats fom pot, reserving the stock. Put drained, rinsed beans into stock and simmer very gently, not letting them boil, until *al dente*. They should be firm but not mushy.

Preheat oven to 425°F (220°C/Gas 7).

Slice the meats and return to the pot. Bring back to simmering point. Spoon out excess stock so that it comes about 1 in under the top of the beans. Sprinkle with the breadcrumbs and cook in the oven 15–20 minutes.

Borage
Borago officinalis

A lovely, though rather undisciplined, addition to the garden, it is not fussy about soil as long as drainage is good and there is plenty of sun.

The dainty blue flowers of borage look lovely scattered through summer salads; floating on top of punches and cold soups (borscht, cucumber); or sugared and used to decorate cakes. The leaves too, when picked young, can be added to salads. Both the leaves and flowers can also be used in vinegars and oils.

SUMMER CANAPES

Cut slices of cucumber ⅛ in thick. Sprinkle with flaky sea salt and let drain in a colander for 1 hour.

Wash off the salt and dry well.

Onto each cucumber slice, put a dab of fresh ricotta or cottage cheese. Garnish with black sesame seeds and a small borage flower.

BORAGE FINGER SANDWICHES

Trim crusts from thinly sliced white bread. Spread with softened cream cheese and sprinkle with a little cayenne or chilli powder and finely shredded borage leaves. Stack the slices to form two layers and cut into bars. Top each canape with a tiny borage flower.

Coriander
Coriandrum sativum

Coriander (cilantro) likes lots of sun and a light, rich, well-drained soil. Sow the seeds in spring. It will grow up to 2 ft in height and is best planted outdoors as it can smell rather unpleasant when growing.

Coriander is a dainty, feathery herb, prone to go to seed quickly. These seeds should be picked before they drop off and, once dried, can be used in curries and preserves and are good with fish.

CHAR-GRILLED JUMBO SHRIMP

A lovely summer lunchtime dish. Serve with a big green salad.

SERVES 6

48 green jumbo shrimp, peeled but with tails left intact
1 large clove garlic, diced
1 chilli, diced
bunch fresh coriander (cilantro), chopped (reserve some sprigs for garnish)
virgin olive oil
white wine vinegar

In a large bowl, mix together the jumbo shrimps, garlic, chilli, coriander and a little olive oil. Toss together well. Let marinate for 2–3 hours.

Heat the char-grill (or barbecue) and cook the shrimps quickly on both sides. Arrange on a plate and brush with a little oil and vinegar. Decorate with a few sprigs of coriander. Serve with wedges of fresh lime.

Dill
Anethum graveolens

With its pretty, feathery tops, dill is a very pretty — and useful — addition to the garden. It likes lots of sun, protection from strong winds and a well-drained soil. A fast-growing annual, it often self-seeds and can grow up to 3 ft in warm climates.

Both the leaves and seeds can be used in cooking. The latter are often used to add flavor to pickles.

CHAR-GRILLED CRAYFISH

SERVES 4–6

12 large uncooked freshwater crayfish (yabbies)
6 tblspns (3 oz) melted butter
¼ cup (2 fl oz) lemon juice
2 tblspns (1 fl oz) honey
2 tblspns chopped dill
2 tblspns snipped chives
freshly ground black pepper

Heat the char-grill or barbecue.

Rinse freshwater crayfish under running water. Snip along both sides of the underside and remove tail plate — this enables marinade to penetrate more effectively.

Mix together the remaining ingredients and brush crayfish with the mixture. Char-grill or barbecue for 8–10 minutes or until cooked, brushing frequently with marinade and turning from time to time.

GRAVLAX

This Swedish way of curing fish has become very popular in many restaurants, but you can do it at home too. It's lovely served cut into thin strips with julienned strips of cucumber and a light dressing.

SERVES 4–6

half side ocean trout or *salmon*
⅔ cup (5 oz) flaky sea salt
⅔ cup (5 oz) white sugar
1 tblspn cracked pepper
2 large bunches dill,
finely chopped
2 lemon leaves, washed and finely chopped
cognac (optional)

Remove any bones from the fish with a pair of tweezers or small sharp knife. Trim off fat and fins. Score the skin to allow brine to penetrate.

Mix together the sea salt, sugar, pepper, chopped dill and lemon leaves in a bowl. Spread half the mixture over the skin of the fish, then lay fish flesh side up on a large sheet of aluminum foil. Cover fish with remaining mixture, packing more onto the fleshier parts and putting only a little on the tail. Add a dash of cognac and more sugar and salt if needed — it needs to be coated like breadcrumbs as the mixture 'cooks' the fish.

Wrap the fish securely in the foil and set on a tray in the refrigerator, covered with a tea towel. Leave for 1–2 days in the refrigerator, turning fish from time to time to distribute the 'cure'.

To serve, scrape off most of the dill mixture, spray with a little cognac if desired and slice very thinly. Serve with wedges of lemon.

Keeps up to 1 week in the refrigerator.

Lemongrass
Cymbopogon citratus

I first came across this lovely herb in my mother's farm garden. It was growing in a large clump amongst the pink hibiscus and purple bougainvillea, and looked to me like long grass. 'Come on', she said, 'I'll make you a pot of lemongrass tea.' She cut some of the long sharp blades with a pair of scissors, took them inside, washed and then snipped them into a warmed teapot.

There are times when I find my mother's ideas wacky, but this wasn't one of them. The tea was delicious, refreshing and subtle. Since that time, I have become a great fan of lemongrass.

The Thai and Vietnamese people use it extensively in their cooking, cutting it from the base of the root (the fleshy white part) where the flavor is more intense.

The leafy green part is not as pungent but can be used for steeping in hot water to make a refreshing tea.

Lemongrass can grow up to 6 ½ ft in height, quickly forming a thick clump. It likes lots of sun, water and rich soil and it spreads rapidly so give it plenty of room.

POACHED SALMON IN COCONUT MILK

Lemongrass is an essential ingredient in this recipe: along with the other herbs and roots, it is used as an infusion with coconut milk. The beauty of this dish is that you don't have to stick to the salmon as the major ingredient. You can substitute chicken (this will need to be cooked for approx 5–6 minutes), mushrooms (try a mixture of oyster, shiitake and Swiss brown) and other fish (like ocean trout or snapper) for the salmon, so it doesn't have to be expensive.

The flavor is better if you take the trouble to make fresh coconut milk but if not, a good-quality, tinned variety will do. Reduce the number of chillies if you don't like your food too hot.

SERVES 4

3 cups (24 fl oz) coconut milk
2 stalks lemongrass, cut on the bias
1 coriander (cilantro) root, crushed
1 knob galangal (Thai ginger), peeled and finely sliced
1 clove garlic, crushed
pinch white sugar
13 oz salmon (or chicken), cut into 1 in cubes,
bones removed
¼–⅓ cup (2–2 ⅔ fl oz) fish sauce
juice of 3–4 limes
3–6 small chillies, crushed
8 kaffir lime leaves (or lime leaves)
3–4 shallots (brown onions), crushed (optional)

In a medium saucepan, infuse the coconut milk with the lemongrass, coriander root, galangal, garlic, brown onions and sugar for about 10 minutes over low heat. Bring to a boil then throw in the salmon. Poach for 1 minute, then stir in the fish sauce, lime juice, chillies and lime leaves.

Remove from heat — it should be soupy and taste sour, salty and hot. Serve with steamed jasmine rice.

Nasturtiums
Tropaeolum majus

Nasturtiums love full sun, except where the climate is very hot, and ordinary soil with good drainage. They spread copiously and both the flowers and leaves can be eaten. The leaves add a zingy taste to a salad and are wonderful for lining platters. The separated flower petals bring any salad alive and are also pretty on top of cakes, pizzas and muffins.

STUFFED NASTURTIUM LEAVES

Wash medium-sized nasturtium leaves and dry well. Spread a thick layer of herbed cream cheese over one half of each leaf; fold the other half of the leaf over and press together lightly to seal. Don't close them up completely. Sprinkle the filling with paprika. Chill and serve with canapes.

HERBED CREAM CHEESE

4 oz softened cream cheese

½ cup (4 oz) ricotta

1 clove garlic, crushed

juice of ½ lemon

4 tblspns freshly chopped herbs (basil, parsley, oregano)

2 tblspns snipped chives

freshly ground black pepper

Put all the ingredients in the food processor and process until smooth. Chill well. Use for filling Nasturtium Blossoms and Leaves; as a filling for Finger Sandwiches (page 132) or spread on crusty French bread. Also nice as a dip for crudites.

STUFFED NASTURTIUM BLOSSOMS

Pipe herbed cream cheese into the center of cleaned blossoms. Chill well and serve with canapes.

Parsley
Petroselinum crispum

There are many different types of parsley, the best known being the tight, curly-leaved one and the flat-leaved (Italian) parsley. They are biennials, usually treated as annuals, and enjoy a sunny spot with rich well-dug, moist soil.

Parsley makes a pretty edging for vegetable beds. Seeds take four to six weeks to germinate and soaking beforehand in tepid water for 24 hours hurries them up a bit.

Parsley is rich in vitamins A, B and C, so if you have it growing, use it generously over salads and savory dishes.

B'STILLA

Although there a number of stages of preparation in this magnificent Moroccan dish, the techniques are not difficult. You can make it the day before and reheat it before serving. Another buttered pastry sheet can be added to the top if the previous one looks tired.

SERVES 8

THE CHICKEN

4 lb chicken pieces (thighs and legs)
1 bunch fresh flat-leaf (Italian) parsley, chopped
4–6 sprigs fresh coriander (cilantro), chopped
2 large onions, grated or minced
1 ¼ tspns ground ginger
1 tspn freshly ground black pepper
½ tspn powdered saffron
¼ tspn turmeric
3 cinnamon sticks
coarse salt
3 cups (24 fl oz) water
½ cup (4 oz) butter

THE ALMONDS

2 ⅔ tblspns (1 ⅓ fl oz) peanut oil
3 cups (1 lb) whole blanched almonds
2 tspns cinnamon
¼ cup (1 ½ oz) confectioners' (icing) sugar
¼ cup (2 oz) butter, cut into pieces

THE EGG MIXTURE

½ cup (4 fl oz) lemon juice
10 eggs, well-beaten
coarse salt, to taste

THE PASTRY

½ cup (4 oz) butter, melted and clarified
8 oz phyllo pastry, approximately 14 sheets

Combine all the ingredients for the chicken in a large pot or saucepan, cover and bring to a boil. Lower the heat and simmer for 1 hour, stirring occasionally.

While the chicken cooks, prepare the almond layer. Heat the oil and brown the almonds lightly, in two batches. Drain well on paper towels. When cool, chop coarsely in food processor, being careful not to over-process. Quickly mix in the cinnamon, confectioners' sugar and butter and set aside.

When the hour is up, prepare egg mixture. Remove chicken pieces from saucepan, put into a bowl and set aside to cool. Discard cinnamon sticks and any loose bones. Bring remaining liquid to boil and reduce to 14 fl oz. Lower heat until simmering and add lemon juice. Pour in the beaten eggs, stirring constantly over a medium heat until they are cooked — they should be curdy, but not dry. Add salt to taste. Transfer to a baking dish to cool.

Shred chicken into pieces, removing skin, bones and gristle. Season with extra salt, pepper and ginger if necessary.

Preheat oven to 425°F (220°C/Gas 7). To prepare pastry, brush a little of the butter over the base of an 11–12 in cake, pizza or paella dish. Cover the pan with a sheet of pastry. Drape another five or six leaves over the pan, overlapping them so that they extend beyond the sides of the dish and the base is completely covered. Lightly brush each one with the melted butter.

Strew the chicken pieces over entire bottom of the pastry-lined tin, making sure they are even. Cover with the egg mixture and then sprinkle over the almond mixture.

Cover with two pastry leaves, folded in half and unbuttered, to make a firm top. Fold the extended pastry leaves over the top of the pie to cover and enclose and then place another four or five buttered leaves on top, tucking them in around the edges to make a neat package. Brush with more butter, drizzling some down the sides of the pan.

Bake in oven for 15 minutes. Remove from oven and use a spatula to loosen the pie around the edges. Invert onto a large baking sheet, return to oven for a further 20 minutes until golden brown.

Remove from oven and dust lightly with icing sugar and cinnamon.

HERB-CRUSTED FRESH SALMON

This is another lovely way to serve fresh salmon or ocean trout. It barely needs cooking. You can serve it for brunch with scrambled eggs and toast or just with a green salad and new baby potatoes for lunch.

SERVES 6–8

1 small bunch fresh watercress
1 bunch fresh parsley
6 scallions (shallots, spring onions)
2 tblspns (1 oz) superfine (caster) sugar
1 tblspn (½ oz) flaky sea salt
1 tblspn crushed black mustard seeds
freshly ground white pepper to taste
all-purpose (plain) flour
half side fresh salmon, approx 1 lb, skin on,
bones removed

Chop together on a board the watercress, parsley and scallions. Throw in the sugar and salt, and mix in the mustard seeds. Add pepper to taste.

Lightly flour the fleshy side of the fish (this helps the herbs to stick) and press herb mixture onto the flesh. They should form a thick crust.

Sprinkle some sea salt onto a plate and place the fish on it, skin side down. Refrigerate for ½ hour to let it settle. It will form a little of its own brine.

Brush a flat, black pan, or barbecue hotplate, with oil, remove excess with paper towels. Make sure it gets very hot. Seal the fish, flesh-side first, for 20 seconds (a few of the herbs will come off), then turn over onto skin side and cook until blackened, 20–30 seconds. Remove and let it rest for 10 minutes before slicing into 1 in pieces.

TABBOULI

I guess everyone has their favorite tabbouli recipe. In this one, the crushed wheat isn't soaked beforehand, which gives the salad more texture.

In a salad bowl, combine ⅓ cup (2 ⅔ fl oz) olive oil, the juice of 2 lemons, 1 tspn each of salt and honey. Add ½ cup (4 oz) of bulgar (crushed wheat). Chop a large bunch of flat-leafed (Italian) parsley and about quarter that amount of fresh mint. Dice 2–3 ripe tomatoes and 2 Lebanese cucumbers. Mix all the ingredients together and garnish with a small, chopped red or green sweet pepper (capsicum). Before serving, let sit for 1 hour, or until wheat has softened. Serves 4–6.

Rosemary
Rosmarinus officinalis

Although it gets off to a slow start, rosemary can live to a ripe old age, 30 years or more. It grows well in a pot and can be trimmed to a nice shape. As a native of the Mediterranean, it likes a sunny spot, preferably near salt water. In Spain, France, Italy and Portugal, its perfume can be smelt far out to sea.

Rosemary prefers sandy, light, loamy soils and is hardy and drought-resistant. The more sunshine it receives, the better for building up stores of oils in its leaves and flowers. Be judicious when cooking with this pungent herb as it can be overpowering if not used carefully.

MEDITERRANEAN BAKED FISH

At the Fifth Symposium of Australian Gastronomy, held in Adelaide, South Australia, participants were asked to bring a basket each of seafood and bread to the Sunday lunch. The idea revolved around the 'loaves and fishes' miracle, with former South Australian premier Don Dunstan placing five loaves and two fishes on the luncheon table, then inviting everyone to bring their food forward.

Restaurateur Maggie Beer had organized three huge round handmade baskets. She had covered their bases with grape leaves and filled them with a mixture of smoked and marinated fish, oysters in their shells and a variety of loaves of many different shapes and sizes. One of the most delicious fish dishes was Ann Oliver's, a whole fish with herbs and olives.

SERVES 8–10

*1 x 6 lb white-fleshed fish (like snapper), cleaned
and scaled
½ cup (4 fl oz) olive oil
½ cup (4 fl oz) lemon juice
handful fresh basil, puréed with a little olive oil
salt and pepper
2 cups (16 fl oz) homemade Italian-style tomato sauce
1 ¼ cups (6 ½ oz) pitted black olives
blanched zest (rind) of 2 lemons, finely grated
leaves from 1 sprig fresh rosemary*

Preheat oven to 400°F (200°C/Gas 6).

Score the fish on both sides with a sharp knife. Combine oil and lemon juice and roll fish in mixture, then brush inside with the basil purée. Season to taste with salt and pepper on both sides, place in a baking dish.

Mix together the tomato sauce, olives, lemon zest and rosemary leaves and pour over the fish, pushing into the scored sections on both sides. Bake in oven for 20–30 minutes, or until flesh is just cooked.

BUTTERFLY LEG OF LAMB

A splendid dish for a summer barbecue.

*1 medium–small leg of lamb, 'butterflied'
½ cup (4 fl oz) olive oil
¼ cup (2 fl oz) lemon juice
¼ cup (2 fl oz) white wine
1 clove garlic, peeled and diced
few strips lemon zest (peel)
freshly chopped rosemary
soy sauce, to taste*

Ask your butcher to 'butterfly' the lamb.

Put it into an earthenware dish. Mix together remaining ingredients and pour over the lamb. Allow to marinate, covered, for a few hours or overnight in the refrigerator. Turn the lamb from time to time.

Barbecue the lamb over hot coals, keeping it flat. Turn and baste it frequently with the marinade. It will need 30–40 minutes and should be pink and juicy inside.

Sage

Salvia officinalis

Sage comes in many different varieties — purple, red, and broad-leaved — but the commonly available garden variety has the best flavor.

It is a hardy perennial shrub which grows about 2 ft high on poor, alkaline soil. It will benefit from plenty of dolomite or lime and dislikes wet weather and overwatering.

In the kitchen, sage is synonymous with stuffing. You will find it used to season game and poultry, not just for its aromatic flavor but because it helps break down the fats and oils in the meat, thereby aiding digestion.

LOIN OF VEAL WITH SAGE AND GREEN PEPPERCORNS

Delicious with a green salad and good cold.

SERVES 8–10

3 ½ lb loin of veal (eye or top loin) or *boneless veal roast*
2 tblspns green peppercorns, drained
20 fresh sage leaves
salt and pepper
6–8 rashers of bacon, rind removed

Preheat oven to 375°F (190°C/Gas 5).

Spread the meat out flat. Put a sheet of plastic wrap over and under the meat. Flatten the meat with a mallet. Remove top layer of plastic wrap, spread over the green peppercorns and the sage and sprinkle with salt and pepper.

Roll up the meat, removing the sheet of plastic wrap from underneath. Tie with string every 1 in. Place on a sheet of aluminum foil, sprinkle outside of meat with salt and pepper. Cover with the bacon, wrap foil around, place in baking dish.

Cook in oven for 45–55 minutes or until juices run clear when pricked in center. Remove from oven and let stand for 10 minutes, unwrap. Remove string and cut into slices.

Variation: Deglaze pan juices with a little cognac and add some sour cream and lemon juice to taste. Serve with the meat. Fresh tarragon or basil are nice substitutes for the sage.

Note: Green peppercorns in brine are available from specialty food shops and delicatessens.

JANICE'S HERBED CHEESE BREAD

Delicious served straight from the oven, but also good wrapped in a tea-towel and packed warm to take on a picnic. Use any fresh chopped herb of your choice.

SERVES 8

TOPPING
2 onions, chopped
¼ cup (2 fl oz) olive oil
2 tblspns fresh herbs (sage and parsley), chopped
2 cloves garlic, crushed
2 tblspns (1 oz) butter

BREAD

4 cups (1 lb) self-raising flour

1 tspn salt

¼ cup (2 oz) butter

1 tblspn fresh sage, chopped

1 ½ cups (6 oz) Cheddar (tasty) cheese, grated

1 ½ cups (12 fl oz) milk and water, mixed together and

soured with juice of ½ lemon

Preheat oven to 400°F (200°C/Gas 6).

In a frying pan, sauté the onions gently in oil until translucent. Stir through the chopped herbs. In another pan, melt butter and sauté garlic lightly, set aside.

Sift the flour and salt into a large mixing bowl. Rub in the butter until mixture resembles fine breadcrumbs. Stir through the fresh herbs and half of the cheese. Make a well in the center and stir in milk, water and lemon juice using a knife.

Gather mixture into a soft dough, turn out onto a lightly floured surface and gather roughly into a round. Do not knead.

Place the round on a lightly greased baking tray and press out to about 1 ½–2 in thick. Score the surface into eighths and brush top with garlic butter. Cover with onion and herb topping and sprinkle over remaining cheese.

Bake in oven for 35 minutes or until well risen and a lovely crusty golden brown.

Tarragon
Artemisia dracunculus

There are two main types — French and Russian. The French is the one to look for because it has the better flavor. It likes a rich soil and plenty of sun. Water in well during the early settling-in period.

It may disappear in winter but its roots will remain and pop up again next spring. Division of the roots is a good idea every three to four years to help keep the plant healthy.

TARRAGON BUTTER

Tarragon goes well with fish and chicken. Put a few sprigs inside the cavity of either when baking or barbecuing. Or use this tarragon butter to add flavor to broiled (grilled) or pan-fried dishes.

You can substitute any herb for the tarragon.

SERVES 4–6

½ cup (4 oz) softened butter

2–3 tblspns freshly chopped tarragon

2 tblspns (1 fl oz) lemon juice

salt and white pepper

Cream together the butter and tarragon in a small bowl. Add lemon juice and season to taste. Spoon onto a sheet of aluminum foil and roll up in a log shape. Refrigerate until firm. Remove and slice into eight rounds.

TARRAGON CHICKEN

SERVES 4

1 medium chicken, approx 3 lb
2 sprigs fresh tarragon
peeled zest (rind) of ½ lemon
1 onion, peeled and quartered
salt and freshly ground black pepper
2 tblspns (1 oz) butter, softened
1 tblspn freshly chopped tarragon
2 cups (16 fl oz) chicken stock (broth)
extra stock (broth) if needed

SAUCE
½ cup (4 fl oz) cream
1 tblspn freshly chopped tarragon
salt and pepper

Preheat oven to 400°F (200°C/Gas 6).

Trim chicken and wipe dry. Put the tarragon sprigs, lemon zest, and onion quarters into the cavity. Season with salt and pepper. Mix together the butter and tarragon and rub over the skin. Truss and place on a rack in a baking dish, adding chicken stock to the baking pan.

Cook for 15 minutes, baste with the stock then turn down the oven to 350°F (180°C/Gas 4). Cook another hour, basting three to four times, adding more stock if needed. Chicken is cooked if juices run clear when a skewer is inserted in thickest part of thigh. Remove chicken and cover with aluminum foil whilst preparing sauce.

Reduce pan juices on top of stove to about 2 ⅔ tblspns (1 ⅓ fl oz). Pour in the cream and add the chopped tarragon. Season to taste. Cut chicken into serving pieces adding juices to the sauce in the pan. Serve with the sauce.

Thyme
Thymus

Thymus vulgaris (or culinary thyme) grows well in a light, well-drained, preferably alkaline soil. It likes full sun. On the hillsides of the Mediterranean, its fragrance is particularly strong. The ancient Greeks burnt it as an offering to the gods, a practice which later spread elsewhere. It was also used as an insect repellent.

HERBED VINEGARS AND OILS

Not only do these look pretty, they also add flavor to all manner of dishes. You can combine two or more herbs and add seeds, chillies and berries to taste. A twist of lemon zest (rind) is also a nice addition.

Pick herbs for vinegars and oils early in the morning after the dew has dried. Wash and dry well, then bruise slightly before putting them into a wide-mouthed glass jar or decorative bottle of your choice. Cover with vinegar at room temperature, filling to the brim. Close tightly. Set the bottle or jar in a sunny window for a couple of weeks, then store in a cool place for another month. Alternatively, you can heat the vinegar and pour it over the herbs and let steep overnight.

Strain the vinegar, if you like, and add a new fresh

herb sprig. This step is not necessary, though, for flavoring. Herb blossoms make pretty additions.

For the oils, choose fresh herbs of your choice, wash and dry them well and put into sterile jars and cover with virgin olive oil.

MARINATED FETA OR GOAT CHEESE

These lovely cheeses will keep for 1–2 weeks in a cool place. Use herbs of your choice — thyme and rosemary are good.
Serve sliced with tossed salad greens as a first course; or eat on pieces of crusty bread for lunch.
If using feta, cut it into 1 in slices and soak overnight in equal quantities of water and milk, drain well and dry on paper towels. If using goat cheese *(chevre)*, slice into rounds and salt it lightly with a flaky sea salt. Let drain overnight in the refrigerator, then scrape off the salt before proceeding.

1 lb block feta or *round goat cheese*
6 sprigs fresh thyme
1 bay leaf
2–3 fresh red chillies
2 cloves garlic, peeled
zest (rind) of ½ lemon
10–15 small black olives
approx 3 cups (24 fl oz) olive oil

Put the cheese into a wide-mouthed clean sterile jar. Arrange remaining ingredients in jar and cover with olive oil.

THE BOOK OF THE MARKET

begins and ends in medias res,
a classically 'indifferent whole'.
We wander through it like Casaubon, clutching
lists we've pencilled on the backs of envelopes.

    Tomatoes kiss
with puckered lips, drooling
ichor from their broken skins.
Their colour clamours to be fed:
we prod them gently, bring our faces
close like mothers bending over babies,
as if to shush that red.
The prawns respond by crooking
helpless fingers, tiny segments
soft as sucking blisters.
The raspberries are nursing nipples . . .

    We potter calmly like Casaubon,
clutching the key to all mythologies,
a shopping list. Among the butcher's
bric-a-brac, a cameo
cut on a conch of Wiltshire ham —
five milky roads divide some reddish fields
ploughed neatly as a fingerprint, calm
as a corpse.

    Everywhere, memento mori —
the turnip's scar is written here;
onions trundle from a pelican scoop
like anarchist bombs; the cobs of corn
are similes for nooses neatly tied;
lobster and crabs, breastplates and pliers,
wirecutters and greaves, blending the vocabulary
of different wars . . .

    Strawberries resume a sub-plot
of revolt, a peasant rising:
the ringleaders' heads arranged in punnets,
sunburnt, pitted, unshaven.
Grapes are held aloft, their shining sacs
jostle like traitorous bowels . . .

    There is no end, except that,
in medias res, the kippers'
quotidian violins assume the antique tones
and smokey varnish of Cremona.
We see the carrots under glass,
as items in a treasure house —
each bunch an old Elizabethan gauntlet,
the tapered fingers creased with wear . . .

CRAIG RAINE

Fruits

Pitted Fruits

Prunus *species*

Plums fallen to the ground
Are singing with sweetness.
Bees are busy in them.

Is it because of the sweetness of the plums
That the bees are so ecstatic?
They roll about like clowns, are drunken with hilarity.

ROSEMARY DOBSON, FROM 'DAILY LIVING — WAITING FOR THE POSTMAN'

A summer's day. The cicadas are singing ecstatically, the sky is a deep blue and a gentle breeze caresses my skin. As I stroll through the orchard with the old Italian farmer, I feel close to heaven.

On the trees I see plums of many different hues (blood red, mauve, purple, blue) and blushing yellow peaches. The farmer picks a dozen for me. He is deft and certain of which ones to pick. He makes no mistake. I am overcome by the beauty of these perfectly ripened, warm fruits. Yet the farmer is fed up, and just nods in acquiescence. He has been picking for days now, in the hot sun, and to him they are just another crop to be sorted and packed.

Growing fruits and vegetables commercially is a vastly different proposition from growing them at home. The competition in the commercial market is intense and often heart-breaking. In addition to natural disasters to contend with (drought, flood, pests) farmers face intense competition from imported produce. With a few trees at home, you're more likely to be able to enjoy the fruits of your labor — and to appreciate their beauty. True, we eat to live but the soul also requires nourishment. I can think of nothing more beautiful than a bowl of ripe aromatic peaches, nectarines and plums on a summer's day. For the cook, the very sight of such beauty is a source of inspiration. When picked fresh, with their leaves intact, it seems a crime to tamper with them, though I admit there are many delicious ways of cooking with pitted fruits.

The peach has a certain sumptuousness, speaking to me of

lushness and long, languorous summer days. I understand why for the ancient Chinese it was so highly venerated: poets, painters and sculptors celebrated it as a symbol of immortality and friends gave each other peaches, real or in porcelain, to show their affection. In the imperial gardens of Changan, the golden yellow peaches of Samarkand grew to the size of goose eggs.

The French author Colette also understood the nature of the peach. In The Ripening Seed, *an older woman is preparing to seduce a chaste young man:*

Mme Dalleray was not expecting him, or so it seemed, for he found her reading. He felt assured of his welcome, however, when he saw the studied half-light in the 'salon' and noticed the almost invisible table from which rose a pervasive aroma of slow-ripening peaches, of red cantaloup melon cut in slices the shape of crescent moons, and a black coffee poured over crushed ice.

Of all the stone fruits, the peach (both its fruits and its flowers) is the one I love most. The others — nectarines, apricots, plums and cherries — come a close second, though, because I am a devoted fan of all stone fruits. I think they're best eaten fresh. Of course there's always the problem of glut, or of having too many of one thing when they're in season, which is why recipes abound for jams, preserves and pickles. Giving away baskets of homemade preserves to friends and neighbors is one answer. They're a lovely gift for anyone, especially if the basket is attractively wrapped in clear cellophane and tied with ribbon.

Nectarines belong to the same species as peaches, Prunus persica. *They are often called smooth-skinned peaches but are less hardy. Their nectar-like taste probably gave the tree its name.*

Plums happen to be one of the most popular of all home-grown fruits. They have been cultivated since classical times and come in a glorious myriad of skin colors — reds, yellows, purples, blues and blacks. The color of the flesh varies enormously too, from yellow to green to purple or blood red; some are sour even when ripe and some are very sweet. The many species and varieties differ greatly in their habits and climatic requirements. The European plum, which is the result of the mingling of many hybrid races, has high winter chilling requirements whereas both the Japanese plum and the cherry plum will grow in temperate coastal areas. Both the Greeks and Romans had a number of cultivars and they were aware of the difference between cooking and eating types.

Cherries too have been cultivated in Europe since Roman times. The sweet cherry is a native of west Asia; the sour cherry is grown as an ornamental tree, but the fruit can be used in jams. Both are native to Europe, though sweet cherries probably originated from somewhere around Turkey and Greece. In Britain during the eighteenth and nineteenth centuries, cherry orchards were often underplanted with strawberries and currants — you can imagine how beautiful they must have looked. In some grand eighteenth century gardens, cherries were produced all year round. Small trees were often grown in pots which enabled their growth to be controlled and the plants to be forced. The trees were taken indoors and the dessert served straight from the branch!

Like cherries, apricots are vigorous growers and begin producing worthwhile crops after three to four years. Picked warm from the tree, they have a beautiful smell and delicious taste. Sadly, because they don't travel well, most people have never had the pleasure of tasting them like this. There are a surprising number of varieties which range in colors from pale yellow to a deep orangey-red. The apricot originated in central Asia and western China; around Beijing, it grows wild in the mountains. From China, it was taken along the old silk routes through India and to the Middle East. It thrives in temperate regions, needing cold winters for good fruit set and warm to hot summers.

Peaches and Nectarines
Prunus persica

A neglected peach tree is a sorry sight. All summer long it drops its bruised and rotten fruit on the ground. I have lived next door to such a one for years, and although its pink blossom in spring always fills me with joy, its wasted fruits make me sad. They're also a nuisance to clean up.

Although peaches and nectarines are distinct fruits, their requirements are so similar that they can generally be regarded as identical. Both are very popular with home gardeners, though the peach is more widely grown.

Peaches and nectarines must be grown in well-drained soil, preferring a light sandy loam (though they will tolerate other soils). They grow well in climates where the summer is mild to hot and the winter cool to cold (or cold enough to induce dormancy and prevent shedding of blossom buds) and are best planted in winter whilst dormant.

Variations in size and color are enormous with fruits classified as clingstone (where the flesh clings to the stone), or freestone (where it separates easily from the stone). Except for the J.H. Hale variety, most peaches and nectarines are self-fertile.

Pruning is essential, otherwise you'll get less fruit each year. Peaches and nectarines are usually pruned to a vase shape, though the central leader or pyramid system also works well. The fruit forms on the previous year's new growth and enough wood must be cut each year to stimulate new growth for next year's crop. Problems include curly leaf, brown rot, rust, aphids and fruit fly. Overall, peaches and nectarines are easy trees to manage, provided they are pruned each year and kept in good health. Fruit is usually produced on one-year-old laterals or shoots.

PEACHES IN CHAMPAGNE

To serve six to eight people, choose 6–8 large white or yellow peaches. Try to keep them all the same size. Peel them by dropping into boiling water for 1 minute and slipping off their skins. Cut in halves, remove the stone, then slice into eighths. Put the pieces into a bowl and sprinkle with some superfine (caster) sugar. Pour some dry champagne over the peach slices and let macerate for a little while. Serve at room temperature.

POACHED SUMMER FRUITS

Poached peaches, at the height of summer, are something to behold. They sparkle and glisten in their syrup and in every way are just heavenly.

Make a sugar syrup, but not a sweet one. For every 2 cups (½ qt) of water allow 1 cup (8 oz) of sugar. Dissolve the sugar in the water and then bring to a boil, adding a piece each of lemon and orange zest (rind) to the water. A vanilla pod is a nice addition but not essential.

Now add some fresh firm (but ripe) nectarines, plums, apricots and peaches. Don't use large peaches —

keep all the fruit to about the same size (medium). Poach gently, about 10–12 minutes. Remove from heat and let cool in the syrup.

Chill in the refrigerator and serve with thick runny (double/whipping) cream or mascarpone cream.

MASCARPONE CREAM
2 eggs, separated
¼ cup (2 oz) superfine (caster) sugar
8 oz mascarpone (Italian cream cheese)
2 tblspns (1 fl oz) brandy or Grand Marnier
finely ground fresh coffee grains

In a bowl, beat together the egg yolks, then add the sugar gradually until mixture turns pale yellow and becomes thick. Blend in the mascarpone and then the liqueur. Make sure mixture is smooth, but don't overbeat it, then fold in the stiffly beaten egg whites to lighten. Spoon half the mixture into a serving bowl, sprinkle lightly with coffee grains, then spoon in remaining mixture and sprinkle with more coffee grains. Refrigerate at least 2 hours before serving.
Variation: Ricotta con Caffe is a nice alternative. Allow 2 ⅔ tblspns (1 ⅓ fl oz) strong black coffee and a sprinkling of sugar to each ¾ cup (6 ½ oz) fresh ricotta. Mix together and serve.

SPICY PEACH CHUTNEY

Let the spices float freely in this delicious chutney. They look pretty in the bottle and the cardamom seeds lend a wonderful flavor.

MAKES 2 CUPS (½ QT)

2 lb medium yellow peaches, washed
2 cups (16 fl oz) white vinegar
2 cups (1 lb) sugar
2 tspns fresh ginger, finely grated
1 small whole red chilli, bruised (optional)
6 cloves garlic, finely chopped
1 cinnamon stick
6 cloves
1 tspn black cardamom seeds

Cut peaches into halves, remove the pit, and cut into quarters. Put into a medium–heavy pan with the other ingredients. Bring to a boil and cook for 40–50 minutes or until thickened. Pour into sterile jars and seal.

FRESH FRUIT KUCHEN

Try plums or apricots, as well as peaches (or a mixture of any of them) as the base for this simple delicious pudding. Apples can also be used.

SERVES 6–8

6 medium, fresh peaches, sliced into eighths
3 eggs

1 cup (4 oz) self-raising flour
1 cup (8 fl oz) milk
2 tblspns (1 oz) brown sugar
¼ cup (2 oz) butter, melted
cinnamon
sugar
almonds, chopped
extra butter

Preheat oven to 350°F (180°C/Gas 4). Put the prepared fruit into a 9 in round tin or ovenproof dish. Beat eggs into flour. Add milk, sugar and butter. Pour over fruit. Sprinkle the top with a mixture of cinnamon, sugar, chopped almonds and melted butter. Bake in oven for 40–45 minutes. Test with a skewer. Serve warm with cream.

MEDLEY OF SUMMER FRUIT

SERVES 6–8

Make this at the height of summer. Choose 6 medium-sized nectarines (or peaches). Leave on their skins, halve them, remove the pits and cut into eighths. Put into a pretty serving bowl and sprinkle with superfine (caster) sugar. A little orange juice or Cointreau is a nice addition. Leave to mingle for 1 hour in the refrigerator. Before serving, carefully add 8 oz each fresh hulled small strawberries, blackberries and blueberries (or any berries in season). Mix together very carefully, trying not to let the berries discolor the nectarines. Serve immediately with yogurt or whipped cream flavored with superfine sugar and a good pinch of cardamom powder.

MOROCCAN PEACHES

In Morocco they peel fresh peaches, sprinkle them with sugar and rose water and refrigerate for a few hours. Before serving, the peaches are sprinkled with ground cinnamon and garnished with mint leaves.

Try them also with fresh pistachio nuts. Omit the cinnamon and mint and strew with fresh, coarsely chopped pistachios and pale pink rose petals. Serve with a bowl of whipped cream. Allow one large ripe peach per person.

BROILED PEACHES AND NECTARINES

Simple and good. Choose ripe peaches, nectarines and plums of about the same size. Wash, cut into halves and remove the pits. Put them cut-side up onto a baking tray or heatproof dish and sprinkle lightly with brown sugar.

Heat the broiler (grill) to hot. Put the fruit under and cook for just a minute or until the sugar is melting and beginning to caramelize. Remove and serve immediately with whipped cream or plain yogurt.

Apricots
Prunus armeniaca

Apricots are also popular with home gardeners, perhaps because they are hardy, vigorous growers and produce abundantly. They also travel badly and don't keep well — another reason for trying them in your own garden.

Apricots like well-drained soils and frost-free areas with good air circulation. They can be grown in frost-prone locations provided there are no frosts at flowering time. Large, unthinned trees are less susceptible to frost damage. If you shape them during the first couple of years, they should need little pruning except to remove excess height. Pruning is best done in summer so that the wounds can heal quickly to help prevent fungal and bacterial infection.

As with peaches and nectarines, the best time for planting is winter. Heavy mulching and plenty of water are necessary for a good crop, especially when the trees are young.

A number of varieties are available. A hybrid, the Plumcot, is also available. This is a cross between a plum and an apricot. Like apricots, the trees are vigorous and need little pruning. The fruit is slightly more acid than apricots.

MOROCCAN LAMB WITH APRICOTS AND PRUNES

I love the combination of meat with fruit in Moroccan cooking. This fragrant tagine can be cooked using quinces, apples or pears. You can substitute beef for the lamb, but I particularly like this combination.

SERVES 4–6

1 ¼ cups (8 oz) prunes
3 lb lean lamb (preferably from the leg), cut in cubes
1 medium onion, grated
2 tblspns (1 oz) butter
2 ⅔ tblspns (1 ⅓ fl oz) vegetable oil
1 tspn cinnamon
½ tspn ground ginger
½ tspn ground coriander (cilantro)
salt and freshly ground black pepper
pinch of saffron (optional)
4 tblspns (3 oz) honey
salt and pepper
1 lb fresh apricots, pitted
1–2 tblspns toasted sesame seeds (optional)

Soak the prunes in water to cover. Put the lamb into a medium–large saucepan and cover with water and add the onion, butter, oil and spices. Bring to a boil, cover and simmer for about 1 ½ hours. Drain the prunes and add to the meat along with the honey. Simmer for a further 30 minutes.

Remove meat and prunes from saucepan with a slotted spoon. Reduce liquid in saucepan by boiling hard. Season to taste. Return meat and prunes to saucepan and add the apricots. Cook for 5–10 minutes, just long enough to heat the apricots. Serve sprinkled with toasted sesame seeds.

APRICOT BUTTER

This recipe is also delicious using peaches instead of apricots.

MAKES ABOUT 8 CUPS (2 QT)

4 lb apricots or peaches
sugar
grated lemon zest (rind) and juice

Wash the fruit. Peel by dropping into boiling water and slipping off the skins. Cut into halves, remove the stones and put into a saucepan. Cook slowly, covered, in their own juice until soft. Remove from heat and purée the fruit, then push through a sieve.

For every cup of pulp, allow ½ cup (4 oz) sugar, and lemon zest and juice to taste. Put this mixture into a wide frying pan and cook over low heat, stirring constantly, until sugar dissolves. Continue cooking, stirring frequently so that it doesn't catch, until mixture thickens up and sheets from the spoon.

You will know the butter is done when no rim of liquid separates from the edge of the butter. Pour into hot sterile jars and seal. Use in pre-baked pastry, cakes or spread on bread, toast and croissants.

APRICOT MARINADE

MAKES APPROX 1 ¼ CUPS (10 FL OZ). ENOUGH TO MARINATE 3 LB QUAIL OR CHICKEN DRUMSTICKS, OR PORK SPARE RIBS

10 fresh apricots
1 ⅓ tblspns (⅔ fl oz) light soy sauce
2 ½ tblspns (2 oz) runny honey
1 tspn roasted sesame oil

Wash the apricots, cut them into halves and cook in a little water in a covered saucepan. They only need a few minutes. Drain off the water and put apricots into a food processor or blender.

Purée apricots, tip into a bowl with remaining ingredients and mix well together.

Use this marinade for quail, chicken pieces, lamb and pork. Good for barbecued or char-grilled meat.

HAZELNUT VACHERIN WITH FRESH APRICOTS

This is a very luscious and spectacular dessert. The fresh fruit is lovely, but you could use Apricot Jam (see below) when fresh apricots are not in season. Fresh peaches, cherries or plums can be substituted. Berries are also nice.

In a humid climate, moisture gets into the sugar. Use fresh sugar straight from the packet so that the egg whites won't become runny.

6 egg whites
1 ⅓ cups (10 oz) superfine (caster) sugar
1 ¼ cups (4 oz) ground hazelnuts
1 lb fresh apricots
2 cups (16 fl oz) cream whipped with 2 ⅔ tblspns
(1 ⅓ fl oz) orange liqueur
toffee shards

Preheat the oven to 250°F (120°C/Gas ½).

Cover three baking sheets with non-stick baking paper and, using a 9 in cake tin, draw outlines of three circles onto the paper.

Whisk the egg whites until stiff but not dry. This is best done in a copper bowl by hand with a whisk. Add ¼ cup (2 oz) of the sugar gradually to the whites, whisking continually. With a spatula or slotted spoon, fold through the remaining sugar and the nuts. Be careful not to overwork the mixture — just fold through lightly.

Spoon evenly onto the three prepared circles and spread out to the edges of each circle with the spoon. Bake in the oven for 1 ½ hours or until the meringue has thoroughly dried out. Remove and cool.

Wash the apricots, remove the stones and cut into eighths. A few hours before serving, assemble the cake. Put one meringue round onto a serving platter, spoon over one third of the cream and scatter with half the apricots. Repeat with the next layer, reserving some cream for the top. Insert shards of toffee into the cream on the top layer.

TOFFEE

Melt 1 cup (8 oz) sugar slowly over low heat in a heavy frying pan. Swirl it around, lifting off the heat occasionally, until the sugar is runny and the color is golden brown. Oil a baking dish or marble slab and pour toffee onto it, spreading out with an oiled spoon. Let cool. Break into longish shards when set and hard.

APRICOT JAM

The rising perfume of apricots from the cooking jam will fill any cook with joy. It is a beautiful jam, full of lovely quarters of gleaming, translucent fruit.

MAKES 4 CUPS (1 QT)

2 lb apricots
3 cups (1 ½ lb) white sugar

Wash the apricots and cut into halves. Remove the stones and cut the apricots again into quarters. Put the apricots into a medium-sized bowl and mix with half of the sugar. Cover well.

The following day, drain the juices into a large pan and add the remaining half of the sugar which has been warmed in the oven. Bring to a boil, making sure all the sugar is dissolved. Add the fruit and simmer gently for about 30 minutes or until the apricots are soft and translucent. Stir occasionally with a wooden spoon. Test for setting by putting a little on a cold saucer. Let cool, then pour into sterile screw-top glass jars.

Variation: The addition of 2– 4 tblspns (1 ⅓ –2 fl oz) brandy is nice. Add to the jam when it has reached setting point and simmer another 5 minutes.

Plums

Prunus domestica, P. salicina, P. cerasifera

The many species and varieties of plums are astonishing. A member of the rose family, plums have been so hybridized that it is very difficult to trace the ancestry of many of the more popular varieties.

There are three major categories — the European (Prunus domestica), the Japanese (P. salicina) and the cherry plum (P. cerasifera). The European plum has high chilling requirements, whereas the latter two will grow in coastal areas with a more temperate climate. The damsons (P. insititia) which produce small tart fruit are seldom grown in Australia. Japanese plums include the wonderful blood plums with their deep red flesh, red-skinned plums, and some yellow- and purple-skinned ones. Japanese plums also need a winter cool enough to induce a dormant or rest period, but they will crop well in places too warm for European plums. European plums all have yellow flesh and are usually smaller than the Japanese although the Japanese are more vigorous growers. The cherry plums are hardy but their fruit is inferior to the other two varieties.

Gage and prune plums are usually regarded as subgroups of European plums — the gages have round, sweet, scented fruit, whilst the prunes are varieties with good drying properties, high sugar content and small stones.

Plums like feeding (especially the European ones) and plenty of moisture. However, they withstand drought well and can be grown in soil which is too wet or heavy for other trees.

European plums do not vary much in their growth habits, and can be trained to conform with the traditional vase shape. Japanese varieties can be upright growers like 'Santa Rosa' and 'Mariposa' or spreading growers like 'Narrabeen' and 'Satsuma'. The idea is to open out the upright grower and train the spreading grower to a more upright form. Correct pruning encourages fruit-bud development and cropping on younger wood.

Plum trees produce worthwhile crops three to four years after planting and are less likely to be attacked by pests and diseases than other stone fruits.

PRUNE PLUM AND MASCARPONE TART

The plums need to be tart for this to work well. You need something sharp to contrast with the mascarpone. Use small prune plums.

1 x 10 in pre-baked pastry shell
(cooked in a flan tin with a removable base)
1 lb mascarpone (Italian cream cheese)
2 tspns superfine (caster) sugar
1 lb fresh prune plums
1 tblspn brown sugar

Mix the mascarpone with the sugar, place in the refrigerator.

Cut the prune plums in half, remove the stones and sprinkle with brown sugar. Bake in a moderate oven (350°F/180°C/Gas 4) for 15 minutes so that they are cooked but still hold their shape. Allow to cool but do not refrigerate.

Just prior to serving, spoon the mascarpone into the cooked pastry shell and place the prune plums on top in a decorative fashion.

PLUM AND POLENTA PIE

SERVES 6–8

2 lb blood plums
¼ cup (1 oz) all-purpose (plain) flour
¼ cup (2 oz) superfine (caster) sugar

finely grated zest (rind) of ½ orange
½ tspn cinnamon

PASTRY
⅝ cup (5 oz) softened butter
⅔ cup (5 oz) superfine (caster) sugar
3 egg yolks
1 ¾ cups (7 oz) plain (all-purpose) flour
½ cup (3 oz) polenta or cornmeal (medium ground)
pinch salt
1 tblspn polenta, extra

Prepare the plums by washing them and cutting into large pieces, discarding the pits. Mix together in a bowl with the flour, sugar, zest and cinnamon.

To make the pastry, cream together the butter and sugar, add egg yolks one at a time. Add flour, polenta and salt and combine well. Turn onto a floured board. Wrap in plastic wrap and refrigerate until well chilled.

Preheat oven to 400°F (200°C/Gas 6).

Roll out a little over half the dough onto a floured board. If dough seems too soft and you are having difficulty with it, add a little more flour. Press dough into the base of a 9–10 in flan tin. Sprinkle the extra tablespoon of polenta on the bottom then spoon in the plums.

Roll out remaining dough and cover plums.

Cook in oven for 40 minutes. Serve warm with thick cream.

Variation: A lattice top is a pretty variation. Using a crimped pastry cutter, cut pastry into ½ in strips. Arrange these in lattice pattern on top of pie. Cook as above.

BLOOD PLUM JAM

Follow the recipe for Apricot Jam (page 153), using blood plums instead of apricots. Port is a nice addition to this jam. Add it when the jam has reached setting point and then simmer for another 5 minutes.

Cherries
Prunus avium, P. cerasus

Keep your mouth open — for a ripe cherry.

SARA MIDDA, FROM *IN AND OUT OF THE GARDEN DIARY* 1984

Sweet cherries (Prunus avium) *are potentially large trees, have a short season and are attacked by birds. Unless pruned rigorously they tend to be too big for the home garden. The problem can be partly controlled by planting two varieties about 6 ft apart. Both trees will be stunted by the other's proximity, and pollination should be excellent.*

Sweet cherries are also fastidious about soil, climate and situation and suffer from more diseases than most fruit trees.

Generally speaking, home gardeners do best to grow the sour cherry (P. cerasus). *These can be grown as bushes in the open soil or fan-trained. Sour cherries (of the Kentish and Morello varieties) are also the best for cooking purposes. They are the ones used by the French for clafoutis, and for all manner of conserves, jams and soups throughout other parts of Europe.*

Ask at your nursery for the most suitable variety for your district. Remember that drainage is very important and if the trees are to be grown against a wall, bank the soil so that it slopes away from the wall to drain well. They will grow on most soil types, though wet soils should be avoided.

Cherries do not produce true to type from seed, so grafted trees are preferred. Planting can take place any time in winter while trees are dormant. Plant in holes large enough to take the roots without crowding. Cherries blossom early (a glorious sight), so should not be grown in late frost areas.

DUCK SALAD WITH CHERRIES AND LYCHEES

Buy a roasted duck from a Chinese grocery for this to save time. If you grow fresh lychees, use them when they're in season after taking off their skins.

SERVES 6

1 whole roasted duck, approx 4 lb
2 ⅔ tblspns (1 ⅓ fl oz) soy sauce
1 ⅓ tblspns (⅔ fl oz) rice vinegar
1 ⅓ tblspns (⅔ fl oz) roasted sesame oil
1 tblspn sugar
1 tblspn finely grated fresh ginger
1 small hot chilli, finely chopped (optional)
6 ½ oz fresh cherries, washed and pitted
1 tin lychees, drained
bunch fresh watercress, washed
1 ½ green sweet peppers (capsicums), slivered

Remove the meat from the duck, retaining the lovely crisp skin, and cut into strips. Take off any extra fat. If roasting at home, try to ensure a crisp skin. Don't refrigerate the duck as the skin will lose its crispness.

In a large bowl, mix together the soy sauce, vinegar, sesame oil, sugar, ginger and the chilli. Add cherries and lychees to marinade, then add the duck meat and half the slivered sweet pepper and toss together well.

Arrange watercress on a platter, put the salad on top and strew the top with the remaining sweet pepper. Serve immediately. *Variation: Fresh mangoes, peaches or apricots can be substituted for the cherries.*

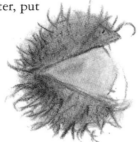

LUSCIOUS CHERRY CHOCOLATE ROLL

When I was a child, I'd often visit the McDonalds who lived down the road. The house was rickety and always looked ready to slide down the hill into the harbor. Its saving grace was that it was almost always filled with the smells of freshly baked cakes. Norene McDonald was a wonderful cook and I would be tempted down the hill by the inescapable aromas.
This recipe was one handed on to her by her mother. She in turn has passed it on to her daughter Deborah. It is the McDonald family birthday cake and when you bake it, you'll know why (it's heavenly). Norene often doubled the quantities, baking the mixture on two separate trays (because the family was so large) and she would put one layer on top of the other with the cream in the middle. She never rolled it.

SERVES 8–10

6 ½ oz cherries
6 ½ oz dark chocolate
¼ cup (2 fl oz) liquid coffee
7 eggs, separated
⅔ cup (5 oz) superfine (caster) sugar
cocoa powder
1 ¼ cups (10 fl oz) thickened cream

1 ⅓ tblspns (⅔ oz) confectioners' (icing) sugar
1 ⅓ tblspns (⅔ fl oz) Kirsch

Prepare the cherries a few hours ahead. You'll need about a cupful of washed, pitted and halved fruit. Dry well on paper towels.

Preheat oven to 350°F (180°C/Gas 4). Line a Swiss roll tin, 12 x 10 in, and about ¾ in deep with non-stick baking paper brought up around the sides.

Break up chocolate, mix with coffee and melt in a moderate oven, or over a pan of simmering water.

Beat yolks with superfine sugar until thick and creamy. Add chocolate mix. Whisk whites until stiff and fold quickly through the egg/chocolate mixture. Pour into the prepared tin. Cook for 18 minutes with oven on, turn off oven, and leave in there for 10 minutes with door slightly ajar. Remove and cover with a damp cloth until cool. Dust top of the cake thickly with cocoa powder, loosen paper around the edges and turn out onto a sheet of non-stick baking paper.

Whip cream with confectioners' sugar until thick, add Kirsch and fold through the cherries. If kept flat, cut the cake into two halves; spread the bottom half with the cream and cherries, top with the other half. Spread more cream on the top and sprinkle with grated chocolate. If rolled, spread with the cream and cherries before rolling, and make it the day before as it cuts better after being refrigerated overnight. Don't worry if the cake cracks when rolled up — it's meant to do that.

CLAFOUTIS

The recipe for clafoutis comes from the Limousin region of France, where batter and fruit desserts are common. You can use any soft fruits for this (apricots, strawberries, pears, nectarines). The beauty of this dish is that you don't need to pit the cherries, a time-consuming and kitchen-spattering job at the best of times. The stones actually add an extra element to the flavor of the dish.

SERVES 6

1 ½ lb ripe black cherries, not pitted
3 eggs
⅓ cup (3 oz) sugar
¼ cup (2 oz) butter, melted
1 tspn each finely grated lemon and orange zest (rind)

1 cup (4 oz) all-purpose (plain) flour, sifted with a pinch of salt
1 cup (8 fl oz) milk
confectioners' (icing) sugar or *vanilla sugar for the top*

Preheat the oven to 400°F (200°C/Gas 6).

Wash, drain and destalk the cherries. Grease an earthenware or quiche dish large enough to hold the cherries in a single layer (about 11 in diameter).

In a bowl, whisk the eggs and gradually add the sugar. Keep beating until pale in color. Whisk in the butter and citrus zests. Stir in the flour and salt and mix well, then pour in the milk. Keep whisking until you have a creamy batter free from lumps.

Pour the batter over the top of the cherries and cook in the oven for 40 minutes. It will rise during cooking and fall again when taken out of the oven. Dust the top with confectioners' sugar or vanilla sugar and serve warm.

Berries

What poet as a child was given blackcurrant jam juice to paint with?

BROWNING

The day I fell off a donkey and into some blackberry bushes is one I shan't forget, nor recommend. Just what those blackberry bushes were doing right in the middle of a grassy paddock, I don't know. When the settlers introduced the blackberry to Australia, little did they realise it would be declared a noxious weed in some areas. Of all the berries, it is probably the prickliest, so I guess I should count my blessings — apart from numerous scratches, the damage wasn't too bad, and it hasn't put me off the berries. The intense flavor of wild blackberries is not to be underestimated.

A day strawberry picking, though, is one I would recommend. I first picked strawberries in Tasmania as a teenager, and I hadn't seen them growing until then. We ate as many as we picked. The owner didn't mind a bit — he had so many. The sweetness and fragrance of those juicy, freshly picked strawberries has lingered ever since.

That is the ideal way to eat berries — picked fresh from the plant. Strawberries are not difficult to grow in the home garden. Apart from their lusciousness, they are pretty, decorative plants which spill over borders and tumble down hills. They also give a quick return, bearing fruit in less than a year. The ones most often grown today are hybrids of various American species, most of which were introduced to Europe during the seventeenth and eighteenth centuries, although some claim that the cultivated berries, even at their best, do not equal the wild berries.

The soft fruits which show the quickest return after strawberries are raspberries, blackberries and loganberries. Eighteen months after planting the canes you will be able to enjoy the fruit. Raspberries are the most popular, probably because they are the most perfumed and have such an intense flavor. White, red and black varieties exist. Over the years raspberries give bigger crops for the space they occupy than any of the other soft fruits.

The word 'berry' can in fact be rather confusing. Strictly speaking, a berry is a fleshy fruit which doesn't split open and has one or more seeds but no stone (pit). It develops from a single enlarged ovary: grapes, tomatoes, eggplants (aubergines), currants, blueberries and cranberries all reside in this category. The popular understanding of berry is somewhat different and for our purposes, we have chosen to follow this rather looser definition.

As far back as 5000 BC, Mesolithic people in northern Europe enjoyed berries in their diet. In Siberia prehistoric people stored them in icy pits, an ancient version of freezing (berries do freeze very well). Neolithic sites dating from 3000 BC in Denmark and Switzerland have yielded the fossilized remains of a number of berries: blackberries, strawberries, bilberries and raspberries, though Waverley Root insists the raspberry is of East Asian origin. This, he puts down to its flavor: 'It breathes of the Orient — rich, exotic, spice-laden and with a hint of musk.' Pliny described it growing wild on Mount Ida in Turkey and it still grows wild in much of Northern Europe. Edward I of England was the first on record to transplant strawberries and raspberries from the wild. He cultivated them in his manorial garden during the thirteenth century and they became a fashionable treat for the gentry. Since then, kitchen gardens have been the traditional place for growing many of the berries.

The sheer variety of soft-fruited berries and brambles is staggering. Included in the latter category are a range of dewberry, raspberry and blackberry hybrids, most of which originated in the United States. The best known hybrid is the loganberry, which has a more acid taste than the blackberry and a larger, longer, reddish-purple fruit which makes it ideal for jam-making and bottling. Thornless loganberries are now available and are good in the home garden. These all belong to the genus Rubus in the rose family, of which there are over 500 species, some authorities recognizing twice that number.

Phenomenalberry is very similar to the loganberry, except that it carries more single berries and the fruit is often larger in size, ripening a week or two later. Youngberries are the result of a cross between phenomenalberry and Mayes dewberry, and thornless varieties are available. Boysenberries are another hybrid, developed by Rudolph Boysen in 1923. A cross between blackberries and raspberries, they are similar in appearance to the loganberry. Mammothberry is a blackberry/dewberry cross with fruit similar to a cylindrical blackberry. All of these brambles will grow and crop in cool climates and are less demanding than raspberries. A reasonably good soil will do for most varieties and they will tolerate a certain amount of shade. Blackberries flower later than raspberries, and loganberries even later, thereby escaping spring frosts.

Some berries only thrive in the wild, including the cloudberry, a small golden-colored fruit which grows in open moorland. It's a rather ornery creature which cannot be relied upon to fruit (or even appear) each year. It loves the long nightless days of the Arctic Circle where its golden fruit glows in the boggy landscape. Its complex, bittersweet taste is much prized in Scandinavia.

Other wild berries are marionberries, with their delicious red fruits and unique flavors; tangleberries; veitchberries, worcesterberries; and honeyberries. The latter, an Arctic brambleberry, is closely related to the raspberry. Its taste inspires berry pickers to search for it endlessly. The Finns call it mesimarja and managed to keep it to themselves until about 100 years ago. Now that the secret is out, its reputation has spread far and *wide. Like the cloudberry, the honeyberry defies cultivation and in some years produces little or no fruit.*

The rowanberry (or European mountain ash) is another popular culinary berry throughout northern Europe. Once considered a magical plant (it was thought to protect people against witches' spells and its branches were used as divining rods on Midsummer Eve to find precious treasure), its taste is disagreeable when raw, but it makes a wonderful jelly.

There are also redcurrants, white currants with their rather sour taste, and blackcurrants, used mostly to make the delicious liqueur cassis. The latter two are considered to have medicinal benefits. Currants and gooseberries take longer than raspberries to come to full cropping, but they then have a longer fruiting life. Then there are mulberries, the fruit of which grows on a handsome spreading tree. There are various species of these too but the white and the black are the most common. You sometimes see mulberry trees lining avenues. They are easily trained to grow as a wall-fruit in the kitchen garden.

Berries are fragile fruits. They don't travel well, a good reason for planting some in the kitchen garden. However, they do freeze well, an excellent way to retain some for year-round use. Hull them or remove stalks beforehand. Put them on trays each separated from the other and pop into the freezer. When frozen, bundle into plastic freezer bags — this way, they won't stick together in a lump. Ask your local nursery about the varieties available, and consult the different seed catalogues. That way, you'll be able to grow some of the more unusual ones yourself.

Strawberries
Fragaria *species*

Doubtless God could have made a better berry, but doubtless God never did.

ASCRIBED TO WILLIAM BUTLER, OR BOTELER IN IZAAK WALTON, *THE COMPLEAT ANGLER*, I, 1653

I once attended a superb art exhibition called 'Flowers and Nature', an overview of four centuries of Netherlandish flower painting. A painting by Jacob Van Hulsdonck entitled Strawberries with a Carnation in a Ming Bowl *caught my eye. Its beauty was breathtaking and the presentation of the red fruits in a blue-and-white Wan-Li bowl exquisite. The strawberries depicted were a cultivated form of the wild strawberry (Fragaria vesca). They gleamed and sparkled, harmonizing with the highlights from the cherries and red and white currants scattered on the table under the bowl.*

Van Hulsdonck would have painted it between 1615 and 1630, at a time when the strawberry was regarded as a heavenly fruit, an interpretation probably deriving from Ovid, who wrote that people of the Golden Age fed on strawberries. Medieval writers also referred to it as a fruit of paradise. By that time, strawberries the size of mulberries were available, as were runnerless sorts and various color variants. Of these the white-fruited was said to have the most delicate flavor and the green (F. viridis) was said to be the sweetest. Small-fruited alpines were also available, though they were not cultivated until the eighteenth century.

Yellow, white and red alpines can be found today at specialist nurseries and are well worth growing in the home garden. They are raised from seed, as they do not produce runners. Ask at your nursery for the best variety to suit your locality and climate.

Strawberries grow well in containers and on walls and look very pretty. However, they require frequent watering and must be protected from excessive heat in summer. In the garden, grow them under black plastic or mulch or in slightly mounted, weed-free beds. They prefer loamy, slightly acid soils and will not tolerate poor drainage. They are usually trouble-free plants, provided that suitable varieties are selected and virus-free stock is planted. Birds and slugs can be a problem.

FRUIT SLICE

This is a wonderfully simple dessert and always popular. Best with summer fruits, when you can mix and match from a wide range, but good at other times of the year. It is rich and luscious if made with the sour cream, but just as nice (and less rich) if you use the ricotta.

SERVES 8

8 oz lady fingers (savoiardi)
scant ½ cup (3 ⅓ fl oz) fresh orange juice
2 ⅔ tblspns (1 ⅓ fl oz) overproof rum or orange liqueur
1 ¼ cups (10 fl oz) sour cream or 1 cup (½ lb) ricotta
⅔ cup (5 fl oz) cream
2 tblspns (1 oz) brown sugar
grated zest (rind) and juice of ½ lemon

approx 1 ¼ lb fresh soft fruit (berries, kiwi fruit (Chinese gooseberry), bananas, pitted cherries, apricots, papaya)
½ cup (4 fl oz) apricot jam
juice of ½ lemon, extra

Combine orange juice and rum, and dip the lady fingers quickly into the mixture. Set them side by side on a large flat platter or tray, about 10 x 15 ½ in, until the tray is covered.

Beat the ricotta or sour cream until smooth, gradually add the cream. Beat in the brown sugar, lemon zest and juice, and keep beating until mixture holds its shape. Spread over base. It is good to do this the night before and keep covered and chilled in the refrigerator — the mixture seeps into the biscuits which become quite soft.

Next day, hull, slice and peel the fruit. Arrange the fruit over the cream forming a pattern.

Heat apricot jam and extra lemon juice until liquid and push through a sieve. Use while still warm to glaze the fruit and cream base. Chill until ready to serve.

Remove from refrigerator about 30 minutes before serving.

ROSIE'S STRAWBERRIES AND CREAM

Food consultant and caterer Rosie Penman once made a lovely simple dessert with raspberries and strawberries. She served it in silver and crystal serving bowls, one inside the other, on a nest of crushed ice.

For four to six people, you'll need 1 ½ lb each fresh raspberries and strawberries. Put the raspberries into the food processor with a little confectioners' (icing) sugar and strawberry or raspberry liqueur to taste. Process briefly.

Place the whole, hulled strawberries into the smaller bowl, adding raspberry sauce as you go and using the sauce to help keep each layer of strawberries upright. Cover and refrigerate for 1–2 hours.

Whip 1 ¼ cups (10 fl oz) fresh cream, flavoring with vanilla. Cover and refrigerate.

Just before serving, pile the cream over the raspberry sauce and strawberries. Crush some macaroons or Amaretti biscuits and sprinkle them over the cream. Decorate with whole fresh strawberries if you like.

STRAWBERRIES AND LYCHEES

Hull some fresh strawberries (for four to six people, allow about 1 lb), wash well, drain. Open a tin of lychees, drain and mix together with the strawberries. Sprinkle with orange flower water and confectioners' (icing) sugar and leave to macerate in the refrigerator. Garnish with fresh mint tips.

BUTTERMILK PANCAKES WITH STRAWBERRIES

These pancakes are delicious served with ice-cream and fresh strawberries (or any fresh berries for that matter).

SERVES 6

2 cups (½ qt) buttermilk
2 eggs
¼ cup (2 fl oz) vegetable oil
1 ¾ cups (7 oz) all-purpose (plain) flour
2 tblspns (1 oz) sugar
2 tspns baking powder
1 tspn baking soda (bicarbonate of soda)
1 tspn salt
good quality vanilla ice-cream
1 lb fresh prepared berries

In a large bowl, beat together the buttermilk, eggs and oil. Sift together the dry ingredients and stir into the buttermilk mixture. Lightly grease a heavy frying pan and set on moderate heat until hot. Ladle on the batter, making the cakes about 4 in in diameter. Cook until small bubbles form on top, flip over and cook until golden on other side. Serve warm with ice-cream and fresh berries.

COEUR À LA CREME

This simple French summer dessert, made here with mascarpone, is both light and elegant. The classic accompaniments are unhulled strawberries (preferably wild) and raspberries.

Fruit sauces also go well with these little heart-shaped cheeses. The quantity specified here will fill four small *coeur à la crème* molds. The molds have small holes in the base to allow excess moisture to drip out while the dessert is setting.

SERVES 4

1 lb mascarpone (Italian cream cheese)
5 tspns (1 oz) superfine (caster) sugar
1–2 tblspns (½ –1 fl oz) Cognac or *Grand Marnier (optional)*

Beat together all the ingredients until thickened, about 1–2 minutes, being careful not to overbeat. Line the molds with fine muslin (to make unmolding easier). Spoon the mixture into the prepared molds and place on a tray. Leave to set and drain in the refrigerator overnight.

Before serving, set out four large white plates. Onto each plate, spoon three fruit sauces in separate groupings, then swirl them together to form a ripple or marbled effect. Unmold the cream cheese hearts, taking great care as they are very soft, and place off-center on each plate.

FRUIT SAUCES

BERRIES

Place 8 oz berries, washed and hulled, into the food processor, add 1–2 tblspns (½ –1 oz) confectioners' (icing) sugar and process, turning on and off until smooth. Strain through a fine sieve and stir in a little lemon juice. If it seems too thick, you can add a little soda water or aerated mineral water. Makes about 1 cup (8 fl oz).

OTHER FRUITS

Process as for berries, using fruits in season, peeling first and removing stones or seeds if necessary (kiwi fruit, peaches, apricots, guavas). Peaches and apricots need to be blanched in rapidly boiling water to remove skins beforehand. Adjust amount of sugar and lemon juice depending on the sweetness of the fruit (and on your tooth).

STRAWBERRIES IN BALSAMIC VINEGAR

Freshly squeezed lemon juice always accentuates the flavor of strawberries. In Italy balsamic vinegar is often used as in this recipe.

SERVES 4

1 lb strawberries
1 ⅓ tblspns (⅔ fl oz) balsamic vinegar
2–3 tblspns (1–1 ½ oz) superfine (caster) sugar, or *to taste*

Place the hulled, washed strawberries in a bowl. Sprinkle over the vinegar and sugar. Cover and chill for not more than 1 hour as the strawberries will begin to go mushy. Just before serving, mix gently.

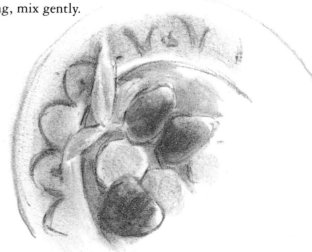

Raspberries, Loganberries, Youngberries, Boysenberries

Rubus idaeus, R. loganobaccus, Rubus *species*

These are usually referred to as trailing berries or brambles. I have grouped these together because they are the four most widely grown berries.

They like a slightly acid soil, temperate–cool climate, protection from wind and a lot of mulching. Berries are perennials, so it is important that the soil is well dressed and prepared before cultivation, and all weeds removed. A green manure crop the year before with ground rock phosphate will get them off to a good start.

Raspberries require a cooler climate than the other three. They grow wild in much of the northern hemisphere and are hardy bushes which usually bear fruit on second-year canes (the name given to the long-fruiting stems). The most common raspberry is the red-fruiting one, but there are also varieties with yellow fruit, known as white raspberries. There is also a pale-colored variety, said to have an excellent flavor. A black-fruited raspberry (R. occidentalis) is also widely cultivated.

Berries are best trained to stakes or trellises, otherwise they just sprawl everywhere. A good support is a parallel wire system with plants held between the wires. Drive in two posts at either end of the row, place wires between them and twist the canes around them as they grow. If using a fence, staple wires along it and tie the canes to them. The trellis system allows more exposure to the sun which improves the yield.

When pruning, the idea is to keep new canes away from the two-year-old canes which bear the fruit. Canes that have fruited are cut down to ground level in winter, leaving half a dozen or so new canes to continue growing. Separation of fruiting from non-fruiting wood makes picking and pruning much easier and helps to reduce the spread of any disease (like spot fungus, where spores can be washed from old to new canes). Pick the berries every morning as they get squashy when ripe; remove any ripe ones after rain to prevent mold spreading.

RASPBERRY JAM

This is the easiest and most flavorsome jam I know. The method has been around for some time and the result is fantastic — especially with pumpkin scones, or spread in the middle of a freshly baked sponge cake with whipped cream.

The same method can be used for very ripe loganberries.

Preheat oven to 400°F (200°C/Gas 6).

Choose firm, ripe raspberries and weigh them. Weigh the sugar (white granulated). For every 12 oz of raspberries, allow 1 ¼ cups (9 oz) sugar. Place the fruit, spread out, on one baking tray. Put the sugar, also spread out, onto another tray. Place both trays into the oven until hot, 15–20 minutes.

Remove trays from oven. Pour berries into a large mixing bowl, then gradually add the hot sugar and stir vigorously with a wooden spoon until all the sugar is dissolved. It will splutter and spit, so be careful.

Pour immediately into warm, sterile jars and seal.

BUTTERMILK JAM CAKE

This is one of those splendid big American jam cakes which keeps well and transports easily. Very good on picnics as it cuts well too. Use the raspberry jam (left) and/or persimmon and apricot jam (see page 241). It looks good if cooked in a 10 in bundt tin and iced with a lemon icing. Decorate with either shredded or flaked coconut, lightly toasted.

1 cup (8 oz) softened butter
¾ cup (4 oz) brown sugar
grated zest (rind) ½ lemon
5 eggs
3 cups (12 oz) all-purpose (plain) flour
1 tspn cinnamon
1 tspn nutmeg or *allspice*
1 tspn baking powder
1 tspn baking soda (bicarbonate of soda)
1 cup (8 fl oz) buttermilk or *sour cream*
¾ cup (6 fl oz) raspberry (or *fig) jam*
¾ cup (6 fl oz) persimmon and apricot jam
½ cup (4 fl oz) blackberry (or *strawberry) jam*
1 cup (4 oz) pecans or *blanched almonds, chopped*

Preheat the oven to 350°F (180°C/Gas 4). Grease and flour the bundt tin.

Cream together the butter and sugar. Add lemon zest, then the eggs one at a time, beating well after each addition. If mixture begins curdling, add a teaspoon of flour with each egg. Sift together the flour and spices, baking powder and soda. Add alternatively to the batter with buttermilk and jams. Fold through the nuts. Pour into the cake tin and bake for 1 hour.

MARBLED CHEESECAKE

A splendid, delectable cheesecake which will serve 12–14. Not only is it luscious, it is also very pretty with the fruit purées swirled through it. Use any berry purée — there is no need to sieve it.

2 ¼ cups (8 oz) crushed sweet crackers (biscuits)
½ cup (4 oz) melted butter
1 tspn ground cinnamon
⅓ cup (3 fl oz) milk
4 eggs, separated
1 cup (8 oz) superfine (caster) sugar
1 tspn vanilla extract (essence)
2 tblspns (1 oz) gelatine
½ cup (4 fl oz) water
1 ½ lb cream cheese, cut up and softened
½ cup (4 fl oz) cream, whipped
⅓ cup (3 fl oz) raspberry purée, approx 3 ½ oz fresh raspberries
extra raspberries for decorating

Preheat oven to 350°F (180°C/Gas 4).

Mix together the cracker crumbs (make these in the food processor), butter and cinnamon and press into a 10 in cake tin with removable base. Chill well, then bake for 15 minutes.

Scald milk in a saucepan. Meanwhile, in a bowl, beat together the egg yolks with half the superfine sugar until thick and creamy, then add the milk very gradually in a thin stream of drops so that the yolks are slowly warmed. Pour back into the saucepan and stir slowly and continuously over low heat until mixture coats the back of a spoon. Don't let the custard get anywhere near simmering point. Remove from heat and stir in vanilla.

Soak gelatine in the water and stir into hot custard until dissolved. Beat the cream cheese or work with a fork to make sure it is smooth, then beat into the custard until well combined.

Whip egg whites until stiff but not dry and gradually beat in the remaining superfine sugar. Fold these into the custard, then fold in the whipped cream. Swirl the berry purée through the mixture to give a marbled effect and pour into the crumb crust. Don't overmix or you will lose the marbled effect. Chill well. Decorate top with fresh raspberries.

MARY'S HOT BERRY SOUFFLÉ

Food lover Mary Beasley, who gave me this recipe once when I was in Adelaide, says she always feels somewhat guilty about the compliments she receives for it. Most people, she rightly observes, are intimidated by serving hot soufflés at a dinner party, but this one has never let her (or itself) down. The bulk of the preparation for this can be done beforehand.

SERVES 4–6

melted butter, for coating
1 tblspn (½ oz) superfine (caster) sugar, for coating
3 tblspns (1 ½ oz) butter
⅓ cup (1 ½ oz) all-purpose (plain) flour
1 cup (8 fl oz) hot milk
½ cup (4 oz) superfine (caster) sugar
1 ⅓ tblspns (⅔ fl oz) vanilla extract (essence)
4 egg yolks
18 oz fresh raspberries, puréed
5 egg whites
1 tblspn (½ oz) superfine (caster) sugar, extra

First, prepare an 8 in soufflé dish by brushing with the melted butter and then swirling the superfine sugar around the inside to coat. Set aside.

Melt the butter in a saucepan, add the flour and cook over gentle heat for 1 minute, stirring continuously. Add milk gradually, stirring until mixture thickens and boils, simmer for 5 seconds.

Remove saucepan from heat, stir in superfine sugar and vanilla, add egg yolks one at a time, beating well after each addition. Set aside, covered with plastic wrap. Reheat gently before using.

Preheat oven to 350°F (180°C/Gas 4).

Prepare the raspberries. Whisk the egg whites until stiff and then stir a large tablespoon of the egg whites into the reheated egg yolk mixture to soften it. Fold through remaining egg whites very lightly. Gently swirl through the berry purée and pour into prepared dish.

Cook in oven for 30 minutes. Pull out and sprinkle extra superfine sugar over the top, gently close the oven door, increase temperature to 375°F (190°C/Gas 5) and cook for a further 5 minutes.

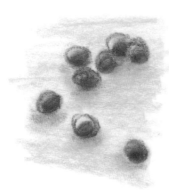

Blueberries
Vaccinium *species*

Native to the United States, these small dark blue fruits are enormously popular there and increasingly popular in Australia. I confess to not being a great fan. Neither their flavor nor texture appeals to me, perhaps because I've never tasted them in their wild form — these apparently have a tartness, which takes the edge off their sweetness.

Blueberries are deciduous, requiring cool to cold weather in winter and disliking spring frosts. The bushes are often prized for their brilliant autumn colors and make a lovely ornamental bush.

It's a good idea to grow two varieties to ensure a good yield. They start bearing at about two to three years of age, producing up to 10 lb of fruit at about seven years. They do best in an acid, peaty soil with lots of organic matter. Reclaimed marsh or swamplands are ideal. Blueberries are best grown from cuttings as they do not breed true from seed. The fruit can be picked when it has been blue for about a week and will keep in the refrigerator, without ripening further, for a long time.

BLACK-EYED SUSAN CAKE

So called because the pattern on this upside-down cake resembles the black-eyed Susan.

2 mangoes
10 oz blueberries, washed
1 ½ cups (6 oz) all-purpose (plain) flour
¾ cup (6 oz) sugar
1 ½ tspns baking powder
1 tspn baking soda (bicarbonate of soda)
¼ tspn salt
1 cup (8 fl oz) buttermilk or sour cream
3 eggs

GLAZE
flesh from mango stones (seeds)
½ cup (4 oz) sugar
¼ cup (2 fl oz) water
2 ⅔ tblspns (1 ⅓ fl oz) lemon juice
overproof rum to taste

Preheat oven to 350°F (180°C/Gas 4). Line a 9 ½ in round or square tin with non-stick baking paper, making sure it comes up around the sides.

Slice the cheeks off the mangoes, remove the skins then slice again into crescent shapes, reserving the stones. Put the crescent slices in the bottom of the tin in the shape of a flower. Fill the center with the blueberries and put more blueberries around the outer edges, filling up the whole of the bottom of the tin.

Sift together the dry ingredients. In another bowl, beat together the buttermilk and eggs. Add sifted ingredients to the egg mixture. Beat until smooth and pour over the fruits.

Bake for about 30 minutes or until a skewer inserted in the batter comes out clean. Remove and allow to sit in tin for 10–15 minutes. Turn out. Whilst still warm, pour over the glaze.

GLAZE

Remove remaining mango flesh from stones with a small sharp knife and put into a blender. Blend until smooth. Combine in a saucepan with sugar, water and lemon juice. Bring to a boil and simmer for 5–10 minutes. Remove and push through a sieve. Stir through the rum. Pour over hot cake, brushing evenly over all the fruit.

LUSCIOUS BERRY GRATIN

The fragrance and flavor of the berries are enhanced when cooked like this, but you need to serve the gratin straightaway. Use a 9 in ovenproof dish that you can serve from. It needs to be only ¾ in deep. A mixture of berries (strawberries, raspberries, blueberries, blackberries) is good.

SERVES 4

1 lb mixed berries
6 egg yolks
3 tblspns (1 ½ oz) superfine (caster) sugar
2 ⅔ tblspns (1 ⅓ fl oz) orange liqueur (Grand Marnier, Cointreau)

Preheat the broiler (grill) to very hot.

If using strawberries, hull them and cut into halves. Put the berries onto the bottom of the dish.

Put the egg yolks and sugar together in a bowl over a saucepan of steaming water. Add the liqueur and whisk until the mixture is thick and creamy, being careful not to scramble the eggs. Pour the sauce over the berries and cook under the hot broiler for 1–2 minutes or until golden brown. Watch it carefully because it burns quickly. Serve immediately.

BLUEBERRY SMOOTHIES

You can, in fact, use any berry for these. Wonderful for children for afternoon tea.

SERVES 2

5 oz blueberries
2 cups (½ qt) buttermilk
3–4 scoops vanilla ice-cream

Put all ingredients in a blender and blend until smooth. Serve immediately in long glasses.

Currants
Ribes *species*

Currants belong to a talented family, whose fruits include the blackcurrant (Ribes nigrum), *native to all Europe and northern Asia, the redcurrant* (R. rubrum), *originally from western Europe and Russia, and its variants the white currant and the gooseberry. They are not cultivated widely in home gardens. Mature blackcurrants do take up a lot of room, but redcurrants and gooseberries can be trained as cordons. Pruning must be done regularly each year in summer and winter, however, or the cordon will get out of hand.*

Currants only fruit in cool climates, though in areas with cold winters and hot summers, they may do well

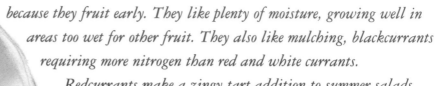

because they fruit early. They like plenty of moisture, growing well in areas too wet for other fruit. They also like mulching, blackcurrants requiring more nitrogen than red and white currants.

Redcurrants make a zingy tart addition to summer salads tossed through grated or julienned raw vegetables. Their sparkling red–blue color adds eye appeal, too.

Generally redcurrants are made into a sparkling jelly which goes well with game and roasted poultry. You can also try dipping them in lightly beaten egg white and frosting with superfine (caster) sugar for a pretty table decoration.

KATE'S SUMMER PUDDING

You can use a mixture of red or black currants, blueberries, mulberries and pitted cherries in this stunning English pudding. It is best if about 1 lb of the fruit is composed of raspberries.

SERVES 4–6

1 ½ lb mixed soft red summer fruits
scant 1 cup (7 oz) superfine (caster) sugar
1 loaf sliced white day-old bread

Wash and destalk fruit. Put into a shallow pan with the sugar. Heat gently until sugar dissolves and juices are running — do not cook beyond this stage.

Put a colander over a basin and tip the fruit into it.

Trim crusts from bread and dip each slice into the reserved fruit juices.

Line a 3 cup (¾ qt) pudding basin with the bread, easing each piece together so there are no gaps. Half fill the lined basin with drained fruit. Cover fruit with one layer of dipped bread, then fill with remaining fruit. Cover the top with bread, tucking in neatly to the edges of the basin.

Put a plate that fits inside the bowl on top of the bread and weight it lightly. Leave overnight in the refrigerator, reserving any left over juice.

To serve, remove plate and tip pudding onto a serving platter, pouring over any of the excess juice. Serve with thick cream.

REDCURRANT AND CHERRY JAM

Yes, you need patience for stoning cherries, but it is a peaceful way to spend part of a summer's afternoon, especially if you sit out under a tree on the grass. Children can help in this part of the preparation too, but watch out for those pips.

MAKES APPROX 4 CUPS (1 QT)

1 ½ lb black cherries
6 ½ oz redcurrants
juice of 1 lemon
warm sugar
¼ cup (2 fl oz) Kirsch

Wash the fruit well. Destalk and stone the cherries. Break a few of the stones and add the kernels to the fruit.

Put the redcurrants into a small saucepan, put on the lid and let them cook gently in their own juice. When soft, strain through a sieve into a larger saucepan, pushing through as much of the pulp as you can. Add the cherries and kernels, bring to a boil and simmer until the fruit is soft but not broken, 15–20 minutes. Add lemon juice. Remove from heat and measure. For every cup of fruit, allow ¾ cup warm sugar. Return pan to heat and stir with a wooden spoon until sugar is dissolved. Bring to boil and cook quickly, 15–20 minutes, or until syrup has thickened and setting point is reached.

Add Kirsch after setting point is reached and simmer another 5 minutes. Pour into sterilized jars and seal.

Note: Warm the sugar in a baking dish in a moderate oven (350°F/180°C/Gas 4) for about 8–10 minutes.

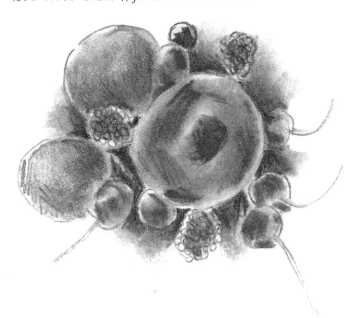

REDCURRANT JELLY

4 lb redcurrants, washed
2 ⅔ cups (22 fl oz) water
sugar

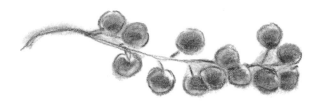

Put the redcurrants and water into a large pan and simmer until the fruit is very soft, about 1 hour. Mash well, then strain through a jelly bag, suspended over a bowl for at least 12 hours.

Measure the juice and pour into a clean pan, bring to a boil. Reduce heat and for every 2 ⅔ cups (22 fl oz) juice, add 2 cups (1 lb) warmed sugar. Cook, stirring constantly, over low heat until sugar is dissolved.

Bring to a boil and boil rapidly for about 10 minutes or until the jelly has reached setting point. Pour into warm sterile jars and seal immediately.

Citrus

Citrus *species*

Oranges and lemons
Say the bells of St Clement's

TRADITIONAL ENGLISH NURSERY RHYME

Through the French doors, I glimpse my neighbor's orange tree dancing in the bright sunlight of a winter's day. Eyeing me cautiously is a large black currawong, sitting nervously on the trellis which runs between the two back gardens.

I have always thought that every back garden should have a lemon tree. Now I think there should be an orange tree as well. In winter, when everything else is dormant, the sight of these vivid orange globes is a delight and, for the cook, a necessity. Where would we be without the orange and lemon to flavor and perfume our food?

And the heavy fragrance of the flowers, when in blossom, is an added bonus for gardener and cook alike. I live in an area where the climate is temperate. In northern Europe, where the winters are colder, the orange has always been a status crop, a sign of opulence. The most famous of these was the Orangerie at Versailles. Built for Louis XIV by Mansart, it housed 1200 orange trees in silver tubs plus 300 other exotic trees. A contemporary version, fruiting kumquats in tubs on either side of a front door, is a sure statement of upper-middle-class comforts. In Seville, the streets are lined with orange trees, introduced there by the conquering Moors who, by the twelfth century, had converted the region between Granada and Seville into a vast citrus orchard. They also introduced the lemon to Spain around this time, and later took it to North Africa where it flourished. The first settlers recognised the importance of citrus fruits when they arrived in Australia. Apart

from the use of lemons and limes as cures for scurvy, citrus fruits were also cultivated for the kitchen garden. George Worgan, the surgeon on the Sirius, *describes the orange, lemon and lime as growing, admittedly with difficulty, from seed on the first farm in the colony in 1788. Such exotics had been picked up in South America en route. By 1790 Reverend Richard Johnson, who had planted orange seeds beside the family cottage near Bridge Street in modern Sydney, could write that they had reached two feet in height and were 'very promising'. By 1820, the eminent colonist W.C. Wentworth was giving advice on the transplanting and pruning of all manner of fruit trees and around that time a charming black and white illustration depicts a healthy orange grove, owned by the Pyes at Parramatta, some 12 ½ miles west of Sydney.*

Citrus trees originated in China and South-East Asia, though plant geographers do not agree about the exact place of their origin. The different species were slowly introduced into Europe during Roman times and the Middle Ages, the citron being the first member of the genus to be carried to Mesopotamia and the Nile Valley. A close relative of the lemon, it was cultivated in the Holy Land, being used by the Jews for ritual observances. Jewish gardeners, much in demand throughout the Roman world for their skill in fruit cultivation, used the citron as grafting stock for other kinds of citrus, particularly the orange.

Apart from the citron, the orange, lemon and lime, there are mandarins (tangerines), grapefruit, calamondin, pummelo, chinotto and the seville (or bitter orange). Kumquats, though closely related to the Citrus *species, belong to a different genus, the* Fortunella. *All are fairly small trees, ranging from the lime which is about 6 ½ ft in height to the orange (13–16 ft). They are generally considered subtropical. Though oranges and grapefruit resist frost better than lemons, and much better than limes, they will not grow in severe frost areas. In general, they prefer warm–hot summers and mild winters. The most cold-hardy is the kumquat, followed by the seville, mandarin and Meyer lemon.*

*You can grow citrus fruits from seed but undesirable side effects can sometimes occur. Valencias grown from seed, for example, produce fruit which resemble Valencias but the tree grows larger and is thornier. Common varieties budded onto a number of specifically grown and suitable rootstocks are available from most nurseries. The most common rootstocks for citrus are trifoliata (*Poncirus trifoliata*), rough lemon and sweet orange, but Troyer and Carrizo citrange, Cleopatra and Emperor mandarin are also used in some localities to propagate trees. Trifoliata and both of the citrange rootstocks are resistant to* Phytophthora *root rot and are used in heavier soil with drainage problems.*

Citrus grow best in deep (20 in), well-drained sandy loam soils and will not tolerate very acidic or alkaline conditions, preferring a pH in the range of 6 to 7.5. They love the sun and don't like frosts or strong winds, especially those from the sea. Best time for planting is when risk of severe frost is past, usually around late winter–early spring. It is important not to disturb the root system when planting. Gently tease out the external roots and dig the planting hole deep enough to allow the tree to be placed at the original nursery or container soil level. This is because citrus roots come very close to the surface, so cultivation must be kept shallow. However, the bud union must be at least 5 in above ground level. Make the hole wide enough for the roots to spread out and don't add any artificial fertilizer to the planting hole. Citrus need to be kept well watered during dry, warm to hot weather and when first planted, so it is a good idea to form a basin around the tree to make watering easier. Pour a little over 2 gallons of water slowly into this basin to help consolidate growth and provide moisture when needed.

Citrus require extra nitrogen to promote growth and fruit size and often suffer from zinc and magnesium deficiencies. They have moderately heavy nutrient requirements: a well-grown tree requires 16–18 oz of a mixed fertilizer annually until the tree is 10 years old, applied in early spring and early fall.

Citrus usually will begin to produce fruit within two to three years of planting. Except for limes, the fruit should be left on the tree until full flavor and color is developed — they do not continue to ripen after being picked. Mature fruits can be held on the tree for some time.

They also make attractive and fragrant potted plants, though some fruit more happily than others, and special care in fertilizing is required. Once again, they like a sunny position for at least part of the day to maintain healthy growth. Patios and small courtyards are ideal, particularly for tub trees like kumquats, calamondin and Meyer lemons. These can be kept ornamental (under 5 ft) by pinching out the tips of stems. They can also be kept indefinitely if removed from the container and repotted in fresh soil when growth is less vigorous.

Limes
Citrus aurantifolia

The green intensity and fragrance of the lime has always drawn me. So, too, its neat perfect shape and its sharp, sour taste, evoking memories of hot, tropical days. I can think of nothing more cooling on a summer's day than a freshly made limeade or gin and tonic with ice and a generous wedge of fresh lime. I can never forget the superb taste of the lime drinks I had in Singapore, after a hot day trudging the streets.

The lime seems to have originated somewhere in South-East Asia and traveled west through India and Persia, reaching southern Spain with the Arabs. Both lime and lemon come from the Arabic limah. *Don't confuse the citrus lime, though, with the lime tree or basswood as in Linden (the European lime tree). Limes are now grown in many tropical countries, often replacing the lemon. Being tropical plants, they dislike frost. A number of varieties are available: the Tahitian (or Persian), which is my favorite; the Mexican (Key lime or Wet Indian), the juice of which is aromatic and has a full lime flavor; sweet limes, which are rather insipid in taste; Rangpur, a hybrid mandarin–lime variety; and the Kaffir lime (or Makrut), the fragrant leaf used in Thai cooking, redolent of lemon verbena, geranium and lemon. In Australia, there are four species of wild limes (Microcitrus) which can be used as substitutes for lemons or limes in cooking. The skin of the small round lime is quite bitter and the flesh acidic; the finger lime is delicious just sucked out of its skin, sweetening the breath. Australia also has a native orange (Capparis), green on the outside and related to the caper, which grows in arid areas.*

For the home garden, the recommended variety is the Tahitian lime (Citrus aurantifolia 'Tahiti'). Good drainage is essential and all citrus love urine diluted with water, which can be poured around the roots from a bucket.

YAM PLA (MARINATED FISH)

It was on Lord Howe Island (off the east coast of Australia) 25 years ago that I first tasted Tahitian fish salad. I remember the night — warm, still, dark and dank. The sky was clear and filled with thousands of stars. We were at a private house, sitting outside on a verandah (the house was timber and quite old) with the vegetation surrounding us on all sides.

The fish salad was served as an entrée. In those days, it was unheard of to eat raw fish and so we felt we were partaking of something mysterious and exotic. The fish had been marinated in lime juice, which 'cooks' it, then fresh coconut milk, cucumber, tomatoes, onions and scallions were added.

The following is a delicious Thai version of the Tahitian dish. Lovely served in a wooden bowl lined with fresh, washed banana leaves as part of a Thai meal.

SERVES 4

*1 ½ lb white fish fillets (coral trout,
ocean perch, snapper)*
½ cup (4 fl oz) fresh lime juice
1–2 tblspns tinned green peppercorns
2 stalks lemongrass, white part only
1 cup (8 fl oz) fresh coconut milk

2 ⅔ tblspns (1 ⅓ fl oz) fish sauce
1 bunch (approx 3 ⅓ oz) fresh mint leaves, shredded

Slice the fish finely, removing all bones, then place in a glass or enamel bowl and cover with lime juice. Set aside. Drain the peppercorns of all brine then crush them with a mortar and pestle (or use the bottom end of a rolling pin and a cup). Slice the lemongrass thinly along the stems. Mix together all the ingredients and stir well to combine. Cover with plastic wrap and refrigerate for at least 4 hours, or overnight.

Note: Whilst fresh coconut milk is ideal, you can use the tinned variety.

TERIYAKI TUNA STEAKS

SERVES 4

4 x ¾ in thick tuna steaks
lime wedges (garnish)

MARINADE
½ cup (4 fl oz) teriyaki marinade
½ cup (4 fl oz) dry sherry or mirin
¼ cup (2 fl oz) olive oil
1 ⅓ tblspns (⅔ fl oz) lime juice
⅓ cup freshly chopped coriander (cilantro) leaves

Place tuna steaks in a shallow dish. Mix all marinade ingredients together, pour over the fish and refrigerate for a few hours. Cook steaks over hot coals, 2–3 minutes on each side, brushing with marinade (the tuna should remain pink inside). Serve with lime wedges.

MARINADE
Combine all ingredients.
Note: Mirin is a sweet Japanese rice wine.

BARBECUED JUMBO SHRIMP

SERVES 6

36 fresh green jumbo shrimp (prawns), approx 2 lb

MARINADE
3–4 cloves garlic, crushed
½ cup each freshly chopped coriander (cilantro) and basil
4–5 tblspns (2– 2 ⅔ fl oz) chilli sauce
sea salt to taste
juice of 10 limes or 5 lemons
2 cups (16 fl oz) olive oil

De-vein jumbo shrimps, but leave their tails on. If you like, you can thread six of the shrimp onto bamboo skewers pre-soaked in water.

Place jumbo shrimps in a bowl and pour over marinade. Let stand a few hours or overnight.

Drain jumbo shrimps and cook on a hot barbecue, 1–2 minutes for each side. Serve with a salad and fresh crusty bread.

MARINADE
Shake all ingredients together in a jar.

LIME, LEMON OR ORANGE SYRUP CAKE

Marvellously simple and very good too, this is really a version of the old stand-by pound cake. As Jane Grigson points out in her *Fruit Book*, the various possibilities for embellishment of this standard recipe (equal measures of self-raising flour, sugar, eggs and soft fat, plus a teaspoon of baking powder) seem to be endless.

The very best thing is the syrup, which adds both intensity of flavor and moisture. You can substitute one lemon or one orange for the two limes if you would prefer a lemon syrup or an orange syrup cake. Both are equally delicious.

finely grated zest (rind) of 2 fresh limes
¾ cup (6 oz) sugar
1 cup (8 oz) soft unsalted butter, cut in pieces
2 cups (8 oz) self-raising flour
1 tspn baking powder
pinch salt
4 large eggs
1 ⅓ tblspns (1 ⅓ fl oz) fresh lime juice

SYRUP

juice of 2 limes

½ cup (4 oz) superfine (caster) sugar

gin or *orange liqueur (optional)*

Preheat oven to 350°F (180°C/Gas 4). Butter and flour an 8 in cake tin or a decorative 8 cup (2 qt) bundt tin (it looks very pretty when turned out).

Put the zest, sugar and butter into a mixing bowl and beat until creamy and white. Sift together the flour, baking powder and salt, set aside.

Add the eggs one at a time to the butter mixture. If it looks like curdling, add 1–2 tspns of the flour with each egg. Fold in the flour. Finally, add the lime juice.

Spoon into the cake tin and bake in the oven for 45–60 minutes. If you have a fan-forced oven, it will cook in a shorter time.

Remove, let stand for 10 minutes, then turn out onto a wire rack and pour the syrup over the hot cake.

It's best if the rack sits over the plate, to catch any dribbling syrup. Pour that back over the cake. Let the cake cool completely before cutting.

SYRUP

Mix together the lime juice and sugar in a saucepan and bring to a boil. When the sugar has dissolved, remove from heat. At this stage you can stir in a little gin (or orange liqueur, if it's an orange cake).

Oranges
Citrus sinensis

Dance the orange. Who can forget it,
how, drowning in itself, it grew
against its being-sweet.

RAINER MARIA RILKE, 'SONNETS TO ORPHEUS' 1, 15

It's not just the look of oranges glowing like lamps from amongst dark leaves that I love, it's their sweet, acidic flavor and diverse culinary uses. According to Jane Grigson, in her Fruit Book, *the word itself goes back to Dravidian India,* narayam *meaning 'perfume within'. The Arabs took it from the Persians as* narandj, *Italians softened it to* arancia *and in medieval France* arancia *slipped into 'orange' because the town of Orange was a great center for the fruit.*

Oranges seem to have come either from eastern India or southern China and to have been cultivated there as early as 2400 BC. Today, in southern China, they are associated with good fortune, orange (along with red and scarlet gold) being a religious color, connected with auspicious events. In Chinese medicine, the nature of the flesh is considered neither hot nor cold, and they are believed to promote a healthy stomach.

Oranges arrived in Italy at the end of the Roman Empire, taken there on Arab dhows, but they were always rare and expensive and not heard about after the collapse of the empire. It was the Moors who, after conquering Spain in the eighth century, gradually revived them.

The early oranges were all bitter, belonging to the Citrus aurantium group, represented today by the Seville orange. This orange has wonderfully perfumed flowers, aromatic skin and sharp juice and is still popular today for making English marmalade. The sweet orange (C. sinensis), with its delicious taste, was introduced to Europe in the sixteenth century and is probably a mutant of the bitter orange. It is widely represented today by the Valencia and navel oranges. Much more prized in China itself were the delicious southern tangerines. The bitterpeel tangerine (C. deliciosa) was much used in medicine and existed in many varieties, among them the vermilion bitterpeel and the winter-ripening golden bitterpeel of the deep south, which we know as the kumquat. Interestingly, the Chinese of the T'ang dynasty (618–907 AD) stored their oranges in salt. Kept this way, they were reputed to have the added virtue of relieving the effects of drinking too much wine.

The Valencia and Washington navels are said to be the best oranges for small gardens, the fruit from both holding on the tree for several months under favorable conditions. The best climate is one in which there are definite winter and summer seasons, though the winters must not be too cold whilst too much heat in early spring or summer can cause 'fruit drop'.

VEAU LUNEL

Chef and boulanger (baker) Franck Francois gave me this recipe. Now settled in Sydney, he originally came from Lunel in the Camargue in the south of France which is famous for its muscatel. Like many of his fellow countrymen, he is vibrant and cheeky. 'Come and see me, come and taste my bread . . . ' he implored when I met him at a reception for Paul Bocuse. His opinions about what constitutes 'real' food are, well, definite. 'A good honest feed is what I like. Not the stuff that requires tweezers to get it into your mouth, or a magnifying glass to see it with.'

His philosophy? 'Everything revolves around the table or the bed. Show me someone who knows good food and I'll show you a good lover.'

SERVES 6

1 onion, finely chopped
softened butter
2 cups (16 fl oz) muscatel
2 cups (16 fl oz) veal stock (broth)
handful seedless raisins, soaked overnight in hot tea
scant ½ cup (3 ⅓ fl oz) cream
12 veal medallions (taken from the sirloin)

all-purpose (plain) flour
salt and pepper
zest (rind) of ½ an orange
handful of walnuts, chopped

In a saucepan, sauté the onion in a knob of butter until soft, add muscatel and boil until all the alcohol is gone, about 5 minutes. Add stock, seedless raisins, half the cream and reduce.

Toss veal medallions in flour, salt and pepper. In a frying pan, sauté both sides in a little butter, being careful that the butter doesn't burn. Don't overcook or they will toughen. Set aside and keep warm.

Just before serving, put the saucepan back on the stove, bring to a boil, add remaining cream. Boil for 2 minutes, throw in orange zest and walnuts. Boil another 2 minutes. Put the veal into the saucepan with its juices. Simmer gently for another 2 minutes, just enough to heat the meat.

Take out the medallions, place on a platter and cover with the sauce.

PICKLED ORANGES

These delicious preserved oranges go well with the Christmas ham, or with duck, pork and turkey. They keep well. Don't worry if the oranges you use are a little sour — they taste even better. Some of my friends even eat them for breakfast!

MAKES APPROX 8 CUPS (2 QT)

8 oranges, unpeeled
1 tsp salt
1 cup (8 fl oz) water
¼ cup (3 oz) honey
2 cups (1 lb) sugar
1 cup (8 fl oz) malt vinegar
1 tspn cinnamon
½ tspn Chinese five-spice powder
8 whole black peppercorns

8–10 cardamom pods, split open
2 star anise
12 cloves

Put oranges and salt into a large saucepan, cover with water and bring to a boil. Reduce heat and let simmer for 40–50 minutes or until tender. Remove from heat, drain and let the oranges cool. Using a sharp knife, cut them into slices, not too thick and not too thin.

Put remaining ingredients into a large saucepan, bring to a boil, reduce heat and simmer gently for 10 minutes. Remove from heat and strain through a sieve to catch all the spices. Return liquid to pan and put orange slices into the pickling mixture. Place over moderate heat, bring to boil, stirring occasionally.

Reduce heat and simmer gently for another 15 minutes. Remove from heat, allow to stand for 10 minutes and then ladle into hot, dry, sterile jars. Seal and label. They look pretty covered with brown paper and tied with string.

Note: The star anise and the cloves can be returned to the pan with the oranges. The spices are pretty left floating in the liquid and give it a more homemade look.

ORANGES WITH CINNAMON AND ROSE WATER

SERVES 6–8

In Morocco, oranges are used extensively. This is a simple and refreshing way of serving them for a summer dessert.

Remove all the white pith from 10 oranges, using a small sharp knife. Slice into circles and overlap on a wide, shallow dish. Sprinkle with rose water and dust with confectioners' (icing) sugar and cinnamon. Decorate with pink rose petals. Fresh pitted dates are a lovely addition to this. In Morocco, slivered green almonds are sometimes strewn over the top.

ORANGE AND ALMOND CAKE

This is Claudia Roden's justly famous orange cake from *A Book of Middle Eastern Food*. It is a stunning, moist and moreish cake. A little goes a long way and it's very easy to make.

2 large oranges
6 eggs
1 cup (8 oz) sugar
2 ¼ cups (8 oz) ground almonds
1 tspn baking powder

Wash the oranges, then boil them unpeeled in water for 1½ –2 hours. Check occasionally to make sure the water hasn't boiled away. Allow them to cool, then cut open and remove the seeds. Turn the oranges into pulp by putting in a food processor or blender.

Preheat oven to 400°F (200°C/Gas 6). Grease and flour a 10 in tin with a removable base (a fluted one looks pretty).

In a large bowl, beat the eggs until fluffy, add the sugar and beat well. Add remaining ingredients and pour into the prepared tin. Bake in oven for 50–60 minutes or until a skewer inserted in the middle comes out clean. Cool a little and remove from tin — don't let it get so cold that it sticks to the tin.

ORANGE CHOCOLATE BALLS

Luscious and rich, these are good with coffee. Use a couverture chocolate, rather than a compound one, for a better taste.

MAKES APPROX 25

6 oz dark chocolate
½ cup (4 oz) unsalted butter
3 egg yolks
¼ cup (3 oz) superfine (caster) sugar
grated zest (rind) of 1 orange
1 ⅓ tblspns (⅔ fl oz) orange liqueur
sifted cocoa

Chop up the chocolate and put it together with the butter in the top of a double boiler. Melt over hot, not boiling, water. Remove from heat.

In a bowl, beat together the egg yolks and sugar until thick and creamy. Add the orange zest and liqueur, then beat in the melted chocolate mixture. Refrigerate until firm but not stiff.

Remove from refrigerator and roll into walnut-size balls. Coat with the sifted cocoa. Store in the refrigerator in an airtight container.

CHICKEN WITH ORANGE MACADAMIA STUFFING

SERVES 6

6 small chickens
ground cinnamon
pepper
melted butter

ORANGE MACADAMIA STUFFING
4 tblspns scallions (shallots, spring onions), finely chopped
1 ⅓ tblspns (⅔ oz) butter
2 tblspns fresh green ginger, grated
3 cups (6 oz) fresh breadcrumbs

1 cucumber, peeled, seeded and diced
2 tblspns fresh coriander (cilantro) leaves and roots, chopped
2 cups (8 oz) unsalted macadamia nuts, chopped
zest (rind) of 1 orange
½ cup (3 oz) seedless raisins
¼ tspn ground cinnamon
½ cup (4 fl oz) orange juice
salt and pepper
1 egg, beaten

Wipe the chickens dry, remove any fat and innards.

Loosely pack the stuffing into the chickens. Rub bodies all over with a little ground cinnamon and grind pepper over them. Place on a rack over a baking dish, brush all over with melted butter and place in a preheated oven (400°F/200°C/Gas 6). Baste every 10 minutes. After 30 minutes, reduce heat to 300°F (150°C/Gas 2) and roast for 15 more minutes.

ORANGE MACADAMIA STUFFING
Sauté scallions and ginger in the butter in a frying pan. Put them into a mixing bowl with breadcrumbs, cucumber, coriander, macadamia nuts, orange zest, seedless raisins, cinnamon and orange juice. Season to taste and add an egg if the mixture doesn't hold.

CANDIED CITRUS PEEL

Candied peel, be it orange, lemon or grapefruit, is delicious added to cakes and puddings — and also good eaten on its own.

The homemade variety is full of flavor and quite luscious and makes a lovely gift to a friend who cooks.

6 oranges, lemons or grapefruit
4 cups (2 lb) sugar
2 cups (½ qt) water
superfine (caster) sugar

Wash and scrub the fruit well. Peel it thickly, including all the white pith which clings to the skin — it turns translucent in the syrup.

Put the peel into a large saucepan, cover with water and bring to a boil. Lower heat and simmer until tender. Drain and boil again in fresh water for 15–20 minutes.

Bring the sugar and water to a boil, stirring to make sure all the sugar is dissolved. Put in the peel and simmer vigorously until syrup has almost disappeared, stirring to prevent burning.

Remove peel from saucepan and spread on trays lined with waxed (greaseproof) paper. Leave to dry in the sun. Alternatively, dry it in a cool oven (approx 120°F/50°C/Gas ½) for 35–40 minutes. Be careful not to overdry.

Roll peel in superfine sugar when dry and store in airtight jars.

CANDIED ORANGE PECANS

These pecans, coated in soft, sugary, orange-flavored candy originate in the deep south of the United States. They make lovely gifts, wrapped in cellophane packages and tied with a bow. If pecans are not available, use walnuts.

vegetable oil
1 ½ cups (12 oz) white sugar
½ cup (4 fl oz) fresh orange juice
1 tblspn (½ oz) butter
grated zest (rind) of 1 orange
2 ½ cups (8 oz) pecans or walnuts

Lightly oil a marble slab or baking sheet with a brush.

In a heavy saucepan combine the sugar and orange juice and stir together over moderate heat until all the sugar is dissolved. Insert a candy thermometer and boil gently until the syrup reaches the soft ball stage (234–240°F/112–116°C).

Remove the saucepan from the heat and immediately add the butter and orange zest. Beat with a wooden spoon until mixture thickens and is about to set. Quickly stir in the pecans or walnuts until they are well coated in the mixture.

Turn out onto the oiled surface and separate the nuts using two forks. Dry on a rack and store in airtight containers.

Kumquats
Fortunella *species*

I love the look of the kumquat tree when it is in full fruit. Such a joy to behold, the tiny orange fruits shining forth from the dark green of the leaves, cheering up a grey winter's day.

The biggest kumquat tree I've seen is at my mother's farm, and it seems to be always in fruit. I don't know why. Perhaps it has something to do with the amount of fertilizer my mother continually throws around it (she is not renowned for her moderation — in anything!). Perhaps it's just a very happy tree. The bantams and peacocks are certainly fond of it, scratching away underneath, much to my mother's annoyance. Sometimes, when the peacocks are showing off and strutting around with their tails open, or are just lazing underneath the tree, the sight of the two together is breathtaking.

Long cultivated in China (kam kwat in Cantonese means 'golden orange'), Japan and Malaya, it was not introduced to Europe until 1846. Robert Fortune, a collector of plants for the Royal Horticultural Society, took it to Europe and the genus (of which there are four known species) was named in his honor. The amber colored rind of the golden kumquat, steeped in honey, was highly prized in the southern province of Lingnan during the T'ang dynasty. Today, the Nagami or oval kumquat is the commonest of the kumquats and is available from most nurseries. It is both tart and sweet. Round kumquats are often confused with calamondins by nurseries. They resemble the Nagami but have a sweeter flesh and rind. Kumquats make ideal pot plants. As well as looking lovely, they are sweetly scented and are well suited to colder climates with late frosts.

Not only does the kumquat look splendid, its fruit is also very good: golden yellow with that pungent acid taste which is so good for cutting through the sweetness or fattiness in different dishes.

SPIRITED KUMQUATS

Brandy is traditionally used for these, but they are also good preserved under gin or vodka. There is no specific recipe —just use your commonsense.

Wash freshly picked kumquats and prick all over with a darning or tapestry needle. Layer in sterilized glass jars (with clip-on or screw-top lids). To each layer, add about ½ cup (4 oz) superfine (caster) sugar.

Pour over the spirit of your choice. Shake the jar each day for the next three weeks, standing it on its lid one day and its bottom the next. This ensures the sugar will dissolve and not adhere to either bottom or top. Store in a cool place for 3–4 months.

Excellent with ham, pork, poultry and game. The liqueur can be used for basting. Mix it with a little honey, Chinese five-spice powder and/or cinnamon for a delicious and fragrant marinade.

Kumquat Marmalade

When we go to my mother's farm, I always try to make a batch of kumquat marmalade. It is absolutely delicious — not just on toast for breakfast, but as a glaze (with brown sugar and five-spice powder) for the Christmas ham, and stirred into the juices of a roast loin of pork with a little stock, reduced and served as a sauce. We sit out under the mango tree when preparing the fruit.

freshly picked kumquats

water to cover

sugar

Wash the kumquats and cut them into halves. Remove the seeds and put into a cup covered with water.

Put halved kumquats into a preserving pan and just cover with water. Put on a lid and let them sit overnight.

Next day, measure the kumquat/water mixture and put into a big pot or preserving pan. For every 1 cup (8 fl oz), allow ¾ cup (6 oz) sugar. Strain the seeds through a muslin cloth, tie up, and put into the pan with the kumquats and water. Bring to a boil on the top of the stove, turn down heat and simmer for 30 minutes. While the kumquats simmer, heat the sugar in a large tray in a moderate (350°F/180°C/Gas 4) oven. Pour the sugar into the pan and stir well with a wooden spoon. Bring back to boiling point, and simmer, uncovered, for 30–40 minutes or until the jam reaches setting point.

Turn off the heat, ladle into warm, sterile jars. Cover with a tight, screw-top lid. The bottles look lovely covered in rounds of brown paper and tied with string.

Lemons
Citrus limon

My sister Skye has a curious affinity with the bush lemon. Wherever she decides to put down roots, she finds a drooping old bush lemon in her back garden. These have usually shot up from seed and have rough thick skins (rather like the kaffir lime) and can sometimes be very good.

If you want a lemon tree in your back garden, it would be wiser to obtain suitable rootstocks from a reliable nursery, the Eureka being most suitable for the coastal home garden. It bears several crops of fruit in winter, spring and summer and is normally propagated on a rough lemon or Benton citrange rootstock. Other popular varieties are the Lisbon, a vigorous, thorny tree that is more cold-tolerant than the Eureka; the Meyer, which produces fruit throughout the year and does well in pots; and the Lemonade, a new Australian seedling recently located in Queensland. It has a lower acid content and a distinctive 'lemonade' flavor.

There is no common agreement on the lemon's origin, though it probably came from either India, Burma or perhaps southern China. By the fourth century AD the fruit and its tree were depicted in Roman mural paintings, the agricultural writer Palladius having planted the first lemon tree in Italy in that century. It was in Italy that I came across potted lemon trees lining the terraces and steps of a number of ancient Italian gardens. Lemons were planted in the Sahara by the Arab invaders in the eighth century and it was they who established the lemon orchards of Andalusia in Spain.

A whole book could be written in praise of the lemon. Whilst its uses in the kitchen are diverse, it is a food rarely eaten on its own (though the Moroccans preserve their lemons whole in salt and in India they are preserved when green in mustard oil with exotic spices). Its juice and zest (rind) are used widely in other cuisines and both the leaves (when crushed) and the flowers smell marvellous. Plant a lemon tree today.

FISH IN LEMON LEAVES

Small pieces of fish are enclosed in lemon leaves, threaded onto skewers and barbecued or broiled.

SERVES 4–6 AS AN ENTRÉE

1 lb firm white fish fillets (snapper, perch, bream)
1 stalk lemongrass (lower 1 in only), finely sliced
2 scallions (shallots, spring onions), finely sliced
2 tblspns (1 fl oz) fish sauce
2 tblspns (1 fl oz) light soy sauce
2 tblspns (1 fl oz) lemon juice
1 tspn turmeric
½ tspn sugar
freshly ground black pepper
large lemon leaves, washed
18 bamboo skewers, soaked in cold water for 1 hour

Trim fish and cut into slices, about 1 ½ x ¾ in. In an enamel or glass dish, mix together the lemongrass,

onion, fish sauce, light soy sauce, lemon juice, turmeric, sugar and a good grind of black pepper. Add fish and toss well, cover and refrigerate for at least 1 hour. Fold a lemon leaf over each slice of fish and push two pieces onto each skewer. Brush with oil and broil or barbecue over medium heat, 4 in from the heat source, for 4–5 minutes each side. Good with Radish Salad (page 100).

CHICKEN WITH CRACKED OLIVES AND PRESERVED LEMONS

The cracked olives are well worth finding as they are very delicious. Otherwise use green jumbo olives. The onions help to thicken the sauce.

SERVES 6–8

1 lb cracked olives
2 medium chickens, cut into serving pieces
1 onion, ground (minced)
3–4 cloves garlic, finely chopped
2 tblspns (1 fl oz) oil
1 tspn ground ginger
½ tspn ground cumin
salt
large pinch saffron
water (approx 4 cups (1 qt))
2 preserved lemons (see page 186)
1 tblspn (⅓ oz) paprika
3 onions, ground (minced), extra
juice of 2 fresh lemons (or to taste)

Rinse the olives and blanch them if they taste bitter. Set aside.

Mix the chicken pieces with 1 ground onion and the garlic, oil, ginger, cumin, salt and saffron. Put mixture into a large saucepan. Cover with the water and bring to a boil, partially cover, reduce heat and cook for 30 minutes. Add olives and washed zest (rind) of 2 preserved lemons, paprika and remaining ground onions. Partially cover again and continue cooking until chicken is very tender — about 30 minutes. Remove chicken from pan and keep warm. Reduce the juices until you have a thickish sauce, then add the lemon juice to taste.

Arrange the chicken pieces in a circle on a large, warm platter. Put the olives in the center. Cut the lemon skins into eighths and place on top of the chicken. Pour over the sauce.

LEMON DELICIOUS PUDDING

Aptly named, this is a very delicious winter pudding, with a golden brown spongy top and a lemon custard underneath. Serve it hot or warm with lashings of cream.

SERVES 6–8

3 tblspns (1 ½ oz) softened butter
1 cup (8 oz) sugar
juice and zest (rind) of 2 large lemons, finely grated
2 whole eggs
4 eggs, separated
¼ cup (1 oz) all-purpose (plain) flour, sifted
1 ⅔ cups (13 fl oz) milk

Preheat oven to moderately hot (375°F/190°C/Gas 5).

Cream together the butter, sugar and grated lemon zest. Add the 2 whole eggs, one at a time, then add the yolks of 2 eggs (set the other 2 yolks aside for another use). Fold in the flour alternately with the milk and lemon juice. Beat to combine well.

Whisk the 4 egg whites until stiff and glossy, then fold through the lemon mixture. Pour into a 7 cup (1.¾ qt) pudding basin and bake uncovered in a pan of water for 30 minutes. Cover top with aluminum foil and bake a further 30 minutes.

PRESERVED LEMONS

In the Middle East, lemons are often preserved in this manner. The salt is available from specialty delicatessens.

Cut washed lemons in four, from the stem end but not right through. Fill the center of the lemons with 1 tspn of flaky sea salt and place them in clean, sterile jars with screw tops.

Push the lemons down with a clean wooden spoon — don't use your hands. Fill the jar completely and seal. After a couple of days, the lemons will soften slightly and more can be added. When the jar is well filled, set aside for 4 weeks. Don't worry if a film forms over the lemons as it can be washed off.

Lemons preserved in this manner are used in Moroccan tagines, in fish dishes and in salads. Only the skin is used — the pith is discarded.

Lemons can also be kept fresh by packing them in salt, but don't let them touch each other.

LEMON ICE

Nice served in the frozen hollowed-out shells of lemons.

MAKES APPROX 4 CUPS (1 QT)

⅔ cup (5 oz) sugar
2 ½ cups (20 fl oz) water
zest (rind) and juice of 3 large lemons

Place sugar, water and grated lemon zest together in a heavy saucepan, stirring over a moderate heat until sugar dissolves. When dissolved, bring to a boil and boil for 5 minutes. Cool and add the strained lemon juice. Strain again into freezer tray and freeze. Check after ½–1 hour and if beginning to set, stir the frozen sides into the more liquid middle part. Do this once more, about 1 hour later. After 2–3 hours (this depends on how deep your freezer tray is) the syrup should have formed into thick mushy granules. Serve with fresh berries and almond tuiles.

LEMON BARLEY WATER

A good refreshing drink to keep in your refrigerator in summer. Try it with fresh lime juice when limes are in season.

MAKES APPROX 6 CUPS (1 ½ QT)

4 tblspns (2 oz) pearl barley
5 cups (1 ¼ qt) boiling water
small piece lemon zest (rind)
½ – ¾ cup (4–6 fl oz) freshly squeezed lemon juice
(or to taste)
3–4 tblspns (1 ½ –2 oz) sugar

Wash the barley and put into a saucepan with the boiling water and lemon zest. Boil, uncovered, until reduced by half. Remove from heat and cool. Pour in the lemon juice and stir in sugar to taste. Strain and chill. Serve with fresh mint, bruised lemon verbena leaves and ice blocks.

Pears and Quinces
Rosaceae family

It was sunset, late evening. It was the season
when the grain had begun to head and the fields
were fair with flowers — flowers beginning to nod
as night came on and on, night which really did wear its
'cloak of darkness.' Tables were being laid outside; candles
lit and placed in the blossoming pear trees
where, shortly, they would assist the moon
to light the homecoming festivities.

RAYMOND CARVER, FROM 'THE OFFENDING EEL'

Hanging in my kitchen is a beautiful pen and ink watercolor by Australian painter Donald Friend. On a stool near some balcony doors sit two pears and an avocado. The painting is alive with color and sensuality, the solid contours of the fruits adding an extra dimension to the light.

Yet when Friend painted this picture, he was going through a difficult time. His health had deteriorated rapidly and he found it difficult to paint the human figure. Instead, he began a series of still lifes reflecting the beauty of objects around him. At the time he wrote:

The greengrocer's shop is crammed with colourful models, attractive vegetable rivals to those warm blooded bipeds in blue jeans who lean provocatively against lamp posts playing pocket billiards or to the polychrome butterfly painted ladies clad in varieties of musical comedy drag.

For sheer loveliness the fruit and

vegetables win hands down. Hinting, by means of smooth rounded contours and stalwart protuberances, at the erotic amenities of harem and slave market, the gay bar, and the massage parlour . . .

Pears have often been described lyrically. Some modern gourmets find them incomparable. Restaurateur Gay Bilson, once wrote of a round, brown, almost apple-shaped pear she had eaten:

It was reminiscent of one I had had in France, and which I longed for ever since. This pear, possibly an *Olivier de Serres* or a *Passé Crasanne*, exhibited every trait that a pear could possibly have to be considered great — a wonderful shape, firmness combined with juiciness, and best of all the texture of sand without the grittiness we all remember from picnics on the beach . . . I could go on and on about pears . . .

That pear was the Winter Cole. She spoke, too, of the varieties of pears originating in France and Belgium which have such beautiful names — Doyenné d'Été, Beurre d'Amanlis, Bergamotte D'Espéren, Passé Crasanne, Sanguinole. She didn't mention the famous Doyenne du Comice, which first appeared in France in 1849. Such varieties were bred by wealthy amateurs in a climate where the summers are warm and the roots receive just the right amount of moisture (pears do not like permanently wet soils). It is in this part of Europe that the pear thrives.

However, food writer Waverley Root points out, pears differ more in size, shape, texture and flavor than almost any other fruit of the orchard. In fact there are said to be over 3000 varieties, only a few of which are cultivated by home gardeners. Variability may operate in either direction, for better or for worse: great variability gives us richness of choice, but versatility makes the pear vulnerable, cautions Root. He advises you pay attention as you taste a perfect pear: its flavor is fragile and delicate, but the slightest imperfection can destroy its subtlety.

Homer called the pear 'one of the fruits of the Gods', so the ancient Greeks must have had some delicious cultivated varieties. No-one, though, has ever sung the praises of wild pears: Alexandre Dumas cites pears as an outstanding example of the improvements which can be brought about by cultivation.

I have often been surprised by a new variety. Recently Nashi pears from Japan and Corella pears, named after the glorious red-crested parrot, have become more available. Even more recently I have come across tiny red-faced pears, sometimes described as gambe di donna *(women's legs). These lilliputian pears are exquisite and are becoming more fashionable, thanks to Sicilian immigrants who took the grafting wood with them from their native home. During the 1950s and 1960s, Sicilian farmers exported these pears to northern European countries where they were very popular and were known as cocktail pears. The Italians often use them in their* mostarda di frutta, *those delicious, piquant preserves made with mustard oil and fermented grape juice* (mosto).

Pears seem to have originated in western Asia and are one of the oldest of fruits. Seeds have been found in a tomb dated 2100 BC in China, and some writers speculate that perhaps that is where they first came from.

When Marco Polo was there, he reported huge pears for sale 'weighing ten pounds apiece, white as dough inside and very fragrant'. Chinese pears are sometimes called sand pears because they have a high proportion of grit cells and can be quite crunchy.

The pears we eat in the West are varieties of Pyrus communis and are grouped into families by shape: round and flattened with rough skins (mostly old varieties); bergamot or top-shaped, which are green when ripe (typical pears of this group come from Bergamo, Italy); conical, yellow or red flushed pears which taper but are not waisted; pyriform, with a distinct waist, which are yellow when ripe; oval, with no red coloring; and calebasse or long pears, which are long and straight and mostly used for cooking.

Like the apple and quince, the pear is botanically a pome. The quince, however, differs from these fruits in that it has many ovules in each section (carpule) whereas the apple and pear have only two. Quinces have often been mistaken for pears and for a long time were in fact classified as Cydonian pears (P. cydonia).

Jewish tradition believes the quince is the oldest of the fruits and that it grew in the Garden of Eden. I had always believed Eve was tempted by an apple, but some say it was a quince tree in which the snake dwelt.

Today, the quince is a much neglected and overlooked fruit, which is a pity. The color transformation that takes place when quinces are cooked, is, for me, a small miracle.

I think the ancient Greeks and Romans knew better. They held the quince in high esteem, dedicating it to both Venus and Aphrodite as a symbol of happiness, love and fruitfulness. Eating one was a necessary preliminary before entering the marriage bed.

Pears
Pyrus communis

In Patrick White's novel, Voss, the heroine's uncle brings her a box of expensive pears, hoping that through this material offering he will be able to express the affection absent from his voice and looks. But these beautiful golden pears are left to rot on a console table in the shadows of the sick woman's room.

It's always sad when something once glorious has been forgotten and left to rot, be it under a tree, in a fruit bowl or tucked away in the refrigerator. Fruit rots are often caused when pears are bruised during picking. They need to be handled carefully if you want the best from them.

European pears are often too large for the home garden,

growing as they can to a height of 40 ft. They do not grow true from seed and should be propagated on a suitable rootstock. Quince rootstocks work well for some varieties. Young trees are best purchased from a reliable nursery.

Williams Bon Chrétien (or Bartlett) is the most popular commercial pear, but there are nicer varieties for the home garden. Shop around. The Beurre Bosc, for example, is a harder, crisper pear which is delicious eaten fresh and also very good cooked. Packhams, Winter Cole, Josephine and the Nashi are other varieties you could explore.

Pears grow best in areas also suitable for apples, that is, where the winters are cool to cold, the summers mild and the spring rainfall is light. They need deep, fertile soil and are slow coming to maturity, often taking seven years before cropping. Too much nitrogen will lead to lush, disease-prone growth; too little will lead to pale leaves. Like apples, most pears are pruned to a vase shape, but the central leader system (which leads to earlier cropping) is also popular. Pears also respond well to trellis training, but you will need to allow more space for spreading than is required for the apple, unless the tree has been propagated on quince rootstock.

STUFFED NECK OF PORK WITH PEARS AND BLUEBERRIES

This is a lovely combination. Some people like their pork well cooked, in which case cook for the longer time, I prefer mine to be a little pink and tend to undercook it.

It used to be considered esssential to cook pork thoroughly, but modern methods of feeding and raising pigs have made this unnecessary.

SERVES 6

2 lb piece of pork neck
3 ⅓ oz blueberries
2 hard pears, peeled and diced
grated zest (rind) of 1 orange
1 ⅓ tblspns (⅔ fl oz) Galliano
Chinese five-spice powder
vine leaves (optional)

Preheat oven to 425°F (220°C/Gas 7).

Ask the butcher to tunnel bone the pork, but not to cut right through to the other end.

Mix together the blueberries, pears, orange zest and Galliano in a bowl. Spoon into the center of the pork, pushing the mixture in firmly with your fingers.

Wipe the pork dry and sprinkle with the five-spice powder. Wrap in blanched fresh vine leaves, cover tightly with aluminum foil, place on a baking tray and cook in the hot oven for 10 minutes. Turn heat down to 350°F (180°C/Gas 4) and cook for 1–1 ½ hours or until a skewer inserted into the meat shows the juices are clear. Remove, let stand for 10 minutes before cutting. Nice with sweet potatoes. Also good cold.

PEAR AND WATERCRESS SALAD

1 bunch watercress, approx 1 lb, washed
4 pears, peeled and sliced
4 oz crumbled blue vein cheese (such as Stilton)

DRESSING
juice of ½ lemon
½ cup (4 fl oz) olive oil
2 ⅔ tblspns (1 ⅓ fl oz) cream

1 dessertspoon poppy seeds
salt and pepper

Arrange the watercress on a platter. Put the pear slices on top and scatter over the crumbled cheese. Spoon over the poppy seed dressing.

To make the dressing, put all the ingredients together in a screwtop jar and shake well to amalgamate. Keep refrigerated.

PEAR AND CORIANDER SALAD

What a delightful and unusual combination this is. A few pecans or walnuts may be added to give it an extra crunch.

SERVES 4

4 large ripe pears
1 bunch watercress, washed, dried and stalks removed
8 oz pear tomatoes
6 tblspns fresh coriander (cilantro) leaves, finely chopped
½ bunch scallions (shallots, spring onions), slivered
½ bunch chives, snipped
2 tspns Dijon-style mustard
3–4 tblspns (1 ⅓ –2 fl oz) lemon juice
½ cup (4 fl oz) olive oil
1 clove garlic, crushed
freshly ground black pepper

Peel pears, halve and core. Slice lengthways and arrange in a salad bowl lined with watercress. Scatter over tomatoes, coriander, scallions and chives.

Place remaining ingredients in a small bowl, whisking together until combined. Pour over salad and lightly toss just before serving.

Note: Pear tomatoes are also known as yellow tear-drop tomatoes. They are very small, about the size of cherry tomatoes.

PEAR GALETTE

You can also make this galette with scraps of puff pastry, and you can substitute apples for the pears.

½ cup (4 oz) butter, softened
½ cup (2 oz) confectioners' (icing) sugar, sifted
finely grated zest (rind) of ½ lemon
1 egg yolk
1 ¼ cups (5 oz) all-purpose (plain) flour
6 ripe pears
superfine (caster) sugar

Combine the butter, confectioners' sugar and lemon zest, and beat together until creamy. Add the egg yolk, then fold in the flour. Wrap in waxed (greaseproof) paper and chill for at least 1 hour in the refrigerator.

Roll out the pastry on a lightly floured board. Cover the flat removable bottom of a round 10 in flan tin. You won't need to use the fluted edge. Return to the refrigerator whilst preparing the pears.

Preheat the oven to 425°F (220°C/Gas 7).

Peel the pears, cut them into quarters and remove the seeds. Slice them very finely. Remove pastry from refrigerator. Starting in the center, arrange the slices in overlapping circles on top of the pastry. Sprinkle liberally with superfine sugar and place the galette on a baking tray. Bake for 25 minutes, then remove from the oven and tip off any excess juices. Sprinkle again with superfine sugar and return to the oven for another 10 minutes or until the sugar has caramelized and the pastry is brown and crisp.

Serve warm with vanilla ice-cream.

GREEN SALAD OF PEARS, AVOCADO AND APPLE

A nice accompaniment to the cheeseboard, this is a creation of television cook Bernard King.

SERVES 6

2 firm ripe avocados
2 green apples, unpeeled
2 firm green pears, unpeeled

DRESSING
½ cup (4 fl oz) olive oil
¼ cup (2 fl oz) lime and/or orange juice
1 kiwi fruit (Chinese gooseberry), peeled and puréed

Peel avocados, cut into halves and then into chunks. Wash the apples and pears and cut into similar size chunks. Toss together with the dressing.

DRESSING
Blend ingredients together in blender or food processor. Pour over prepared fruits.

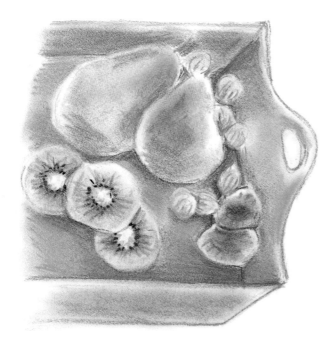

GLISTENING PEARS

These glistening golden pears are like the jewels from Aladdin's Cave. Presented on a white oval platter and served with plenty of thick cream, they look superb. They are time consuming and do need to be watched carefully, but don't worry that they'll fall apart (they won't). You can substitute peaches for the pears. The peaches need to be a hard variety, like the Golden Queen, and their skins should be peeled by plunging in hot water.

SERVES 6

12 small or 6 large hard green pears, peeled
equal quantities of sugar and water
generous pinch saffron threads

Place the pears standing up in a preserving pan or saucepan which will hold them snugly. Measure equal quantities of sugar and water (1 cup:1 cup) and let this mixture cover about three-quarters of the pears. Bring to a boil, making sure the sugar has dissolved first, add the saffron, then cover with a lid and simmer very gently for 1 hour.

Remove cover, turn up the heat a little and allow syrup to reduce and the pears to caramelize, which will take another hour. It is easier to do this in a heavy baking pan on top of the stove: remove pears with two spoons, being careful not to mark them and place in the pan, then very carefully pour in the sugar syrup. Watch this part of the process carefully, stirring from time to time to make sure the pears don't stick on the bottom of the tray and catch, and also that the syrup doesn't burn towards the end. Don't rush this — the pears need to be a rich, golden color and be sticky with the caramelized syrup mixture.

Remove from the pan and spoon onto the platter. Serve at room temperature. Don't refrigerate as the caramel will water out.

Quinces
Cydonia oblonga

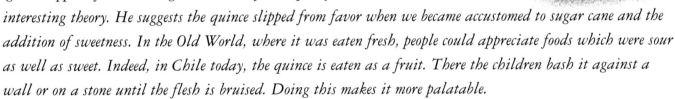

Another unsung, old-fashioned fruit, sometimes referred to as the 'golden apple'. It is one of the wonders of the kitchen, transforming itself during the cooking process from beige to pink. Along with the persimmon and pomegranate, it evokes for me the mellow fruitfulness of autumn with all its lovely tawny, russet colors. The ancient Greeks and Romans loved the quince — in fact many believe it to be the 'golden apple' of classical legend. Waverley Root puts forth an interesting theory. He suggests the quince slipped from favor when we became accustomed to sugar cane and the addition of sweetness. In the Old World, where it was eaten fresh, people could appreciate foods which were sour as well as sweet. Indeed, in Chile today, the quince is eaten as a fruit. There the children bash it against a wall or on a stone until the flesh is bruised. Doing this makes it more palatable.

Quinces were popular throughout Europe up until the sixteenth century when they were eaten baked and whole at the end of a meal. Indeed, anything made with quinces was popular. They were also treasured for their cosmetic and medicinal properties. It is not the quince that has changed, it is our gastronomic education. The tree itself is quite lovely, with large pinkish or white flowers, oval leaves covered with thick down, and golden, pear-shaped fruit with a wonderful perfume.

A number of varieties are available including, in order of fruit maturation, 'De Vrajna', 'Smyrna', 'Champion' and 'Pineapple'. A single tree will crop satisfactorily but will do better if cross-pollinated. They are fairly adaptable, growing well in a range of climates from the subtropics through to cool highlands. Fleck diseases (or small reddish-brown spots) can be a problem in coastal areas with high rainfall.

Quinces are deciduous and so are best planted in winter when dormant. Use plenty of organic mulch to help with moisture retention and water frequently during the growing season. Like pears and apples, they are usually trained to grow into an open-centered, vase-shaped tree. Cropping begins after about five years.

PORK WITH QUINCE

SERVES 6

3 lb stewing pork, cubed
2 ⅔ tblspns (1 ⅓ fl oz) oil
2 tblspns (1 oz) butter
1 large onion, grated
1 cup (8 fl oz) red wine
1 cup (8 fl oz) water
pinch saffron
salt and pepper
1 tspn powdered ginger
1 cinnamon stick
strip of orange zest (rind)
3 medium quinces, approx 2 lb, well-washed
cinnamon and sugar

In a heavy frying pan, brown the pork on all sides in the oil and butter. Remove to a plate. Add onion to the pan and cook gently until soft. Return pork to the pan, add the red wine and water to cover. Add saffron, salt and pepper to taste, powdered ginger, the cinnamon stick and orange zest. Cover and simmer gently for 1 hour.

Meanwhile, cut the quinces into eighths, removing their seeds but leaving on the skin. Rinse them and poach in lightly sugared water for 15–20 minutes or until just tender. Remove and drain.

Place quince slices on top of the pork and sprinkle lightly with sugar and cinnamon. Cover and cook until pork and quinces are tender, approx 45 minutes.

Nice garnished with freshly chopped parsley or coriander (cilantro) and served with saffron rice or steamed couscous.

Note: For a richer sauce, caramelize the drained quince slices before adding to the pork.

DESSERT QUINCES

This recipe was given to me by restaurateur Maggie Beer, who was in turn given it by a woman who lives in the Barossa Valley, South Australia, whose grandmother had passed it on to her. Such is the way of many recipes, especially those handed on over generations. There is a generosity in such sharing and much pleasure and joy when a recipe becomes a treasured part of a family.

These quinces, when cooked, can be served whole. Because they are so soft and luscious, every part can be eaten, including the core. Maggie serves hers with a crème anglaise and just a little of the glorious translucent red jelly, which is very sweet. Keep the leftover to spread on toast and scones, or to serve with roast pork or turkey. The quinces are a nice alternative to apples with pork and good, too, sliced on breakfast cereal.

SERVES 6

6 whole quinces
6 cups (1 ½ qt) water
4 cups (2 lb) sugar
juice of 3 lemons

Rub skins of quinces and wash. Place in a pot packed fairly tightly with water and sugar. Boil at a reasonably high temperature, uncovered, for up to 3 hours, turning two or three times during the cooking process.

Add juice of 3 lemons to take away excessive sweetness in the last stage of cooking, and turn temperature down to prevent jelly burning. Finish the cooking on a simmer pad to prevent sticking or burning.

UPSIDE-DOWN QUINCE CAKE

My mother makes this cake every weekend when quinces are in season. The cake base comes from English cookery writer Jane Grigson.

QUINCES

4 medium, ripe quinces, approx 10 oz each

1 lemon

1 orange

sugar

TOFFEE

¼ cup (2 oz) butter

⅓ cup (3 oz) superfine (caster) sugar

¼ cup (2 fl oz) reserved quince syrup

1 tspn cardamom seeds

CAKE

½ cup (4 oz) butter, softened

⅓ cup (3 oz) superfine (caster) sugar

1 ⅔ cups (7 oz) self-raising flour

4 eggs

1 ½ tspns baking powder

1 tspn ground cardamom

½ cup (2 oz) ground almonds

scant ½ cup (3 ⅓ fl oz) preserved quince syrup

QUINCES

Wash quinces, remove core and seeds, cut into eighths. Place all the parings in a saucepan, cover with water. Add a thinly sliced lemon and a thinly sliced orange. Simmer until soft, strain and reserve the liquid.

Weigh the quince slices. Weigh an equal quantity of sugar and warm it in the oven. Put reserved liquid, quince slices and warm sugar into a saucepan and simmer until quinces are tender adding more water if necessary to cover quinces. Remove quince slices and reduce syrup until thick. Set aside and reserve.

TOFFEE

Grease a 10 in tin or line with non-stick baking paper. Put the butter in a small, heavy saucepan, melt over low heat and add the sugar. Stir with a wooden spoon until mixture is a pale toffee color. Add quince syrup and remove from heat. Pour mixture into prepared tin, scatter cardamom seeds over evenly and arrange the poached quince slices in a sunflower pattern on bottom of tin.

CAKE

Preheat oven to 350°F (180°C/Gas 4).

Put all the ingredients for cake mixture into a food processor and process until smooth. Pour over top of quinces and bake for 50–60 minutes until edges are coming away from the side of the pan and a skewer inserted in the middle comes out clean.

Cool on a wire rack and run a knife around the edges. Place a large plate over the top and tip out. As the cake tips onto the plate, juices from the toffee will run down the sides, ensuring a moist and very delicious cake. Serve hot or cold with cream.

PICKLED QUINCES

Pickled quinces complement rich game and poultry dishes beautifully, cutting through the richness. They also go well with terrines and patés.

MAKES 7 CUPS (1 ¾ QT)

3 lb quinces, approx 5 medium quinces

3 tblspns (1 ½ oz) coarse salt

sugar (see method)

white wine vinegar

2 star anise

6 cloves

½ tspn black cardamom seeds

Peel and core the quinces, cut into eighths and remove the seeds. Put into a large saucepan, cover with water and the salt and bring to a boil. Boil for 10 minutes, strain and measure the juice.

For every 2 cups (½ qt) juice, add ¼ cup (2 oz) sugar and ⅔ cup (5 fl oz) vinegar. Taste the mixture and add more vinegar or sugar to suit your taste. Bring to a boil, put the fruit back and simmer until almost tender. Let stand overnight. Next day, drain off the syrup. Pack the fruit into clean sterile jars with the spices. Reboil the syrup and pour over the fruit.

QUINCE PASTE

Wonderful on the cheese board or delicious with coffee.
Make it when quinces are in season — it will
keep for ages.

2 lb quinces
sugar (see method)
juice of 1 lemon
blanched almonds or *pistachio nuts (optional)*

Preheat oven to 300°F (150°C/Gas 2).

Wash the quinces and put them whole into a large
baking dish. Place in the oven for 2–2 ¼ hours or until
cooked through. If you pierce them with a skewer they
should be soft. Remove and cool.

When cool, peel and cut into quarters. Rub the flesh
through a sieve — or put it into a food processor,
processing until smooth.

Weigh the pulp. Weigh an equal amount of sugar.
Put the sugar and lemon juice into a large heavy pan
with about ⅔ cup (5 fl oz) water. Bring to a boil and
simmer, stirring, until sugar is dissolved. Add the
quince pulp and cook over very low heat, stirring
occasionally with a wooden spoon, until the paste
thickens and comes away from the sides and bottom of
the pan, 45–60 minutes.

Turn into a wide shallow tray or baking dish (lined
with non-stick baking paper or edible rice paper) and
spread out evenly. Leave to dry for several days. To speed
up this process, you can also put it into a very low oven
or into an airing cupboard.

Cut the paste into small squares or triangles and
store between sheets of waxed (greaseproof) paper or foil
in an airtight container.

It looks pretty when studded with blanched almonds
or pistachio nuts.

Apples
Malus *species*

The silver apples of the moon,
The golden apples of the sun.

YEATS, FROM 'THE SONG OF WANDERING ÆNGUS'

Apples and comfort somehow go together. In the Western world, they are probably the most familiar and best loved of all the fruits. Mothers tuck one or two into their children's lunchboxes each day, having been told as children themselves that an apple a day will keep the doctor away.

In Chinese medicine, they are said to invigorate and promote vital energy, benefit the spleen and stop diarrhea whilst their nature is said to be neither hot nor cold.

If the vegetable kingdom has a royal family, it is the 'Rosaceae' which includes the queen of all flowers, the rose, and king of all fruits, the apple.

Apples are one of the oldest fruits, having been gathered, dried and stored as far back as the Stone Age. Evidence of carbonized apples were found by archeologists in ancient dwellings in Turkey, and Neolithic sites in Denmark and Switzerland have revealed the fossilized remains of crab-apples. Some claim the first apples grew not far from the Baltic, though others say that the modern apple developed from the wild crab-apple, whose origins are in the Balkans and south-west Asia. Their direct history is hard to trace because wild crab-apples are to be found growing through Britain, Europe, western Asia and the Himalayas.

Cultivation probably started in the thirteenth century BC when Ramses II had apple trees planted in the delta of the Nile. Records remain of how the apples were transplanted. The Greeks were cultivating them in Attica by

the seventh century BC, *but they were rare and expensive. Solon ordered newly married couples to eat an apple before going to bed on the first night of the marriage. By the fourth century* BC, *one writer could refer to 37 different varieties which suggests they had already been cultivated a very long time.*

When Europeans began exploring the world, they took apples with them. They went on the Mayflower *to America, where apple planting was among the first tasks of the new settlers. They also went on the* Bounty *with Captain Bligh to Australia (Bligh planted the first apple seedlings on Bruny Island in Tasmania, off the south coast of mainland Australia in 1788) and also to Canada, South Africa and New Zealand. From these countries, cultivation continued to spread. By 1833 the Van Diemen's Land* Almanac *could report 'that the success (of the apple plantings) was so astonishing it needs to be seen'. By 1895, the Bismark (a bright crimson cooking apple) was first sent to Britain from Tasmania. Many seedlings raised in the colonies were so good they were sent back 'home'. Few, however, did well away from their place of birth. Tasmania was, in fact, to become Australia's apple isle, due to its favorable climate. If you look at a map of Tasmania, it even looks a bit like an apple.*

Apples are selective about the areas in which they grow which is why one which thrives in one country fails to thrive in another. This also accounts for the fact that each country tends to rely on seedlings locally grown and tested rather than on imported stocks. It also accounts for the huge variety of apples.

Where would we be without apples? Today there are tens of thousands of known varieties, though, unfortunately only a few outstanding ones are grown for commercial production.

Myths, magic, folklore and science are full of apples: the golden apples of the Hesperides were given to Hera as a wedding present when she married Zeus; in ancient Greece, tossing an apple to a girl was a proposal and catching it an acceptance; on Twelfth Night in some English villages, 'apple wassailing' is still respected as a means of ensuring a good crop, the apple signifying fertility; at Halloween, the apple is also prominent, believed by some to hark back to some ancient Druid rites and by others to the Roman harvest festival of Pomona, the goddess of fruit and gardens. The apple led Isaac Newton to propound the theory of gravity; William Tell used an apple placed on his son's head to show the accuracy of his shot; and many people today refer to New York City *as 'The Big Apple'. Cezanne celebrated them in* Still Life: Apples and a Pot of Primroses *as did Lucas Cranach the Elder in* Virgin and Child under the Apple Tree.

Today, sadly, many commercial growers spray and wax them so much, then put them into cold storage, that they lose their appeal. True, they may look shiny and big and be perfectly shaped, but in the process, they have lost their taste and many of their life-giving properties. Apple trees are popular with home gardeners, though, because of the apple's many uses and excellent keeping qualities. They are the most widely cultivated fruits in temperate climates and grow well in a wide range of soils, but do prefer those which are slightly acidic with a pH of about 6 and require good drainage. Like many other fruits, apples may be grown in containers.

They do best where the winters are cool to cold because they require a dormant period of about two months to restore their strength. Ideally, summers should be mild and spring rainfall light. Most apple trees are not self-

fertile, so two varieties should be planted to ensure cross-pollination. To ensure this takes place, they must be no more than 32 ft apart.

All major pruning should be done in winter. Most apple trees have traditionally been pruned to a vase shape, but the central leader system (which produces a pyramid-shaped tree similar to the natural growth habit) is now preferred. Espalier-trained trees (with a stout central stem and 'ladder' of four or five branches on each side, parallel and about 1 ft apart and all on one plane) can be grown against a wall or fence or can be supported by wires. They look lovely flanking a garden path.

Varieties

Apple tree, Apple tree, bear Apples for me;
Hats full, laps full,
Sacks full, caps full;
Apple tree, Apple tree,
Bear Apples for me.

WILLIAM BUTLER

The many varieties of apples can be divided into two main categories: dessert (those which can be eaten fresh) and cooking. They tend to overlap: many dessert apples are also delicious when cooked. Apart from these two main categories, there are also perishable apples (which don't keep); winter apples (which keep well in storage), and apples which are most suitable for cider-making and for drying.

It's not always easy to give a particular apple its varietal name or origin as varieties differ so much in size, flavor, aroma, color, keeping quality and uses. As well, different varieties mature at different speeds, some maturing on the tree, others not maturing until harvested and stored. Generally speaking, the earlier an apple matures, the softer its flesh and the less likely it is to last long and keep its flavor. Apples which mature later in the year are harder and many need a long ripening period.

Some varieties are recognized worldwide, like Jonathon, Delicious, Granny Smith and Cox's Orange. Each country seems to have its favorites, and often each region within a country also has its favorites. As previously stated apples themselves are selective about where they will grow, often thriving in one area and failing in another. But no matter where you live, if you believe Horace, you'll pick your apples by the light of the waning moon to get the best taste.

The names given to the different apple varieties are interesting, the most popular in the United States and

Britain include Cox's Orange Pippin, McIntosh and Bramley. Other popular varieties in Australia are the Jonathon, Delicious, Star Crimson, Crofton, Yates and Democrat for eating; and the Golden Delicious, Sturmer, King Cole, Pippin, Granny Smith and the rarer Five Crown for both cooking and eating. Others not seen around so much include Tasman's Pride, Greeveston, Fanny, Rokewood, Spartan, Scarlet and Pearmain. Much of the important genetic diversity of the older and rarer varieties is being lost, so if you have room for (and are lucky enough to find) some unusual ones, do try them.

His poem was growing. It would have the smell of bread, and the rather grey wisdom of youth, and his grandmother's kumquats, and girls with yellow plaits exchanging love-talk behind their hands, and the blood thumping like a drum, and red apples . . .

PATRICK WHITE, *THE TREE OF MAN*

A RUSTIC TART OF APPLE, RHUBARB AND GINGER

7 oz softened cream cheese
1 cup (8 oz) unsalted butter, softened
3 cups (12 oz) all-purpose (plain) flour, sifted

FILLING
7–8 large Granny Smith apples, approx
2 lb prepared weight
1 bunch rhubarb (10 oz prepared weight)
grated zest (rind) of 1 lemon
2 in piece ginger, finely grated
¼ cup (1 ⅓ oz) cornstarch (cornflour)
apricot jam
sugar to taste or *⅓ cup (3 oz)*

Preheat oven to hot (400°F/200°C/Gas 6).

Cream together the cheese and butter. When combined, add the flour and mix until just incorporated. Wrap into a ball in waxed (greaseproof) paper and refrigerate while preparing the filling. Use the warmth of your hands to make it come properly together if it's crumbly. When filling is ready, roll out the pastry on a floured bench and free-form it onto a baking tray. You can roll it out as thinly as you like as it should be very pliable. Place the prepared filling onto the pastry and spread out evenly, folding pastry over the edges of the fruit. Leave the center free of pastry, trimming off any excess. Glaze pastry with egg yolk and sprinkle with sugar.

Bake in oven for 15 minutes, then turn heat down to 350°F (180°C/Gas 4) for a further 20 minutes. When cooked, glaze the fruit with warmed, sieved apricot jam.

FILLING
Peel, core and slice the apples. Wash the rhubarb and slice it. Mix together in a large bowl with remaining ingredients.

GOOD-FOR-YOU-CAKE

An easy, wholesome cake, especially good for taking on picnics. You can make one large or two smaller ones — freeze one for later use.
A number of variations are possible.

4 eggs
1 ¼ cups (10 oz) raw (demerara) sugar
1 ¼ cups (10 fl oz) vegetable oil
grated zest (rind) of 1 lemon
11 oz grated green apples, approx 4 medium apples
1 ½ cups (5 oz) wheatgerm
1 ⅔ cups (8 oz) all-purpose (plain) whole-wheat
(wholemeal) flour

3 tspns baking powder

1 tspn salt

1 ½ tspns cinnamon

½ tspn nutmeg

¾ cup (4 oz) golden raisins (sultanas)

½ cup (3 oz) walnuts, chopped

½ cup (3 oz) sunflower seeds

⅓ cup (3 fl oz) sour cream

Preheat oven to 350°F (180°C/Gas 4). Grease one large cake tin (11 x 9 ½ x 2 in) or 2 x 9 in cake tins.

In a large bowl, beat together the eggs and sugar until light and creamy. Add oil, beating constantly. Stir in lemon zest, apple and wheatgerm. Sift together the dry ingredients and fold through thoroughly. Stir in the golden raisins, nuts and seeds then fold through the sour cream.

Pour into prepared tin (tins). If using large tin, cook for 1–1 ¼ hours or until a skewer inserted in the middle comes out clean. If using smaller tins, cook for 45–50 minutes.

Turn out onto a wire rack and cool. Nice with a lemon or lime cream cheese icing.

LIME CREAM CHEESE ICING

4 oz cream cheese, softened

2 tblspns (1 oz) butter, softened

1 ⅔ cups (8 oz) confectioners' (icing) sugar, sifted

grated zest (rind) and juice of 1 lime or lemon

Beat together the cream cheese and butter until smooth. Add confectioners' sugar, zest and juice slowly. Beat well. Spread over cooled cake. Sprinkle with shredded or flaked coconut. Pretty decorated with 'impatiens' flowers.

Variations:

• *Substitute grated carrot for the apple.*

• *Substitute orange or lime zest (rind) for the lemon.*

• *Use nuts of choice.*

SMOKED HAM HOCKS WITH APPLES AND CABBAGE

The hocks swell as they cook and the aroma fills the house. A good one for hungry appetites in winter. Ask the butcher to break the knuckle of each hock, giving you 4 pieces.

SERVES 4 (OR 6 IF YOU ADD ANOTHER HOCK)

½ heading cabbage, shredded

2 green apples, peeled and sliced

2 cups (16 fl oz) apple juice

2 ⅔ tblspns (1 ⅓ fl oz) cider vinegar

1 tblspn (½ oz) brown sugar

2 tspns caraway seeds

2 large onions, peeled and sliced

2 smoked ham hocks, approx 1 ¾ lb each

Preheat oven to 350°F (180°C/Gas 4).

Combine the cabbage, apples, juice, vinegar, sugar and caraway seeds and place in a large heavy casserole. Top with the onion rings, then place the smoked ham hocks over the top. Cover with a tightly fitting lid.

Cook in oven for 2–2 ½ hours.

Serve with mashed potatoes and hot English mustard.

CHRISTMAS MINCE PIES

Our modern fruit mince recipes differ markedly from the original. Only the suet remains to remind us of the meat which was preserved in this way. Gervase Markham's 1615 recipe for mince pie includes a boned leg of lamb or mutton. After the mid-seventeenth century, the addition of juice and grated peel of citrus fruits developed.

Make the fruit mince mixture 3 weeks before you intend using it. This quantity makes about 2 lb and will keep for up to 6 months if kept airtight and in a cool place.

MAKES 3 LB OR ENOUGH FOR 48 PIES

2 x 2 lb pre-rolled shortcrust or puff pastry
milk
confectioners' (icing) sugar

FRUIT MINCE
8 oz beef suet, finely chopped
zest (rind) of 1–2 lemons
1 ⅔ cups (8 oz) currants
1 ½ cups (8 oz) seedless raisins, chopped
2 medium apples (approx 8 oz prepared weight), peeled, cored and chopped
¾ cup (4 oz) golden raisins (sultanas), chopped
¾ cup (4 oz) chopped mixed peel
¾ cup (4 oz) blanched almonds, chopped
1 ¼ cups (10 oz) superfine (caster) sugar
½ tspn each cinnamon, nutmeg and ground cloves
½ cup (4 fl oz) good-quality brandy or overproof rum

FRUIT MINCE
Put the suet into a bowl and add the lemon zest. Add the fruits, nuts, sugar and spices, mixing well to combine, then add the brandy to moisten. Pack into an airtight glass jar and store in a cool place. Add more brandy or rum to taste. Cover and allow to mature for 3 weeks before using.

PIES
Preheat oven to moderate (350°F/180°C/Gas 4).

Handle pastry according to directions on pack. Stamp out rounds with a large cookie cutter or glass dipped in flour. Fill into patty pans and stamp out matching lids of pastry. Fill the lined patty pans with 1–2 tablespoons fruit mince, smooth into neat shape and cover with lid, moistening edges with beaten egg. Brush lids with milk and put a little slit in the top of each pie before placing in oven. They'll need about 25–30 minutes cooking. Remove, cool and dust with confectioners' sugar.

APPLE AND GREEN TOMATO PIE

This is a lovely and unusual combination, lending a satisfactory tartness to the apples. If green tomatoes are not available, use all apples.

1 cup (4 oz) all-purpose (plain) flour
¾ cup (4 oz) all-purpose (plain) whole-wheat (wholemeal) flour
¼ cup (1 ½ oz) confectioners' (icing) sugar
¼ tspn salt
½ cup (4 oz) butter, frozen, cut into chunks
2 eggs
1 tblspn poppy seeds
1 ⅓ tblspns (⅔ fl oz) water
milk and extra sugar and cinnamon for top

FILLING
4 medium Granny Smith apples, approx 14 oz prepared weight, peeled and sliced
5 medium green tomatoes, approx 15 oz prepared weight, washed and sliced
½ cup (4 oz) sugar
¼ cup (1 ⅓ oz) cornstarch (cornflour)
1 tspn lemon zest (rind), finely grated
1 tspn cassia cinnamon
3 tblspns (1 ½ oz) butter

Preheat oven to hot (425°F/220°C/Gas 7).

Put the flour, confectioners' sugar and salt into the food processor with the steel blade in place. Add the butter. Process, turning on and off until the butter is cut through the flour and the mixture resembles coarse breadcrumbs. Lightly beat the eggs, poppy seeds and water together. Pour egg mixture through the feed tube, with motor running. When dough has formed into a ball around the blade, stop pouring. Wrap in waxed (greaseproof) paper and chill in refrigerator for 20–30 minutes before using. Line a 9–10 in pie plate with a little over half the pastry. Reserve remainder for top.

Layer filling into pie shell and dot with the butter. Roll out remaining pastry, prick it and crimp the edges. Brush with milk, sprinkle with some sugar and cinnamon mixed together.

Bake in oven for 10 minutes, turn down to 350°F (180°C/Gas 4) and cook until done, about 40–45 minutes.

FILLING
Put all ingredients, except the butter, into a bowl and stir well until the apples and tomatoes are evenly coated.

APPLE, SEEDLESS RAISIN AND CREAM CHEESE CAKE

A family standby, this three-layered cake is rich and creamy and great for winter desserts. Granny Smith apples are good in this cake.

¾ cup (6 oz) butter, softened
⅓ cup (3 oz) superfine (caster) sugar
finely grated zest (rind) of 1 lemon
1 egg yolk
1 ½ cups (6 oz) all-purpose (plain) flour
1 ⅓ tblspns (⅔ fl oz) cold water

CREAM CHEESE FILLING
8 oz cream cheese, chopped up
2 eggs
⅓ cup (3 oz) superfine (caster) sugar
1 tspn vanilla extract (essence)

RAISIN MIX
¼ cup (1 ½ oz) seedless raisins, soaked in ¼ cup (2 fl oz) rum
4 green apples, peeled and sliced
2 tspns cinnamon

Preheat oven to 350°F (180°C/Gas 4).

Cream together the butter and sugar, add zest and egg yolk. Fold in the sifted flour and water. Form into a ball with your hands and wrap in waxed (greaseproof) paper. Chill for ½ –1 hour.

Remove pastry from the refrigerator and press over the base of a 9 in spring-form pan, reserving a third (4 oz) for the top.

Pour cream cheese filling over pastry base and top with seedless raisin mix.

Divide reserved pastry into five pieces. Press the pieces between the palms of your hands into small circles. Lay over the top to form a pretty pattern.

Bake for 1–1 ¼ hours or until a skewer inserted in the middle comes out clean.

When cool, remove from spring-form pan, and dust with confectioners' sugar.

CREAM CHEESE FILLING
Blend all ingredients together in food processor or beat together well in electric mixer.

SEEDLESS RAISIN MIX
In a bowl mix together the soaked seedless raisins with the apples and cinnamon.

RED CABBAGE, APPLE AND SPINACH TOSS

SERVES 8–10

½ head red cabbage, finely shredded
½ bunch fresh spinach or Swiss chard (silverbeet), washed and shredded
2 red or green eating apples, unpeeled and chopped
1 green sweet pepper (capsicum), slivered
2 stalks celery, cut on the diagonal
1 small Spanish (purple) onion, finely chopped
½ cup (2 oz) chopped pecans or walnuts
vinaigrette made with olive oil and lemon juice

Put all the ingredients into a large salad bowl. Mix together well, and taste for seasoning. Serve immediately.

Melons

Cucurbitaceae family

O sweet grassy snake, crawling on a green bed.

For me, summer and wedges of chilled watermelon go hand in hand. With its crisp texture, sweet flavor and watery consistency, there is nothing more thirst-quenching.

When the children arrive home from school, I'd rather provide a platter of watermelon wedges than an ice block to cool them down. Much more nutritious and sustaining. And such a glorious sight with its thick green and white rind, pinky-red flesh and lustrous black seeds. Occasionally a hose is also required — to remove the dripping pink juice!

Honeydew and cantaloupe (rockmelon) are also firm favorites, though perhaps not quite as thirst-quenching as watermelon. Just to walk into a room where one of these melons has been cut evokes memories of summers past for me.

Melons are members of the Cucurbitaceae family and as such are usually classed as vegetables along with other cucurbits like cucumbers, squash and pumpkins. I must admit to having difficulty with this classification, as I've always thought of melons as fruits, but so be it. Classifying melons can be a tricky affair for cook and gardener alike, because there are so many different hybrids among the netted or cantaloupe varieties. Watermelons are the exception as they do not cross-pollinate with other melons.

In Lorenza de Medici's book The Heritage of Italian Cooking, *there is a glorious full-page reproduction of a* Still Life *(c. 1687) by Giovanni Paolo Spadino. In it is depicted, among other things, a splendid cantaloupe melon. Draped alongside is a slice of prosciutto. The delicate flavors of these two are combined to form an antipasto dating back to Renaissance times. The melon depicted there looks like a nuggety pumpkin and is the one first cultivated in the papal garden of Cantalupo near Rome. A similar melon is also shown in David Stuart's informative book,* The Kitchen Garden, *in a drawing from Hooker's* Drawing of Fruits *(1817), but there it is called a 'Black Rock Melon'.*

Melons were popular in Europe during the Renaissance, so much so that according to French writer Georges Blond, 'Renaissance France smelled of melon'. Introduced to France at the end of the fifteenth century, melons were all the rage, so much so that Succinct Treatise on Melons *was written in 1583 by Professor Jacques Pons. He listed 50 different ways of eating it — including as an hors d'oeuvre, chilled, with sugar, salt or pepper, cooked, in soups and in fritters. The rind was also used in compotes. Exactly which type of melon was so popular I'm not sure, though the glorious Charentais was probably not around until the seventeenth or eighteenth centuries.*

Even today in France, melons remain popular. In summer at harvest time the perfume of the Charentais melons can knock you out. These melons are so fragrant that their scent permeates the air as the smell of lavender does from the lavender fields. People who specialize in growing these melons know exactly when to pick them and can choose which day each melon will be best. To help intensify their flavor, the melons are hardly watered during the last six weeks of growing.

Melons, it seems, originated in Africa, though some claim it was the Middle East, probably Persia. Watermelon leaves and seeds have been found in New Kingdom tombs in Egypt and pictures of a fruit which some have identified as melons are depicted in Egyptian paintings dated at 2400 BC. The Greeks had melons (but not watermelons) by the third century BC, evidenced by a wall painting in Herculaneum depicting what seems to be a melon. By the third century AD, Roman manuals were giving directions for growing them, though apparently the Romans preferred to import their melons from Armenia. At the time they were only about the size of our oranges today.

According to David Stuart, the melon seems to have arrived in Asia late for there is no Sanskrit word for it, though there is a Tamil one. The earliest reliable report from the Far East is from the tomb of a Chinese noblewoman dated between 175 and 145 BC. In the lady's oesophagus, stomach and intestines were found yellowish-brown musk melon seeds, clearly indicating she had eaten musk melons not long before she joined her husband, the first Marquis of Tai (Han dynasty, eastern outskirts of Ch'ang-sha, Hunan).

Melons were extremely popular on the Chinese medieval table (T'ang dynasty, 618–907 AD). Among the available species were the pickling melon of the south, the cucumber, the white gourd or winter melon and the bottle gourd. The Chinese today are still keen on melons of all kinds. I remember a couple of years ago being taken to a nightclub in a village in Guangzhou in southern China and being offered wedges of watermelon for supper. The locals dipped theirs in hot tea! Winter melons too are very popular and are among some of the largest vegetables grown. The Chinese use them mostly for soup.

If you live in a hot climate, growing melons should be no problem. In fact the explorer David Livingstone found 'great tracts of water-melon growing wild in the Kalahari desert' in the 1850s. You can imagine the sight — luscious, thirst-quenching watermelons in the desert — but it was no mirage. Mother Nature had provided well.

Melons don't like a humid climate, however, as they are subject to a lot of fungal diseases. Excessive wet weather can cause fruit drop and root rot, and high humidity encourages powdery mildew. They are also frost-sensitive and can be killed by frost. Their growth is severely checked by cool temperatures and cold winds. High temperatures during the growing season are essential for good-quality and good-tasting melons. Although they don't require a lot of water, an adequate and uniform supply of moisture in the soil is necessary during the growing period, though watering should be reduced towards harvest time.

KINDEST CUTS

The Thai people do magnificent things with melons. They carve exquisite flowers and designs through the skin and into the flesh, revealing the pink, green and white of the melon. Such expertise requires a fine hand and eye — and training.

If you have a canelle knife, you could try experimenting with carving for unusual effects. I once copied an Australian Aboriginal design onto a watermelon which looked really splendid sitting on a long table alongside other summer fruits. (The Aborigines carve patterns onto the baobab nut, the shape of which is similar to oblong watermelons.)

The canelle knife pares ¼ in strips of skin from fruit and vegetables and is easier to control than a regular knife. It can also be used to cut thin grooves or channels. Draw it upwards in a paring action, letting the strips of skin fall as you go. It helps if you mark patterns on the skin with a pen before you start. It is also advisable to brush the scored sections of the skin with lemon juice to prevent browning.

Of course there are many things you can do with melons. You can cut a lid off and hollow out the middle. You can leave a handle on so that you end up with a basket. Pumpkins (squash), zucchini (courgettes), pineapples, lemons and oranges also lend themselves to different carvings. Use your imagination. Here are a few suggestions:

PINEAPPLES I first came across baby pineapples — such sweet, juicy fruits — carved like this in Mauritius. Sadly, in many parts of the world, they are often grown so big by commercial growers that they have lost their lovely sweetness. Holding the leaves and using a medium-sized sharp knife, shave the skin off carefully so that the imprint of the pineapple skin leaves its diamond-like design still showing on the flesh. Using a smaller sharp knife, cut grooves in a spiral effect so that the 'eyes' come away. The canelle knife will come in handy for this.

LEMONS Use a small sharp knife to cut a slice off the bottom of the lemons so that they sit up straight. Using the same knife, cut a Vandyke design (jagged, triangular border) from the skin through to the center of the flesh, about three-quarters of the way through the fruit. Remove the lid and scoop out the pulp. Fill with a lemon or raspberry sorbet or ice-cream. Return to freezer and before serving, put the lid back on.

ZUCCHINI (COURGETTES) Using the canelle knife, cut interesting swirls and diagonal patterns across the skin. Plunge zucchini into rapidly boiling salted water and serve with your main course.

PUMPKINS These make an interesting centerpiece for a table in winter. The canelle knife is best for cutting into the tough pumpkin skin. Use it to sculpt different patterns and designs before brushing with a little lemon juice. Smaller golden nugget pumpkins lend color to the table — you can carve into their skins or Vandyke the edges. Candles look good set alight inside their carved-out hollows.

And don't forget Halloween. Pumpkins make wonderful jack o'lanterns, though admittedly the carving of them is best left to someone with strong hands. Place them at your front door or on a window ledge in a front room. When it gets dark, set a candle alight inside the pumpkin and watch the face flicker and change into myriad shapes. It's spooky, but children love it. Watch them around the candles, though.

ORANGES Use a felt-tipped pen to mark out your chosen pattern on its skin. Following your lines, cut away the skin through to the pith with the canelle knife being careful not to pierce the flesh. Brush exposed pith with lemon juice. If you like, you can press lines of cloves into the exposed pith — this gives a wonderful fragrance. Alternatively, stud the whole outer surface of an orange with cloves, dust with orris root powder and put aside for Christmas. These oranges look wonderful piled in a glass stand or heaped up in pyramid shapes in blue and white bowls.

Watermelon
Cucumis citrullus lanatus

In Australia during the mid-nineteenth century, the chief vegetable was the pumpkin and the chief fruit was the watermelon, 'the size, the colour, and delicious refreshing coolness of which, eaten during the three hours of mid-day heat when most farming people pause for a time from their field labour, it would be impossible for me to describe by mere words'. Such were Alexander Harris's impressions when he came to Australia. He subsequently wrote a book entitled Settlers and Convicts: Or, Reflections of Sixteen Years in the Australian Backwoods.

One approved method of eating these melons was to cut a hole, pour in a bottle of Madeira or sherry and mix it into a cold pulp. This reminds me of the British custom of pouring port into a wheel of Stilton.

There are many different varieties, sizes and shapes of watermelons today. At present the most popular variety is the Warpaint which is medium large, round to slightly elongated and distinctly striped with dark green on a bright green base. It weighs 24–28 lb. Others include the Charleston Grey, Allsweet, Sugar Baby (this is a small watermelon, weighing 6 ½ – 9 lb and is one of the easiest and sweetest for the family garden), Sunnyboy and Madera. A good one for the home gardener is the

Sugar Bush which grows as a compact bush, needing only about 6 sq ft of space to produce two to four fruit weighing 6 ½ –9 lb each. It does well even in a cool climate but if you put it in a hot position, you'll have table melons in 12 weeks.

When planting melon seeds, the soil temperature should be over 68°F (20°C) and sowing depth not more than ½ – ¾ in. Well-manured soil and ample water are necessary, but water the roots, not the leaves, to prevent mildew. Unlike the cantaloupes, watermelons will not cross-pollinate. Watermelons are ready to harvest when their surface skin is tough and hard to puncture with a fingernail, and the bottom of the melon has turned yellow.

WATERMELON AND BLACKBERRY BASKETS

SERVES 10–12, DEPENDING ON SIZE OF THE MELON

The French have a wonderful way with late watermelon and early blackberries which is simple and stunning.

Cut the melon in half and make lots of little balls from the flesh, using a baller. Remove as many black seeds as you can. Scoop out all the remaining flesh so that you have two baskets. Put the balls back into one of these and mix through some blackberries. Depending on the watermelon, add a little sugar. Sprinkle with Kirsch, toss together well and chill in the refrigerator.

The blackberries take the place of the seeds and add a tartness to the melon. This also looks splendid heaped in a pyramid in an ice bowl. Lovely for late summer entertaining.

WATERMELON ICE

SERVES 6

3 cups (24 fl oz) watermelon purée, approx 3 ½ lb unpeeled watermelon
½ cup (3 oz) superfine (caster) sugar (more or less depending on sweetness of melon)
juice of 1 lemon or 2 limes

Remove flesh from melon, discarding the black seeds. Chop up and put into a blender in batches. Purée until smooth. Push through a sieve to remove any remaining seeds. Stir in sugar and lemon or lime juice. Combine well and place in the freezer in a rectangular tray (about 11 x 8 inches). When almost set, remove and beat well. Re-freeze. Remove from freezer 15 minutes before serving.

WATERMELON RIND PICKLE

A marvellous, tasty way of using up the rind of watermelons.

½ watermelon, approx 6 ½ lb
¼ cup (2 oz) salt
water to cover, approx 2 cups (16 fl oz)
2 cups (1 lb) sugar

2 cups (16 fl oz) cider vinegar
1 orange, thinly sliced
1 lemon, thinly sliced
1 cinnamon stick
2 star anise
few black cardamom seeds

Cut melon in half, scoop out the pink flesh and seeds and use for making an ice or for eating. With a very sharp knife, peel the dark green skin off and chop the white rind into ¾ in cubes. Leave on a little of the pink flesh for eye appeal. Soak overnight in a bowl with the salt and water.

Next day, drain, rinse and cover with cold water. Cook until just tender or *al dente*. Drain, reserving the water.

Combine reserved water with remaining ingredients in a saucepan, simmer for 15 minutes and add watermelon rind. Simmer gently a further 5 minutes. Ladle into sterile jars.

Cantaloupe (Rockmelon) and Other Melons
Cucumis melo

The taste of melons is a complex subject as they can vary so much. They can be musky, sweet, aromatic, spicy, earthy, floral and cucumber-like. When they're not in their prime, though, they can be flat, watery, tasteless and even fermented — and there's nothing worse than a fermented melon. They can also be juicy, succulent and ravishing — or mushy, rubbery and stringy.

It's important, therefore, to know when to pick your melons: they must remain on the vine until fully ripe, as their sugar content is not reached until the very last days of growing. Most cantaloupes (rockmelons) will 'slip' from the vine when ready, which is when the netting has turned from green to tan and a crack has formed on the stem near the area attached to the melon. Honeydews are ready when they begin to turn slightly yellow.

These melons have the highest heat needs of any vegetable and will not germinate well below 68°F (20°C). Some varieties, though, like the Ambrosia Hybrid, will grow in cooler areas and are resistant to powdery mildew. There are many varieties available including the Casaba Golden Beauty (its flesh is white with a spicy flavor), Hales Best (popular because of its orange flesh and resistance to mildew), Honey Bush (salmon-fleshed, extremely sweet), the aromatic Charentais, the pineapple-tasting Annenais and the yellow egg-shaped Japanese melon. I've also recently come across the champagne melons which are a very pale gold. Included in this category is the Honeydew with its light green, sweet flesh and creamy, light green rind. As they are slow growing, they are only suitable for warm and hot areas.

CHICKEN WITH MELON AND GINGER MAYONNAISE

Lovely and light with a soothing green color.

SERVES 4

4–6 chicken fillets, approx 10 oz–1 lb, skinned and trimmed
2 cups (16 fl oz) water
½ cup (4 fl oz) white wine
1 small stalk of celery
1 small carrot, peeled
½ small onion, peeled
3 black peppercorns
1 green sweet pepper (capsicum), slivered
1 small honeydew melon

DRESSING
½ cup (4 fl oz) mayonnaise
1–2 tspns freshly grated ginger
2 ⅓ tspns lemon or lime juice
1 tblspn freshly chopped coriander (cilantro)

Put chicken in a saucepan with water and wine — or enough to just cover. Add celery, carrot, onion and peppercorns. Bring to a boil, turn down and let simmer very gently for 8–10 minutes. Do not overcook. Remove chicken, cool and cut into slivers.

Put chicken on a pretty serving platter. Toss through slivers of sweet pepper, reserving a few for the top. Halve and seed melon. Using a melon baller, make balls from the flesh and add to chicken.

Combine dressing ingredients well and toss through the chicken, sweet pepper and melon mixture. Garnish with reserved sweet pepper slivers and chopped coriander.

GINGERED MELON AND ORANGE FRUIT SALAD

Garnish this refreshing salad with nasturtium flowers for a pretty effect.

SERVES 4

1 honeydew melon
3 oranges
juice 2 fresh limes
finely grated zest (rind) of 1 fresh lime
3 tblspns (2 oz) honey
1 tblspn slivered preserved ginger
1 ½ tblspns (⅔ fl oz) ginger syrup (from the preserves)

Halve and seed the melon and scoop out the flesh with a melon baller. Put into a dessert bowl. Peel the oranges, removing all their pith. Cut out the segments from them and add to the melon. Mix together the lime juice, zest, honey, slivered ginger and ginger syrup and pour over the melon and oranges. Toss together well. Chill before serving.

SHALIMAR ICE

Simple and delicious. A little red or pink fruit is lovely because it adds a pinkish tinge.

SERVES 4

1 cup (8 fl oz) fruit purée (cantaloupe (rockmelon),
watermelon, strawberries, kiwi fruit (Chinese gooseberries))
1 cup (8 fl oz) water (or you can use half water,
half fruit juice)
1 cup (8 oz) sugar
1 small banana
juice of 1 orange and 1 lemon
2 egg whites

Place all ingredients, except egg whites, in a blender and purée until smooth. Pour into freezer tray and place in freezer. When almost set, remove, blend again and pour onto the stiffly beaten egg whites. Mix well and re-freeze.

MELON SAGO WITH SOY MILK

A lovely light dessert based on old-fashioned sago. Unlike most sago dishes, however, this one does not set hard. Rather, the melon balls float in the milk, echoing the shape of the sago, and look very cooling. Good after curries or spicy dishes. Make sure you use unsweetened soy milk.

SERVES 8–10

1 honeydew melon
1 cantaloupe (rockmelon)
7 oz sago
3 cups (24 fl oz) soy milk
1 cup (8 fl oz) water
⅓ cup (3 oz) superfine (caster) sugar (or to taste)

Cut the melons into halves and scoop out balls with a melon baller. Put the balls into a large dessert bowl.

Wash the sago under cold running water and drop into rapidly boiling water. Cook for 7–10 minutes until transparent. Drain through a sieve and wash again under cold running water. Put into the bowl with the melon balls, pour in the soy milk and water and stir through the sugar until it is dissolved. Taste — add more sugar if desired. Cover and chill well before serving.

MARINATED MELON BALLS

SERVES 6–8

1 cantaloupe (rockmelon)
1 honeydew melon
2 ⅔ tblspns (1 ⅓ fl oz) fresh lime juice
1 ½ tblspns (1 oz) honey
½ tspn ground coriander (cilantro)
⅛ tspn nutmeg
bunch fresh coriander (cilantro), chopped

Halve and seed the melons, and scoop out the flesh with a melon baller. Put the melon balls and their juices into a large bowl. Mix together remaining ingredients, pour over melon balls and toss to coat. Chill in the refrigerator for a couple of hours before serving. Good with barbecued pork spareribs and kebabs.

Melon Ice

Use honeydew or cantaloupe (rockmelon) for this, but not watermelon because it requires a different method of preparation. You can also use the following method for pineapple ice, substituting pineapple for the melon.

SERVES 6–8

1 cup (8 oz) sugar
3 cups (24 fl oz) water
1–2 melons (you need approx 4 ½ lb)
¼ – ⅓ cup (2–2 ⅔ fl oz) lemon juice
1–3 tblspns (⅔ –1 ⅓ fl oz) Kirsch

Place sugar and water together in a heavy saucepan. Dissolve sugar over moderate heat and when dissolved, boil for 5 minutes. Allow to cool.

Halve the melons, remove seeds and purée flesh in a food processor or blender. There should be about 4 cups (1 qt) of purée. Combine with the syrup, lemon juice and Kirsch, pour into scooped-out melon halves or freezer trays and place in freezer. When it starts to set, blend again and re-freeze. Remove from the freezer 10–15 minutes before serving.

Tropical Fruits

I will have the gardeners come to me and recite
many flowers, and in the small clay pots
of their melodious names I will bring back
some remnant of the hundred fragrances.
And fruits: I will buy fruits, and in their sweetness
that country's earth and sky will live again.
For that is what you understood: ripe fruits.

RAINER MARIA RILKE, FROM 'REQUIEM FOR A FRIEND'

My mother was born in Townsville, Queensland. Although she has lived most of her life in Sydney's more temperate climate, her center is located in Queensland — it has always pulled her back.

I understand this, because I, too, was born in Queensland. The first seven years of my life were spent in the south-eastern part. There is a 'blood-remembering' (a term used by the German poet Rilke to describe memories and experiences which have turned to blood within us) about those years. Veiled memories of large-limbed, dark, mosquito-filled mango trees; lush, dense foliage; hibiscus and frangipanis; steamy heat; flying foxes in the bananas; and ant-ridden monsteras.

Memories of the lushness and abundance of tropical gardens remain like a spell. Something mysterious and half-forgotten resides therein — a part of my childhood I abandoned when we left Queensland to move south. To this day I prefer a full, overgrown garden to a trimmed, spick-and-span one.

Twenty years ago, my mother reclaimed her own childhood by purchasing a property in a valley on the hinterland of the Queensland Gold Coast. It is a magnificent place, alongside a winding river. My uncles catch mud crabs in the river and there are peacocks, ducks, chickens, geese, horses, fan-tailed pigeons, foxes, tree frogs, snakes and, yes, cane toads. I know it has already cast

its spell over my children. My daughter, in particular, has a very strong affinity for the place — a sort of 'blood remembering' of her own.

Whenever I visit tropical or subtropical places, I feel a sense of belonging, of coming home. A few years ago, my work took me to far northern Queensland to interview actress Diane Cilento on her property, Karnak, north of Mossman. I immediately felt at home. The landscape there is lush and dense, and the colors of the bougainvillea so vivid that my eyes ached.

Diane Cilento has long been a follower of different esoteric teachings, and this place became a retreat or refuge for her in the mid-seventies. In England she was involved with the Gurdjieff Work when J.G. Bennett was still alive; when I visited, her interest had shifted to Sufism which explains this 'Notice to Cooks' which I found hanging in the main kitchen of this spiritual community:

Now know this, that cooking is an art. It is also an integral part of esoteric training because it is a two-fold means of service: service to humanity and service to the food prepared. There is no higher state than that which a man can reach . . . It should be undertaken only in an attitude of deep respect and consideration and full awareness of the bounty and clemency in the divine order . . .

The notice alludes to Jalaludin Rumi, the great Sufi mystical poet whose sect, the Mevlevis, referred to the esoteric (or spiritual) education of novices as 'cooking' and to achievement as 'taste':

Those who use ingredients of food without consideration of providing the best possible means of an ingredient's expression are devaluing service, awareness and value of life.

Karnak is a working farm where students come to study and work. The preparation and cooking of meals is an integral part of the life. So is gardening. There's a vegetable patch, full of snake beans, carrots, Chinese cabbages, herbs, corn, eggplant (aubergines) and chicory, which requires constant weeding and watching (nocturnal animals visit frequently). The vegetables are a winter (or dry season) job, as it's impossible to grow vegetables in the far north in summer. The sun is so hot that they scorch.

There are numerous exotic fruit trees on the property, most planted by Cilento. Her friend, Deirdre Scomazzon, who lives down the road, is one of the biggest commercial growers of these fruits and they frequently swap information. The Scomazzons have over 40 varieties of exotic fruits including the uvilla (a South American grape-like fruit with purple skin), jackfruit (which is very good for flavoring stews and curries), guavas, breadfruit, durian and rambutan. One of the Scomazzons' favorites is the black sapote, or chocolate pudding fruit. Its soft brown flesh makes a delicious healthy dessert, commonly eaten in Mexico with a dab of cream. It is also good flavored with a little sugar, lemon and orange zest (rind) and eaten with yogurt.

At Karnak, there are carambolas (five-star fruit), mangoes, lychees, pomelos, sapodillas, papayas, guavas, grenadillas and a number of arabica coffee trees. Citruses are also abundant. The fruits are picked in season and used in cooking. When we visited we were treated to soursop juice in the morning for breakfast, hot black arabica coffee, fresh goat's yogurt and a choice of kumquat or orange-lemon marmalade (both homemade) on homemade whole-wheat (wholemeal) bread. The soursop also makes a delicious daiquiri.

Everything grows abundantly in the tropics. There is often so much fruit that it doesn't really matter if the flying foxes or possums get a few (except, of course, if you're a commercial grower). At my mother's farm we often have so many mangoes we can't give them away.

You need to live in the tropics — or at least the subtropics — to grow the more exotic tropical fruits like sapotes, sapodillas, pumelo, breadfruit, durian, abiu, mangosteen, jaboticaba, tamarind, Malay roseapple and the Barbados cherry. Most tropical fruits deteriorate within days of picking and are best eaten ripe and fresh from the tree. In 1979 the Rare Fruit Council was established in Queensland, northern Australia, to help encourage growers and disseminate information. Since its inception, seeds and hundreds of varieties from Central and South America, Borneo, Indonesia, the Philippines, Malaysia and China have been imported to Australia. Thanks to the efforts of this group, Australia now has the world's largest collection of rare and exotic fruit.

Bananas
Musa *species*

The banana is actually not a fruit at all, but really a giant herb. Now grown throughout the world, the banana is believed to be one of the first fruits gathered and cultivated by humans. The genus itself originated in prehistoric times in the region stretching from New Guinea to India.

Joseph Banks, the botanist who traveled with Captain Cook to Australia, reported the banana growing wild in Queensland. He declared it was 'a kind of Wild Plantain whose fruit was so full of stones that it was scarcely eatable'. Today's fruits are the result of much selection and later hybridization. The seeds have slowly been bred out so that they are now sterile and only reproduce with human help.

Bananas are popular in home gardens and will produce crops outside the tropics, though bunches do not develop as well in cooler areas. The common edible bananas are cultivated varieties of Musa acuminata *and include the well-known Cavendish, the popular Williams, Lady Fingers and Sugar Banana. They are vulnerable to wind and sun and to flying foxes and birds. A plastic cover helps to protect the fruit and also improves the quality and increases the yield.*

Young trees need to be fed properly with a complete fertilizer. They are heavy feeders and need good mulching. Keep them free of weeds.

FISH IN BANANA LEAVES

Banana leaves are used as enclosures for cooking many
foods in the tropics. This is a simple and very lovely way
of cooking fish.

Choose a medium-sized white-fleshed fish like
snapper, and make sure it is cleaned and scaled. Slash it
two or three times on the diagonal across the thickest
part of the flesh — this allows the marinade to
penetrate.

Wash some banana leaves and lay them in a baking
dish. Put in the fish.

In a saucepan, put 2 tblspns (1 oz) butter, ½ cup (4 fl
oz) soy sauce, 2 cloves crushed garlic, a chopped small
chilli (with seeds) and some lemon or lime juice to taste.
Heat enough to melt the butter, swilling to combine.
Pour this mixture over the fish and inside the cavity,
then wrap the fish well in the banana leaves.

Bake in a preheated moderate oven (350°F/180°C/
Gas 4) for about 30 minutes. Don't let the fish
overcook.

BANANA CHUTNEY

MAKES ABOUT 12 CUPS (3 QT)

12 bananas, peeled and chopped
1 lb dates, chopped
1 lb apples, chopped
2 lb onions, peeled and chopped

4 oz fresh ginger, peeled and finely chopped
2 tspns hot curry powder
2 tspns salt
½ tspn cinnamon
2 ½ cups (20 fl oz) white wine vinegar
1 ¼ cups (10 fl oz) water

Preheat oven to 350°F (180°C/Gas 4).

Put all the ingredients into a baking dish, cover with
foil and cook in the oven for a couple of hours. Spoon
into hot sterile jars and seal.

BANANA ICE-CREAM

SERVES 6–8

4 cups (1 qt) cream
1 cup (8 oz) sugar
pinch salt
½ tspn vanilla extract (essence) or 1 ⅓ tblspns (⅔ fl oz)
overproof rum
3–4 bananas
½ cup (4 fl oz) lemon juice
handful shredded coconut

Warm a quarter of the cream gently. Stir in the sugar
and salt and keep stirring until sugar is dissolved. Chill
in the refrigerator. Stir in remaining cream, add vanilla
or rum and pour into freezer tray. Freeze until mushy.

Purée bananas and lemon juice in the blender and
beat into the partly frozen cream. Freeze again, beating
every 30 minutes until solid. Remove from freezer
10–15 minutes before serving.

FRUIT DAIQUIRIS

One evening in November some friends and I drank
daiquiris to celebrate the beginning of summer and its
long lazy days. None of us quite knew how to make

them, but after a little experimentation, the results were stunning.

We tried a strawberry one first. A pint of strawberries went into the blender followed by some sugar syrup and a handful or two of ice cubes. This was whizzed around until the ice cubes had broken up into a fine snow-like texture. Then we added white rum and a squeeze of lemon juice. The next was an unusual combination of fresh banana, peach and apple juice, ice, white rum and a little lemon juice.

Try the following combinations, experimenting until it tastes good to you:

SERVES 4

10 oz prepared fruit (strawberries, mangoes,
peaches, bananas)
1 cup (8 fl oz) crushed ice
½ cup (4 fl oz) white rum
⅓ cup (3 fl oz) lemon or lime juice
1–2 tspns superfine (caster) sugar (or to taste)

Place all ingredients in a blender and blend until mixture is thick and shiny. Serve immediately in elegant glasses.

Note: Peach and banana are delicious mixed together — use one of each fruit and proceed as above.

BANANA CARAMEL PIE

An old-fashioned dessert. Years ago, the caramel was made by boiling an unopened tin of condensed milk for 2–3 hours. My grandmother, Pearl Douglas, used to make caramel pie for her five sons this way and it was always a special treat. The result is a very rich satiny filling which was used straight, or folded through an equal quantity of mock cream. To save fuel, the tin was put into the same pot as the steamed pudding. This recipe is not as rich, but very delicious.

SERVES 6–8

sweet crust pastry
2–3 oz toasted flaked coconut
1 tblspn (⅓ oz) cornstarch (cornflour)
1 cup (8 fl oz) milk
2 egg yolks, beaten
1 ½ cups (8 oz) brown sugar
1 ½ tblspns (⅔ oz) butter
2 ⅔ tblspns (1 ⅓ fl oz) overproof rum
4 bananas, sliced on the diagonal
lemon juice
1 ¼ cups (10 fl oz) freshly whipped cream

Make a sweet crust pastry, enough to line a 9 in pie plate. Bake it blind in a hot oven (400°F/200°C/Gas 6) for 15 minutes. Remove the weights and give it another 5 minutes to crisp the bottom. Allow to cool.

Toast the coconut on a tray in a moderate oven (350°F/180°C/Gas 4), just letting it become golden around the edges. Remove, cool and set aside.

Mix together cornstarch and milk until smooth and add to beaten egg yolks. Put egg mixture, sugar and butter into a saucepan and bring to boil slowly, stirring well. Allow to simmer for 2–3 minutes, stirring constantly. Stir in rum and remove from heat.

Spoon into the pie shell. When cool, top with the bananas and brush them with a little lemon juice to prevent discoloring. Smother the top of the pie with cream and scatter over the flaked coconut.

Mangoes
Mangifera indica

mangoes are not cigarettes

mangoes are fleshy skinful passionate fruits

mangoes are hungry to be sucked

mangoes are glad to be stuck in the teeth

mangoes like slush & kissing

mangoes are not cigarettes

mangoes are idiosyncratic seasonal seducers

mangoes are worse than adams apple

mangoes are what parents & parliaments warn against

mangoes like making rude noises

mangoes are not cigarettes

mangoes are greedy delicious tongueteasers

mangoes are violently soft

mangoes are fibrous intestinal lovebites

mangoes like beginning once again

mangoes are not cigarettes

mangoes are tangible sensual intelligence

mangoes are debauched antisocialites

mangoes are a positive good in the world

mangoes like poetry

RICHARD TIPPING, 'MANGOES'

Debauched antisocialites? Mangoes? And yet . . .

One year at my mother's farm, we were awoken in the middle of the night by drunken mangoes dancing on the kitchen table. There'd been such a surplus that year and we didn't want to waste them. Even the fruit bats couldn't keep up. A recipe for brandied mangoes appealed. My mother and I spent the day peeling and cutting and putting them in sterilized jars with sugar syrup and brandy. But something was amiss, for that night they went berserk. It was a reminder that we were dealing with living things.

I think it was that year, too, that the snake came into the kitchen. Mangoes and snakes. I wouldn't be surprised if, in some Indian cookbook, there is such a combination. I have come across many such odd combinations of mangoes with other foods and most of them I don't like. My preference is to eat them ripe from the tree, or in very simple combinations like the one below with smoked chicken.

The mango, which some call the 'king of fruits', is one of the earliest known tropical fruits and is a native of Indonesia and Malaysia. Grown extensively in India, it has been cultivated there for so long (4000 years) that many believe India to be its place of origin.

Because of its size, it is best suited to large gardens in tropical areas. It will grow in subtropical regions too, but does best in areas where there is a definite dry season, ideally in spring. Its requirements for producing fruit are quite exacting — at least 26 in rainfall per year for good fruit production with dry weather during flowering and the early stages of fruit development.

Mangoes vary in size, color, flavor, and skin color. Some are yellow-green when ripe, others a deep orange, red or straw-colored or a combination of all three. For the most reliable results, purchase a named variety from a nursery. Otherwise you can try growing one from seed by placing the seed point-end downwards in a good potting mix. When the strongest shoot is 4–6 in tall, cut off the weaker ones and plant the seedling in its permanent position in the garden.

MANGO TART

This tart also looks pretty if you substitute pink papaya for half of the mango topping. Passionfruit pulp can also be spooned over the top. Use your imagination with other fruits: for example, sliced kiwi fruit (Chinese gooseberry) and pink guava.

Use a pre-baked 10 ½ –11 in pastry crust, brushed during the last 5 minutes of cooking with the yolk of an egg mixed with 1 ⅓ tblspns (⅔ fl oz) of water. Let cool before filling.

SERVES 8–10

3 egg yolks
¾ cup (5 oz) plain yogurt
3 tblspns (1 ½ oz) superfine (caster) sugar
3 tblspns (1 oz) cornstarch (cornflour)
1 cup (8 fl oz) milk
finely chopped zest (rind) of 1 lemon or lime
2 ⅔ tblspns (1 ⅓ fl oz) fresh lemon or lime juice
3–4 large mangoes, peeled
lemon or lime juice, extra

Mix together the egg yolks, yogurt and sugar in a bowl. Stir cornstarch into a little of the milk and whisk into the yogurt mixture. Heat remaining milk with lemon zest, but don't let it boil. Pour into the yogurt mixture, return to saucepan, bring to a boil and cook gently for 2–3 minutes, stirring continuously. Remove from heat, add lemon juice and spread into prepared shell.

Slice the cheeks from the mangoes, then slice into crescent shapes. Arrange the slices in a pretty fashion on the filling. Brush lightly with extra lemon or lime juice. Chill before cutting.

MANGOES IN CHAMPAGNE

A simple and lovely way to serve mangoes for dessert is to peel and slice off the cheeks. Put these into pretty glass dessert dishes and sprinkle with a little Grand Marnier. Put in the refrigerator until ready to serve. Just before serving, pour champagne over the mangoes and serve immediately.

FRULLATI

A refreshing drink in summer can be made by liquidizing fresh fruit (peaches, strawberries, mangoes, fresh pineapple, passionfruit) in a blender with ice-cubes and a little freshly squeezed lemon or lime juice. For one drink, chop up the flesh of the fruit (about ¼ lb) and put in the blender with a handful of ice-cubes and 1–3 tblspns (⅔ –1 ⅓ fl oz) water. Add a squeeze of citrus juice and blend, turning on and off until fruit is puréed and ice cubes are crushed. Pour into a long tall glass and serve immediately. Children love these.

MANGO SALSA

I have seen this served with grilled ham hocks and a mustard aioli — a lot of preparation for the home kitchen. However, it will go equally well with pieces of warm, sliced ham or barbecued pork or chicken kebabs. Also good with Merguz sausages (the hot spicy sausages from North Africa) and couscous.

SERVES 4–6

4 mangoes, peeled and cut into ⅓ in cubes
1 medium red onion, finely chopped
2 chillies, seeded and finely chopped
¼ cup (2 fl oz) peanut (groundnut) oil
2 ⅔ tblspns (1 ⅓ fl oz) water
1 cup (⅔ oz) mint leaves
¼ cup (2 fl oz) fresh lime juice

1 tspn salt
1 tspn freshly ground pepper

Put the chopped mangoes into a mixing bowl. Mix the onions, chillies, oil and water in a saucepan. Cover and cook over very low heat until the onion is transparent, about 10 minutes. Do not let the mixture brown. Remove from heat and cool, then add to the mangoes.

Blanch the mint leaves in boiling water for 1 minute. Cool in ice water, drain, squeeze dry and chop finely. Add to the mangoes, stir in lime juice, salt and pepper. Let stand for 1 hour to macerate.

SMOKED CHICKEN SALAD WITH FRESH MANGO

This makes a lovely entrée, and is also a good dish to put on a Christmas buffet table along with the glazed ham and a variety of fresh, mixed salads.
It is simple to prepare and the combination of flavors is superb. You can prepare it well ahead and keep, covered, in the refrigerator.

SERVES 6

1 smoked chicken, approx 2 lb
baby carrots
celery
chives
white pepper
olive oil
red or white wine vinegar
2 fresh mangoes

Remove all chicken flesh from bones, separating the dark meat (thighs and legs) from the white (breast). Cut the dark meat into julienne strips using a small, sharp knife. Cut white meat into thicker strips. Place in a bowl.

Peel the carrots, string the celery and cut into julienne strips. Snip chives. There should be about 6–7 tablespoons of vegetables for the chicken (be careful not to overdo these), they are used to contrast with the chicken in texture and color. Season with white pepper and moisten with a little olive oil and a few drops of vinegar. Add to chicken. Cut the fresh mango into thin slices and toss through.

FRESH MANGO AND PITTED FRUIT PRESERVE

After spooning into hot sterile jars, let the preserve cool and then store in the refrigerator. It will keep for 2–3 weeks. It's a good idea to give jars away to friends as gifts. Tie a tag around it instructing them to keep it in the refrigerator and tell them it goes well with cold ham, pork or duck.

MAKES 8 CUPS (2 QT)

2 cups (16 fl oz) orange juice
1 cup (8 fl oz) sugar syrup (see note below)
¼ cup (1 ½ oz) brown sugar
5 cloves
1 cinnamon stick
3 tblspns (1 ½ fl oz) orange marmalade
⅓ oz tamarind pulp

juice of 1 lime
juice and zest (rind) of 1 lemon
zest (rind) of 1 orange
1 ⅓ tblspns (⅔ fl oz) champagne or white wine vinegar
5 mangoes
3 peaches
2 nectarines
5 blood plums
5 apricots
5 plums
fresh mint

Combine all ingredients except mangoes and pitted fruit in a large saucepan, bring to a boil and simmer until reduced by half. Strain.

Peel the mangoes and slice.

Skin the stone fruit by plunging into boiling water. Refresh under cold water and then cut in quarters. Don't chop the fruit. The beauty of this preserve lies in the lovely crescents of fruit all through it.

Add the fruit to the reduced liquid and let it simmer for 10 minutes. Take off the heat and cool. Then add 2–3 tblspns of freshly chopped mint, or to taste.

Note: For the sugar syrup, combine ½ cup (4 oz) sugar and ½ cup (4 fl oz) water in a saucepan. Stir over medium heat until sugar is dissolved then simmer for 5–10 minutes.

Passionfruit
Passiflora edulis

Passionfruit are perennial vines native to Brazil. The flower is supposed to picture all the instruments of the Crucifixion, hence the name.

The best home garden species are the purple or black variety (Passiflora edulis) *and the golden passionfruit* (P. flavicarpa). *With the purple passionfruit, the fruit looks wrinkled and old when ripe and at its best. Banana passionfruit and granadilla are other species, the latter requiring more tropical conditions.*

Passionfruit will grow in a wide range of soils and it likes plenty of organic matter and mulching. However, soil that is waterlogged or that drains slowly is unsuitable, as it increases the risk of root rot.

The vine needs support and for best results, training. A trellis is ideal or, where space is limited, plants can be trained over wire fences. Use only seed from fruit which has come from disease free vines. The virus disease bullet, or woodiness, can easily be transferred from a diseased to a healthy plant when pruning.

Passionfruit pulp can be frozen easily. Spoon out the pulp and spoon into ice-cube trays. When frozen, transfer to freezer bags. The ice cubes are delicious added to Frullati (page 220).

PASSIONFRUIT ORANGE SYLLABUB

SERVES 2–4

1 orange
1 ¼ cups (10 fl oz) cream
2 passionfruit
3 tblspns (1 oz) confectioners' (icing) sugar
1 ⅓ tblspns (⅔ fl oz) Grand Marnier
2 egg whites

Remove zest (rind) from the orange with a zester and squeeze out the juice. Chop the zest finely. Lightly whip the cream and as it starts to thicken, add the orange zest, the pulp from the 2 passionfruit and one-third of the confectioners' sugar. Continue whipping, gradually adding remaining confectioners' sugar and the orange juice. When all the juice has been incorporated, add Grand Marnier.

In a clean, dry bowl, whisk the egg whites until stiff and fold gently into the cream mixture. Serve immediately in individual glasses decorated with slivers of orange zest and a little passionfruit. Toasted, slivered almonds are also nice on top of this.

PAVLOVA ROLL

A lovely, old-fashioned and very Australian recipe. You don't have to stick to passionfruit. Strawberries, kiwi fruit (Chinese gooseberries), raspberries, peaches and apricots can be substituted.

SERVES 8

cornstarch (cornflour)
4 egg whites
¾ cup (6 oz) superfine (caster) sugar

1 tblspn (½ oz) sugar
1 tspn cinnamon
1 cup (8 fl oz) cream, whipped
pulp of 3–4 passionfruit

Preheat oven to 375°F (190°C/Gas 5).

Line a jelly roll pan (Swiss roll tin) measuring 12 x 10 x ¾ in with non-stick baking paper and dust lightly with cornstarch.

Beat egg whites until stiff but not dry. Gradually beat in the superfine sugar to form a meringue. Spread mixture evenly over baking paper and sprinkle the surface with the combined sugar and cinnamon. Bake for 10 minutes or until the meringue is firm, turn out onto a sheet of waxed (greaseproof) or non-stick baking paper. Let cool.

When cool, spread with cream and passionfruit (or fruit of your choice), roll up carefully and chill.

LADYBIRD BUTTER

Spread this on fresh bread or spoon into small pastry cases.

MAKES ABOUT 3 CUPS (¾ QT)

½ cup (4 oz) butter
1 ¼ cups (10 oz) sugar
4 eggs
⅔ cup (5 fl oz) passionfruit pulp, approx 12 passionfruit

Put the butter and sugar into a saucepan and melt over low heat. In a bowl, beat the eggs, add the passionfruit pulp, and pour in the butter mixture. Simmer the mixture very gently until it is the consistency of honey. Store in sterile, screw-top jars.

Papaya
Carica papaya

Papaya, papaw, pawpaw and papita are all names given to this delicious native of tropical South America.

They are popular with home gardeners and will grow where bananas grow. Whilst they grow best in areas where temperature, humidity and rainfall are high all year, they can also be grown in temperate regions. However, low winter temperatures slow down the growth rate and affect the quality of the fruit.

To grow successfully they need maximum sunlight and protection from frosts and cold winds. Their shallow root systems require mulching and good drainage is essential as they are susceptible to root rot.

The papaya has an interesting sex life — plants may be male, female or bisexual (hermaphrodite). Female plants produce only female flowers and cross-pollination with a male or bisexual is necessary for the fruit to set. Male plants produce mainly male flowers but can also produce bisexual flowers on the ends of branches: these develop into long fruit that are edible although lacking the flavor of fruit from the female or bisexual trees. Bisexual trees produce flowers capable of self-pollination and the fruits are generally of excellent quality. The shape of the fruit on the tree reminds me of full, pendulous breasts.

Papayas produce an enzyme, papain, which breaks down protein. If you wrap papaya leaves around tough meat, they will tenderize the meat before cooking. Papaya flesh added to casseroles and curries also helps to tenderize tough meat.

SOM DTAN (GREEN PAPAYA SALAD)

You need to like Thai food to enjoy the bold flavors in this salad. The recipe comes from north-east Thailand where it is a traditional lunchtime dish. It's popular throughout the rest of the country too, and is often accompanied by grilled chicken or beef, and sticky or white rice.

You'll need a mortar and pestle to prepare it properly. Because it is a peasant dish, the ingredients need only be pounded coarsely.

For four people, pound together 2 peeled garlic cloves and 3–4 small hot green chillies. Add 1 medium chopped tomato, ⅓ cup (2 oz) roasted peanuts (groundnuts) and 2 oz snake beans, sliced in ¾ in lengths. Add 6 ½ oz shredded green papaya, pounding once or twice, then add 2 ⅔ tblspns (1 ⅓ fl oz) fresh lime juice, 1 ⅓ tblspns (⅔ fl oz) fish sauce and 1 tspn brown or palm sugar. The Thais throw in 2 oz dried jumbo shrimps, but you can add 3 ½ oz freshly cooked jumbo shrimp or crabmeat.

It should taste hot, sour and salty, with a hint of sweetness.

KING SALAD

If you layer the salad in a glass bowl, it will look wonderful. Spoon the dressing over, don't mess it up by tossing until you take it to the table. The passionfruit is added at the very end.

SERVES 6

½ firm ripe papaya
1 firm ripe avocado
¾ lb smoked turkey or *chicken* (or *smoked pork loin*)
1 small white onion, peeled and thinly sliced

DRESSING
reserved papaya pips
½ cup (4 fl oz) vegetable oil
¼ cup (2 fl oz) fresh lime or *orange juice*
salt
1 large passionfruit

Peel the papaya. Scoop out the pips and reserve. Slice papaya into elegant slices. Peel and halve avocado, remove seeds and cut into elegant slices. Cut turkey or chicken into slivers.

Blanch onion rings in iced water for a few minutes.

Layer the papaya slices alternately in glass serving bowl with the avocado slices, smoked turkey or chicken and onion slices. Pour over the dressing. Spoon over the passionfruit pulp and toss at the table.

DRESSING
Put half the reserved papaya pips into a blender or food processor with the oil and citrus juice. Blend or process until the pips look like cracked pepper. Add salt to taste. Combine well and pour over salad. Remove pulp from passionfruit, spoon over just before serving.

FRUIT SALAD ICE-BLOCKS

Thirst-quenching and very delicious, they're also good for you and fun to make with children. Spoon the mixture into plastic or polystyrene cups and push a wooden stick down through the middle of the fruit. Sometimes it is better to do this when the fruit is partially frozen so that the stick sits up straight. I particularly love papaya, banana and passionfruit in these ice-blocks. The soft texture of the banana and papaya are quite lovely.

Choose from a mixture of fruits, including papaya, banana, apple, orange, plum, peach, passionfruit, kiwi fruit (Chinese gooseberries), watermelon and cantaloupe (rockmelon). Peel the fruits (do this over a large bowl to catch all the juices), then cut them up into bite-sized pieces. Remove pips and seeds from oranges, apples, watermelon and cantaloupe. Put all the fruits together into the bowl and toss them together well. When well mixed, spoon mixture into cups, filling about three-quarters full.

Fill to the top with freshly squeezed orange juice. Insert a wooden stick into each one and put them in the freezer. Leave until frozen solid.

When you want one, remove from freezer and let sit for 5–10 minutes (depending on the heat), then pull the ice-block out of its plastic container. Alternatively, put the cup under a tap of running warm water to loosen the ice-block.

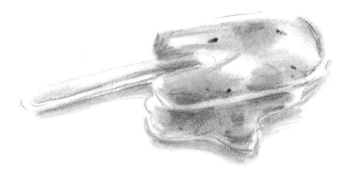

Pineapples
Ananas comosus

The pineapple is native to Brazil and is one of the most popular and delicious of the tropical fruits. It belongs to the bromeliad family and is indeed a regal fruit.

Christopher Columbus is said to have brought the pineapple to Spain. It had already been cultivated by American Indians for a long time before the Europeans came across it. When Columbus's men found it on Guadeloupe, it was love at first sight — its flavor and fragrance astonished and delighted them. The great fruit lover Louis XIV had them growing at Versailles and they were the craze of the European hot-houses during the eighteenth century.

Pineapples do best in tropical areas but can also be grown in warmer parts of the subtropics if the garden is frost-free. They need to have a warm aspect and protection from cold winds. In cooler areas, they are grown mainly as ornamentals. Good pot specimens can be grown in cooler areas on warm patios or verandahs.

The main varieties are the Smooth-leaf Cayenne whose fruit is large and juicy, Common Queen and Ripley Queen, both high-quality dessert varieties with small sweeter fruit.

Pineapples can be grown from tops, slips (tiny pineapples pulled from the base of the plant) or suckers (a shoot from the leaf axil of a stem). Tops cut from plants are excellent for planting — stand the top, butt upwards, in a cool airy place to allow the base to dry out before planting. This 'curing' reduces the possibility of rotting once they are in the soil.

Pineapples grow in a wide range of soil types but do not like heavy clays. A deep, well-drained sandy loam rich in organic matter is best. Plant them in a warm, frost-free position, protected from winds.

PINEAPPLE AND SWEET POTATO CAKE

Use fresh pineapple for this and chop it finely. The orange sweet potato (kumera) is the best one to use. This is a big, light, moist cake, which is good to take on picnics.

1 ¼ cups (6 ½ oz) all-purpose (plain) whole-wheat (wholemeal) flour
1 ½ cups (6 oz) all-purpose (plain) white flour
1 ⅓ cups (11 oz) raw (demerara) sugar
2 tspns baking powder
2 tspns baking soda (bicarbonate of soda)
2 tspns cinnamon
1 tsp ground cardamom
½ tspn ground ginger
½ tspn salt
6 ½ oz grated sweet potato, approx 10 oz unpeeled
6 oz diced fresh pineapple, approx 10 oz unpeeled
1 ¼ cups (10 fl oz) polyunsaturated vegetable oil
4 eggs, well beaten
1 cup (4 oz) walnuts or pecans, chopped

Preheat oven to 350°F (180°C/Gas 4). Line a large tin (11 x 9 ½ x 2 in) with non-stick baking paper — or grease and lightly flour it. You can also use 2 x 9 in cake tins, and store one cake in the freezer for later use.

Sift all the dry ingredients together into a large bowl. Make a well in the center.

Put the pineapple and sweet potato into the middle of the dry ingredients. Stir in the oil, eggs and walnuts and thoroughly combine.

Pour into prepared tin/tins. Cook the larger cake for 1–1 ¼ hours, the two smaller ones for about 45–50 minutes. Test by inserting a skewer in the center — if it comes out clean, the cake is cooked.

Nice with a lemon or lime icing.

CORNED BEEF WITH PINEAPPLE

A rather old-fashioned dish but very good, and easy to do. Serve hot with potatoes, sweet potatoes, green beans and baby squash.

SERVES 4–6

3 lb corned beef
1 ⅓ tblspns (⅔ fl oz) vinegar
1 onion, peeled
1 carrot
1 bay leaf
1 stalk celery
few peppercorns
6–8 cloves
10 oz fresh pineapple, cut into small pieces
2 tblspns (½ oz) seedless raisins
¾ cup (4 oz) brown sugar
⅓ cup (3 fl oz) white vinegar
2 tspns dry mustard

Put beef into a large pot, cover with water and add vinegar, onion, carrot, bay leaf, celery and peppercorns. Bring to a boil and let simmer until cooked, approximately 1 ½ hours.

Remove the beef from the water, put it into a baking dish, fat side up, and stud it with some cloves.

In a bowl, mix together remaining ingredients and pour mixture over meat. Bake for 30 minutes at 350°F (180°C/Gas 4), basting frequently with the juices.

TROPICAL BEEF KEBABS

There are so many delicious, inventive marinades for meats, poultry and game. Here is one for beef. The meat looks pretty if it is sliced thinly and then woven onto the bamboo skewers.

SERVES 4–6

1 ½ lb round steak, trimmed of fat

½ cup (4 fl oz) pineapple juice

1 ⅓ tblspns (⅔ fl oz) cider vinegar

2 tspns honey

2 tspns freshly grated ginger

pinch cayenne

1 clove garlic, crushed

3–4 freshly sliced pineapple rounds, skin on

1–2 red (Spanish) onions, peeled

1 green sweet pepper (capsicum), cut into chunks

bamboo skewers, soaked in water for 15 minutes

Cut the beef into ¼ in strips across the grain then put it into a glass or enamel bowl. Mix together pineapple juice, vinegar, honey, ginger, cayenne and garlic and pour over the beef. Cover and refrigerate a few hours or overnight.

Cut the pineapple rounds into wedges. Cut the red onions into 6–8 wedges.

Remove beef from marinade. Thread a wedge of pineapple onto the top of each skewer, then weave on the strips of meat interspersing with wedges of onion and sweet pepper as you go.

Barbecue over hot coals or cook on a char-grill, being careful not to overcook the meat.

Guavas
Psidium species

You can't mistake the fragrance of guavas — once smelt, they are unforgettable. I happen to like them as they evoke strong memories for me, but some people dislike their pungency.

The guava was another fruit served to Christopher Columbus in the Caribbean. Before that, only American Indians had set eyes on them.

There are over 150 varieties of guava, all originating in tropical America. They belong to the genus Psidium, which is Greek for 'pomegranate'. Like that fruit, the guava is also full of small seeds enclosed in the pulp. Botanically it is a berry and may be white, yellow, green, purple or red according to species and variety.

I know of two types of guava — the Psidium guajava and P. cattleianum. The former, known as the tropical or tree guava, includes the apple, yellow and pear guavas, and thrives in warm to hot climates. The latter, which will grow in cooler conditions, includes two types — the cherry or strawberry guava, which is small, delicious and very pretty with red-purple fruit; and the yellow cherry guava, which has yellow fruit.

The common guava (P. guajava) is easy to grow from seed and reproduces mostly true to type. It can also be propagated from cuttings taken in spring or summer. Cherry guavas are easily propagated from seed.

Guavas grow in a wide range of soils but dislike low temperatures and will not tolerate frost. They grow well where oranges thrive, if planted in a sunny spot protected from winds.

GUAVAS IN SYRUP

One of the nicest ways I know to eat guavas. The smell of these while cooking will fill the whole house. It is a magical, evocative smell — but not for those who dislike guavas. I happen to love them.

MAKES ABOUT 6 CUPS (1 ½ QT)

4 cups (1 qt) water
3 cups (1 ½ lb) sugar
2 lb firm ripe guavas
juice of 1–2 fresh limes, strained
2–3 slices fresh lime (optional)

Make a sugar syrup by putting the water and sugar into a saucepan. Bring to a boil, making sure all the sugar is dissolved, and boil for 10 minutes. Remove and cool.

Wash and dry the guavas, then peel, halve and core them. Put the peel and seeds into a saucepan with a little water, bring to a boil and let simmer for 10 minutes or until very soft. Strain through a fine sieve and add to the sugar syrup along with the lime juice (to taste) and slices of fresh lime. Return to the saucepan and put in the guava halves. Bring very gently to a boil, being very careful not to let the fruit disintegrate. They need to soften but remain firm. Test with a knife point. Remove fruit with a slotted spoon and place in clean sterile jars or a pretty dessert dish.

Bring syrup back to a boil and reduce by half. Cool. Pour over the guavas. Add lime slices. Seal jars, if using, and store in refrigerator. Keeps up to two weeks.

ARNIE'S GUAVA FLAN

The flan is a beautiful pink color and wonderful served warm. You need to use the pink-fleshed guavas.

SERVES 6–8

1 pre-baked 10 ½ –11 in pie shell, at least 1 in
in height
8 medium guavas
1 cup (8 fl oz) cream
8 eggs
⅓ cup (3 oz) sugar
2 tspns lime or lemon juice

Preheat oven to cool (300°F/150°C/Gas 3).

Peel the guavas. Chop flesh (with seeds) roughly and put into blender or food processor with cream. Blend well, then push through a sieve to remove all the seeds.

In a bowl, beat together eggs, sugar and lime juice. Beat in guava–cream mixture. Pour into pre-baked pastry shell and bake for 30 minutes or until custard is just set — don't let it overcook or bubble. Cool slightly before cutting.

Note: The guavas, skin on, can be put through a juicer. This makes for an even more intense flavor. You need about 2 ¼ cups (18 fl oz) guava juice if done this way.

Other Fruits

Season of mists and mellow fruitfulness,
Close bosom-friend of the maturing sun;
Conspiring with him how to load and bless
With fruit the vines that round the thatch-eves run; . . .

KEATS, FROM 'TO AUTUMN'

In the midst of fall, when farmers have laid by their harvest and a full moon hangs in the sky, pause for a while. How many city dwellers are aware of the harvest? Of its ancient significance, or the fact that of all seasonal festivals, harvest was undoubtedly the most important?

In fall many plants come to fruition, among them the grape, the fig, the persimmon, pomegranate and tamarillo. When you think of their colors — the reds, pinks, purples, mauves, blacks, yellows and oranges — they summon up fall. Along with the olive tree and wheat, the fig and vine provided the Mediterraneans with their four basic foods until modern times. Without them, they could not live. All the tales and myths surrounding the fig, olive and grape reflect their central place. If you plant one or two of these trees in your garden, they will be constant reminders to you of the importance of the harvest and its significance to peoples since early times.

In times past, numerous seasonal pagan rituals were developed as insurance against the perils of an untamed world. Throughout Europe, the concept of a Demeter-like corn mother was retained for centuries. It was thought that the corn mother or earth goddess controlled the seasons, all forms of nature and even the continuance of life itself. If the harvest was good, there would be plenty of food to last the winter, but if the harvest had been poor, she had been vexed and famine would follow.

In Greece, the corn mother was known as Demeter; the Romans called her Ceres (grain crops have been called 'cereals' ever since) and in Britain she was sometimes known as the 'white lady of death'. Some believed the corn spirit lived in the very last sheaf and that whoever cut it killed the spirit. This would almost certainly bring bad luck, so all the reapers threw their sickles at the sheaf from a distance, so that no-one would reap misfortune with the final bundle. They would then make a 'corn dolly' out of the corn to represent the corn mother and the dollies would be hung up in the kitchen where they served to protect the household throughout winter from evil spirits and pestilence. In North Pembrokeshire the doll was called 'the hag'; in Poland it was called 'Baba' (old woman), and there it would be made by two girls who delivered it with a garland to the farmer. Similar customs are recorded in various European countries.

At La Palisse in France, a man made of dough is hung on a fir tree carried on the last harvest wagon. The tree and the dough man are taken to the mayor's house and stay there till the vintage is over. In Wermland in Sweden, the farmer's wife uses the grain of the last sheaf to bake a loaf in the shape of a young girl. The loaf is then divided up and eaten by all the members of the household.

In Germany, fall is festival time. Celebrations still take place at the end of harvest and the country is rich in fairs. In the United States, Thanksgiving is a modern version of more ancient European customs.

In Honey From a Weed, *Patience Gray pays due attention to seasonal changes and their significance. She evokes the life of a woman living and working in stone-built primitive homes on the shores of the Mediterranean. There, the rhythm of living is the rhythm of planting, growing and gathering, of wine-making and olive harvesting. She also stresses the importance of food being grown to be eaten, not handled.*

I am interested in growing food for its own sake and in appetite. The health-giving and prophylactic virtues of a meal depend on the zest with which it has been imagined, cooked and eaten. It seems to me appropriate to show something of the life that generates this indispensable element at a time when undernourishment bedevils even the highest income groups.

In One Continuous Picnic *Michael Symons pointed out that Australia is the only land which has never enjoyed agrarian society. It has a history without peasants, which means Australians have been either conservationists or developers, without appreciating the cultivated landscape. In our own small way, each of us can help to redress that balance by growing a fruit tree or two in our own back gardens. These trees — the fig, pomegranate and tamarillo — and the vine are not difficult to grow, and they will reward you in countless ways.*

A bubble of milk
will ooze out of the taut stem
when you pick a fig —
don't drink, the milk tastes bitter
though it looks like a man's juice.
When ripe to bursting

figs pass a drop of syrup
that glows at their pink
puckered holes. Put your mouth there.
Open the red seed-bellies.

BEVERLEY FARMER, 'FIGS'

Figs
Ficus carica

Fig-tree, for such a long time I have found meaning
in the way you almost completely omit your blossoms
and urge your pure mystery, unproclaimed,
into the early ripening fruit.

RAINER MARIA RILKE, FROM 'THE SIXTH ELEGY'

'Ancient, mysterious and delicious, the fig should be more widely grown than it is,' writes David Stuart in The Kitchen Garden. *He points out that if you plant a fig tree in your garden, you will have something that grew in the earliest gardens of all. The fig and the grape were two of the plants that survived the Ice Age (the others were the vine, olive, carob, myrtle, oleander, plane, lentisk and Judas tree). Since then, painters and writers have been celebrating these hardy bearers, weaving myths and legends around them.*

A member of the mulberry family, the fig is one of the most ancient plants, popular everywhere in the Middle East (where it seems they originated) since at least 3000 BC. Figs grew in the Garden of Eden and in the hanging gardens of Babylon. They were dried for preservation by burying in the hot sands. They were also a favorite of the ancient Greeks, who believed they were a special gift from Ceres to the city of Athens and who planted a grove of fig trees in the city's market place.

The genus Ficus *includes over 750 species. Some ripen underground, others grow high in the air, some grow on low trailing shrubs in the desert. There are large figs, small figs, round figs and ovoid figs, black, brown, red, green, purple, yellow and white. The most famous of all is the Smyrna fig, which comes from Western Turkey, home of the domesticated fig.*

I love figs and think they should be more widely grown. The very best way to eat them is either fresh from the tree, or gathered in the early morning, set on a fig leaf in a dish in pyramid form and eaten warm from the sun at midday. You know they are ripe when a bead of nectar appears at the opening of the fruit. I remember seeing them presented like this in the film The Belly of an Architect, *in which the protagonist was obsessed by green figs. And in* Women in Love, *Alan Bates bites into a fig to expose, to his amazed guest, the deep red mass of flowers inside the soft skin: an aura of sexuality has always surrounded this sublime fruit.*

They're delicious as an entrée with thinly sliced prosciutto; or as a dessert on warm toasted slices of brioche spread with honey, some mascarpone on the side. Or serve them on a cheese platter with fresh goat cheeses and soft brie. Don't peel them. Eat them skins and all.

Figs are quick-growing, deciduous trees that grow 10–16 ft tall, and up to 33 ft under ideal conditions. For the kitchen gardener, they are an ideal plant because many varieties bear a better crop if their roots are constricted. This also makes them excellent container plants. The main varieties grown in home gardens are self-fertile and will produce fruit even when the flowers are not pollinated by the fig wasp, which means you only need one tree. Varieties include the Brown Turkey, Preston Pacific, Cape White, Black Genoa and White Adriatic. Figs will grow easily from cuttings which need to be about 8 in long and taken in late winter from one-year-old wood.

They require a light, well-drained loamy soil and a warm, dry climate. During summer they need plenty of soil moisture if they are to bear good-quality fruit. Little pruning is needed as they naturally form a well-balanced framework. Birds are a real problem as the fruit is ripening. Trees are usually netted or banners hung to distract the birds.

RABBIT WITH MUSTARD SAUCE AND FRESH FIGS

I had this one lunchtime at The Pheasant Farm, Maggie Beer's marvellous restaurant in the Barossa Valley, an hour and a half's drive from Adelaide in South Australia. It was superb and I asked her for the recipe. There are a number of steps involved — the paws and legs need to be cooked first; the fillets, liver, kidney and figs pan-fried and a sauce needs to be made.

SERVES 4

2 rabbits (paws and legs, fillets, liver, kidney)
2 tblspns (1 oz) butter
20 fresh sage leaves
6 chopped shallots (brown onions)
1 ⅓ tblspns (⅔ fl oz) good-quality French mustard
½ cup (4 fl oz) white wine
6–8 cups (1 ½ –2 qt) rabbit or chicken stock (broth)
4–6 fresh figs
extra butter and fresh sage leaves
scant ½ cup (3 ⅓ fl oz) cream

Ask the butcher to remove the fillets from the rabbits; to cut the legs from the saddle and through the pelvis, and to cut off the paws.

In a heavy frying pan, melt the butter and gently brown the paws and legs. Toss in the sage and shallots and allow to soften, then add mustard. Pour in the white wine and reduce until there are 2 ⅔ tblspns (1 ½ fl oz) liquid left. Transfer to a heavy-based pot and cover with stock. Cover, bring to a boil, turn down heat and sit the pot on a simmer pad. Simmer very slowly for 2 hours. Remove from heat. Take out the paws and legs and keep covered in a warm place until ready to serve.

Measure 2 cups (16 fl oz) of the stock and put in a saucepan with the cream. Bring to a boil and reduce until you have a nice smooth sauce-like consistency. Adjust mustard to taste, being careful it's not over-salty.

Quickly pan-fry the fillets, livers and kidneys (if used) in foaming butter just to color. Remove and keep warm. Toss in legs and paws to reheat.

In another pan, quickly sauté cross-sections (that is, cut from the top through the stem) of fresh figs with some more fresh sage leaves, sprinkle with freshly ground black pepper.

To serve, remove the rabbit fillets, livers and kidneys from pan. Slice the fillets on the diagonal and place one fillet per person on plates. Allow one leg and one paw per person. Spoon sauce over the meat and garnish with figs.

FROZEN FIG PARFAIT

This is nice served with fresh raspberries and quarters of fresh figs.

SERVES 6–8

1 lb very ripe, dark purple figs
1 cup (8 oz) superfine (caster) sugar (adjust according to ripeness of figs)
juice of ½ lemon
¼ cup (2 fl oz) white wine
3 egg yolks
vanilla extract (essence)
1 ½ cups (12 fl oz) cream

Wash figs and cut in quarters. Cook, covered, in saucepan for about 15 minutes with half the sugar (adjust to taste), the lemon juice and wine. Remove from heat. When cool, purée in a blender.

Place egg yolks and a few drops of vanilla in a bowl. Beat well, then add remaining sugar gradually until thick and creamy. Place over a pan of simmering water and continue beating for about 5 minutes till warm and thickening. Keep scraping down sides as you do this. Remove from heat and beat until cool. Whisk in the fig mixture. Lightly whip the cream and fold in. Pour into 6 cup (1 ½ qt) mold and freeze until set. To unmold, dip quickly into a basin of warm water and turn out onto a platter.

Cut into wedges or slices and allow to thaw a little before serving.

FIG JAM

This is heaven just eaten from the spoon. The figs retain their shape and flavor and fall off the end of the spoon surrounded by a lovely clear jam. Don't do what I did once and leave the bowl near an ant trail. Fig and ant jam is not one I can recommend.

MAKES APPROX 3 CUPS (24 FL OZ)

2 lb green figs
3 cups (1 ½ lb) sugar
grated zest (rind) and juice of 2 limes or *lemons*
½ cup (3 oz) blanched almonds (optional)

Wash figs and remove stems. Cut into quarters and place in an earthenware bowl. Sprinkle with 1 lb of sugar, cover well and leave overnight.

Next day, place fig mixture in a large saucepan, add lime zest and juice. Simmer gently for 30 minutes. Warm remaining sugar and have jars clean and warming in the oven. Add the hot sugar to the pan and bring to a rapid boil. Boil for 10–15 minutes or until setting point is reached. Be careful not to overcook. Add almonds. Spoon immediately into the prepared jars.

Pomegranates
Punica granatum

Like the fig, the pomegranate is one of the oldest fruits in cultivation, and as such is steeped in myths and legend. Its glistening grain-like seeds seem always to have captured the imagination. Again, like the fig, its origins are somewhere in the Middle East.

Because of the number of its seeds and their bright assertiveness, it has been a symbol of fertility since earliest times. In Greek mythology, Persephone, daughter of Demeter, goddess of agriculture, made the fatal mistake of eating six of the seeds when in the underworld. This condemned her to spend six months of the year there with Hades, her dark husband. The story is an allegory of the dormancy of vegetable life during the winter and the promise of rebirth in the spring. Even today, Sephardic Jews set bowls of pomegranates on the table at New Year (Rosh Hashanah).

Biblical references abound: Moses promised the wandering Israelites 'a land of wheat and barley and vines and fig trees and pomegranates'; Solomon had a pomegranate orchard. Its juice was much prized and was used by herbalists for many disorders. Granada in Spain is thought to have been named after the pomegranate and the Moors planted an avenue of its trees there.

Fortunately for the home gardener, pomegranate trees are easy to grow and also thrive in containers. With their translucent pink, white or vermilion flowers, their flushed, scarlet-golden fruit and glorious autumn colors, they are a great joy to behold. Pomegranates are deciduous shrubs or small trees with bushy habits, 16–23 ft in height, and they are suitable as hedge plants. The dwarf varieties are ornamental only, producing inedible fruit.

They like hot, dry conditions, dislike humidity and low temperatures, and are moderate in their demands for water. Propagation from cuttings is recommended. Take hardwood cuttings about 12 in long in winter and almost cover with soil, leaving one or two buds exposed. Mature trees need a dressing of citrus fertilizer each winter. Fruit can be picked before full maturity and ripened in storage — if rain falls during harvest, pick before the skin becomes waterlogged and splits. Pomegranates do not usually bear well until they are five or six years old.

The sparkling red fleshy seeds of the pomegranate are often eaten out of the hand, with a little sugar or salt. They have a sweetly acid flavor. The bitter kernels can be eaten, though they are usually discarded.

Pomegranate seeds are frequently used for garnishing and the juice can be used in sauces, drinks, soups, jellies and ices. To extract the juice, cut the fruits in half, scoop out the seeds, discarding all the pith (which can be very bitter) and put into a blender or food processor. Blend for a few seconds, then pour through a sieve into a bowl, squeezing out all the juice. Depending on the variety of the pomegranate, the juice will vary from sweet to sweet-sour. The juice is very good for basting roast turkey or chicken.

A few seeds in a flute of champagne make a pretty addition.

FAISINJAN

This is a sweet-sour dish originally from Iran. Taste as you go to ensure the delicate mix of sweet and sour is to your liking. Make sure you use fresh walnuts. Don't grind them too finely — they need to have some texture. Serve with saffron rice.

SERVES 4

1 medium chicken, cut into serving pieces
2 ⅔ tblspns (1 ⅓ fl oz) vegetable oil
2 tblspns (1 oz) butter
1 medium onion, finely chopped
1 ¾ cups (6 ½ oz) ground walnuts
4 pomegranates
juice of 1–2 lemons
¾ cup (6 ½ fl oz) chicken stock (broth)
2–3 tspns sugar
salt and pepper

Trim the chicken and wipe dry. In a large heavy frying pan, heat the oil and butter and brown the chicken pieces all over. Remove and keep warm.

Add onion to pan and cook until soft and golden. Stir in the walnuts and cook gently, stirring well, for 2–3 minutes.

Extract the juice from 3 ½ pomegranates, reserving one half for garnishing. You should have about 1 cup (8 fl oz). Add to the pan along with the remaining ingredients, checking the sweet-sour flavor as you go.

Season to taste. Bring to simmering point, then add the chicken pieces and cook for about 1 hour, partially covered, or until chicken pieces are tender. Garnish with reserved seeds.

POMEGRANATES AND MELON

SERVES 4

Pomegranate seeds tossed through balls of pink and green melon are both stunning and delicious. With a melon baller, remove the flesh from one medium honeydew melon and half a small watermelon. Put into a glass serving bowl and pour over some white rum or rose water to taste. Scatter through the seeds of two medium pomegranates. Serve chilled, garnished with pink rose petals.

Fruit Flan

A version of the famous French dessert fruit tarts, this one is made with a filling of cream cheese. It is easier to prepare and a nice change from the ubiquitous (and often heavy) crème pâtissière. It is also very pretty, especially if you lay the fruit out imaginatively on top of the cream cheese base.

Serves 6–8

Sweet Pastry

1 cup (4 oz) all-purpose (plain) flour
¼ cup (⅔ oz) cornstarch (cornflour)
2 tblspns (1 oz) confectioners' (icing) sugar
½ cup (4 oz) frozen unsalted butter, cut into chunks
1 egg, beaten together with 1 ⅓ tblspns (⅔ fl oz) water

Filling

8 oz cream cheese, softened and cut into small pieces
½ cup (4 oz) superfine (caster) sugar
2 eggs
2 ⅔ tblspns (1 ⅓ fl oz) Madeira
selection of fruits in season: kiwi fruit (Chinese gooseberries),
guava, mango, persimmons, pomegranates, berries, banana,
grapes, peaches, apples, pineapple

Glaze

½ cup (4 fl oz) redcurrant jelly
dash brandy (optional)
lemon juice

Preheat oven to 400°F (200°C/Gas 6).

Sift together the flours and confectioners' sugar and put into the food processor with the butter. Process quickly, turning on and off, until mixture resembles fine breadcrumbs. Pour the beaten egg through the feed tube and process until mixture forms a ball around the blades; remove and wrap in waxed (greaseproof) paper. Chill in refrigerator for 1 hour.

Roll pastry out to fit a 9 in flan tin and bake the pastry blind in oven for 10–12 minutes.

Reduce oven temperature to 350°F (180°C/Gas 4). Beat together the cheese, sugar, eggs and Madeira and pour into the pre-baked pastry shell. Cook for 20–30 minutes or until just set. Remove and cool.

Peel the fruits and slice into attractive shapes — slices of firm ripe persimmon and pomegranate seeds look pretty, banana looks good sliced on the diagonal; mango can be cut into fine wedges and fanned out; you can leave small seedless grapes whole; raspberries also look good kept whole. Arrange over the cooled filling, either in the design shown or in concentric circles.

Put the redcurrant jelly into a small saucepan with a dash of brandy and a squeeze of lemon juice. Bring to a boil and cook, stirring well, until it is smooth. Cool, then brush over fruit with a clean pastry brush.

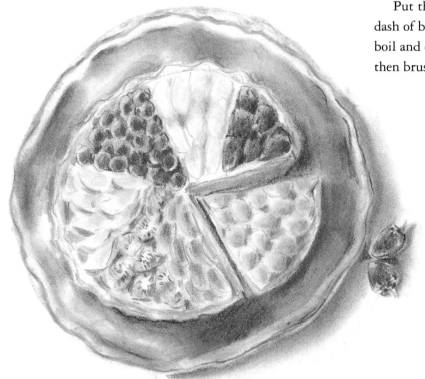

Tamarillos
Cyphomandra betacea

I'd never seen a tamarillo tree until my mother planted one near her back gate. For many years, it gave us the most beautiful crops of fruit, delighting us with the fragrance of its flowers and its abundance. Sadly, it died after about five years. I subsequently discovered that tamarillos are short-lived plants (about five to seven years). Unlike the fig, grape and pomegranate, the tamarillo, also known as the tree tomato, is a relatively new fruit. Its tart, egg-shaped, red or yellow fruit is a matter of taste (a cross between a tomato and a passionfruit), and there are those who do not enjoy the tartness. Also, many people avoid them because they're not quite sure what to do with them. If you peel, slice and sprinkle them with sugar, they are delicious. Always make sure you peel them or their skin will 'shrink your mouth'.

Originally from Peru or Brazil, tamarillos have been grown widely in New Zealand. They are ideal for the small garden in tropical and subtropical climates, because they are neat and easily tended.

The tree is a shrubby, soft-wooded evergreen which grows up to 13 ft tall. It flowers in spring and the tree droops with fruit from early fall to spring. Red and yellow seedling varieties are available, although the yellow ones are difficult to find. They can be grown from cuttings taken in summer and also grow easily from seeds taken from mature fruit.

Tamarillos are frost sensitive and dislike wind. They require a light, well-drained soil. Poor soil can cause root rot and viral diseases. Once established, give annual dressings of compost or manure to maintain a high level of organic matter in the soil.

TAMARILLO AND ALMOND FLAN

Make the pastry the day before — it is a soft one, so handle with care. The filling is rich but superb. Figs can be substituted for the tamarillos, but you won't need to sugar them. They look pretty if splayed out into flower petals by cutting a deep cross in each of their top ends.

SERVES 6–8

2 cups (8 oz) all-purpose (plain) flour
½ cup (2 oz) ground almonds
¾ cup (6 ½ oz) unsalted butter, cold
½ cup (4 oz) superfine (caster) sugar
pinch salt
1 egg yolk
zest (rind) of 1 lemon
2 tblspns (1 fl oz) overproof rum
few drops almond extract (essence)
8 tamarillos
sugar

ALMOND CREAM
⅝ cup (5 oz) butter, softened
1 ¼ cups (6 ½ oz) sifted confectioners' (icing) sugar
1 ¾ cups (6 ½ oz) ground almonds
2 eggs
¼ cup (1 oz) cornstarch (cornflour)
few drops bitter almond extract (essence)
1 ⅓ tblspns (⅔ fl oz) overproof rum

Put the flour and ground almonds into the food processor bowl. Cut butter into chunks and add to the flour and almonds with the sugar and salt. Process, turning on and off, until mixture forms breadcrumbs. Add the yolk, lemon zest, rum and almond extract and process until it forms a ball. Wrap in plastic wrap and refrigerate overnight.

Next day, preheat oven to 400°F (200°C/Gas 6). Remove from the refrigerator 30 minutes before rolling out. Roll out between sheets of non-stick baking paper or plastic wrap to fit an 11 in flan tin. Prick well and bake in oven for 12–15 minutes or until light golden and brown. Allow to cool.

Meanwhile, peel, slice and sugar the tamarillos and set aside for 2 hours.

For the filling, beat together the butter and confectioners' sugar until pale-colored and light, and continue beating as you add the remaining ingredients. Spread the almond cream over the pastry with a spatula and arrange tamarillo slices in concentric circles on top. Color contrast can be added by using sliced kiwi fruit (Chinese gooseberries), strawberries, or green or purple grapes. Glaze with sieved warm apricot jam. Alternatively, slice the figs and arrange in a pretty pattern over the top.

POACHED TAMARILLOS

Very delicious.

SERVES 4

2 cups (16 fl oz) water
2 cups (1 lb) sugar
8 ripe tamarillos
1 lime, orange or lemon

Make a syrup with the water and sugar, making sure all the sugar has dissolved, simmer for several minutes then add a long thin piece of citrus peel.

Leaving the stems on the tamarillos, nick the other end with a sharp knife. Drop them gently into the simmering syrup and simmer until the skins peel off easily, about 1–2 minutes. Peel, leaving stems on, and leave in the syrup until ready to serve.

Before serving, remove from syrup. Reduce syrup over high heat and drizzle over the poached fruits. Serve with coconut ice-cream or whipped cream flavored with orange liqueur or a lemon sorbet.

Variation: Try poaching the tamarillos in a red wine and sugar syrup. Leave them to stand in the poaching liquid overnight, then serve with a coconut junket. Make this by infusing milk with shredded coconut, then straining. Add junket powder to the coconut milk and proceed as usual.

Persimmons
Diospyros *species*

Now prove these promised joys,
What scraping bitterness, what clawed acridity,
What griping, green, unseasoned, thin acidity,
The palate ploughed, the puckered lip awry.
    But wait: wait till the crackled stars turn brown,
The slackened skins in sagging scrollwork creep,

Or stickily in oozy patches weep.
Then boldly bite. The luscious flesh glides down,
    So those to whom fair-seeming youth proves sour,
In shrivelled age may see their sweetness flower.

JOHN BRAY, FROM 'THE PERSIMMONS'

Once when working on a photographic shoot, food stylist Robin Duffecy turned up with a basket of burnt gold persimmons, some with their stalks still attached — she had picked them the day before from a friend's tree. She set them in a beautiful blue and white Chinese bowl and put the bowl on a wooden stool in front of some artists' easels. Artist Sharne Weidland, the photographer's wife, saw the photograph and painted a still life from it. There is a Zen quality about the painting which captures the glowing persimmons against the oriental bowl.

The Japanese love persimmons, most particularly of the P. kaki *species, welcoming in the New Year with them. There, they are left to ripen on the tree until there is a heavy frost. The flesh becomes frozen and they eat them on the spot, iced. The sight of these glowing golden globes hanging on leafless trees against the snow is breathtaking. It is probably the latest ripener of any fruit, and it is ripeness, even over-ripeness, that makes them edible. At home, if your persimmons are not ripe, put them in the freezer to ripen. As with its cousin, the tropical sapote, the flesh is best eaten with a spoon straight out of its skin.*

Persimmons are native to China and are generally known as kaki *though they are also known as date plums and keg-figs. There are over 150 species of* Diospyros, *but only five are eaten regularly. Persimmons are well adapted to extremes of climate and grow in both subtropical and temperate areas. They will also tolerate a wide variety of soils, preferring deep, rich, well-drained ones. Grafted plants are recommended as they do not grow well from seed. Selected named varieties are grafted onto* D. kaki *rootstock.*

They are slow-growing trees, not reaching full maturity for about 12 years, though they will begin to bear after three years. They require only light pruning but should be planted at least 20 ft from other trees as they spread. Plenty of water during the growing season is recommended for good fruit, as is a dressing of citrus fertilizer each winter.

DESSERT PERSIMMONS

When ripe and soft, scoop the pulp from 4–6 persimmons, leaving their shells intact. Put the shells in the freezer whilst you prepare the filling.

Remove seeds and mix the pulp with some mascarpone, or whipped cream. Add Kirsch or Maraschino to taste. Spoon back into the shells and return to the freezer for 1–2 hours. Remove and garnish with crumbled macaroons or Amaretti biscuits.

Note: It is best if the filling is only partially frozen. Don't let it set hard.

PERSIMMON AND APRICOT JAM

MAKES 8 CUPS (2 QT)

13 oz dried apricots
8 cups (2 qt) water
1 ½ lb persimmons, approx 6 medium persimmons
juice of 2 lemons
6 cups (3 lb) warmed sugar

Wash the apricots thoroughly, cut them into halves and soak for 12 hours overnight in the water.

Next day, peel the persimmons, chop the pulp and put into a large pan with the apricots and soaking water. Add the lemon juice and warmed sugar. Stir over low heat until the sugar is dissolved. Bring to a boil and simmer until thick, about 1 ½ hours, stirring

occasionally and removing any scum which forms on the top. Pour into clean sterile jars when cold and seal.

PERSIMMON BREAD

3 eggs
1 ½ cups (11 oz) superfine (caster) sugar
1 cup (8 fl oz) light vegetable oil
finely grated zest (rind) of 1 lemon or *lime*
15 oz persimmon pulp, approx 6 persimmons
1 ½ cups (6 oz) all-purpose (plain) flour
1 ⅓ cups (6 oz) all-purpose (plain) whole-wheat
(wholemeal) flour
1 tspn baking soda (bicarbonate of soda)
1 tspn mixed spice
1 tspn cinnamon
½ tspn baking powder
pinch salt
¾ cup (3 oz) walnuts, chopped

Preheat oven to 350°F (180°C/Gas 4). Line 2 x 9 in loaf tins with non-stick baking paper.

In a mixing bowl, beat the eggs and sugar until thick then add oil and lemon zest. Stir in persimmon pulp. Sift together the dry ingredients and fold through the persimmon mixture with the nuts. Pour into prepared tins and cook for about 1 hour or until a skewer inserted in the center comes out clean. Turn out and cool.

Nice iced with Lime Cream Cheese Icing (see page 201).

Table Grapes
Vitis vinifera

The vine makes the true savour of the earth intelligible to man. With what fidelity does it make its translation! It senses, then expresses, in its clusters of fruit the secrets of the soil.

COLETTE, FROM EARTHLY PARADISE

The sight of clusters of plump grapes intertwined amongst vivid green leaves is one of the delights of late summer. As the grapes ripen and the leaves turn yellow and red and brown, we are reminded that winter is on its way.

The vine is one of the oldest plants in cultivation. Of the 8000 varieties available, both natural and cultivars, all those of the Old World developed from the Vitis vinifera. *This is the best wine grape, but it has also been developed to produce many good table grapes. Just when the distinction between wine grapes and dessert grapes was made, we do not know. By the first century BC, the Greeks were cultivating special varieties for the table and the Romans followed their example. They also made a distinction between those meant to be eaten fresh and those for drying in the form of raisins.*

Viticulture (the cultivation of the grape) seems to have begun around the Caspian Sea. From there, with the movement and spread of people, it found its way south through Asia Minor and west to Greece, Italy and France, and thence to Britain. The Bible is full of references to it; grapes were cultivated in ancient Egypt (a jar marked 'unfermented grape juice' was found in the tomb of Tutankhamen, dating from 1350 BC) and in the hanging gardens of Babylon.

Those of us fortunate enough to live in a climate where the summers are warm—hot and the winters cool can grow grapes. In Belgium, the most expensive (and perfect) grapes are grown in greenhouses — these tear-shaped beauties, covered with fine, silvery dust, are packed in cotton wool and sold at huge prices in luxury food shops. However, even if the climate is right, a certain amount of daily attention is necessary once new growth begins if the grapes are to develop properly. Selection of the site is important. Grapes like a sunny position, and will tolerate ordinary soil, though it must be fertile and well drained.

They do not like windy or very hot positions.

Propagation is from cane cuttings taken in winter when the vines are dormant. Named varieties are available from local nurseries, and it is wise to consult with a specialist nursery before selecting a particular variety for your garden. Organic matter should be dug in before planting. Vines can be grown on a free-standing trellis or the side of a fence or building. They look wonderful draped around the eaves of a balcony. Correct pruning is essential to encourage the growth of large, evenly ripened grapes in attractive clusters.

GRAPE IDEAS

As with many of the fruits, I think grapes are best eaten fresh. I love nothing better than a cluster of cold grapes on a hot day. They go well on a cheese platter, and look festive dipped in egg white and covered with superfine (caster) sugar. Piled up on a glass stand and presented this way, they are truly spectacular.

On the island of Naxos in Greece, large firm rosy grapes called rosakí are preserved in syrup and served in summer on a saucer with a spoon, a remedy against heat and exhaustion.

Grapes are also good added to the sauce made from deglazing a pan after roasting meat, especially if the deglazing has been done with verjuice (the sour juice from unripe grapes, similar to lemon juice). They're also good served with rich game pâtés.

For a very simple dessert, combine seedless grapes with sour cream, to which a little brown sugar and slivered orange zest (rind) have been added. Serve chilled. Seedless green grapes also combine well with melon balls and freshly chopped mint.

BOILED CHOCOLATE AND RAISIN CAKE

This cake is a marvel. I have included it because it is so popular, even though it uses dried, not fresh, grapes. It is surprisingly moist but you need to be careful to dissolve the soda properly.

1 ½ cups (12 fl oz) water
1 cup (5 oz) raisins
1 cup (8 oz) butter
1 cup (8 oz) sugar
½ tspn cinnamon
½ tspn ground cloves
¼ cup (1 oz) cocoa
¼ tspn salt

1 tspn baking soda (bicarbonate of soda)
¼ cup (2 fl oz) boiling water
2 cups (8 oz) all-purpose (plain) flour, sifted

Preheat oven to 350°F (180°C/Gas 4). Grease a 9 in cake tin.

Put all the ingredients, except for the soda, boiling water and flour, into a medium, heavy-bottomed saucepan. Stir together well, bring to a boil, then simmer for 5 minutes. Remove from heat and allow to cool.

When cool, dissolve the soda in the boiling water and add to the saucepan along with the flour. Stir to combine well and pour into the tin. Cook 40–50 minutes or until a skewer inserted in the center comes out clean.

GRAPE FLAN

Not too sweet. You can use red seedless grapes for this,
or the green sultanas.

1 ½ cups (5 oz) walnuts
½ cup (4 oz) butter, softened
2 tblspns (1 oz) superfine (caster) sugar
1 ½ cups (6 oz) all-purpose (plain) flour
1 egg yolk, beaten
½ tspn vanilla extract (essence)

FILLING
1 lb green or red seedless grapes
3 eggs
⅓ cup (3 oz) sugar
2 ⅔ tblspns (1 ⅓ fl oz) brandy
2 tblspns (1 fl oz) sour cream
⅓ cup (1 ½ oz) ground walnuts

Preheat oven to 350°F (180°C/Gas 4).

Put the walnuts into the food processor and process
quickly until they resemble coarse breadcrumbs. Be
careful not to overprocess. Remove and put into a bowl
with the butter, sugar and flour. Rub together with the
tips of your fingers, then add the egg yolk and vanilla
and combine well.

Press the pastry into the bottom and sides of a
9 ½ in flan tin and pre-bake in oven for 12–15 minutes.

Wash the grapes, pluck from the stems and place in
a bowl.

Beat together the eggs, brown sugar, brandy, sour
cream and ground walnuts.

Put grapes in the pre-cooked pastry shell, pour over
the liquid and cook in the oven for 40–50 minutes or
until custard is set. Cover lightly with aluminum foil if
becoming too brown.

Glossary

AAMCHUR: A greenish-gray powder made from dried, unripe mango. It has a tart lemony taste. Substitute 1–3 tblspns (⅔ – 1 ⅓ fl oz) lemon juice if it is not available.

ACIDULATED WATER: Water to which lemon juice or vinegar has been added. The proportion is 1 ⅓ tblspns (⅔ fl oz) lemon juice to about 2 cups (½ qt) water. Cut fruit and vegetables are dipped in this mixture to prevent them from discoloring.

ALMOND TUILES: This is my favorite recipe for almond tuiles. These biscuits go well with ice-cream and mousses.

Preheat oven to 350°F (180°C/Gas 4). Lightly grease three or four baking trays (to allow for the biscuits spreading).

Beat 2 egg whites and gradually add ½ cup (4 oz) superfine (caster) sugar. Add ½ cup (2 oz) sifted all-purpose (plain) flour, ½ tspn vanilla extract (essence) and ¼ cup (1 oz) blanched, slivered almonds. Melt ¼ cup (2 oz) butter. Make sure butter is cool, then add to the egg white mixture. Place mixture in teaspoonfuls at least 4 in apart on the baking trays. Cook until they are brown at the edges and a pale biscuit color in the middle.

Remove from oven and cool, then lift off carefully with a palette knife. While still warm, lay the biscuits over a rolling pin to form a slightly curved shape. When cold, store in airtight container to keep crisp. Re-crisp in hot oven for a few minutes if necessary.

ARBORIO RICE: Starchy Italian rice which can be bought from specialty delicatessens.

ASAFOETIDA: Seasoning powder obtained from the milky resin in the stems and roots of giant fennels. It helps to bring out the flavors in stews, curries and sauces. (It also helps to relieve flatulence.)

BAIN-MARIE (or 'hot-water bath'): A large pan of boiling hot water in which smaller pans or dishes (like custards, puddings, patés and terrines) can be placed. The smaller dish is placed in the larger one and the water, which should be boiling, is brought about halfway up.

BAKE BLIND: Pastry cases for flans and tarts are usually baked 'blind', that is, without a filling. A case can be cooked completely if a filling is not to be cooked with it, or partially to crisp and color the pastry before adding a filling.

BALMAIN BUGS: Small crustaceans also known as shovel-nosed, bay or sand lobsters. Their flesh, which is mostly in the tail, is similar to that of lobster and they can be prepared in any way, hot or cold, that is suitable for lobster, crayfish or yabbies.

BLANCH: *Kitchen usage*: prepared vegetables are plunged into rapidly boiling salted water for 1 minute, then drained and 'refreshed' under cold running water; *garden usage:* vegetables (like celery and asparagus) are excluded from light to whiten the stalks and make them less bitter. This can be done by hilling up the soil around them or covering them with dampened newspaper.

BOLT: The premature flowering of a plant which causes it to 'run' to seed.

CLARIFIED BUTTER: Sold as ghee in Asian food stores. You can make it at home by cutting butter into pieces and melting it slowly (don't let it brown). Remove from the heat, allow to stand a few minutes. A milky residue will sink to the bottom — the clear yellow liquid at the top is the clarified butter. Pour off and allow to solidify. The residue can be used to enrich sauces.

CORDON: A fruit tree trained, usually, as a single stem. Double and triple-stemmed trees also exist.

CREME ANGLAISE: A light custard.

CREME FRAICHE: Mix together scant 2 ½ cups (19 fl oz) cream with scant ½ cup (3 ⅓ fl oz) cultured buttermilk in a bowl over gentle heat, stirring, until it is warm to the touch, about blood temperature.

Cover bowl and leave in a warm place for 8–10 hours, or overnight, until it thickens. Will keep up to 1 week in the refrigerator.

DE-GLAZE: A method of capturing all the browned juices left in the bottom of a cooking pan. Wine, water or cream is added to the pan and brought to a boil whilst scraping all the browned bits and incorporating them into the liquid.

GOLDEN SYRUP: Liquid sweetener made from evaporated sugar cane juice. In England it is called light treacle. Karo or cane sugar syrup can be substituted.

GRAVLAX: A Swedish way of curing fish with sugar, salt and dill (see recipe on page 134).

JAM SETTING POINT: Put a saucer into the freezer for 5 minutes, then remove. Drop a little of the hot jam onto the saucer, cool for 20 seconds. If it wrinkles when you run a finger through it, the jam is ready.

JULIENNE: A way of cutting any vegetable, fruit or meat into very fine strips.

MASCARPONE CHEESE: Mascarpone is a fresh Italian cream cheese sold unripened. It is very luscious and needs to be eaten within 2–3 days of opening.

MAYONNAISE: You cannot compare homemade mayonnaise with the stuff we get in the shops. Make your own — there is no substitute. I do it in the food processor, which makes it easier.

Place 2 egg yolks, 1 tspn lemon juice, ½ tspn dry mustard, and a pinch salt and pepper in the food processor or blender. Blend for a few seconds. With motor running, pour in 1 cup (8 fl oz) olive oil very slowly to begin with, ensuring each addition has been absorbed before adding more. As mayonnaise thickens, the sound of the machine becomes deeper. Taste for additional lemon juice, salt and pepper. Store, covered tightly, in refrigerator.

Freshly chopped herbs are a good addition to homemade mayonnaise.

SCAMPI: Relatives of jumbo shrimp and shrimp, in the United States scampi are known as freshwater crayfish; you can also substitute yabbies.

SWEET SHORTCRUST PASTRY SHELL: This basic recipe for sweet shortcrust pastry is suitable to use for dessert pies and makes 1 x 9 in shell.

Sift together 1 cup (4 oz) all-purpose (plain) flour, ¼ cup (1 oz) cornstarch (cornflour) and 2 tblspns (1 oz) confectioners' (icing) sugar and put into the food processor with ½ cup (4 oz) frozen unsalted butter, chopped. Process quickly, turning on and off, until the mixture resembles fine breadcrumbs. Beat 1 egg together with 1 tspn water. Pour the beaten egg through the feed tube and process until mixture forms a ball around the blades. Remove and wrap in waxed (greaseproof) paper. Chill in refrigerator for 1 hour before rolling pastry out. Preheat oven to 400°F (200°C/Gas 6).

For a partially baked shell, bake the pastry blind in oven for 12 minutes.

SAVORY SHORTCRUST PASTRY SHELL: This basic recipe for savory shortcrust pastry is suitable for quiches and savory tarts and makes 1 x 9 in shell.

Place 2 cups (8 oz) all-purpose (plain) flour, pinch salt and ½ cup (4 oz) butter, frozen and cut into pieces, in food processor and process until mixture resembles breadcrumbs. Add 2 eggs and continue to process until mixture forms a ball. Add a little water to bind if needed, approx 1 ⅓ tblspns (⅔ fl oz). Wrap the dough in waxed paper and refrigerate for 1 hour. Roll out to line a spring-form cake tin or deep flan dish about 9–9 ½ in in diameter, reserving remainder for further use. Crimp edges and prick with a fork. Return to refrigerator to relax for a further 15–20 minutes. Heat oven to moderate (350°F/180°C/Gas 4). Line pie shell with aluminum foil and put in a layer of beans or rice. Cook for 10 minutes, remove foil and beans. Cook a further 5 minutes until golden. Remove and cool.

TAHINI: A thick paste made from sesame seeds.

VANDYKE: Strictly, in the style of dress with pointed borders, common in the portraits by Van Dyck; in cooking, to cut into fruits and vegetables (for example, melons) in a V-shape.

VINAIGRETTE: A classic French dressing made from good-quality olive oil and wine vinegar. Classically made from three parts olive oil to one part vinegar, and seasoned to taste with salt and pepper. A little Dijon mustard is often added, or, as in southern France, some crushed garlic.

There are many variations on this classic: different oils are used (for example, walnut, hazelnut or sesame); different vinegars (balsamic, red wine, raspberry, tarragon); lemon juice or lime juice is substituted for the vinegar. Experiment to suit your taste. The following recipe for walnut oil vinaigrette is an example of the possible variations. Whisk together ½ cup (4 ⅔ fl oz) walnut oil; ¼ cup (2 fl oz) vegetable oil; ⅓ cup (2 ⅔ fl oz) white wine vinegar; 1 clove garlic, crushed; flaky salt and freshly ground pepper to taste, or shake in a screw-top jar.

YABBIES: A species of freshwater crayfish. They resemble miniature northern hemisphere lobsters. Before cooking kill them by placing in the freezer for 30 minutes.

SPOON AND CUP MEASUREMENTS
(All countries use the same teaspoon measures)

	AUST	NZ	UK	US
1 tablespoon	20 ml	15 ml	15 ml (½ fl oz)	15 ml (½ fl oz)
1 cup	250 ml	250 ml	300 ml (10 fl oz)	240 ml (8 fl oz)

Endnotes

Leaf vegetables

p. 5 CYNTHIA ADEY'S SALAD: At Darling Mills Restaurant in Glebe, Sydney, the garden literally spills onto the table. Fresh greens picked daily from the owner's garden at Castle Hill, north of Sydney, are served in the restaurant tossed with various edible flowers.

p. 10 SPINACH WITH PANIR: There are many versions of panir — this one is from Meera Blackley who runs the charming Meera's Dosa House in Crown Street, Sydney.

p. 13 WARM SALAD OF SMOKED CHICKEN OR PHEASANT: I came across this one year at the Gouger Street Fair in Adelaide, Australia. It was the best thing there, probably because Maggie Beer of the Pheasant Farm Restaurant was cooking.

Brassicas

p.28 VEGETABLE CURRY: This recipe comes from Artoosh Voskanian who runs the very popular Flavour of India restaurant in Glebe, Sydney. Artoosh lived in Calcutta for 20 years and the food from that area is not as rich or creamy as that from other parts of India.

Fruit Vegetables

p. 60 DRIED CHERRY TOMATOES: I was given the pot of dried cherry tomatoes to take home and try by Stefano Manfredi, one of Sydney's smart young chefs.

p.61 PASTA AL PESTO DI OLIVA: I stumbled across this idea one day when eating lunch with specialist cheesemaker Richard Thomas at his house in Milawa in north-eastern Victoria. His friend Sarah Gough had tossed a green salad with a little vinaigrette and some black olive paste. Strewn over the top were roughly broken pieces of one of his superb goat cheeses. I decided to try the idea with pasta. It too is delicious.

p. 63 BAKED EGGPLANT WITH PESTO: I first tasted this lovely dish at Brown's Restaurant in Armadale, Melbourne.

p. 68 PRESERVED SWEET PEPPERS IN OIL: I was given this recipe by Bill Langas who runs Myahgah Mews Delicatessen in Sydney's northern suburbs. He is originally from Akrata in Greece and his mother passed the recipe onto him. She grew her own vegetables and this is how she preserved them.

p. 69 CHICKPEA SALAD WITH RED SWEET PEPPERS: Millie Sherman, a wonderful cook and cookery teacher, had just finished making this one day when I went to visit her. It looked very appetizing piled up in the bowl.

Bulbs

p. 91 MEGADARRA: At Howqua Dale, a marvellous gourmet retreat and cooking school in north-eastern Victoria, Marieke Brugman cooks the onions in the fat left over from a *confit* of duck rather than in the oil and butter.

p. 92 JENNY'S PUFF PASTRY PIZZAS WITH ONION AND PROSCIUTTO: Sydney chef and cookery writer, Jenny Ferguson makes simple, elegant onion pizzas from leftover puff pastry pieces.

Root Vegetables

p. 102 CARROT PUDDING: This recipe comes from Vo Bacon, a well-known Australian cookery writer. It was her mother's tried-and-tested Christmas pudding and is a nice alternative to the more common plum pudding.

Tubers

p. 119 PICKLED JERUSALEM ARTICHOKES: Maggie Dougan (Maggie Blinco of *Crocodile Dundee* fame) has become a celebrated preserve maker. Her chutneys and pickles are especially popular as are her Pickled Jerusalem Artichokes.

Herbs

p. 130 BELINDA'S SAVORY TART: When Belinda Jeffrey ran the Good Health Cafe in Mosman, Sydney, this tart was often on the board for lunch.

p. 135 POACHED SALMON IN COCONUT MILK: David Thompson, a talented Sydney chef, spent a couple of years in Thailand. Whilst living there he ate and learnt about the Thai cuisine from an elderly woman in one of the old palaces. His adaptations of this gracious, feminine cuisine are superb. He gave me this wonderful recipe in which lemongrass is an essential ingredient.

Citrus

p. 185 CHICKEN WITH CRACKED OLIVES AND PRESERVED LEMONS: Millie Sherman gave me this recipe. She teaches Moroccan and North African cooking and is also a fabulous 'chocolatier'.

Pears and Quinces

p. 191 PEAR AND CORIANDER SALAD: My friend Janice Baker, a wonderful cook and superb food stylist, introduced me to this combination.

Tropical Fruits

p. 216 FRUIT DAIQUIRIS: One balmy November evening, I drove with the children up the northern peninsula of Sydney to Palm Beach. We were going to visit Katie Highfield and her mother Rosemary Penman, both well-known in the catering business in Sydney. They live in a wonderful light-filled house overlooking the water.

The jacarandas were out, the white gumnut blossoms were in flower and the scarlet and purple bougainvilleas startled us at every turn. Once we reached Pittwater, the vivid blue of the water was speckled with yachts and big cruisers, a sure sign that 'summer madness' had begun. Katie's husband, Alan, made the best daiquiris I'd tasted anywhere — an unusual combination of fresh banana, peach and apple juice, ice, white rum and a little lemon juice.

p. 220 MANGO SALSA: Melbourne restaurateur, Gloria Staley has been a great advocate of Californian cuisine in Australia. Through her restaurants — Fanny's (Melbourne), Chez Oz (Sydney) and Le Beach Club (Gold Coast) — she has introduced Australians to the bold and often surprising flavors of this style of cooking. Gloria gave me the recipe for Mango Salsa a few years ago.

p. 220 SMOKED CHICKEN SALAD WITH FRESH MANGO: I was given this recipe years ago by Damien Pignolet who was then at Butler's Restaurant in Sydney's Kings Cross and who now owns Claude's in nearby Woollahra.

p.221 FRESH MANGO AND PITTED FRUIT PRESERVE: This delicious preserve was served at a gourmet picnic held outside of Picton, 100 or so kilometers south-west of Sydney. Serge Dansereau, executive chef at The Regent, Sydney, had organized it and many of Sydney's leading food suppliers and chefs were present. The preserve was made with mangoes only and served with cold smoked duck. It was superb.

p. 224 KING SALAD: Flamboyant showman and cook, Bernard King is the creator of this spectacular salad. Originally from Queensland in tropical north Australia, such colorful, exotic combinations are perfectly natural to him. This salad has evolved over the years — the papaya pips weren't in the original recipe. Smoked trout was his preferred choice then, but he now uses either smoked turkey or chicken. Smoked pork loin can also be used.

p. 224 FRUIT SALAD ICE-BLOCKS: We stumbled across these one hot Sunday afternoon on our way back from the Byron Bay markets in northern New South Wales. For a change we had taken the back road which leads up over the mountains, rather than continuing along the nightmarish Pacific Highway. The road goes out along the river plains, passing by fields of sugar cane before climbing up through banana trees and plunging down again into the magnificent Currumbin Valley. The roadside stall we stopped at sold fresh tropical fruits and homemade jams. They also had these wonderful ice-blocks in the freezer.

p. 228 ARNIE'S GUAVA FLAN: This stunning recipe was given to me by Arnold de Jong, a Sydney chef who works at Bronte Epicurean in Sydney's eastern suburbs.

Acknowledgments

Sheridan Rogers: *Kim Anderson for her inspiration and encouragement; Ruth Sheard, Liz Seymour and Katie Davis for all their help and hard work; Margaret Connolly for her support and encouragement; Jill Aldiss for her help and commonsense in the kitchen; Rosie Penman, Janice Baker and Sue Whitter for their friendship; Peter Young for his wry observations; Warwick Quinton for his enthusiasm for gardening and growing nutritionally sound food; John Coco, The Garden Advisory Service, Royal Botanical Gardens, Sydney for all his help and advice; my father for building my vegetable patch; my children, Natali and Linden for their freshness and openness; my sisters Skye, Justin and Brett for their love of gardens; Gyalsay Tulku Rinpoche, Dzongsar Khyentse Rinpoche and His Holiness the Gyalwang Drukchen for their loving kindness; Bridget Wilson-Gebbie for caring; and Lisa Highton for opening the door.* **Skye Rogers:** *Clare for finding me first.*

Documents

Bilson, Gay, from 'Please Don't Peel Me a Pear', *National Times*, Mar 29–Apr 4 1981. Reprinted by permission of Gay Bilson.

Bray, John, from 'The Persimmons', in *Poems 1961-1971*, Jacaranda Press, Milton, Vic., 1972. Reprinted by permission of John Bray.

Carver, Raymond, from 'The Offending Eel', in *A New Path to the Waterfall*, Atlantic Monthly Press, New York, 1989. Copyright © 1989 by the Estate of Raymond Carver. Reprinted by permission of Atlantic Monthly Press and Tess Gallagher.

Chekhov, Anton, excerpt from *The Unknown Chekhov*, translated by Avraham Yarmolinsky, retitled 'An Unpleasantness' in *A New Path to the Waterfall* by Raymond Carver, Atlantic Monthly Press, New York, 1989. Copyright © 1954 by Avraham Yarmolinsky. Renewal copyright © 1982 by Ms Babette Deutsch Yarmolinsky. Reprinted by permission of Farrar, Straus and Giroux, Inc.

Dobson, Rosemary, from 'Waiting for the Postman', in *The Three Fates and Other Poems*, Hale and Iremonger Pty Ltd, Sydney, 1984. Reprinted by permission of Hale and Iremonger.

Dobson, Rosemary, from 'The Good Host', in *The Three Fates and Other Poems*, Hale and Iremonger Pty Ltd, Sydney, 1984. Reprinted by permission of Hale and Iremonger.

Dumay, Raymond, quote in *Food — An Authoritative and Visual History and Dictionary of the Foods of the World*, by Waverley Root, Simon and Schuster, New York, 1980. Copyright © 1980 Waverley Root. Reprinted by permission of Simon and Schuster.

Farmer, Beverley, 'Figs', in *A Body of Water*, University of Queensland Press, St Lucia, 1990. Reprinted by permission of University of Queensland Press, Australian Literary Management and Beverley Farmer.

Friend, Donald, quote on the greengrocer, in *Donald Friend 1915-1989 — Retrospective*, by Barry Pearce, Art Gallery of New South Wales, Sydney. Reprinted by permission of the Estate of the late D.S.L. Friend.

Gray, Patience, quote from *Honey From a Weed*, Papermac, London, 1987.

Gray, Robert, from 'Pumpkins', in *Selected Poems*, Collins/Angus & Robertson, Sydney, 1990. Reprinted by permission of Robert Gray.

Gray, Robert, from 'To The Master, Dogen Zenji', in *Selected Poems*, Collins/Angus & Robertson, Sydney, 1990. Reprinted by permission of Robert Gray.

Llewellyn, Kate, 'Planting', in *Honey*, Hudson Hawthorn Publishing, Hawthorn, Vic., 1990. Reprinted by permission of Kate Llewellyn.

Neilson, John Shaw, from 'May' in *The Poems of John Shaw Neilson*, Angus & Robertson, Sydney, 1965. Reprinted by permission of Jack McKimm.

Midda, Sara, quotes from *In and Out of the Garden Diary 1984*, Sidgwick and Jackson Ltd, London, 1983.

Raine, Craig, 'The Book of the Market', reprinted from *The Onion, Memory* by permission of Oxford University Press, Oxford, 1978. Copyright © Craig Raine 1978.

Rilke, Rainer Maria, quotes from *The Selected Poetry of Rainer Maria Rilke*, edited by S. Mitchell, Random House Inc., New York, 1982. Copyright © 1982 Stephen Mitchell. Reprinted by permission of Random House, Inc.

Root, Waverley, quotes on fruit, in *Food — An Authoritative and Visual History and Dictionary of the Foods of the World*, Simon and Schuster, New York, 1980. Copyright © 1980 Waverley Root. Reprinted by permission of Simon and Schuster.

Tipping, Richard, from 'Mangoes', in *Domestic Hardcore*, University of Queensland Press, St Lucia, 1975. Reprinted by permission of Richard Tipping.

White, Patrick, quotes from *The Tree of Man*, Jonathon Cape Ltd, London, 1955. Reprinted by permission of Barbara Mobbs.

Recipes

p. 5 Cynthia Adey's Salad
Cynthia Adey
Chef/Manager
Darling Mills Restaurant
134 Glebe Point Road
Glebe NSW 2037

p. 8 Swiss Chard and Chicken Terrine
Vamps B.Y.O Bistro
227 Glenmore Road
Paddington NSW 2021

p. 10 Spinach Salad with Bacon,
 Pinenuts and Hard-boiled Eggs
Tony Pappas
Bayswater Brasserie
32 Bayswater Road
Kings Cross NSW 2011

p. 10 Spinach with Panir
Meera Blackley
Meera's Dosa House
567 Crown Street
Surry Hills NSW 2010
Ph: (02) 698 5395

p. 13 Warm Salad of Smoked Chicken
 (or Pheasant)
Maggie Beer
Pheasant Farm Restaurant
Samuel Road
Barossa Valley
Nuriootpa SA 5355

p. 28 Vegetable Curry
Artoosh Voskanian
Flavour of India
142a Glebe Point Road
Glebe NSW 2037
Ph: (02) 692 0662

p. 38 Ken Hom's Vegetable Pasta
Ken Hom

p. 43 Stuffed Artichokes
Beppi Polese
Beppi's Restaurant
Cnr Yurong Street and Stanley Street
East Sydney NSW 2010
Ph: (02) 360 4558

p. 49 Anitra di Campagna
Beppi Polese
Beppi's Restaurant
Cnr Yurong Street and Stanley Street
East Sydney NSW 2010
Ph: (02) 360 4558

p. 50 Meera's Spicy Peas and Potatoes in
 Yogurt
Meera Blackley
Meera's Dosa House

567 Crown Street
Surry Hills NSW 2010
Ph: (02) 698 5395

p. 56 Mixed Vegetables in Coconut
 Milk
Margaret Fulton
adapted from *My Very Special Cookbook*,
Octopus Books, Sydney.

p. 65 Ratatouille
Geoff Parsons

p. 68 Preserved Sweet Peppers in Oil
Bill Langas
Myahgah Mews Delicatessen and
Gourmet Centre
Shop 5, No. 3, Myahgah Road
Mosman NSW 2088
Ph: (02) 969 8973

p. 69 Chickpea Salad with Red
 Sweet Pepper
Millie Sherman
I Piatti
Darling Street
Balmain NSW 2041

p. 70 Panthay Kauskwe
Doris Ady
from *Curries From the Sultan's Kitchen*,
Reed Books, Sydney, 1968.

p. 83 Frittata Primavera
Beppi Polese
Beppi's Restaurant
Cnr Yurong Street and Stanley Street
East Sydney NSW 2010
Ph: (02) 360 4558

p. 90 Deep Dish Onion Tart
Jenny Ferguson
from *Cooking For You and Me*, Methuen
Haynes, Sydney, 1987.

p. 91 Megadarra
Marieke Brugman
Howqua Dale
Gourmet Retreat
P.O. Box 379
Mansfield Vic 3722

p. 92 Jenny's Puff Pastry Pizzas with
 Onion and Prosciutto
Jenny Ferguson
from *Cooking For You and Me*, Methuen
Haynes, Sydney, 1987.

p. 95 Braised Leeks
Marieke Brugman
Howqua Dale
Gourmet Retreat
P.O. Box 379
Mansfield Vic 3722

p. 102 Carrot Pudding
Vo Bacon

p. 110 Crab Soup
An adaptation of the recipe by John
Oakes

p. 114 Karen's Roësti Potatoes
Karen Kerby
Old Emu Restaurant
Milawa Vic 3678

p. 116 Madhur Jaffrey's Potatoes with
 Whole Spices and Sesame Seeds
Madhur Jaffrey
from *Eastern Vegetarian Cooking*,
Jonathon Cape Ltd, London, 1981.
Copyright © 1981 by Madhur Jaffrey.
Reproduced by permission of Rogers,
Coleridge & White Ltd and Random
Century Group.

p. 118 Sweet Potato Salad
Raymond Sokolov, *Natural History*
magazine, New York. Adaptation of
recipe by Eileen Yin-Fei Lo.

p. 124 Cold Chicken Pie
Janice Baker

p. 129 Rhonda's Pasta and Basil Salad
Rhonda Hertz

p. 130 Belinda's Savory Tart
Belinda Jeffrey

p. 135 Poached Salmon in Coconut
 Milk
David Thompson
Darley Street Thai
Darley Street
Newtown NSW 2042

p. 139 Mediterranean Baked Fish
Ann Oliver
Mistress Augustine's Restaurant
145 O'Connell Street
North Adelaide SA 5006

p. 140 Janice's Herbed Cheese Damper
Janice Baker

p. 163 Rosie's Strawberries and Cream
Rosemary Penman

p. 167 Mary's Hot Berry Soufflé
Mary Beasley

p. 178 Veau Lunel
Franck Francois
La Gerbe D'or Bakery
225 Glenmore Road
Paddington NSW 2021

p. 180 Orange and Almond Cake
Claudia Roden
from *A New Book of Middle Eastern Food*,
Viking Penguin Books, London, 1986.

p. 185 Chicken with Cracked
    Olives and Preserved
    Lemons
Millie Sherman
I Piatti
Darling Street
Balmain NSW 2041

p. 191 Pear and Coriander Salad
Janice Baker

p. 192 Green Salad of Pears, Avocado
    and Apple
Bernard King

p. 194 Dessert Quinces
Maggie Beer
Pheasant Farm Restaurant
Samuel Road
Barossa Valley
Nuriootpa SA 5355

p. 200 A Rustic Tart of Apple,
    Rhubarb and Ginger
Fiona Baxter
Bronte Café
467 Bronte Road
Bronte NSW 2024

p. 220 Mango Salsa
Gloria Staley
Chez Oz
23 Craigend
Darlinghurst NSW 2010

p. 220 Smoked Chicken Salad
    with Fresh Mango
Damien Pignolet
Claude's
10 Oxford Street
Woollahra NSW 2025

p. 221 Fresh Mango and Pitted Fruit
    Preserve
Serge Dansereau
The Regent Hotel
199 George Street
Sydney NSW 2000

p. 224 King Salad
Bernard King

p. 228 Arnie's Guava Flan
Arnold de Jong
Bronte Epicurean
59 Birrell Street
Bondi Junction NSW 2022
Ph: (02) 369 3404

p. 234 Rabbit with Mustard Sauce
    and Fresh Figs
Maggie Beer
Pheasant Farm Restaurant
Samuel Road, Barossa Valley
Nuriootpa SA 5355

Bibliography

Adams, John F., *The Epicurean Gardener*, E. P. Dutton, New York, 1988.

Alexander, Stephanie, *Feasts and Stories*, Allen and Unwin, Sydney, 1988.

Alexander, Stephanie, *Stephanie's Menus for Food Lovers*, Allen & Unwin, Sydney, 1985.

Apicius, *De Re Coquinaria*, Joseph Dommers Vehling (trans.) as *Cookery and Dining in Imperial Rome*, Dover Publications, New York, 1977.

Bacon, Vo, *The Fresh Fruit Cookbook*, Regency.

Bacon, Vo, *The Fresh Vegetable Cookbook*, Regency.

Beck, Simone, & Child, Julia, *Mastering the Art of French Cooking*, Vol. 2, Penguin Books, Middlesex, 1978.

Becker, Marion Rombauer & Rombauer, Irma S., *The Joy of Cooking*, J. M. Dent & Sons Ltd, London, 1963.

Cameron-Smith, Marye, *The Complete Book Of Preserving*, Marshall Cavendish, London, 1976.

Carey, Nora, *Perfect Preserves — Provisions from the Kitchen Garden*, Stewart, Tabori and Chang, New York, 1990.

Castelvetro, Giacomo, *The Fruit, Herbs and Vegetables of Italy*, Viking, British Museum, London, 1989.

Chang, K. C. (ed.), *Food in Chinese Culture — Anthropological and Historical Perspectives*, Yale University Press, New Haven, 1977.

Coupe, Christian, *Good Things From the Deep*, Golden Press, Sydney, 1987.

Creasy, Rosalind, *Cooking From the Garden*, Sierra Club Books, San Francisco, 1988.

Culpeper, Nicholas, *Complete Herball*, 1651.

David, Elizabeth, *French Provincial Cooking*, Penguin Books, Ringwood, 1986.

David, Elizabeth, *Italian Food*, Penguin Books, Ringwood, 1963.

David, Elizabeth, 'Mad, Despised and Dangerous', *Petits Propos Culinaires*, Prospect Books, London, 1981.

David, Elizabeth, *Summer Cooking*, Penguin Books, London, 1978.

Davidson, Alan & Jane (trans.), *Dumas on Food*, Oxford University Press, Oxford, 1978.

Davidson, Alan, *On Fasting And Feasting*, MacDonald & Co. Ltd, London, 1988.

Deans, Esther, *Esther Deans' Gardening Book: Growing Without Digging*, Collins/Angus & Robertson, Sydney, 1990.

De Cieza de Leon, Pedro, *Chronicle of Peru* 1532–1550, Clements R. Markham (trans.), B. Franklin, New York, 1964.

Department of Agriculture NSW, *Home Fruit-Growing*, Sydney, 1985.

Dioscorides, *De Materia Medici*, 77.

Dowell, Philip & Bailey, Adrian, *The Book of Ingredients*, Mermaid Books, 1983.

Esbensen, Mogens Bay, *A Taste of the Tropics*, Viking O'Neil, Ringwood, 1988.

Ferguson, Jenny, *Cooking For You and Me*, Methuen Haynes, Sydney, 1987.

Fitzgibbon, Theodora, *The Food of the Western World*, Hutchinson & Co. Ltd, London, 1976.

Forsell, Mary, *Herbs: The Complete Guide to Growing, Cooking, Healing and Pot-pourri*, Anaya Publishers Ltd, London, 1990.

Forsell, Mary, *The Berry Garden*, MacDonald Orbis, London, 1989.

French, Jackie, *The Organic Garden Doctor*, Angus & Robertson, Sydney, 1988.

French, Jacqueline, *Organic Gardening in Australia*, Reed Books, Sydney, 1986.

Fulton, Margaret, *Encyclopaedia of Food and Cookery*, Octopus Publishing, Sydney, 1983.

Gerard, John, *The Herball*, 1597.

Giobbi, Edward, *Italian Family Cooking*, Vintage Books, New York, 1978.

Gray, Patience, *Honey From A Weed*, Papermac, London, 1987.

Hall, Dorothy, *The Book of Herbs*, Angus & Robertson, Sydney, 1972.

Harris, Alexander, 'An Emigrant Mechanic', in *Settlers and Convicts: Or, Reflections of Sixteen Years in the Australian Backwoods*, London, 1847.

Holt, Geraldene, *Recipes From A French Herb Garden*, Conran Octopus Ltd, London, 1989.

Hom, Ken, *The Taste of China*, Simon & Schuster, New York, 1990.

Jaffrey, Madhur, *Eastern Vegetarian Cooking*, Jonathon Cape Ltd, London, 1983.

Johns, Leslie & Stevenson, Violet, *The Complete Book of Fruit*, Angus & Robertson, Sydney, 1979.

Jonas, Stephanie, *The Fruit Cookbook*, Reed Books, Sydney, 1985.

Kuo, Irene, *The Key To Chinese Cooking*, Thomas Nelson, Melbourne, 1978.

Medici, Lorenza de, *The Heritage of Italian Cooking*, Weldon Russell, Sydney, 1990.

Montagné, Prosper, *Larousse Gastronomique*, Hamlyn Publishing Group Ltd, London, 1961.

Mortimer, John, *The Whole Art of Husbandry*, 1707.

Pellegrini, Angelo M., *The Food Lover's Garden*, Lyons & Burford, New York, 1970.

Pellegrini, Angelo, *The Unprejudiced Palate*, North Point Press, San Francisco, 1984.

Phillipps, Karen & Dahlen, Martha, *A Popular Guide To Chinese Vegetables*, South China Morning Post, Hong Kong, 1982.

Pliny, *Natural History*.

Reader's Digest Illustrated Guide to Gardening, Sydney, 1979.

Reid, Wynwode, *New Australian Cookery Illustrated*, Colorgravure Publications, Melbourne, 1950.

Roads, Michael J., *The Natural Magic of Mulch*, Greenhouse Publications, Elwood, Vic., 1989.

Roden, Claudia, *A New Book of Middle Eastern Food*, Penguin Books, London, 1986.

Romer, Elizabeth, *The Tuscan Year — Life and Food in an Italian Valley*, Hodder and Stoughton, Sydney, 1984.

Root, Waverley, *Food — An Authoritative and Visual History and Dictionary of the Foods of the World*, Simon & Schuster, New York, 1980.

Seddon, George & Radecka, Helena, *Your Vegetable Garden in Australia*, Rigby Ltd, Adelaide, 1978.

Simpson, Maureen, *Australian Cuisine*, Methuen Haynes, Sydney, 1985.

Stobart, Tom, *Cook's Encyclopaedia*, Papermac Macmillan, London, 1980.

Stuart, David C., *The Kitchen Garden — A Historical Guide to Traditional Crops*, Robert Hale, London, 1984.

Symons, Michael, *One Continuous Picnic*, Duck Press, Adelaide, 1982.

Tannahill, Reay, *Food in History*, Eyre Methuen, London, 1973.

White, Patrick, *The Tree of Man*, Penguin Books, Middlesex, 1955.

White, Patrick, *Voss*, Jonathon Cape Ltd, London, 1980.

Wolfert, Paula, *Good Food From Morocco*, John Murray, London, 1989.

Worlidge, John, *Systema Horticulturae*.

Yin-fang, Dai & Cheng-jun, Liu, *Fruit As Medicine*, The Rams Skull Press, Kuranda, Qld, 1986.

Index